★ BEST
LITTLE
STORIES

★ FROM THE ★

Published by Cumberland House, an imprint of Sourcebooks, Inc.
P.O. Box 4410, Naperville, Illinois 60567-4410
(630) 961-3900
Fax: (630) 961-2168
www.sourcebooks.com

Library of Congress Cataloging-in-Publication Data

Kelly, C. Brian.
   Best little stories from the Civil War : more than 100 true stories / by C. Brian Kelly;
with Ingrid Smyer.—2nd ed.
       p. cm.
   Includes bibliographical references and index.
   1. United States—History—Civil War, 1861-1865—Anecdotes. I. Smyer-Kelly,
Ingrid II. Title.
   E655.K25 2009
   973.7—dc22
                              2009042114

Printed and bound in the United States of America.
VP 10 9 8 7 6 5 4

Other Books by C. Brian Kelly
& Ingrid Smyer

BEST LITTLE STORIES
FROM THE AMERICAN REVOLUTION

BEST LITTLE STORIES FROM THE LIFE AND
TIMES OF WINSTON CHURCHILL

BEST LITTLE STORIES
OF THE BLUE AND THE GRAY

BEST LITTLE IRONIES, ODDITIES & MYSTERIES
OF THE CIVILWAR

BEST LITTLE STORIES
FROM THE WHITE HOUSE

BEST LITTLE STORIES
FROM THE WILD WEST

BEST LITTLE STORIES
FROM WORLD WAR II

BEST LITTLE STORIES FROM VIRGINIA

For our children,
Beth, Charlie, Fran, Hal, Jimmy, Katheryn, Sid

CONTENTS

Introduction

HERE'S OUR PREMISE: HISTORY CAN BE TOLD IN LITTLE BITS AND PIECES AS WELL AS in heavyweight and multi-volume tomes.

All too often, even the best recitals of great events can overlook the basic human story lurking behind those same great events. And that's where our series of Best Little Stories historical books comes into the picture. That's us—history as short, narrative bits.

But...can that work?

Reviewer Craig. K. Allen seemed to think so, seemed to catch both the intent and flavor of our approach in the Macon (Georgia) *Telegraph* when he described our *Best Little Stories from the White House* as "a genre not quite practiced by anyone else" and said the book's stories "possess the immediacy of a front-page newspaper article."

Also gratifying was the reaction of Bill Ruelhmann, Books columnist at the Norfolk (Virginia) *Virginian Pilot*, back in 2002 to our newly published *Best Little Stories from the Wild West*. Our digging for "historical gold" in "mundane earth," he wrote at that time, had enabled us to "prise forth glittering nuggets of nifty narrative that, packed tight in the thick treasure boxes of their paperbound anthologies, make for truly priceless reading."

Thanks of course to Craig and Bill. But how does it work, you may be asking. *Best Little Stories*, we say? Exactly what does that mean? Well, as I wrote in an earlier edition of this, the first of our three Best Little Stories Civil War books, I once was a newspaperman. I always looked for the good, i.e., the *best*, story. Be it cheerful, light and frothy, or hard-hitting, sad, poignant—it didn't matter. Just the good story. The kind the reader would read. No "message," just the unusual, the obscure, the fascinating...the gripping, the touching *human* story.

When I turned to history as the first editor of *Military History* and *World War II* magazines, I was inclined from the start to treat history as journalism—to look for the little nuggets gleaming with pathos, cheer, tragedy, irony—the human-interest stories in history.

Together with my wife and book collaborator Ingrid, I came to call them *Best Little Stories* in this and our companion historical books (there are nine total as of this writing). *Little* in part because, yes, the stories may be shorter than historical accounts. But also because in most cases, they focus more on the individual person at, say, Gettysburg, rather than simply report the size of the armies, who won the battle and how they did so.

Rather than write a straightforward, fact-filled—but potentially dull—short biography of U. S. Grant as the Union general who finally won the Civil War for Abraham Lincoln, it's far more interesting to recall the *little* moment when he led his troops toward his first conflict of the entire Civil War with very human fear and trepidation: "[M]y heart kept getting higher and higher until it felt to me as though it was in my throat. I would have given anything then to have been back in Illinois."

And then, delicious irony, the enemy he expected to meet just over the brow of the next hill was gone, decamped.

In like fashion, it's one thing to take note that the landscape of the Civil War was often peopled by black slaves (keyword: *peopled*), but it's important also to cite their own individual experiences, whether it's Booker T. Washington recalling his first moments of freedom, Frederick Douglass reciting his brutal treatment before escaping to freedom, or other, far lesser-known slaves telling their own stories. Or, for that matter, the tale of how the young, newly freed black youth named Booker finally acquired a last name.

But this isn't a book all about soldiers and slaves, which, to judge by many historical accounts, were the principal parties of the Civil War. Instead, our Civil War stories often are about the average civilian, sometimes even special groups. For instance: Congress.

Or, more precisely, read in the pages to follow about a member of Congress who had to ride to his nation's capital in an unheated freight car, then had to wear unlaundered shirts and socks for many days at a time, while his wife and children remained at home under constant threat of invasion. Such was life, not all that unusual a case, actually, for a member of Congress from Georgia—the *Confederate* Congress meeting in Richmond, that is.

Were conditions that much better in Washington, D.C., the Union capital and home to the United States Congress? Undoubtedly, yes. But it's easy for us to forget that the Federal capital was an incomplete, even primitive urban center by modern standards. "Not a sewer blessed the town, nor off of Pennsylvania Avenue was there a paved gutter," wrote Ohio Congressman Albert G. Riddle, albeit with perhaps some exaggeration.

Meanwhile, First Bull Run in the first July of the Civil War was a rout of the Federal forces defending the same Washington, D.C., correct? Quite so, and so easy to recite today as part of any listing of the major battles of the Civil

War. But the real sense of the panic among the retreating Union forces comes through from the onlooking Congressman Riddle's own eyewitness account of the retreat.

As he later recalled, "The poor, demented, exhausted wretches, who could not climb into the high, closed baggage wagons, made frantic efforts to get onto and into our carriage."

The same terrified soldiers grabbed at every handhold they could find, he added with little apparent sympathy. "We had to be rough with them and thrust them out and off." Even so, one of the fleeing "wretches"—a Union major at that—managed to pull himself aboard the congressman's carriage, "and we lugged the pitiful coward a mile or so."

And then? "Finally I opened the door, and he tumbled—or was tumbled out."

Women, too, make up the annals of history, along with history's best little stories, to be sure. So it is that my wife and collaborator Ingrid has written the twin biographies appearing at the end herein of the Civil War's twin First Ladies, Mrs. Jefferson Davis (*Varina: Forgotten First Lady*, page 266) and Mrs. Abraham Lincoln (*Mary Todd Lincoln: Troubled First Lady*, page 279).

As indicated a few lines ago, this is not the first edition of *Best Little Stories from the Civil War* but rather the third—with brand new material added—thanks to a kind reception by the reading public for which we, the authors, are exceedingly grateful.

While hoping our latest set of readers will enjoy our approach to history, I can still wonder, as I did in the introduction to our 1998 edition: Is journalism but a facet of history, or is history but another form of journalism?

C. Brian Kelly
Charlottesville, Virginia, 2010

Select Guide to Battles & Personalities

★ BATTLES ★

★ MAJOR PERSONALITIES ★

BOYD, BELLE: see *Parallel Spies*

BRECKINRIDGE, JOHN C.: see *Jaws of Death*

CHESNUT, MARY BOYKIN (AND HUSBAND, JAMES, JR.): see *Hello, Richmond; Unnecessary Tragedies; What Does a Slave?; Varina: Forgotten First Lady*

CUSTER, GEORGE ARMSTRONG: see *Swinging His Arms*

CUSTER, TOM: see *So Very Personal*

DAVIS, JEFFERSON: see *Portents; Fresh Start Sought; Who the South Was; Social Notice Taken; Hello, Richmond; Davises Everywhere; Close Connections; War's Sting Delayed; Varina: Forgotten First Lady*

DAVIS, VARINA: see *Portents; Social Notice Taken; Hello, Richmond; What Does a Slave?; Close Connections; Varina: Forgotten First Lady*

DOUGLASS, FREDERICK: see *Portents*

FARRAGUT, DAVID: see *They Also Served*

FORREST, NATHAN BEDFORD: see *Injury Added to Insult; Brave Men Spared*

FRÉMONT, JOHN C.: see *They Also Served*

GARFIELD, JAMES A.: see *Hello, Washington; Miss Kate's Brief Run; Surviving to Serve Again*

GORDON, JOHN BROWN: see *"Shot for You"; Coincidences at Gettysburg*

GRANT, ULYSSES S.: see *Heart in the Throat; Complete Conquest Required; Sidling Down to Richmond; Longest Siege; Embarrassing Outing; Close Connections; Julia Reads a Note; Always a Clear Course*

HAYES, RUTHERFORD B.; MCKINLEY, WILLIAM; HARRISON, BENJAMIN; CLEVELAND, GROVER; AND ARTHUR, CHESTER A.: see *Surviving to Serve Again*

HILL, AMBROSE POWELL: see *Hello, Richmond; Two More to Mourn; Final Glimpses*

HOOD, JOHN BELL: see *Unlucky John Bell Hood*

JACKSON, THOMAS J. ("STONEWALL"): see *A "Bear" Installed; Perfect Storm of Bullets; Jackson's Odd Failure; They Also Served*

LEE, ROBERT E. AND FAMILY: see *Portents; Who the South Was; Robert and Mary; A "Bear" Installed; "Granny" Lee; Jackson's Odd Failure; Hello, Richmond; More Than a Few Ghosts; Antietam; Gettysburg; Lee Family Saga, Continued; Sidling Down to Richmond; Close Connections; Lee's Final Order; Final Glimpses; An Arlington Postmortem*

LINCOLN, ABRAHAM AND FAMILY: see *Portents; Racing to War; Better Angels Invoked; Lincoln Wins Rebel Debate; Sherman's Threat Appealed; Spank the Boys; Faces in the Crowd; More Than a Few Ghosts; "Down, You Fool!"; Friendly Boost Given; Christmas; Embarrassing Outing; Close Connections; Julia Reads a Note; Final*

★ PORTENTS ★

1809

ON A BED OF CORNHUSKS INSIDE A CABIN WITH ONE DOOR AND ONE WINDOW and a dirt floor, a young frontier woman bore down hard one February morning and squeezed out from her womb a baby...a boy.

A little later that Sunday, a nine-year-old cousin asked the mother what she was going to name the newborn child. "Abraham," she said, "after his grandfather."

The next morning, the same boy held his new cousin for the first time. But the baby cried, and young Dennis Hanks quickly gave him up. "Take him," he said. "He'll never come to much."

1810

ANOTHER FAMILY...A FATHER IMPRISONED FOR OWING MONEY, RELEASED IN THE spring of the year. Mother and father considered their situation and decided they could not afford to remain at the grand family estate in Westmoreland County, Virginia. They traveled north by carriage to take up residence in a small house in Alexandria, across the Potomac from the newly established Federal capital.

Young Robert was three years old as his parents passed into "genteel poverty." But not into a gentle life. Two years later, his military-hero father, Henry "Lighthorse Harry" Lee, once governor of Virginia and a congressman, was beaten and mutilated by a mob in Baltimore. Recovering with difficulty, left disfigured, broken in spirit, he made his farewells in 1813 to family, commonwealth, and country...all for a new life in Barbados. He meant to return soon, and after a few years, he was indeed on his way back. But he fell ill aboard ship, went ashore at Cumberland Island, Georgia, and died there March 25, 1818. Son Robert E., by then, was just eleven years old.

1832

FOR THE SECOND TIME IN FOUR YEARS, SOUTH CAROLINA ACTED TO *NULLIFY* tariffs imposed by the Federal government in Washington. Andrew Jackson, president at the time, was on the Federal side of the issue, while his vice president, South Carolina's own John C. Calhoun, was on the other side—so much so that he resigned the vice presidency to carry on the fight in the U.S. Senate. For months the air was full of impassioned, dangerous words for the still-young Republic: nullification, states' rights...*secession.*

After winning reelection in 1832 with Martin Van Buren of New York as his ticket mate, Tennessee's "Old Hickory" still had to deal with the South Carolina thorn in his side. By now, the disgruntled state had canceled its earlier nullification actions, only to try another—this time to nullify congressional action authorizing the use of Federal force against the state.

Here was a most delicate dilemma for President Jackson. In the midst of deliberations with Cabinet members, senators, and others, he called for a faithful comrade-in-arms from old wars against the Creek Indians in Alabama and the British at New Orleans. Closeted in the White House, they shared a decanter of whiskey and talked of old times and new...and new issues. Like the thorny nullification issue.

To Sam Dale, Jackson said, "They are trying me here; you will witness it; but by the God in heaven, I will uphold the laws."

Dale said he hoped things would go right. Whereupon Jackson slammed his hand down on a table so hard he broke a pipe and replied, "They *shall* go right, sir!"

It wasn't long after Dale's visit that Andrew Jackson sent fighting ships to Charleston Harbor, denounced any state's pretension to rights of nullification or secession, and on December 10, 1832, issued his Proclamation on Nullification, after which the storm died down for the time being.

In Illinois, meanwhile, a country lawyer named Abraham Lincoln read Jackson's Proclamation most carefully. He would read it again when composing his inaugural address of 1861.

1833

NEARLY FIFTEEN, FRED WAS HIRED OUT TO A FARMER AND "PIOUS" CHURCHGOER named Edward Covey. This was in Maryland. "I had been at my new home but one week before Mr. Covey gave me a very severe whipping, cutting my back, causing the blood to run, and raising ridges on my flesh as large as my little finger." Fred was whipped about once a week for the next six months or so, until he fought back. Even then, he remained a slave, and it would be years before he found freedom, his means of escape to the North still a secret when he published his autobiography in 1845.

Beyond his own experiences, his book presented quite an indictment. As a young child he saw a black woman, "Aunt Hester," beaten with hands tied above her head and the rope looped over a joist above. He told of an overseer named Austin Gore who shot a slave named Demby in the face for refusing to stand still for a whipping. Another white man, Thomas Lanham, killed two slaves, "one of whom he killed with a hatchet, by knocking his brains out." A Mrs. Giles Hicks, angered at a slave teenager who fell asleep while babysitting, hit the girl with a stick and injured her fatally. An old black man oystering on the Chesapeake Bay strayed over a neighbor's property line...and was shot by the neighbor.

And so on. Mere whippings are hardly worth mention, there were so many. The Reverend Rigby Hopkins, for instance, "always managed to have one or more of his slaves to whip every Monday morning." There was always some excuse.

It would astonish one, unaccustomed to a slave-holding life, to see with what wonderful ease a slaveholder can find things, of which to make occasion to whip a slave. A mere look, word or motion—a mistake, accident or want of power—are all matters for which a slave may be whipped at any time. Does a slave look dissatisfied? It is said, he has the devil in him, and it must be whipped out. Does he speak loudly when spoken to by his master? Then he is getting high-minded, and should be taken down a buttonhole lower. Does he forget to pull off his hat at the approach of a white person? Then he is wanting in reverence, and should be whipped for it. Does he ever venture to vindicate his conduct, when censured for it? Then he is guilty of impudence—one of the greatest crimes of which a slave can be guilty. Does he ever venture to suggest a different mode of doing things from that pointed out by his master? He is indeed presumptuous and getting above himself, and nothing less than a flogging will do for him. Does he, while plowing, break a plow? or while hoeing break a hoe? It is owing to his carelessness, and for it a slave must always be whipped. Mr. Hopkins could always find something of this sort to justify the use of the lash, and he seldom failed to embrace such opportunities.

Fortunately, Fred found his way out of slavery. On his personal journey to freedom, he secretly learned to read and write. He learned so well, in fact, that he later became a famous orator, abolitionist, and diplomat. A leader among blacks, he was known by his later name, Frederick Douglass.

1843

NEAR CHRISTMASTIME THE SEVENTEEN-YEAR-OLD PLANTER'S DAUGHTER WAS ON her way to a festive visit at the plantation of one Joseph Davis. His niece came for her, "accompanied by a servant-man leading a horse with a lady's side-saddle." The young visitor's "*impedimenta*" went along in a carriage, and in short order they rode over "rustling leaves" and through "thick trees" to the Davis home, known as "The Hurricane."

There the young lady became acquainted with the owner's younger brother, then thirty-six…and the real object of the visit.

Her impression was that he looked closer to thirty than thirty-six, that he was "erect, well-proportioned, and active as a boy." Moreover: "He rode with more grace than any man I have ever seen and gave one the impression of being incapable of either being unseated or fatigued."

That very day, the impressionable but sophisticated young woman wrote to her mother that she couldn't tell if he was "young or old." She added: "He looks both at times; but I believe he is old, for from what I hear he is only two years younger than you are."

Even so, he impressed her "as a remarkable kind of man, but of uncertain temper, and [he] has a way of taking for granted that everybody agrees with him when he expresses an opinion, which offends me." To his credit again, he had a winning manner of expressing himself and a "peculiarly sweet voice."

She went on to write that he was the "kind of person I should expect to rescue one from a mad dog at any risk, but to insist upon a stoical indifference to the fright afterward."

But then again, "I do not think I shall ever like him as I do his brother Joe." And, a real shocker—"Would you believe it, he is refined and cultivated and yet he is a Democrat!"

So wrote the little miss from a staunch Whig household of Joe's young (but, oh, so old!) brother. Even so, the next month Varina Howell became engaged to her host's graceful sibling. The next year, February of 1845, they were married—Mr. and Mrs. Jefferson Davis.

1858

IN THE HOUSE OF REPRESENTATIVES, WASHINGTON, D.C., GALUSHA GROW OF Pennsylvania uttered a few antislavery remarks, then wandered over to the Democratic side of the aisle to talk to a colleague. From there he responded to still another member's remarks, even though he was not at his seat…or even among his fellow Republicans.

None of this was lost upon South Carolina's Democratic representative, Laurence M. Keitt, who told the Pennsylvanian to "go back to your own side of the hall."

Grow replied: "This is a free hall and every man has a right to be where he pleases. I will object when and where I please."

Whereupon Keitt said, "Sir, I will let you know that you are a black Republican puppy."

Grow then said the hall belonged to the American people, he could stay where he pleased, "and no slave driver shall crack his whip over my head."

Seconds later, the fists flew in the House chamber. Keitt went down, knocked out cold by Grow's punch to the jaw. But the fight didn't end there…or with them.

It wasn't as shocking as the time, in 1856, that South Carolina's representative, Preston Smith Brooks, strode into the Senate chamber and broke his gutta-percha cane beating on stridently abolitionist Senator Charles Sumner of Massachusetts, but the Keitt-Grow tiff was a bona fide fight on the House floor all right. Others immediately plunged into the melee. It is said that knives and even pistols were in evidence. Someone hurled a large spittoon, and Representative William Barksdale of Mississippi lost his wig to a Wisconsin member. When Barksdale got it back, he put it on backward. The levity that resulted helped restore order to the House.

In 1863, Barksdale was killed at Gettysburg, Pennsylvania. In 1864, Keitt was killed at Cold Harbor, Virginia.

1859

FOR SALE, HEADLINED THE ADVERTISEMENT IN MAJOR SOUTHERN NEWSPAPERS.
LONG COTTON AND RICE NEGROES.
Followed by:

A gang of 460 Negroes, accustomed to the culture of Rice and Provisions, among whom are a number of good mechanics and house servants. Will be sold on the 2nd and 3rd of March next, at Savannah, by

> *JOSEPH BRYAN*
> *TERMS OF SALE—One third cash; remainder by bond, bearing interest from day of sale, payable in two equal installments, to be secured by mortgage on the Negroes, and approved personal security, or for approved city acceptance on Savannah or Charleston. Purchasers paying for papers.*
> *The Negroes will be sold in families, and can be seen on the premises of Joseph Bryan, in Savannah, three days prior to the day of sale, when catalogues will be furnished.*

How much for a good, strong Negro male in 1859, on the eve of the U.S. Civil War? According to a story appearing March 9, 1859, in the New York *Tribune*, the figure was $1,600.

Slaves, though, did not wish to be sold at top price. Not at all. They would rather be, or at least appear to be, less than physically perfect, since at top price they had little hope of earning and saving the money needed to purchase freedom. Said the *Tribune* account of Bryan's sale: "But let him [the slave] have a rupture, or lose a limb, or sustain any other injury, that renders him of much less service to his owner, and reduces his value to $300 or $400, and he may hope to accumulate that sum, and eventually to purchase his liberty."

The advertised sale, the largest slave sale in the South for several years, "went on for two long days, during which time there were sold 429 men, women and children." They generated a total take of $303,850.

They were sold by an absentee owner, a recently divorced man from Philadelphia who afterward, the *Tribune* said, was seen "solacing the wounded hearts of the people he had sold from their firesides and their homes by doling out to them small change at the rate of a dollar a head."

1860

IT WAS NO ACCIDENT THE BLUE COCKADES WERE SEEN ON THE MEN'S HATS OUTSIDE A meeting hall in Charleston, South Carolina, on the twentieth day of December. The blue cockade deliberately recalled the nullification controversy that had upset President Andrew Jackson three decades earlier. Only now the movement that was in the air was secession!

The hall was the gathering place for the South Carolina Convention, which by a vote of 169 to 0 adopted an ordinance cutting the state's ties with the Union. The reaction in Charleston was jubilation: parades, bonfires, pealing church bells, even cannons speaking their piece. After the fateful document was signed that evening, wrote elderly Virginia agronomist (and avid secessionist) Edmund Ruffin, "Every man waved or threw up his hat & every lady waved her handkerchief."

Another onlooker was Samuel Wylie Crawford, a U.S. Army doctor recently assigned to duty in Charleston. Outside the hall, he wrote, "the whole city was wild with excitement as the news spread like wildfire through its streets." Indeed, "old men ran shouting down the streets."

To be sure, not everyone in Charleston looked with favor upon the action making South Carolina the first state to quit the Union. Judge James L. Petigru understood better than most of his fellow citizens the trials ahead. "I tell you there is a fire," he warned. "They have this day set a blazing torch to the temple of constitutional liberty, and, please God, we shall have no more peace forever."

In far-off Washington it was South Carolina's fiery Representative Laurence M. Keitt who carried the news to a wedding reception attended by President James Buchanan. Hearing the commotion behind him as Keitt arrived, Buchanan asked Virginia Congressman Roger A. Pryor's wife Sara what was going on. She found Keitt "leaping in the air, shaking a paper over his head, exclaiming, 'Thank God! Oh, thank God! South Carolina has seceded!'"

She returned to Buchanan's side, bent over, and told him, "It appears, Mr. President, that South Carolina has seceded from the Union." Stunned, Buchanan fell back into his chair, clutching its arms. He asked her to call his carriage; he would be leaving right away. "There was no more thought of bride, bridegroom, wedding cake or wedding breakfast," wrote Sara.

1860

FUTURE PRESIDENT OF THE UNITED STATES TO FUTURE VICE PRESIDENT OF THE Confederate States of America: The USA would not—that is, *not*—attempt to dictate policy on slavery within the CSA.

So wrote Abraham Lincoln to Georgia Representative Alexander H. Stephens on December 22. "The South would be in no more danger in this respect," wrote President-elect Lincoln to his onetime colleague in the U.S. House, "than it was in the days of Washington. I suppose, however, this does not meet the case. You think slavery is a right and ought to be extended; while we think it is wrong and ought to be restricted. That I suppose is the rub."

★★★

If President Buchanan was stunned by the secession of South Carolina (no real surprise to most political onlookers), South Carolina in turn was about to be outraged by the audacity—the effrontery—of the U.S. Army officer commanding a few troops at Fort Moultrie in Charleston Harbor.

On the night after Christmas, without notice or warning, he moved his entire garrison from the exposed, unprotected spit of land known as Sullivan's Island to the real and more isolated island out in the harbor—Fort Sumter.

Moultrie, as Abner Doubleday noted, to South Carolinians, "was almost a sacred spot, endeared by many precious historical associations, for the ancestors of most of the principal families had fought there in the Revolutionary War."

Doubleday, later famous for his dubious claim of "baseball pioneer," was a young Federal officer taking part in the nighttime move on December 26. His commander at Fort Sumter, the man who decided his men would be safer, his delicate position in a sea of hostility stronger, was Major Robert Anderson. And never mind that Anderson's own father had fought the British at the same Fort Moultrie and had been kept prisoner in Charleston! All that aside, Charleston was outraged.

As Anderson's small command of sixty-one enlisted men, seven officers, and thirteen musicians debarked from their boats on the wharf at Sumter, local workers engaged in improvements at the island fort "rushed out to meet us," recalled Doubleday. Most of them were angry and called out, "What are these soldiers doing here?" A "demonstration" with bayonets forced them back, "and the disloyal workmen were shipped off to the mainland."

On that mainland, meanwhile, Charleston was agog over Major Anderson's surprise move. Diarist Mary Boykin Chesnut, wife of a former U.S. senator from South Carolina, wrote that Anderson had "united the Cotton States." Reflecting the mood of those around her, she also noted: "Those who want a row are in high glee. Those who dread it are glum and thoughtful."

The talk in Charleston the next day, December 27, was, "Fort Sumter must be taken," even though Sumter was one of the strongest Federal bastions in the South. With obvious trepidation, Mary Chesnut had to wonder: "How in the name of sense are they to manage it? I shudder to think of rash moves."

1861

THE TROUBLE WITH FORT SUMTER WAS THAT IT REALLY WAS AN ISLAND SITUATED in hostile waters. As the year began, it was, by order of South Carolina's authorities, cut off from the mainland—no communication, no supplies for Major Anderson and his garrison of eighty souls.

In Washington, the policymakers of the Federal capital awaited a change in presidents at the very moment of the young Republic's worst crisis ever. Winfield Scott, general in chief of the U.S. Army, had obtained permission to send Major Anderson help in the form of supplies, ammunition, and additional troops.

The supplies and 250 reinforcements set sail in an ordinary, civilian merchant ship called *Star of the West*. But at Fort Sumter, Anderson was expecting his resupply and reinforcement to be accomplished by U.S. Navy warships.

The *Star of the West* arrived off the harbor entrance at 1:30 in the morning on January 9, then hove to in the main shipping channel to wait for daylight before proceeding farther.

As daylight began to reveal her outlines, she was moving again. Artillery hidden in nearby sandhills opened fire. The first shot was traditional—across the bow. When the *Star of the West* kept moving, the cannon fire continued. Two rounds struck the merchant ship, which ran a flag up and down a forward mast as if pleading for Anderson to tell her what to do. Now Fort Moultrie lay in the ship's path, manned by hot-eyed South Carolina secessionists. And Moultrie's guns, while not yet in range, opened fire.

At Fort Sumter, all was confusion and disarray at the ship's unexpected appearance. Army surgeon Samuel Crawford, one of Major Anderson's seven officers at the island outpost, later wrote that Anderson didn't know what to do, since he had anticipated a warship rather than a merchant vessel. And further, snarled halyards prevented his men from replying quickly to the *Star's* signals.

The *Star of the West* was not about to present her vulnerable broadside for a raking by the batteries at Fort Moultrie, and so the rescue ship turned and pointed toward the open sea. Major Anderson was about to order Fort Sumter's own guns into action—against Fort Moultrie. But he saw the ship turn away. "Hold on," he told his men. "Do not fire."

It was all over in just a few minutes. "The flag of the country had been fired on under our very guns, and no helping hand had been extended," wrote Dr. Crawford, who soon would give up his medical bag to become an active combat commander—and eventually a major general—in the Union Army.

★★★

After a flutter of messages between Major Anderson at Fort Sumter and various authorities representing the newly formed Confederate States of America, there came a final, most formal, notice to the U.S. Army officer at 3:30 a.m. on April 12.

Sir: By authority of Brigadier General Beauregard, commanding the provisional forces of the Confederate States, we have the honor to notify you that he will open fire of his batteries at Fort Sumter in one hour from this time.

★ BEGINNINGS ★

First Time Out

WHAT WAS IT LIKE, THAT FIRST TIME UNDER FIRE? IN REAL BATTLE DURING the U.S. Civil War? Brothers of the native soil against brothers of the same good earth?

Said (or wrote) an officer from Maine sometime after: "The behavior of those who were hit appeared to be singular; and, as there were so many of them, it looked as if we had a crowd of howling dervishes dancing and kicking around in our ranks."

Said (or wrote) a Confederate cavalry colonel: "Barely in position, I heard a distant cannon, and at the same instant saw the ball high in the air. As near as I could calculate, it was going to strike about where I stood, and I dismounted with remarkable agility, only to see the missile of war pass 60 feet overhead."

An unnamed soldier added: "For the first time in your life you listen to the whizzing of iron. Grape and canister fly into the ranks, bomb-shells burst over-head, and the fragments fly all around you."

Maine officer again: "A bullet often knocks over the man it hits, and rarely fails by its force alone to disturb his equilibrium. Then the shock, whether painful or not, causes a sudden jump or shudder."

Rebel colonel: "I felt rather foolish as I looked at my men, but a good deal re-lieved when I saw that they, too, had all squatted to the ground, and were none of them looking up at me. I quickly mounted and ordered them to 'stand up.'"

Unnamed soldier: "A friend falls; perhaps a dozen or 20 of your comrades lie wounded or dying at your feet; a strange, involuntary shrinking steals over you, which it is impossible to resist."

Maine officer: "Now, as every man, with hardly an exception, was either killed, wounded, hit in the clothes, hit by spent balls or stones, or jostled by his wounded comrades, it follows that we had a wonderful exhibition. Some reeled round and round, others threw up their arms and fell over backwards, others went plunging backward trying to regain their balance; a few fell to the front, but generally the force of the bullet prevented this, except where it struck low and apparently knocked the soldier's feet from under him. Many dropped the musket and seized the wounded part with both hands, and a very few fell dead."

Rebel colonel: "We were soon ordered to charge, and drove the enemy through the tall prairie grass, till they came to a creek and escaped. We passed some of the dead and wounded, the first sad results of real war that I had ever seen."

Unnamed soldier: "You feel inclined neither to advance nor recede, but are spell-bound by the contending emotions of the moral and physical man. The cheek blanches, the lip quivers, and the eye almost hesitates to look upon the scene."

Maine officer: "The enemy were armed with every kind of rifle and musket, and as their front was three times ours, we were under a crossfire almost from the first. The various tunes sung by the bullets we shall never forget....The fierce zip of the Minié bullets was not prominent by comparison at that particular moment, though there were enough of them certainly. The main body of sound was produced by the singing of slow, round balls and buckshot fired from a smooth-bore, which do not cut or tear the air as the creased ball does.

"Each bullet, according to its kind, size, rate of speed, and nearness to the ear, made a different sound. They seemed to be going past in sheets, all around and above us."

Rebel colonel: "At night the heavens opened wide, the rain fell in torrents; not even a campfire could be kept to light up the impenetrable gloom, and I sought a comfortable mud-hole to sleep as best I could.

"The pale rigid faces that I had seen turned up for the evening sun appeared before me as I tried in vain to shield my own [face] from the driving rain, and as the big foot of a comrade, blundering round in the darkness, splashed my eyes full of mud, I closed them to sleep, muttering to myself, 'And this is war.'"

Unnamed soldier: "In this [frozen] attitude you may, perhaps, be ordered to stand an hour, inactive, havoc meanwhile marking its footsteps with blood on every side. Finally the order is given to advance, to fire, or to charge. And now, what a change! With your first shot you become a new man. Personal safety is your least concern. Fear has no existence in your bosom. Hesitation gives way to an uncontrollable desire to rush into the thickest part of the fight. The dead and dying around you, if they receive a passing thought, only serve to stimulate you to revenge."

Further: "You become cool and deliberate, and watch the effect of the bullets, the shower of bursting shells, the passage of cannon-balls as they rake their murderous channels through your ranks, the plunging of wounded horses, the agonies of the dying, and the clash of contending arms, which follows the charge, with a feeling so calloused by surrounding circumstances that your soul seems dead to every sympathising [sic] and selfish thought."

So it was for the newcomer to battle, it seems. But when it's all over, what then?

"Walking the battleground, among the dead and groaning wounded," said the unknown soldier, "[you] begin to realize the horrors of war, and experience a reaction of nature." Wondrously, "the heart opens its floodgates, humanity reasserts herself again, and you begin to feel."

You now help the wounded, friend or foe. Foe, too? Yes. "The enemy, whom, but a short time before, full of hate, you were doing all in your power to kill, you now endeavor to save."

You provide water, food, whatever he needs. "All that is human and charitable in your nature now rises to the surface." Amazing. And, oh, so true: "A battlefield is eminently a place that tries men's souls."

Fresh Start Sought

HOW TO START AN "INSTANT" GOVERNMENT? THAT WAS THE CHALLENGE FOR A mere thirty-eight men representing the "secesh" states early in 1861, and the solution they came up with—in an amazingly short time—was a mirror image of the very government they were so avowed to leave behind.

They wished for a president and for a congress, and of course a constitution, all very much like the democratic system they knew so well. All in all, their creation wasn't that different in its framework from the government seated in Washington, D.C.

In framework, yes, but in substance, a few major differences! One, the very issue that affected all differences between the two governments—slavery.

The Union—the Federal government of the United States—had not yet banned slavery. That was yet to come. Lincoln had not yet written his Emancipation Proclamation. Fort Sumter, in fact, had not yet been fired upon.

No matter. The secession leaders, gathering in Montgomery, Alabama, to form a new union, chose to have a constitution very similar to the familiar U.S. Constitution, to have a president and congress all their own (although *their* president would be limited to one six-year term only).

The delegates assembled made no bones about their view of slavery. It would stay! Their constitution ruling all matters of law within their nation (just like the U.S. Constitution) expressly sought out and addressed this most acerbic issue. No law, the new charter said, would be allowed if it had the effect of "denying or impairing the right of property in Negro slaves." In short, the institution of slavery would be protected by constitutional mandate (although in the same breath the African slave trade was banned outright).

The thirty-eight delegates of six seceding states (with Texas soon expected, as well) had gathered on February 4, 1861, weeks before the firing on Fort Sumter. Howell Cobb of Georgia had been elected president of the convention of secesh states that convened in Montgomery at the noon hour, and he lost no time in stating their common cause. "The separation is perfect, complete, and perpetual," he said. "The great duty is now imposed upon us of providing for these States a government for their future security and protection."

In Washington on the same day, a Virginia-sponsored Peace Convention also convened. There, 131 delegates from twenty-one states searched for a way to mend the national rift. Former President John Tyler, himself a Virginian, presided over this convention.

Congress, too, was meeting, and the Electoral College presidential vote approved by Congress this day was: Abraham Lincoln, 180 votes; John C. Breckinridge of Kentucky (a future Confederate general), 72; John Bell of Tennessee (the Constitutional Union's presidential candidate), 39; and Stephen Douglas, Democrat and senator from Illinois, Lincoln's famous debate rival, only 12.

Also on February 4 in Washington, Louisiana's two U.S. senators, Judah Benjamin and John Slidell, left their Federal seats to join Louisiana in the secession. Benjamin would serve as attorney general, and later as secretary of state, for the new nation.

The next day, February 5, John Tyler told his convention that "the eyes of the whole country are turned to this assembly, in expectation and hope." Unfortunately, not *all*, for in Montgomery, at that other convention, the Confederacy's future vice president, Alexander Stephens of Georgia, pushed through a slate of rules for the secesh convention's business. Then South Carolina's Christopher Memminger submitted a fateful resolution urging the creation of "a Confederacy of the States which have seceded from the Federal Union." A committee was to study on it and present a plan for forming the new nation's government.

Events clearly were moving beyond redemption.

On February 6, Abraham and Mary Todd Lincoln were hosts at a farewell reception for friends, neighbors, and politicians at the Lincoln home in Springfield, Illinois—like Montgomery, a state capital. He would be leaving February 11, the day before his birthday, for the journey to Washington, never to return.

February 7 dawned, and before that day's end Christopher Memminger's Committee of Twelve brought forward its plan of government. The entire convention now met in secret to debate the content of the report. Details of the South's fresh start would be argued *in camera*.

The day of the nation aborning was February 8, and the vote taken that evening for a provisional constitution was without a single dissent. It was provisional because the document still had to go before the several seceding states for their ratification. That, too, would be accomplished with surprising speed for such a weighty matter.

Why all the rush? The purpose was to have everything in place and functioning by the time Lincoln was sworn in—March 4—as the *unacceptable* new president of the Federal Union. Amazingly, the Southern secessionists had their provisional bylaws and governmental framework in operation within a week of their first meeting. And it only took a month for the various states to ratify a permanent constitution just slightly different from the provisional one, and both hardly at odds with the original U.S. Constitution—*except for the slavery clause*.

Such similarity was no accident, really. As one of the secesh delegates later wrote, "There was a marked and purposed agreement with the Constitution of the United States." It wasn't that the South left the U.S. Constitution behind, but rather that it withdrew from "wicked and injurious perversions of the compact."

A name was needed for the new nation, and what should it be? The "Republic of Washington"? Or another "United States of America," and fie to those who thought that name already secured by the Union's perversion of the old order? In the end, the new nation's name simply reflected the Memminger resolution's language calling for a "Confederacy of the States" seceding from the Union. And so it became the Confederate States of America (CSA).

All this, in its record-setting time, took place at the hands of the thirty-eight delegates who had repaired for their work to Montgomery, Alabama, still a barren-looking new city, which, although a state capital, was situated on the bluffs of the Alabama River and marked by a handsome Greek-revival capitol building. The town of forty years' duration thus far offered only two hotels of any size, the Montgomery and the Exchange House.

At this new news center, the famous British journalist William Howard Russell of the *Times* of London found slave pens and slave auctions quite active. The visiting Englishman, whose own government had banned slavery throughout the British Empire in 1834, compared hapless Montgomery to some woebegone town in central Russia. Not too complimentary of what today is one of the most striking assemblages of government structures in the world.

Who, meanwhile, were the men (indeed, all the delegates were white and male) who devised convention, constitution, congress, executive branch, and, in such short time, electoral machinery designed to give the new republic a chief executive?

Said Alexander Stephens afterward: "They were men of substance as well as of solid character—men of education, of reading, or refinement, and well versed in the principles of government." Stephens and others wrote that the secret deliberations—press and public were barred—were orderly, calm, even dignified in tone. They were also brief, with little fire-eating oratory. But still secret; no public access allowed, although some people did object.

Still another reason for all the haste, aside from presenting the hated Lincoln with an already existing government, was for the new government to be in place before the more wild-eyed rebels could let their guns loose on stubborn Major Robert Anderson and his Federal troops quartered at Fort Sumter in Charleston Harbor. Furthermore, future allies among the wavering border states and the onlooking outside world must be convinced, posthaste, as to the legitimacy of the new American Revolution, the new Montgomery declaration of independence from tyranny, the grave manifestation of states' rights.

By February 9, then, all were ready to move a step farther and elect a president and a vice president. In the politicking that went on the night of February 8 and all day February 9, the name of a moderate from Mississippi gradually rose to the fore as more extreme candidates were cast aside (along with a few favorite sons offering no compelling appeal overall). That man, no raging secessionist himself, a West Point graduate, a Mexican War veteran, a son-in-law at one time to the late President Zachary Taylor, a former U.S. senator and secretary of war under a thoroughly "Yankee" president (Franklin Pierce of New Hampshire)—that man was at his Mississippi plantation, called Brierfield, peacefully pruning rosebushes with his wife, Varina, when the word came on the Sunday morning after the Saturday evening session in Montgomery officially nominated and elected him president.

So it was that a still fairly young United States of America was presented with a mirror image of itself, small in leadership numbers, weak in resources, but vast in territory. So alike were the two nations that even their day-to-day, more mundane, laws would be the same, since the delegates assembled in Montgomery had made no bones about this aspect, either. All laws of the Federal Union, they had decided, would be the laws of the Confederacy as well, except, of course, when they were in conflict with the new Confederate Constitution.

Eerily, we might say how, so many years later, the incoming presidents of the two nations had both been born in Kentucky, a border state that itself would be torn asunder and see its people play mirror-opposite roles in the war to come. Moreover, Abe Lincoln and his counterpart from the South, Jefferson Davis, both left their homes on the same day, Monday, February 11, 1861, to travel to their respective capitals for their inaugurations as president.

Who the South Was

IF YOU THINK ABOUT IT, THE SOUTH THAT FORMED THE CONFEDERACY WAS A FAR cry from the aristocratic Southland that provided one U.S. president after another following the Revolutionary War. During the Revolutionary period itself, the South produced George Washington, Thomas Jefferson, George Mason, James Madison, James Monroe, George Wythe, and a host of other striking leaders. It was the old Southland, too, that gave the New World its model legislative body—the Virginia Assembly—and that provided the Supreme Court its first historical "superstar," John Marshall.

Consider, too, that the same region produced the author of the Declaration of Independence and led in the framing of the U.S. Constitution. And yet you could say it failed in its statesmanship during the Civil War.

The fact is the Southland that produced the Confederacy was not the same Southland that had contributed so much to the nation earlier. It was in 1861 a region with a shifted center of gravity; it was now a land of rugged, rough-and-tumble frontier types and nouveau riche rather than aristocratic gentry, as noted by Burton J. Hendrick in his 1939 work, *Statesmen of the Lost Cause*.

Its leaders, wrote Hendrick, also bore little resemblance to the traditional Southern aristocrats. "Really, the Confederate States of America rose in a region as recently frontier in character as the West that produced Abraham Lincoln. Of the seven states that formed the Montgomery government, only two—South Carolina and Georgia—existed before 1787."

Indeed, four of the Confederacy states—Florida, Louisiana, Arkansas, and Texas—plus a good part of Mississippi, were Spanish-owned and Spanish-ruled at the time of the Union's birth in the eighteenth century. Conspicuously absent at the Confederacy's formation in the mid-nineteenth century (but joining in later) was that font of early American leadership, Virginia, to say nothing of Tennessee and North Carolina.

The fact is, argued Hendrick with persuasive merit, traditional "Southern aristocrats" were hard to find in the Confederacy's ranks of civic leadership. Jefferson Davis and Abraham Lincoln were born in log cabins a mere 120 miles away from one another in Kentucky. Davis and his fellow leaders of the first Confederate states "hardly resembled" the leaders produced in the tobacco lands of old Virginia and the Carolinas. The Confederacy of 1861 was a South moved westward, "a land of newly acquired wealth, not particularly well-mannered or cultured, but pushing, self-assertive and arrogant."

It wasn't even all-Southern, "for the hordes that had rushed into the cotton El Dorado of the Southwest were composed not only of quick fortune-hunting sons of Dixie, but of adventurers from the North and New England." Here were the breeders of the new South's civilian leadership. "Merely to catalogue the most important of these [Confederate] chieftains shows how the insurgent South, in its social and economic aspects, differed from the land of Washington and Jefferson."

Not only had President Davis been swaddled in a log cabin like his counterpart Lincoln, but Vice President Alexander Stephens had been a "corn dropper" on his father's "slaveless farm and [a] chore boy in tasks usually assigned to Negroes." Further, "The Secretary of State…was the son of the keeper of a dried fish shop in London. The Secretary of the Treasury, born in Germany, spent his childhood in a Charleston orphanage. The Secretary of the Navy, son of a Connecticut Yankee, started life as assistant to his widowed mother in running a sailors' boarding house in Key West, Florida. The Postmaster General, son of a tanner, had for a time engaged in an occupation that made any man an outcast in the South—that of plantation overseer." And so on.

That they were somewhat more plebeian in background than their Revolutionary forebears becomes obvious under such examination. But if the South failed to produce great civil leaders, what about the military side of things?

Here it cannot be denied that the South excelled in the commanders it found. And look, noted Hendrick again, where they came from—the superstars at any rate. "Of the five Confederate generals who won worldwide fame—Lee, Jackson, Stuart, Joseph E. Johnston, Longstreet—four most suggestively were from Virginia; Longstreet came from Georgia, also a state of the Old South. That is to say, the leaders who gave the Confederacy prestige were mostly Virginians of superior breed, while the cotton belt was the region that provided the politicians who failed."

Whether of "superior breed" or not, however, in the end those distinctly superior military men couldn't do the trick, either. New or old, the South that went to war against the North in 1861 simply didn't have the resources to prevail.

Fate Makes a Choice

IT WAS A PRETTY LITTLE SPEECH, AND A SENSIBLE ONE...BUT WITH WAR AFOOT, every man's fate was all atangle. The place was Alcatraz Island in San Francisco Bay, future site of the notorious Federal prison. The principals were two U.S. Army officers: Lieutenants James B. McPherson and Edward Porter Alexander. The time was antebellum by just days, since it was in the fateful April of 1861.

Young Alexander, a West Point graduate and native of Georgia, had learned of his home state's secession from the Union, and he was determined to do the same: resign and join the newly formed Confederacy. He had orders to transfer back east from his posting with the Army Corps of Engineers in Washington State, and his thought was to boat homeward with wife, Bettie, via the Panama Isthmus before taking the ultimate step. Arriving at San Francisco, however, he found two complications. Their ship for Panama already had left, and he had new orders directing him to McPherson's small command on Alcatraz Island.

The fresh orders meant that Alexander must resign on the spot and find some way to convey himself and his wife across the continent on their own. Looking back, it seems incongruous, but Alexander evidently felt no hesitation in explaining his predicament to fellow Union officer McPherson, even though Alexander very shortly could be (and indeed would be) at war against the Federals, McPherson among them. The two young men obviously liked one another and had no problem in discussing Alexander's request to submit his resignation to McPherson for forwarding to higher command. Alexander would take a leave of absence to travel on home to Georgia and be in place when the acceptance came through the chain of command. All so very proper!

McPherson promptly agreed to place no impediment in Alexander's way if he must go. He, in fact, would do all in his power to facilitate Alexander's plans. But, he pleaded, don't go. "Those urgent orders to stop you here [at Alcatraz] are meant to say that, if you are willing to keep out of the war on either side, you can do so."

It was a real siren song: Don't go. Stay and avoid fighting against your own people. Stay, McPherson said, and spend the war on the West Coast on fortification duty. The pending war would be no ninety-day affair, as some were predicting, but would be fought to the bitter end. "If you go, as an educated soldier, you will be put in the front rank. Only God knows what may happen to you individually, but for your cause, there can be but one result. It must be lost."

And why so?

Your whole population is only about eight millions, while the North has twenty millions. Of your eight millions, three millions are slaves who may become an element of danger. You have no army, no navy, no treasury and practically none of the manufactures and machine shops necessary for the support of armies and for war on a large scale. You are but scattered agricultural communities, and you will be cut off from the rest of the world by blockade. Your cause must end in defeat, and the individual risks to you must be great.

McPherson was correct in every particular, and to his baleful outlook for Southern fortune he added the postscript that Alexander could stay safely on the West Coast, advancing rapidly in rank while senior officers went east and were consumed by the war; he could make wise investments from a knowledge of local land values to be gained as an Army engineer in the San Francisco Bay area. In four years' time, he would be a rich man. "Briefly, remaining here you have every opportunity for professional reputation, for promotion and for wealth. Going home, you have every personal risk to run, and in a cause foredoomed to failure."

Alexander was impressed by his comrade's earnest warning. Indeed, "it made me realize, as I had never done before, the gravity of the decision which I had to make."

Even so, the young Georgian was unswayed. When all was said and done, his choice came down to one thought: "I must go with my people." And his people were those of Georgia, not the United States.

He conceded that McPherson's dire warnings would probably prove true but explained that his people believed their cause was liberty, and that was that. "If I don't come and bear my part, they will believe me to be a coward. And I shall not know whether I am or not. I have just got to go and stand my chances."

As fate would have it, future Confederate general Alexander would provide great service to his Army. He introduced wigwag signaling to the Confederate cause, was the Confederacy's first aerial balloonist for reconnaissance purposes, and, most important, emerged from the Civil War as one of its leading artillerists.

His signals warning of a Union flank attack at First Bull Run (First Manassas) contributed to the Southern victory there, and his artillery was instrumental in turning back Ambrose Burnside at Fredericksburg. On an anecdotal note, it was one of his guns that sent a brick caroming off the head of "Fighting Joe"

Hooker at Chancellorsville, after which the stunned Hooker remained uncharacteristically timid and ineffective in his command position and was relieved by Lincoln shortly before the Battle of Gettysburg. Alexander's artillery also served admirably at Gettysburg, Spotsylvania, Cold Harbor, and during the siege of Petersburg. He was with Robert E. Lee at the surrender at Appomattox (which he advised against). After the war, he became a railroad president and author of a widely hailed memoir of his Civil War days. In short, he emerged a Southern hero, a ranking figure of the Civil War…his reputation far greater than any he would have built by remaining safe and out of the way on the West Coast as his would-be mentor McPherson had urged.

As for McPherson, also outstanding and widely admired, fate was not so kind. Also reaching the rank of general, McPherson served through U. S. Grant's Tennessee campaign of 1862, in the siege of Vicksburg, and in William Tecumseh Sherman's Atlanta campaign of 1864 until cut down and killed by desultory Confederate gunfire outside Atlanta.

They say that his commander, Sherman, cried when he heard of McPherson's death.

Alexander never saw his fellow West Pointer again after their parting at San Francisco in early 1861. "Our sad parting," Alexander called it in his post–Civil War *Military Memoirs of a Confederate*.

Racing to War

THE EVENTS AFTER SOUTH CAROLINA'S SECESSION VOTE ON DECEMBER 20, 1860, came in sporadic bursts. Fort Sumter was not always the focus, although it is true that on December 27 South Carolina seized nearby Federal facilities Fort Moultrie and Castle Pinckney. South Carolina sent a delegation to Washington with the demand, delivered before New Year's, that Federal troops leave Charleston and its environs. To this President James Buchanan, surprisingly stern in this instance, said no; Fort Sumter would defend "against all hostile attacks, from whatever quarter." By New Year's Day, South Carolina had also taken over the Federal arsenal at Charleston.

Fast-forward from there:

January 3, 1861, Georgia seizes Fort Pulaski at Savannah.

January 9, Mississippi secedes, and South Carolina fires upon the Fort Sumter relief ship *Star of the West*.

January 10, Florida secedes.

January 11, Alabama secedes.

January 19, Georgia secedes.

January 26, Louisiana secedes.

January 29, Kansas becomes a state—slave-free.

February 4, A provisional Confederate government takes shape in Montgomery, Alabama, and the Virginia-sponsored Peace Convention meets in Washington.

February 9, Jefferson Davis selected as Confederate president.

February 13, Electoral College count: Lincoln officially designated as the new U.S. president.

February 18, Jefferson Davis inaugurated as president of the CSA, and the stirring tune "Dixie" breaks out in Montgomery.

February 23, Lincoln secretly trains into Washington to foil any rumored assassination plots. Texas secedes.

February 26, Federals abandon Camp Colorado, Texas.

February 27, Jefferson Davis names three would-be peace commissioners to negotiate with Washington. The Peace Convention in the capital city sends its recommendations to Congress after much internal argument—no salvation for the Nation here.

February 28, North Carolina says no to secession and stays in the Union... for a while.

March 1, Military control of the Charleston area officially passes from state control to that of the Confederate government. President Davis names Brigadier General Pierre G. T. Beauregard commander.

March 2, The Confederacy welcomes its first convert, Texas. Texas seizes the Federal revenue cutter Henry Dodge at Galveston.

March 3, On this Sunday in Washington, a busy Abe Lincoln hosts his Cabinet appointees at dinner and visits the Senate. In Charleston, Beauregard takes command of his troops.

March 4, Lincoln is inaugurated as sixteenth president. In a time of unprecedented crisis, the nation has a new president, a new administration from the Cabinet on down, and a political party—Republican—that is new to the seat of power. How will it all end?

Better Angels Invoked

AT HIS INAUGURATION ON A CLOUDY BUT MILD MARCH 4, LINCOLN DOFFED HIS black silk hat prior to delivering his inaugural address and…hesitated. Where to put it? Two men reached for it. One was a young reporter named Henry Watterson, who in just a few weeks would be a Confederate soldier and later a journalist for Southern newspapers often on the run from Mr. Abe Lincoln's Yankee troops. The other reaching for the hat, and more successfully at that, was the senator from Illinois, Lincoln's own rival and debating opponent of considerable fame, Mr. Stephen Douglas. Douglas, a Democrat, had been defeated by Lincoln in the presidential race of 1860 (although, it is true, the rebellious Southern Democrats had been represented in the same contest by Vice President John C. Breckinridge of Kentucky).

Not yet sworn in, Lincoln said in his inaugural speech that while he had no intention of interfering with "the institution of slavery," he also felt, "No state, on its own mere action, can get out of the Union." He waxed a bit poetic and was obviously appealing for good will on all sides when he said to a nation not yet one century old (the American Revolution took place only about eighty years earlier): "The mystic chords of memory, stretching from every battlefield, and patriot grave, to every living heart and hearthstone, all over this broad land, will yet swell the chorus of the Union, when again touched, as surely they will be, by the better angels of our nature." More bluntly, he warned: "In your hands, my dissatisfied fellow countrymen, and not in mine, is the momentous issue of civil war. The government will not assail you. You can have no conflict without being yourselves the aggressors. You have no oath registered in Heaven to destroy the government, while I have the most solemn one to 'preserve, protect and defend' it."

And so the immediate issue was not slavery but secession. Or, as Lincoln saw it, the Union, the Union, the Union. He was sworn in after his speech, incidentally, by Chief Justice Roger B. Taney, the jurist famous for his majority opinion in the Dred Scott case, which declared a slave was not a citizen with the right to sue in a Federal court. Taney was from Maryland, a Democrat, and a former slave-owner himself.

Lincoln had spent the night at Willard's Hotel, and he rode to the Capitol in an open carriage, accompanied by outgoing Democratic President James Buchanan. Security was tight, and almost everybody knew war was imminent. Just that morning Buchanan had received word that Major Robert Anderson, commander of the garrison trapped on the island of Fort Sumter in Charleston Harbor, could not hold out against the forces arrayed against him unless he was reinforced by twenty thousand men. That word was passed along to Lincoln even before he rose to speak on the wooden platform erected for his inauguration at the East Portico of the Capitol. Begun around one o'clock, the inaugural speech took about thirty minutes, during which time, it is reported, Senator Douglas held Lincoln's hat for him.

Social Notice Taken

SOCIAL NOTES FROM ALL OVER—

At the recent inaugural festivities for His Excellency Mr. Davis in Montgomery, the noted hostess Aurelia Blassingame Fitzpatrick, wife of the former U.S. Senator, raised more than a few eyebrows when she boldly poked the Confederacy's newly installed leader in the back with her parasol, merely to gain his attention so that she might have a word with him.

It is said also that she was not hesitant, whether then or on other occasions, to urge her own husband upon Mr. Davis as a candidate for his Cabinet. The audacious Aurelia shocked some of the other ladies yet again upon telling Mr. Davis that his reference to a possibly long war was "too gloomy" a remark to make.

Far from gloomy were the bright balls and dinner parties attended by fabulous Southern belles whose encouragement would mean so much to their men at war. One young lady, Ida Rice, was so popular that her countrymen named a cannon in Charleston harbor for her.

Returning to the inaugural ceremonies themselves, wasn't it a sight when all those pretty young ladies on a balcony above the swearing-in let loose a cascade of flowers upon Mr. Davis!

Quite a flutter of attention has been stirred also by adoption of the official Confederate flag—a handsome and eye-catching standard of red, white, and blue (like the Yankee flag in colors only!). How fitting that the flag should be hoisted at the new capital for the first time by Letitia Tyler, granddaughter of the former President and Virginia Governor John Tyler—namesake also of his first wife, Letitia, who bore him seven children before her passing during his presidency.

Speaking of Washington and things Union, one true Southern lady who would prefer to put true embarrassment behind her is Elodie Todd of Selma, Alabama, half-sister to Mary Todd Lincoln, who sits in the Union White House presently as wife of Abraham. It may be fact that Miss Elodie is engaged to her handsome Captain Nathaniel H.R. Dawson, but that perfectly proper liaison has not protected her from hearing the most ugly sentiments expressed within her hearing about the husband of her sister. Said the future Mrs. Dawson in a letter to her beloved, "People constantly wish he may be hung and all such evils may attend his footsteps."

Doing her utmost to bear up, Miss Elodie donated the Captain's "Magnolia Cadets" of Selma a silken banner to take into battle with them—battle against her sister's Union, quite naturally.

All over Alabama in these exciting and turbulent days, the ladies have been making many a wondrous contribution to the cause. Nor have they shirked at patriotically offering their men to the gods of war!

For instance, Maria Ellington of Russell County recently marched into the field where her own two sons were busy at their work and told them to join the army and serve until whenever the war against the Union should end. Further, an anonymous letter-writer not only told readers of a Montgomery newspaper that mothers should offer their sons to battle, but also advised those same sons "they must die" facing the enemy and entrust themselves "in His care Who is the God of war."

In Selma, meanwhile, at least one lady took it upon herself to avoid stepping out with any man who was not in uniform. Another Selma lass broke off an engagement to a young man who had not yet enlisted. Adding deepest sort of insult to injury, she sent him a skirt and ladies' undergarments, together with her tart advice, "Wear these or volunteer."

With activities and sentiments like these, can there be any doubt as to the future prospect of the Confederate cause!

Indeed, if the ladies could only join their menfolk at the front lines, there would be no lingering doubts whatsoever. For example, word has been received of the confrontation off Appalachicola, Florida, where a Yankee ship had the audacity to stop and board a Confederate blockade-running ship. As the Confederate flag sadly fluttered down from its proud perch, Mrs. F. Holland of Greenville snatched it up before any onlooker, Yankee or Rebel, could move. Wrapping the proud flag about her own body, she told the startled onlookers that she would die rather than surrender the "holy banner." Even her husband was aghast, but the Yankee officer in charge honored her stand (perhaps somewhat sardonically, true) with a single-gun salute. With heroes, or heroines, like Mrs. Holland, how can the South lose? Truly now?

Lincoln Wins Rebel Debate

WEEKS BEFORE THE FIRING ON FORT SUMTER, ABE LINCOLN SAW THAT WAR WAS inevitable. He did not wish it, but he was girded for it. It would be a calamity for the nation, but it must be. After all that had passed since the time of his inauguration March 4, 1861, there seemed no other way to preserve and protect the Union. Secession had frozen in place; a new Confederate government had sprung into being in Montgomery; and at Charleston, the guns were aimed at Major Robert Anderson's Fort Sumter. The fireeaters were dancing in impatience.

Lincoln had only to say the word, to touch fire to fuse, and it would begin: War!

But Lincoln was wiser than that. And in the South, it took a fireeater to see "Old Abe's" strategy and to warn against falling into his trap.

The fireeater was Georgia's former U.S. Senator Robert Toombs, who only weeks before had risen in the august Senate chamber at Washington to castigate the Republicans as "black" and "perfidious," to denounce the newly elected Lincoln as "an enemy of the human race…who deserves the execration of all mankind." The same Georgian dared the North to make the Southerners stay in the Union. Like a schoolboy thumbing his nose at a potential adversary, he cried: "Come and do it!" Georgia, he declared, was on the warpath. "We are as ready to fight now as we will ever be! Treason? Bah!"

Those hot words marked his swan song as a senator, for minutes later, in January 1861, Toombs was gone, resigned to join his state in secession (but not before visiting the U.S. Treasury to collect the remainder of his Federal salary and mileage compensation funds for his return home).

Oddly, it was the same Toombs who just a few weeks later, as the newly installed Confederate secretary of state, stood alone to beg Jefferson Davis and his Cabinet to forbear rather than allow guns to open fire in Charleston Harbor. This surprising but astute reaction from Toombs took place April 9 (an auspicious date for any Civil War calendar!). Word had just been received of President Lincoln's message to Governor F. W. Pickens of South Carolina that he, Lincoln, felt constrained to supply the isolated garrison at Fort Sumter. It was a courteous message with serious implications.

In fact, it was a gauntlet. Lincoln knew the South must act…or back down. And if it be war, Lincoln needed the South to strike the first blow in order to have a unified Union behind him. If only war could resolve the crisis, it must be war initiated by the other party—who, indeed, had already fired upon a supply ship once in December 1860 and who had already cut off and trapped the garrison of men on the island of Fort Sumter.

It was Toombs, then, who saw what Lincoln was about. All the Rebel Cabinet was ready to back Jefferson Davis, the new Confederate president, in giving the order to allow force against Fort Sumter—all but Toombs, who came to the meeting late on April 9, but not too late to warn that "firing on Fort Sumter would inaugurate a civil war greater than any the world has ever seen."

He stalked about the room, then suddenly faced Davis. If the South attacked, he declared, "it is suicide, it is murder, and it will lose us every friend at the North. You will wantonly strike a hornet's nest which extends from the mountains to the ocean; and legions, now quiet, will swarm out to sting us to death." And an epitaph that also was true: "It is unnecessary, it puts us in the wrong. It is fatal."

Despite the Georgian's entreaty for caution, Lincoln "won" the debate in the Confederate Cabinet meeting, for the word that went out by a messenger boy to a telegraph office across the street suited Lincoln's sad purpose very well. Pierre G. T. Beauregard's forces at Charleston were authorized to proceed with the seizure of Fort Sumter. The firing began three days later.

Sumter's Silence

BOTH DOUBLEDAY AND BEAUREGARD WOULD LATER AGREE THAT THE FIRST SHOT fired at Fort Sumter came from a Confederate mortar battery at Rebel-held Fort Johnson. Abner Doubleday was the Union captain of artillery, and General Pierre G. T. Beauregard was, of course, the colorful Confederate commander of Rebel forces gathered at Charleston.

Here are their running accounts, spliced together for parallel perspectives:

Doubleday: The first shot came from the mortar battery at Fort Johnson. Almost immediately afterward a ball from Cummings Point lodged in the magazine wall.
Beauregard: The peaceful stillness of the night was broken just before dawn. Fort Johnson's mortar battery, at 4:30 a.m., April 12, 1861, issued the first and, as many thought, the too-long-deferred signal shell of the war. It sped aloft, describing its peculiar arc of fire and, bursting over Fort Sumter, fell with crashing noise in the very center of the parade.

Doubleday: *In a moment the firing burst forth in one continuous roar, and large patches of both the exterior and interior masonry began to crumble and fall in all directions.*

Beauregard: *Thus was "reveille" sounded in Charleston and its harbor on this eventful morning.*

Doubleday: *Nineteen batteries were now hammering at us, and the balls and shells from the 10-inch Columbiads, accompanied by shells from the 13-inch mortars which constantly bombarded us, made us feel that the war had commenced in earnest.*

Beauregard: *In an instant all was bustle and activity. Not an absentee was reported at roll call. The citizens poured down to the battery and the wharves, and women and children crowded each window of the houses overlooking the sea—rapt spectators of the scene.*

Doubleday: *When it was broad daylight, I went down to breakfast. I found the officers already assembled at one of the long tables in the mess hall. Our party was calm and even somewhat merry.*

Beauregard: *At ten minutes before five o'clock all the batteries and mortars which encircled the grim fortress were in full play against it.*

[At Fort Sumter, meanwhile, an unfortunate waiter in the mess hall was visibly terrified, Doubleday noted. The meal itself was "not very sumptuous." Then came time to respond to the Rebel fire. Doubleday had a historic role at this point.]

Doubleday: *In aiming the first gun fired against the Rebellion, I had no feeling of self reproach, for I fully believed that the conflict had been inevitable. My first shot bounded off from the sloping roof of the battery opposite without producing any apparent effect. It seemed useless to attempt to silence the guns there, for our metal was not heavy enough to batter the work down.*

[Ashore, Beauregard and his compatriots had been surprised by Sumter's absolute silence for two hours or more. But, as noted by Doubleday and now by Beauregard, the silence didn't last.]

Beauregard: *At last, however, near seven o'clock, the United States flag having previously been raised, the sound of a gun, not ours, was distinctly heard. Sumter had taken up the gage of battle, and Cummings Point had first attracted attention.*

[Beauregard and his fellow Rebels were almost happy to see Sumter astir and shooting back.]

Beauregard: *It was almost a relief to our troops—for gallantry ever admires gallantry, and a worthy foe disdains one who makes no resistance.*

Stomach Pumping Questioned

THERE WAS NOTHING PRO FORMA ABOUT THE FIRING ON FORT SUMTER. IN thirty-four hours, the little island fortress in Charleston Harbor was shelled into submission. A few words from its commander, Major Robert Anderson, effectively give the picture. He described quarters "entirely burned, the main gates destroyed by fire, the gorge walls seriously impaired, the [powder] magazine surrounded by flames and its door closed from the effects of the heat."

By then, April 13, 1861, the Federal garrison's sole provision was pork, and only "four barrels and three cartridges of powder" were accessible because of the jammed door to the fort's magazine. Outside the inner harbor the Federal resupply ships whose deployment had finally triggered the war's start merely stood by as Sumter suffered bombardment, their commanders unwilling to sacrifice ships or men to a now-hopeless rescue mission.

It was on the evening of April 13 that Anderson agreed to surrender. "The fort was a scene of ruin and destruction," wrote its U.S. Army surgeon Samuel Crawford later. "For 34 hours it had sustained a bombardment from seventeen 10-inch mortars and heavy guns, well placed and well served."

The moment of the inevitable at last had come, he noted. Pierre G. T. Beauregard, later hailed as the hero of Charleston, wrote of the end in calm, simple terms: "The flag over Fort Sumter at last was lowered, and a white flag substituted for it. The contest was over. Major Anderson had acknowledged his defeat."

While no one on either side was killed in this first real exchange of gunfire in the Civil War, former U.S. Representative Roger A. Pryor of Virginia—now a Confederate colonel—almost became a casualty. Sent to Sumter as one of Beauregard's surrender negotiators, Pryor took a seat at a table in the dark dispensary and, feeling quite thirsty, poured himself a drink from a black bottle on the table without thinking much about what he was doing.

As it turned out, he gulped down a poisonous compound, iodide of potassium. Doctor Crawford quickly pumped his stomach and probably saved Pryor's life, which raises a few questions.

"Some of us," wrote Union Captain Abner Doubleday, "questioned the doctor's right to interpose himself in a case of this kind." The thought was, "If any Rebel leader chose to come over to Fort Sumter and poison himself, the Medical Department had no business to interfere."

Crawford, though, had a well-nigh unassailable response, according to Doubleday. Since the good doctor was responsible for all his medicine as Federal government property, "he could not permit Pryor to carry any of it away."

Robert and Mary

THEY LIVED IN A COLUMNED MANSION ON A HILLSIDE OVERLOOKING WASHINGTON from the south banks of the Potomac, 1,100 gorgeous acres with an unparalleled view of the Federal city. Unparalleled, too, were their historical ties to the generation that fought and won the American Revolution, the very event that created the city spread before them. Off and on over the years, theirs had been a household bustling with visiting children, kissing cousins and other such relatives, friends, and associates. For here was an abode known for warm, gracious living—a wondrous stopping place for the visitor to Washington or the traveler to South or North.

But time had taken its usual toll. People died, children grew up and went their ways, other events intervened. And soon, managing her late father's plantation estate was an aging woman crippled by arthritis and often left alone by her husband's U.S. Army duty assignments elsewhere.

It was then that Robert E. Lee decided he had better take leave and stay home to help his wife, Mary Custis Lee, manage the inherited Arlington estate built by her late father, George Washington Parke Custis (the grandson of the widowed Martha Washington and her first husband, later adopted by Martha's second husband, George Washington. With the death of Custis in 1857, the mantle of ownership had passed to only child Mary. The Lee children by then were scattered, with two sons serving in the Army like their father, and Robert E. Lee himself stationed far away at San Antonio, Texas.

Once he heard of his father-in-law's death, Lee—son of the famous Revolutionary War figure Henry "Light-Horse Harry" Lee—took official leave and hurried home. Once there he was shocked at the state of his wife's health. As she herself had written to a friend, "I almost dread his seeing my crippled state." She meant her difficulty in walking unassisted, the pain that kept her sleepless at night, her useless right arm and hand.

Lee, a former superintendent of West Point, extended his leave indefinitely to become, in essence, a farmer.

As he took over the reins at Arlington four years before the Civil War began, however, he still was able to accept spot duty with the Army headquartered in nearby Washington. (He crossed the river between—the Potomac—via the low-lying wooden span known as the "Long Bridge.") His temporary duties usually involved dull service such as a seat on a court-martial, but a startling exception to that rule was the tumultuous and historic moment he spent in October 1859 quelling John Brown's bloody raid at Harpers Ferry, upstream on the same Potomac that flowed so lazily below Arlington.

For a time during this period, with Lee at home, the great columned house was busy once again with visitors of all kinds—relatives and friends. In the Federal city below, of course, the final debates over slavery and states' rights, union versus disunion, were taking place among the solons of Congress and in the salons and saloons of the politically charged capital city.

After three years at home, Lee finally had to return to Army duty, again posted to Texas. Alone again on the Arlington hillside above, Mary Custis Lee was not unaware of what transpired in the city below and in the country at large. With husband Robert gone, she was managing Arlington again, but also maintaining a wary vigil as the momentous events unfolded. And among them came the day, Monday, January 21, 1861, when five Southern Senate members, Mississippi's Jefferson Davis among them, announced before a packed audience in the Senate galleries that their respective states had seceded. And with that, each gathered his papers from the schoolhouse desks on the chamber's floor and departed.

Not long after, in February, Mary Custis Lee wrote to daughter Mildred: "The papers are now filled with Mr. Lincoln's arrival in Washington & this week will, I presume, decide our fate as a nation." She would be slightly distracted from such momentous national events by the arrival of a son, wife, and grandson for a visit—son William Fitzhugh "Rooney" Lee, wife Charlotte, and "the Boy."

In the meantime, Texas at last seceded, and Lee was ordered home to Washington to report to the Army's ranking officer, General Winfield Scott. Lee arrived at Arlington on March 1, and he very shortly faced a momentous personal decision.

"When my husband was summoned to Washington," his wife later wrote, "where every motive and argument was used to induce him to accept command of the Army destined to invade the South, he was enabled to resist them all, even the sad parting voice of his old Commander [Winfield Scott]."

It was almost a week after the fall of Fort Sumter that, by authority of President Lincoln, Lee so famously was offered command of a Federal army charged with subduing the rebellious South. He declined, saying, "Though opposed to secession and deprecating war, I could take no part in an invasion of the Southern States."

After the firing on Fort Sumter, Lee had been distraught in any case, quite unlike the excited, enthused crowds in Richmond. With the offer to command the Union Army and Virginia's subsequent vote to secede, the heartfelt sadness at Arlington only deepened.

The colonel went into nearby Alexandria on business the morning of April 19. He returned with a copy of the Alexandria Gazette reporting Virginia's secession vote and handed it to his wife. He still held out faint hope—perhaps the report was in error. He knew, though, that it was not, and after their supper together he went alone to his upstairs bedroom. Below, Mary Custis Lee listened as he paced the floor above, then heard a mild thump as he fell to his knees in prayer. Below, she also prayed.

Hours later, about midnight, he rejoined her. He showed her two letters he had written. In one he resigned his commission in the United States Army. In the other he expressed personal thoughts to General Scott. Later, his wife would write: "My husband has wept tears of blood over this terrible war, but as a man of honor and a Virginian, he must follow the destiny of his State."

Later still, she also would write: "It was the severest struggle of his life, to resign a commission he had held for 30 years." More immediately, though, to daughter Mildred again, Mary Custis Lee wrote of her "sad heavy heart" and said: "As I think both parties are wrong in this fratricidal war, there is nothing comforting even in the hope that God may prosper the right, for I see no right in the matter."

The following April Sunday was the last day and night that Robert E. Lee would spend at Arlington—for the rest of his life. Summoned to Richmond by Governor John Letcher of Virginia, he left by train out of Alexandria Monday morning. He would not see his wife for another fifteen months.

They both knew at parting that their beloved Arlington estate would fall into Union hands as soon as the defenses were organized around Washington. Neither could remotely guess how quickly that would come or what the final outcome might be, but certainly neither had any idea that in the upheaval of war the grand old Custis home would be turned into a Union cemetery and later into a hallowed national burial ground, still crowned by those stately columns overlooking the Federal city.

Spy with a Future

THE BAND PLAYED "DIXIE," AND THE STUDENTS HAULED THEIR WINDOW SHADES up and down as a homemade semaphore system sending messages to eager Confederate onlookers across the Potomac River. And what did their headmaster think of such nefarious goings-on in the middle of the nation's—the Union's—capital? Why, he put them up to it in the first place!

No matter, indeed, to Thomas N. Conrad, headmaster of a boys' school in town. No matter at all, safe to say, since he also allowed inflammatory, anti-Union speeches on that memorable school-graduation day in June of 1861. The same day he was arrested as prelude to being booted out of town, deported across the Potomac to the rebellious Southland beyond.

It was not a great beginning, true, to a budding spy career—a Confederate spy operating in the same Federal city of Washington. But Conrad was not a man easily discouraged, even if he was a bit too flamboyant at times for his own good. Typically, he didn't stay away from Washington for long. After a brief sojourn as a chaplain among "Jeb" Stuart's cavalry troopers, Conrad made his arrangements with officials in Richmond and headed back for Washington. He made contact with foreign diplomats and escorted them to Richmond—a job that was somewhat risky but not too complicated.

Conrad changed his appearance for this. He boasted a reshaped beard, a new hairstyle, and machine-made Northern boots instead of Southern handmades; he also chewed his tobacco Northern style rather than Southern. It wasn't long before he was engaged in real espionage.

As anyone watching would have noticed, he developed a habit of visiting the War Department around lunchtime. It seems he had cultivated a coterie of Southern sympathizers among the department clerks. His habit was to drop by their desks, and if they had gone to lunch and left important papers out on their desks, all the better.

It is no surprise, then, that Headmaster and occasional Reverend Thomas Conrad was able to warn Richmond of Union General George McClellan's Peninsular campaign in the spring of 1862 and of General Ambrose Burnside's pending attack on Fredericksburg later the same year.

Conrad would suffer his minor setbacks, sometimes barely eluding capture. Fortunately for him, he had "developed" a double agent on the staff of the Union counterespionage agency, and this man, one Edward Norton, warned

Conrad in 1863 that he was under suspicion and about to be arrested again. After again unceremoniously leaving Washington—he had little time to pack—he spent the next few months maintaining a Confederate courier station in Boyd's Landing, Virginia, about thirty-five miles south of Washington. Working for the Confederate Secret Service, "he built a hut there and named it 'Eagle's Nest,'" reported Donald E. Markle in his book, *Spies & Spymasters of the Civil War*. "[At] this location he received communiques from agents in the North and with the assistance of two mounted couriers was able to have the information in Richmond within 24 hours."

Conrad did not always see things eye to eye with his superiors in Richmond. They once had to reject his proposal to assassinate the U.S. Army's presiding general, the aging Winfield Scott. Another unfulfilled Conrad plot was to kidnap Abraham Lincoln on one of his trips from the White House to his summer quarters at the Soldiers' Home on the outskirts of Washington. Oddly enough, just days after Lincoln's assassination in April 1865, Conrad was arrested because he looked so much like John Wilkes Booth, Lincoln's assassin. The head of the Union's counterespionage service, Lafayette Baker, not only ordered Conrad released, but, with the Civil War over, shook his hand.

And what does a successful Confederate spy do after the war is over? In Conrad's case, it was a choice in keeping with his antebellum career: He eventually became a college president. And he married, to a woman named Minnie Ball. (Yes, as in the famous bullet of the Civil War, the so-called "Minié ball," after its creator, Frenchman Claude Etienne Minié.)

Swinging His Arms

"TRIFLING IN RANKS," READ THE FIRST CITATION CALLING FOR DEMERITS AGAINST the young West Point cadet. That was in 1857. So was, "Highly unmilitary & trifling conduct throwing stones on post." And 1858 was hardly any better. February 1: "Unauthorized articles in ventilator." March 8: "Cooking utensils in chimney." April 3: "Hair out of uniform"—Mark that one! May 14: "Gazing about in ranks. " And so on, until his graduation from the Military Academy in June of 1861—after the Civil War had begun with the firing on Fort Sumter and a few other clashes.

As the demerits and behavior pattern might suggest, he graduated thirty-fourth in a class of thirty-four—dead last. And highest of all in total demerits earned.

And for what further activities had he been cited in those years, beyond gazing about in ranks on May 14, 1858? Well, they found rubbish behind his tent one time. He had a bad four days in January of 1859: late to parade one day, to company formation for dinner another day, to supper itself that same day, and to breakfast still another January day.

In February, just days later, he was officially chastised for laughing and talking at the wrong time and place, for throwing snowballs (again at the wrong time and place), and in March for throwing bread in the Mess Hall!

Over the next few months they got him again and again: for boisterous noise in the sink (yes, sink), for idle laughing and talking, for defacing a wall with his pencil, for a room "grossly out of order, bed down & floor not swept."

Nor did his demeanor ever really improve, indication of his future pattern in life. He liked to do things his own way. He did not buckle easily before authority. He had bread, butter, potatoes, even plates, knives, and forks in his quarters one day in March 1860—the same day that his room was cited for being such a mess.

On July 4 that year, not yet abashed, he was spotted swinging arms while marching from dinner. He now gave strong clues to the future man and soldier. February 3, 1861: "Long beard at inspection," and March 10, 1861: "Long hair at insp."

He finished out his career at the Point with once more throwing snowballs (in a rare April snowstorm), sitting at a window in shirtsleeves "with feet on sill, wearing an unofficial ornament on his coat," packing too much "furniture" in his tent, and finally, twice more swinging his arms while on march.

Upon his graduation from West Point, the Civil War interceded just in time for him to avoid a court-martial for a minor offense. He was able to report for duty one July morning and fight the Battle of Bull Run later the same day. A lieutenant to start with, he was a brigadier general of volunteers two years later at age twenty-three.

He finished the war at U. S. Grant's side at Appomattox with the temporary rank of major general—and a name that already was legend, at least in the North. As a reward, Phil Sheridan presented this bright young officer with the small pine table that was at Grant's side for the historic surrender ceremony in the Wilmer McLean home at Appomattox.

An old West Point chum was at Appomattox, too—the Confederate Fitzhugh Lee. They embraced, then fell on the ground and "rassled." Just like the old days.

Earlier in the war, things weren't quite so amicable between this young soldier and the Confederates. Daring, flamboyance, and something more—a real cruel streak—all contributed to his meteoric reputation.

Daring? At Bull Run he was cited for bravery. In the Peninsular campaign not quite a year later, "Little Mac" McClellan was looking for a place to ford the Chickahominy River east of Richmond. With the Rebels thick on the far side, anyone testing the river's depth would be a tempting target. Our West Pointer plunged into the water and pushed slowly across. McClellan was so impressed he promoted the young man to captain and made him a staff aide.

That summer came a battle at White Oak swamp in which the young man killed an enemy officer by chasing him down on horseback, shouting for him to surrender, then shooting him in the back when the Reb continued riding on instead. The West Pointer later came across the victim's riderless horse. He decided to keep it and the saddle—"a splendid one, covered with black morocco and ornamented with silver nails." He also garnered a handsome double-edged sword from his unknown Confederate victim.

It was possibly his first "kill," said biographer Evan S. Connell, and possibly he didn't even think of the horse, sword, and handsome saddle at the outset. But George Armstrong Custer did write his sister Lydia Ann, "I selected him as my game."

A "Bear" Installed

FOR AN INTERVAL AFTER THE FIRING ON FORT SUMTER, A VAST, AS YET uncommitted never-never-land stood between the two nations of North and South: Virginia. More populous than any state in the newly formed Confederacy, it was also more heavily populated than all but four states in the Union.

Extending westward as far as Wheeling in today's West Virginia—425 miles from Atlantic beaches to western mountains—Virginia would be a latecomer to Confederate ranks. She did not secede until late April of 1861, months after the core states of the Confederacy had formed their new government. Even then, Virginia did not rush pell-mell into Confederate arms. While there was much sentiment in favor of such action, many arrangements had to be made before it would happen.

Two men who arrived in Richmond in civilian dress were key figures in the scenario that would play out. Traveling from the North by train, hiring a room at the Spotswood Hotel, and then taking his supper before visiting Governor John Letcher on Monday, April 22, Robert E. Lee, late of the U.S. Army, was asked by the governor if he would accept the Virginia Convention's offer to command the commonwealth's naval and land forces.

Yes, he would, and on the morning of April 23 he began his new military career in a temporary office not even staffed by a clerk. His General Order No. 1 announced that he was assuming the Virginia command as a major general.

The second man who appeared at the state capitol in mufti, with fateful impact to follow, was the new Confederacy's vice president, Alexander H. Stephens. He had come to seek—and negotiate—Virginia's alliance with the rebellious South. In the event of such an alliance, Virginia's military fortunes would, of course, be determined by a higher command—the Confederacy's.

Secession fever had certainly gripped eastern and central Virginia since Sumter, especially after Abraham Lincoln's subsequent call for seventy-five thousand volunteer troops from loyal states to help stamp out the rebellion. Before long Virginia had not only joined the Confederacy, but had invited the government led by Jefferson Davis to sit in Richmond rather than Montgomery, Alabama. The invitation was promptly accepted, although this meant the capital of the new nation would be much closer to Washington and more vulnerable to possible invasion from the North.

It was Robert E. Lee's job to organize his beloved Virginia's defenses against possible assault from any direction. To the east, likely invasion routes for the Union were the Chesapeake Bay and major river highways inland such as the James, the York, and the Rappahannock. To the north were the Potomac and Union territory contiguous with Virginia's borderline. To the west was a vast mountainous land peopled largely by Union loyalists. Only the vista south from Richmond posed no worry for the new commander.

He began his new work with largely untrained, inexperienced militia at his disposal, few arms, a mere handful of veteran officers and virtually no navy. In just eight weeks, however, Lee had organized a Virginia army of forty thousand or so, found forty-six thousand small arms for his men, and brought in cadets from the Virginia Military Institute (VMI) to drill and train many of the new recruits.

He did not accomplish his feat with consistently cheerful mien, it seems. "It was an open secret," wrote one confidant later, "that when he was organizing Virginia's forces at the beginning of the war he was regarded by the militia and other colonels who brought their regiments to Richmond as a sort of 'bear' that when aroused should be avoided by wise people."

A good soldier, an honorable man, and soon to be recognized as the South's great, kindly, and symbolic leader of leaders, Robert E. Lee did not yet look like the legendary figure we all know today. He as yet had no grandfatherly white beard flowing down from chin and cheeks. Only a dark mustache adorned his face in early 1861.

Certainly, he had much on his mind that might excuse an occasional show of temper. The Union military apparatus, after all, sprawled out from Washington, held the Potomac and the Chesapeake Bay, and was entrenched (even after losing Norfolk) at Fort Monroe in a key corner of the Hampton Roads harbor complex, while also crowding Virginia at every foot of its northern and western borderlines. "The war may last 10 years," Lee wrote to his wife before the end of April.

He faced a deadline of sorts at first. When Lincoln issued his call for seventy-five thousand new troops on April 15, he had given the Southern forces seizing Fort Sumter and other Federal properties (Norfolk's naval shipyard among them) just twenty days to "disperse and return peacefully to their respective abodes." Quite possibly that meant Lee had only, from his first day of business as Virginia's military chief, twelve days to get ready for whatever the North would do next—from his start on April 23 until May 5, the expiration of Lincoln's twenty-day ultimatum.

Lee was quite aware, too, that his wife's beloved Arlington estate across the Potomac from the enemy camp was at risk for easy seizure almost any day. Mrs. Lee must not tarry there too long.

In the meantime, Lee had begun to assemble a core group of capable officers—many to become historic figures themselves. They included Joseph E. Johnston, John Bankhead Magruder, Richard S. Ewell, J. C. Pemberton, and Henry Heth.

The prize catch, though, was the major from VMI who appeared at Lee's office one day to discuss the use of the military academy's cadets. Quickly seized upon as colonel of infantry and sent to hold the newly captured Federal arsenal at Harpers Ferry as long as possible, he was Thomas J. Jackson, later known as "Stonewall" Jackson.

A state convention had voted to secede, a decision that was to be submitted to the voters for ratification on May 23. On April 25, three days after Lee took the reins of military command, the same state convention voted to join the Confederacy. But where would that place Lee, a major general in his own Virginia hierarchy, in respect to the Confederate military apparatus, whose highest ranks issued thus far were those of mere brigadier generals? Would he have a problem with lesser-ranking chieftains issuing him orders from higher up the chain of command?

According to Confederate Vice President Stephens, Lee told him he would be "perfectly satisfied" with the alliance. Further, Lee said "that he did not wish anything connected with himself individually, or his official rank or personal position, to interfere in the slightest degree."

In practical terms, the alliance not only meant the arrival in Virginia of military units from the various Confederate states to the south, but some preliminary confusion as to the validity of the commissions of Virginia officers. With the confusion also came minor friction. "Conflict was in the air," wrote Lee's biographer Douglas Southall Freeman, "and the personal representative of the [Confederate] Secretary of War began to crowd the wire with suspicions of Lee and Letcher, intimating that Lee was 'troubled about rank.'"

But Lee assured President Jefferson Davis he was happy with his role as commander of Virginia forces: He and Davis were destined to respect one another and to get on well, in any case. Further, on May 10 Lee was authorized by the Confederacy itself to assume command of all Confederate forces in Virginia, and that largely removed the potential of any further divisive conflict. He also was given the Confederate rank of brigadier general. Thereafter, Lee for a time served both his new nation and his commonwealth.

Early in May, too, Lee and his colleagues were becoming painfully aware of the wide state of disaffection in the western provinces of antebellum Virginia. They worried also over the possibility of a Union movement south from Washington, which was the reason for Lee's buildup of forces at Manassas Junction on the Manassas Gap Railroad below Washington.

Lincoln's apparent deadline of May 4 had come and gone with no major change in the North-South standoff following Fort Sumter. On May 23, however, Virginia voters did ratify their state convention's call for secession. The very next day, Federal troops moved out of their Washington area encampments and occupied the Virginia shoreline on the Potomac. As Lee had feared, Arlington then fell into Federal hands—forever, at that. His invalid wife, though, had left the grand estate ten days earlier. She was fortunate in this instance, but in the days ahead she would find herself in "Yankee" hands, at the mercy of Federal authority after all.

Death of a Congressman

AS A MEMBER OF THE PROVISIONAL CONFEDERATE CONGRESS THAT ORIGINALLY met in Montgomery, Alabama, he helped form the new Confederacy, but it wasn't long before he set out to make his mark on the battlefield as well. The

"Provisional's" second session, removed to the new capital city of Richmond, had just adjourned when Captain Francis S. Bartow and his Company B, 8th Georgia, marched off—for the duration, it was vowed.

Bartow, an attorney and politician back home in Georgia, had led his Oglethorpe Light Infantry at the seizure of Federal Fort McAllister close on the heels of Georgia's decision to secede in late 1860. Now, leaving Richmond in the spring of 1861, he bravely told his wife not to expect him back. If he must die, he hoped to die fighting for Southern liberty on the battlefield, which he did. He was Georgia's first martyr to the war cause.

Future Confederate Congressman Warren Akin, also from Georgia, was in Richmond and listening when Bartow's death was announced in the House chamber with appropriate eulogies by several members of the body. A colonel by midsummer of 1861, Bartow had commanded the 8th Georgia and then the 2nd Brigade of the Army of the Shenandoah in the Shenandoah Valley. He and part of his brigade rushed to the aid of General Pierre G. T. Beauregard at the First Battle of Bull Run (Manassas) on July 21. There, Bartow's command joined other Rebel forces in trying to hold off Yankee pressure against the Confederate left flank.

North of the Warrenton Turnpike and at Henry House Hill, the fighting was difficult. At one point, a Union battery manned by Regular Army men proved especially troublesome for the Southern volunteers. A greatly moved Warren Akin told the essentials of Bartow's story in a letter to Mrs. Akin, penned on the same day that the eulogies were expressed: "After Bartow's 8th G. Regt. was much cut to pieces late in the day, he rode to General Beauregard and said: 'What is now to be done? Direct me and it shall be done if within human power.' Beauregard replied, 'That battery must be taken.' Bartow immediately rallied the remnants of the 8th & ordered the 7th Georgia and one Va. Regt. with the 8th to take it. The charge was made & soon Bartow's horse was shot under him & he was wounded in the leg."

But Bartow was not yet stopped, nor even slowed down all that much, it seems. "He then went from company to company, cheering the men & officers onward, telling them 'the day is ours; onward and take the battery!'"

The Rebels did go onward, but forty yards out from the U.S. line the Rebel standard-bearer was cut down.

Far from being left behind, the wounded Bartow was right there still. "Bartow seized the colors, waved it over his head, with his cap in hand, waving it also and bidding his men to follow him—his men falling at every discharge from the battery, almost like wheat stalks before the scythe."

And just then…

"Just then a bullet pierced his breast."

But Francis Bartow, Georgia's first hero of the Civil War, wasn't quite to be counted out. He told the men who gathered 'round him in a sorrowful knot: "They have killed me, but the day is ours. Never give up the field."

Minutes later his fired-up volunteers overran the battery manned by Yankee Regulars, who "were routed and fled from the field."

Bartow died in the arms of another prominent Georgia politician, former U.S. Congressman and future Confederate Congressman Lucius Jeremiah Gartell, present at Bull Run as a colonel with the 7th Georgia. In the same battle Gartell lost a son, and Bartow, wrote Warren Akin to Mrs. Akin, "had an adopted son who was badly if not fatally wounded in the same fight." Already the bitter toll was being felt.

Most Famous Shooter

"OLD RUFFIN" THEY CALLED HIM. BORN IN '94—1794, THAT IS—HE REALLY WAS old, by comparison with the combatants of the Civil War. *Other* combatants, one should keep in mind, since he himself took part in the fighting and indeed fired two famous and significant artillery rounds still noted in many histories of the Civil War.

Virginia-born Edmund Ruffin, in fact, remains at the center of a very old dispute: Who fired the first shot of the war?

For years—decades even—many said it was the fire-breathing secessionist Ruffin himself. Others said no. In any case, it apparently is true that he fired one of the very first rounds at hapless Fort Sumter in Charleston Harbor.

A gentleman of Virginia's plantation society, Ruffin studied for a time at the College of William and Mary and in his prime as a serious farmer was a progressive agronomist, an advocate of crop rotation, and president of the *Farmer's Register*. Also a veteran of the War of 1812, he eventually became consumed by the issue of slavery versus abolition. He attended the hanging of abolitionist John Brown and made it his business to present every Southern governor with one of the pikes that Brown would have used to arm rebelling Virginia slaves. Ruffin traveled throughout the South years before the Civil War, urging secession, calling for the creation of a new country, and writing articles in the same vein. One of his publications was *Slavery and Free Labor Described and Compared*.

It was no surprise, then, that he was present when South Carolina led the way to secession with its defiant vote of December 20, 1860. He happily noted the wild cheers of the onlookers at the signing of the secession ordinance that evening.

Early on the morning of April 12, he was at Charleston's Cummings Point at the tip of Morris Island. There, as an honorary member of the Palmetto Guards, the sixty-seven-year-old was accorded the privilege of firing the first round from Columbiad No. 1 at Fort Sumter out in the harbor.

Confederate General Pierre G. T. Beauregard later said, however, the historic Ruffin shot was not really the first one of the entire Civil War, as often was alleged ever after. "The peaceful stillness of the night was broken just before dawn," wrote Beauregard. "From Fort Johnson's mortar battery, at 4:30 a.m., April 12, 1861, issued the first—and, as many thought, the too-long deferred—signal shell of the war. It was fired, not by Mr. Edmund Ruffin of Virginia, as has been erroneously believed, but by George S. James, of South Carolina, to whom Captain Stephen D. Lee issued the order."

Even if Ruffin's gun came into action shortly after the shell that signaled the start of the Civil War, the fanatical long-haired oldster cut quite a figure in his uniform of South Carolina's Palmetto Guards. After the younger men of the same outfit were sent to Virginia, Ruffin was still much in evidence. "Old Ruffin has honored our company with a visit," wrote Palmetto member Charles M. Furman in May 1861. "The old gentleman intended presenting us with a flag, but finding us well supplied in that particular, he made a donation of one hundred dollars. The old man is a real patriot, his purse, his pen & his aged frame are all in turn called upon to contribute to the great cause upon which his heart is fixed."

Nor was this elderly legend-in-process through with his activity as an amateur artillerist. His next famous shot would come in July—it also is alleged—during the fighting near First Bull Run. The hated Yankees were in retreat on the Warrenton Turnpike in the direction of Washington. The roadway crossed two bridges, and Honorary Private Ruffin was nearby, watching the Union flight with members of a Virginia artillery battery. The younger sharpshooters of Delaware Kemper's Battery asked the famous "first-shooter" if he would like to fire an honorary round with a gun aimed at one of the turnpike bridges: the Cub Run span.

He was more than happy to oblige. And wonder of wonders, it allegedly was Ruffin's own shot that squarely hit the bridge and upended a wagon across its roadway, blocking it.

"Wagons waiting to cross the bridge were now abandoned by their terrified drivers, who chose to wade the creek," wrote Glenn Dedmondt in his book *Southern Bronze*. "A great quantity of wagons and equipment would be later captured by the South as a result of this single artillery round."

It was to no avail, of course, and in the end the South bowed to the superior manpower and resources of the Union. That was too much for Edmund Ruffin, who in June 1865—two months after Lee's surrender at Appomattox—died an untimely death as a suicide who refused to live in the restored United States.

Perfect Storm of Bullets

IT STARTED OUT AS A "REVOLVING DOOR" BATTLE, THIS FIRST GREAT CLASH OF THE Civil War. Each of the two opposing generals—classmates at West Point some years earlier—planned a feint to his battle line's left and a real lunge forward to the right. Had their strategy prevailed without deviation or the confusion of combat, Beauregard might well have marched on into Washington and McDowell into Richmond.

There had been skirmishes along the small creek line below Washington for two days, but it was on July 21 that the real fight ensued. With it, some famous names and amazing events emerged.

Pierre G. T. Beauregard, for instance, had his headquarters at the McLean House, home of civilian Wilmer McLean, whose farm bordered Bull Run. As Beauregard himself later wrote, he and his staff were interrupted during a meal by a Union shell that landed in the fireplace. Such events, both during First Bull Run and again a year later at Second Bull Run, were more than enough for McLean. In 1863 he moved his family out of the war's path…or so he thought. In fact, the second Wilmer McLean House would be the site of Robert E. Lee's surrender to U. S. Grant at Appomattox.

It was at Bull Run also that Thomas Jackson, Southern general, acquired a well-known, even revered, nickname. He and his men had arrived as badly needed, eleventh-hour reinforcements for Beauregard. An excited fellow Rebel, General Barnard Bee, sought to inspire his own troops by pointing out Jackson and his brigade: "Look. There stands Jackson like a stone wall! Rally behind the Virginians." (Another version has Bee saying after the "Stonewall" reference, "Let us determine to die here, and we will conquer. Follow me.")

Unfortunately, Bee was fatally wounded minutes later and soon forgotten. However, the name Stonewall has endured.

Also killed in the fighting for Henry House Hill was the battle's only civilian casualty, the home's elderly owner, the widow Judith Carter Henry.

Returning to the battle scenario, Confederate Colonel Nathan Evans of South Carolina had seen through Union commander Irvin McDowell's diversionary feint to his own left that morning. As explained later by Beauregard, "Evans, seeing that the Federal attack at the [Stone] bridge did not increase in vigor, and observing a lengthening line of dust to the left of the Warrenton Turnpike [the Confederate left, the Union right, that is], became satisfied that the attack at his front was a feint, and that a column of enemy was moving around through the woods to fall on his left flank from the direction of Sudley Ford."

Indeed, that was the case. Then-colonel Ambrose E. Burnside's brigade marched at the head of the eighteen-thousand-man Union column. In the fight that followed, Bee, Evans, Jackson, and others did their best to contain the Union wave, which also included a brigade led by William Tecumseh Sherman.

The fortunes of battle ebbed and flowed through the day. A Richmond journalist watched at mid-morning as both Beauregard and newly arrived General Joseph E. Johnston, senior to the hero of Charleston, dashed "at a headlong gallop" to a threatened sector of their line—the very moment, in fact, that Bee and Evans fell back and Jackson's brigade planted itself as a stone wall in the path of the enemy.

And what a "thrilling moment!" wrote the onlooking journalist. "General Johnston seized the colors of the 4th Alabama, and offered to lead the attack. General Beauregard leaped from his horse, and turning to his troops, exclaimed, 'I have come here to die with you!'"

More ebb and flow followed, with the Rebs barely holding out and awaiting still more reinforcements. Finally, to the rescue from left and right, came both E. Kirby Smith and Richard Ewell with their respective commands, and not a moment too soon. A Confederate private who was with a Maryland regiment rushing from the rail depot at Manassas to Beauregard's aid encountered a dismaying retreat on the way. "Wagons in great numbers were coming to the rear at headlong speed," wrote Private W. W. Goldsborough of the 1st Maryland Infantry, "and demoralized fugitives by the hundreds from the battlefield were rushing frantically by, crying out, 'All is lost, all is lost, go back, or you'll be cut to pieces! The army is in full retreat.'"

That, of course, was not entirely true. Nor was it a lasting situation, since shortly thereafter Goldsborough and his fellows took part in a highly successful charge. "At the command, with one wild, deafening yell, and amidst a perfect storm of bullets, we drove the enemy pell-mell from their strong position into the thicket in their rear."

Minutes later, Johnston, Beauregard, and Confederate President Jefferson Davis himself rode up to congratulate the 1st Maryland's commander, Colonel Arnold Elzey. Davis was "beaming with excitement and enthusiasm."

While Elzey did not himself win the Battle of First Bull Run, he earned promotion on the spot to brigadier general and effusive praise from Jefferson Davis. The battle was won, though, by their side—the Confederacy. It was the first real battle of any size in the Civil War. It was an uplifting victory for the South, but it at the same time spelled ultimate disaster for the South, for while it created euphoria in Dixie, it showed a shocked Union that the war was serious business—that the enemy was real, was capable…and would fight. The Union response, while often inept, would be serious, no-holds-barred warfare until the issue was settled.

At Every Shot a Convulsion

NEWSPAPERMAN HENRY VILLARD FOUND UNION COLONEL AMBROSE E. BURNSIDE, future general and commander of the Army of the Potomac, riding hatless and swordless in apparent pursuit of the rear during the Federal retreat at First Bull Run. "I am hurrying ahead to get rations for my command," was Burnside's entirely transparent explanation.

Another newsman, William Howard Russell of the London *Times*, later called home for displaying a pro-Union bias in his reportage of the American Civil War, was certainly unsparing in his description of the Union rout at First Bull Run—"'Turn back! Retreat!' shouted the men from the front. 'We're whipped, we're whipped!' They cursed and tugged at the horses' heads and struggled with frenzy to get past." A veteran war correspondent, Russell had never seen anything like this "cowardly rout—a miserable, causeless panic." Not even as "alarms among camp followers" had he seen the like. "Negro servants on led horses dashed frantically past; men in uniform, whom it were a disgrace to the profession of arms to call 'soldiers' swarmed by on mules, chargers, and even draft horses, which had been cut out of carts or wagons, and went on with harness clinging to their heels, as frightened as their riders. Men literally screamed with rage and fright when their way was blocked."

And their only reply when Russell asked what had happened was the refrain, "We're whipped" or "We're repulsed."

The Englishman, a witness to the Crimean War and other British conflicts, wrote that the road from Centreville to the rear toward Washington presented the scene of a totally demoralized army. "Drivers flogged, lashed, spurred, and beat their horses, or leaped down and abandoned their teams and ran by the side of the road; mounted men, servants and men in uniform, vehicles of all sorts, commissariat wagons thronged the narrow ways. At every shot a convulsion, as it were, seized upon the morbid mass of bones, sinew, wood, and iron, and thrilled through it, giving new energy and action to its desperate efforts to get free from itself."

This was the battle, of course, that had attracted innocent—ignorant, too—sightseers from the nation's capital. They had gone over the Potomac with picnic baskets to see the Rebs chased away with a whiff of Union grapeshot.

Among the onlookers, Republican Representative Albert G. Riddle of Ohio and two other House members, plus a constituent from Cleveland, went forth early that Sunday morning with "a strong carriage, a pair of stout horses, a good driver, a hamper of lunch, and four of the largest Navy revolvers," Riddle later wrote. They traveled beyond Centreville, site of Irwin McDowell's headquarters. They passed William Tecumseh Sherman's troops. The Union soldiers they encountered said the enemy—the Rebs—were in retreat. But later in the day, that tide turned. More and more of the men they saw seemed to drift, then hurry, back toward Centreville.

Unsuccessful in finding defined front lines, Riddle's own party was now headed back, but at fairly leisurely pace. From his seat in the right-hand front of the carriage, the congressman was surprised to see "a small body of cavalry turn the angle of [a distant] wood, and head toward us at full speed."

It was a puzzle. "Of course I supposed they were our men, or why were they there? But why were they in such a hurry? The whole army I thought was between them and the enemy."

The explanation dawned when Riddle saw the Union stragglers around his carriage spring to life and run to a nearby fence with their weapons "in position to fire." Riddle leaped from the carriage with his revolver after shouting to his companions, "These are Rebs! Jump out and be ready for them."

They were Rebs at that, but they halted fifty or sixty yards away, their charge discouraged by the "stout Virginia fence" between the congressmen and the cavalrymen. They fired their carbines, however, and killed at least one Union man, David McCook, "a private and a hospital guard." (For more on the McCooks, see *The Fighting McCooks* on page 172.)

Riddle's fellow Yankees returned the fire. As a result, "two or three horses" ran off riderless with the Confederate cavalry troop.

It was right after this that Riddle and his companions saw what had begun as an orderly Union retreat turn into absolute, mindless panic. Nothing—no plea nor threat—could stop the terrified Union soldiers or their wagon drivers (teamsters). "Off they went, one and all, off down the highway, over across their fields towards the woods, anywhere, everywhere, to escape."

The Riddle carriage itself was swept up in the surge, he reported. It could be upset or broken up at any moment, but the driver's skill and the strength of the two horses kept the carriage intact and stable. Yet another danger also loomed. "The poor, demented, exhausted wretches, who could not climb into the high, closed baggage wagons, made frantic efforts to get onto and into our carriage."

As Riddle's "wretches" grabbed at every handhold offered by his tossing vehicle, their sheer weight slowed it down to a standstill. "We had to be rough with them," Riddle explained in an account that later propelled him into controversy back home in Ohio, "and thrust them out and off." He and one companion guarded the doors with their pistols.

But then, "one poor devil did get in, and we lugged the pitiful coward a mile or two. He wore major's straps, was hatless, and had thrown away his sword; finally I opened the door, and he tumbled—or was tumbled out."

Minutes later, Riddle and party came across a "poor drummer boy struggling under the horses' feet." Riddle rescued the boy "with much difficulty" and took him in the carriage. They also took aboard an exhausted New York soldier who had somehow lost hat, coat, and even shoes. They dropped both off at Centreville and resumed their journey back to Washington. On the way, however, they halted and joined forces with two U.S. senators and a visiting Michigan officer to form a line across the road to stop the headlong retreat toward Washington. The seven "with loud cries…confronted the on-sweeping multitude filling the broad road…and with our weapons we commanded an immediate halt then and there, on pain of instant loss of brains, which none of them would miss."

It was a dangerous moment. An angry teamster who had cut his horse loose from a wagon for the flight from the battlefields shot the visiting Michigan officer in the wrist with a revolver, then dashed on down the road. Still, if Riddle's story is to be entirely believed, the others held their thin line. "As the multitude, thus damned up, swelled and raged, the pressure upon us became very great. Loud cries and threats reached us in the deepening twilight."

Just when Riddle's small congressional line was about to be burst asunder by the swelling mob, a colonel with the 2nd New York turned out his men from their encampment at nearby Fairfax Courthouse and "took the tumultuous mass of fugitives off our hands."

As Riddle said, it was getting dark by this time. He didn't reach his boarding-house quarters in town until 2 a.m., and he was too keyed up after the day's events to sleep even then.

The next day Washington, of course, was full of "the wildest rumors" and a good many fears. Wouldn't the Rebs now take advantage of their good fortune and march on into Washington?

First Postmortem

FEW OF THE PARTICIPANTS AT GROUND LEVEL, LIMITED TO A WORM'S-EYE VIEW OF the battle, realized at first what had happened...or why. Only later, after the smoke had cleared, did the many facets of the clash become evident. For start-ers, Irwin McDowell had marched southwest from Alexandria, Virginia, on the Potomac to Centreville in northern Virginia, nearly thirty miles. He had with him a veritable host of thirty-five thousand troops, but many were raw militia with short-term enlistments...and precious little training.

McDowell at first faced Pierre G. T. Beauregard's twenty thousand Confederates at the strategic Manassas rail depot. McDowell then moved out on July 18, 1861, and took two entire days to reach the creek called Bull Run, just beyond Centreville. In the interim, the Confederates were using the time to rush reinforcements, commanded by Joseph E. Johnston, from the upper Shenandoah Valley near Harpers Ferry (they came by train to Manassas, a feat considered the first strategic use of rails in the history of warfare). Johnston brought nine thousand troops, and they enabled Beauregard to hold the line and even to counterattack after McDowell finally mounted his main assault on Sunday, July 21.

Following the feint to his left, McDowell drove against his foe's left with three divisions that crossed Bull Run at Sudley Springs. The left Rebel flank was pushed back to Henry House Hill, where Thomas Jackson and his brigade so famously held like a "stone wall."

This was in the morning, and the front stretched for fourteen miles. Meanwhile, both sides rushed more men to the west, in the direction of McDowell's main attack. It was about four o'clock in the afternoon when the tide changed direction, and instead of a Union attack, it was suddenly a Confederate one. At first the retreat of the Federal right toward Centreville was orderly, but then the famous panic set in, and the retreat became a rout. The South had won the first major battle of the Civil War, with casualties for both sides that were a shock… and yet nothing in comparison with what was to come. On this day 2,896 Federals were killed, wounded, or captured, compared to 1,982 Confederates.

Why did the victorious Confederate forces not pursue the foe all the way into the nation's capital, possibly to end the Civil War then and there?

General Johnston once explained:

My failure to capture Washington received general condemnation. Many erroneously attributed it to the President's prohibition; but Mr. Davis expressed neither wish nor opinion on the subject.

The conditions forbade an attempt on Washington. The Confederate army was more disorganized by victory than that of the United States by defeat.

Besides, the reasons for our course were unfitness of raw troops for assailing entrenchments; the fortifications upon which skillful engineers had been engaged since April; the Potomac, a mile wide, bearing the United States vessels of war, which commanded the bridges and the southern shores.

The Confederate army would have been two days in marching from Bull Run to the Federal entrenchments, with less than two days' rations, or not more. It is asserted that the country could have furnished food and forage in abundance. Those who make this assertion forget that a large Federal army had passed twice over the route in question. As we had none of the means of besieging, an immediate assault upon the forts would have been unavoidable; it would have been repelled, inevitably, and our half supply of ammunition exhausted; and the enemy, increased by the army from Harpers Ferry, could have resumed their march to Richmond without opposition.

And, if we had miraculously been successful in an assault, the Potomac still would have protected Washington and rendered our further progress impossible.

As for McDowell, he had explanations, too:

It was now about 3 o'clock in the afternoon. Three times had the enemy been repulsed and driven back from the Henry House plateau. The third time it was supposed by us all that the repulse was final, for he was driven entirely from the hill, so far beyond it as not to be in sight, and all were certain the day was ours.

The enemy was evidently disheartened and broken. But we had then been fighting since 10:30 o'clock in the morning, the men had been up since 2 o'clock and had made what to those unused to such things seemed a long march, though the longest distance gone over was not more than nine and a half miles; and although they had had three days' provisions served out to them the day before, many, no doubt, either had not gotten them or had thrown them away, and were therefore without food. They had done much severe fighting.

It was at this time that the enemy's reinforcements came to his aid from the railroad train. They threw themselves in the woods on our right and opened fire on our men, which caused them to break and retire down the hillside. This soon degenerated into disorder, for which there was no remedy. Every effort was made to rally them, even beyond the reach of the enemy's fire, but in vain. The battalion of regular infantry alone maintained itself until our men could get back to the position we had occupied in the morning.

The retreating current passed slowly through Centreville to the rear. The enemy followed us and, owing to the rear becoming blocked, caused us much damage, for the artillery could not pass, and several pieces and caissons had to be abandoned. In the panic the horses hauling caissons and ammunition were cut from their traces and used for escape, and in this way much confusion was caused, the panic aggravated and the road encumbered.

By sundown it became a question whether we should endeavor to make a stand at Centreville. The condition of our artillery and its ammunition, the want of food for the men, and the utter disorganization and demoralization of the mass of the army seemed to admit of no alternative but to fall back. Our decision had been anticipated by the troops, most of them being already on the road to the rear.

Sherman's Threat Appealed

AT FIRST BULL RUN, THE UNION SIDE WAS NOTED IN SOME QUARTERS FOR ITS ninety-day wonders, men whose three-month enlistments were up just about the time of the great battle. The *New York Herald*'s Henry Villard, for instance, rushing to file his story on its outcome, encountered an entire regiment of Pennsylvania ninety-dayers leaving the scene because, they said, their enlistments had expired.

Villard could only report the fact, but William Tecumseh Sherman, encountering one such ninety-day wonder in his own command, resorted to sterner measures. Sherman, a colonel and a Union brigade leader at the time, was busy in the days after the disastrous rout preparing his men for the possibility of a renewed Rebel drive. "We took it for granted," he later wrote, "that the Rebels would be on our heels and accordingly prepared to defend our posts."

Among his problems, however, were the short-termers in his command. They were "extremely tired of the war and wanted to go home," he reported. "Some of them were so mutinous, at one time, that I threatened to open fire on them, if they dared to leave camp without orders."

Sherman kept his men busy and under control with drills, exercises, and roll call that only he, in person, could dismiss. But then came the open, highly visible, defiance of an officer from New York, a lawyer in civilian life who had the nerve to approach Sherman after reveille one morning. He announced that he was leaving for New York that very day. Sherman replied, "I do not remember to have signed a leave for you," and would have moved on.

But that was not the end of the encounter. As "a good many soldiers" stopped to listen, the errant officer said he had signed up for three months, his three months were up, and he was going home. Sherman realized that if this officer defied him, the onlookers also would. "So I turned on him sharp and said: 'Captain, you are a soldier and must submit to orders till you are properly discharged. If you attempt to leave without orders, I will shoot you like a dog!'" For the moment, that was an end to their conversation.

Later the same day, Sherman spotted a carriage approaching with both President Lincoln and his secretary of state, William Seward, sitting side by side inside the open hack. Sherman had posted himself by the roadside by the time they drew abreast. They stopped, and he asked if they were going to his encampment. Lincoln said, "Yes, we heard that you had got over the big scare [of First Bull Run], and we thought we would come over and see the boys."

Sherman joined them in their carriage to show the way while one of his men was sent racing ahead to alert Sherman's command that the president was coming.

On the way, Sherman was pleased to discover that Lincoln "was full of feeling and wanted to encourage our men." But when he announced he wished to address them, Sherman asked Lincoln "to discourage all cheering" and said there had been enough of that "to ruin any set of men." What was needed now, Sherman said, were "cool, thoughtful, hard-fighting soldiers—no more hurrahing, no more humbug."

Lincoln "took my remarks in perfect good nature," then delivered "one of the neatest, best and most feeling addresses I ever listened to, referring to our late disaster at Bull Run, the high duties that still devolved on us and the brighter days to come."

Before finishing, Lincoln assured the troops that they could appeal to him in person to right any wrongs done to them. That was when Sherman again heard from the New York captain who had buttonholed him that very morning. The man's "face was pale and his lips compressed" as he pushed his way forward to the presidential carriage and addressed Lincoln with words that Sherman would never forget. "Mr. President," said the New York advocate, "I have a cause of grievance. This morning I went to speak to Colonel Sherman, and he threatened to shoot me."

Lincoln coolly glanced from one man to the other, Sherman later related, then stooped low and told the complaining officer in a perfectly audible stage whisper, "Well, if I were you and Colonel Sherman threatened to shoot, I would not trust him for, by Heaven, I believe he would do it." And that was that. Lincoln never even asked what their dispute was about.

Head of the Passes

IF FIRST BULL RUN (FIRST MANASSAS) WAS THE FIRST MAJOR LAND BATTLE OF the Civil War, and a stinging defeat for the Union at that, what was its equivalent on water? And who came away the victor?

One early sea battle between North and South came on October 12, 1861, at the Head of the Passes below New Orleans in the delta of the mighty Mississippi River. Here were both an early clash and a historic engagement for an ironclad. Here, too, Lilliputians did their best to entrap a few "Gullivers." The action that took place would probably have come about at some early point anyway, but it was U.S. Navy veteran George N. Hollins who had the aggressive instinct to move events along to their climax.

The great river, a pulsating artery leading into the heart of America, was vital to commerce and crucial to both sides' military strategies. Whoever controlled the Head of the Passes controlled access to and from the seas beyond.

Leading to the Gulf of Mexico from the lower Mississippi was a fan of outgoing channels. Above the fan, however, was a single channel, a "handle" to the fan that was navigable to large ships—the Head of the Passes. It was no surprise, then, that the Union Navy moved quickly to establish there a blockading flotilla of four ships: the screw steamer *Richmond* as flagship, the paddlewheel steamer Water Witch, and the sailing vessels *Preble* and *Vincennes*.

The *Richmond*, carrying sixteen guns, encountered some problems crossing the delta sandbars before reaching the small bay that was the Head of the Passes, but she made it. As of September 29 all four Federal warships were on station—a cork in the river's mouth. The South would either strike back—try to drive off the enemy warships—or tamely accept their presence as a choke-point to commerce in and out of New Orleans.

As one indication of the trouble soon to come, the Confederate gunboat *Ivy*, a small steam-powered towboat mounting a single fifteen-pounder gun, had taken on the four Federal warships by herself on October 9 and left their gun crews fiercely gritting teeth since her lone gun outranged all forty-one guns aboard the Union ships. She withdrew, no harm done to either side, but the Federals learned a lesson.

Meanwhile, to the north up in New Orleans was a busy man planning the real trouble for the Federals, former U.S. Navy officer Hollins. Just entering his sixties, the Baltimore native had been going to sea with the U.S. Navy since he was fifteen, but that didn't stop him from immediately quitting his hard-earned rank as a naval captain to join the Confederate naval service…also as a captain, but with no assurances for his future security. Hollins, a veteran of the Barbary Coast Wars and other conflicts, was a man of action. Before taking up his Confederate posting to New Orleans in mid-1861, he had spent a short interval leading a raid against the Federal steamship *Nicholas* on the Potomac River. Former subordinates would have been startled to see their one-time commander dressed as a woman and boarding the vessel to surprise those defending it.

After arriving in New Orleans and taking note of the scanty naval resources available to the Confederacy there (as, indeed, everywhere else), Hollins did not hesitate when he heard a local entrepreneur was building an ironclad ram with plans to hire it out to the Confederate Navy for a handsome profit. Wasting no time on troublesome details, Hollins simply sent his steamer, the *McRae*, alongside the ram and had it seized by a boarding party.

The addition of the ram *Manassas* rounded out a small flotilla consisting of the ironclad; Hollins's own flagship, the *McRae*; and a handful of seagoing tugs and river towboats with only a few guns among them. The chief weapon of the *Manassas*, though, was not her immovable thirty-two-pound bow gun but her ram of heavy armor.

It all along had been the intention of Hollins and his superiors at New Orleans to clear the Federals out of the Head of the Passes. But until all was ready in mid-October of 1861, the Rebels had not been able to offer much protest to the Union blockade. With the "acquisition" of their ram, the time for action had come.

In the early-morning darkness of October 12, 1861, *Manassas* slipped into the Head of the Passes undetected, Rebel gunboats strung out behind her like Cub Scouts marching behind their scout master. Aboard the Federal ships, all was quiet, all was calm. "Despite the lateness of the hour [it was about 3:45 a.m.]," wrote John D. Pelzer in the December 1994 issue of *Military History* magazine, "a supply schooner had been lashed alongside the squadron's flagship, the USS *Richmond*, and the warship's crewmen were busy onloading coal." Nearby, on the sloop-of-war *Preble*, Commander Henry French, the skipper, was asleep in his cabin.

Things would not remain so quiet for very long.

On *Preble*, a midshipman burst into his skipper's cabin to announce, "Captain, there's a steamer alongside of us!" Indeed, as French saw moments later from a gunport, there was a shape in the darkness just twenty yards away—"like a huge whale in the water," he later said.

It was the ram *Manassas*, and the monster was headed for the unsuspecting *Richmond* beyond *Preble*. In fact, it was almost immediately that *Manassas* crunched into the port side of the *Richmond*. She backed off, then tried again, but by now the *Richmond* and her naval companions were firing at the ram—and moving on, aiming for the South West Pass and the open sea beyond.

The gunfire presented quite a spectacle to onlookers such as a Confederate aboard the *McRae*, a mile distant. "Instantly the heavy broadsides of the United States ships blazed forth as they shot holes in the darkness," he said.

As the Northern vessels picked up speed, the ungainly *Manassas*—armored by plating made from rail ties and somewhat damaged by her own ramming lunge—fell behind and, in fact, ran afoul of a marsh.

That left her Cub scouts to pursue the heavy Federal ships alone, and they did, releasing three fire rafts in the process. The rafts didn't do much, but the speedy little Confederate gunboats could chase and brave the fire of the behemoth Federal warships ahead because the *Ivy* had on October 9 already shown that the Federals didn't have long-range guns. The smaller Reb boats could pursue fairly closely without fear of retaliation, and their own few guns might score a lucky hit or two.

It was then that disaster struck for the Federals. Reaching the same sandbars that had been crossed with difficulty coming into the river delta, the Yankee *Richmond* and *Vincennes* both beached on the sandbars—helpless prey.

"While return fire from the Northern warships fell well short, the Confederate rounds burst all around the stranded Northern ships," wrote Pelzer. "Only the tiny steamer *Water Witch*, with its rifled 12-pound howitzer, had sufficient range to engage the enemy."

In short order, the captain and crew of Vincennes abandoned their ship. But then the fortunes of war again intervened. The river current turned *Richmond* so that her broadside faced the Rebel gunboats, while outside the bar the on-looking Federal *Santee* maneuvered and fired upon the smaller Reb gunboats.

The Confederates were forced to turn back, but with both the *Richmond* and the *Vincennes* knocked out of action for a time—and the Head of the Passes cleared for Southern river traffic—Hollins and his flotilla had achieved a resounding victory. A "gallant exploit," proclaimed the *New Orleans Daily Picayune*.

The euphoria would burst when the great port city fell to the Yankees in April 1862, but for the time being the Confederacy had a naval feat to rank alongside its victory at Bull Run, just north of Manassas, Virginia—the very reason, of course, for the name given the ironclad ram whose actions brought about the Federal rout below New Orleans.

Heart in the Throat

HE STARTED OUT AS THE MODERATOR AT A MEETING OF WAR-FEVERED CITIZENS IN Galena, Illinois. It was not so much the firing on Fort Sumter that stirred things up, but Lincoln's appeal for seventy-five thousand troops. "As soon as the news of the call for volunteers reached Galena," he wrote, "posters were stuck up calling for a meeting of the citizens at the courthouse in the evening."

They say people in the South were hot—fire-eaters. Well, one should look at Galena and, by extrapolation, much of the North. "Business ceased entirely; all was excitement; for a time there were no party distinctions; all were Union men, determined to avenge the insult to the national flag."

It was no surprise, then, that the courthouse that night was packed. But who would lead the meeting?

"Although a comparative stranger," continued Ulysses S. Grant many years later in his *Personal Memoirs*, "I was called upon to preside; the sole reason, possibly, was that I had been in the army and had seen service [at West Point and in the Mexican War of the 1840s]."

And so, with "much embarrassment and some prompting," Mexican War veteran Grant "made out to announce the object of the meeting," then subsided while others, the postmaster and a pair of local politicians, made speeches. Afterward, the townsmen formed a company of volunteers and elected their officers and noncoms. Grant turned down a captaincy before the vote but offered to help in any way he could.

A few days later, Grant went with the volunteers when they traveled to the state capital at Springfield for duty assignments. In the meantime, he had already been helpful—by drilling the locals and advising the townswomen on how to design the U.S. Army infantry uniforms they volunteered to make for their menfolk. Grant was so busy after that first courthouse meeting, in fact, that he never returned to the family leather-goods store where he had worked as a clerk—not even "to put up a package."

At Springfield he and the men from Galena found a governor and his legislature so overwhelmed with volunteers that they authorized the creation of ten short-term regiments. This was in addition to the six that had previously been established as the state's quota for a somewhat longer term. The new regiments were to serve one month paid by the state, but they would be available to go into Federal service if needed.

The Galena company was soon swallowed up by the 11th Illinois Volunteer Infantry, and Grant prepared to return home, his duties done. Or so he thought.

He was staying at the same hotel in Springfield as Governor Richard Yates. The very evening that Grant was ready to leave, the governor stopped Grant at the front door after supper and asked him to come see him the next morning. When Grant did, he was offered a post in the State Adjutant General's office—his first job would be mustering in the ten new regiments. Grant took the post and over the next few weeks did the mustering required, visited St. Louis for a few days, sought a more permanent Federal post from the U.S. Army's Adjutant General in Washington, tried to see fellow West Pointer George McClellan (already considered a Union Army "comer") and generally stirred around looking for a way to reunite himself with the U.S. Army.

Finally, after Lincoln called for three hundred thousand more troops to serve a full three years or the duration of the war, Grant was appointed colonel of one of the ten new regiments—the 21st Illinois—since its men didn't have confidence in the commander they had selected beforehand. Grant had from about June 15 until mid-July to work with his new command before he and his men were sent into camp in Missouri, close by the Mississippi River. After a quiet two weeks, Grant next was ordered to "move against" a Southern colonel's command at Florida, Missouri, about twenty-five miles south.

Even though he had seen considerable combat during the Mexican War, Grant was anxious as he marched his men southward. Noting the countryside and houses along the way were all deserted, Grant felt "anything but easy." The only sign of life he and his men saw on the entire march was two horsemen on an intersecting road. "As soon as they saw us they decamped as fast as their horses could carry them," he wrote later.

Grant and his men marched on, over hill and dale, quite literally, expecting the worst at every step. They followed a creek, with ominous hills on each side that insisted upon rising "considerably," to a hundred or more feet.

They neared their goal at last. "As we approached the brow of the hill from which it was expected we could see [Confederate Colonel Thomas] Harris' camp, and possibly find his men ready formed to meet us, my heart kept getting higher and higher until it felt to me as though it was in my throat. I would have given anything then to have been back in Illinois, but I had not the moral courage to halt and consider what to do; I kept right on."

So it was that Ulysses S. Grant, future leader of all the Union armies in the Civil War—the general most widely credited with bringing about the victory over the South—so it was that he and his command of a thousand marched right over the brow of the hill into the unknown.

And what did they find? Nothing. Harris and his own command were gone. The marks of their encampment were still visible, but they had decamped for parts unknown, as Grant immediately realized.

"My heart resumed its place," he later wrote. And it did so for the remainder of the Civil War. For Grant suddenly realized his potential enemy had been "as much afraid of me as I had been of him."

Here was a valuable lesson that Grant would never forget: "From that event to the close of the war, I never experienced trepidation upon confronting the enemy, though I always felt more or less anxiety."

Good Times ... and Bad

For Candis Goodwin of Cape Charles, Virginia, slavery apparently wasn't half bad. In fact, once recalling the games of her childhood, she said years later, "Dem was good ole times."

Her white people, she said in an interview in the 1930s, were good to her. They didn't beat their slaves. As a child, she was just like one of their own children. She played with them, ate with them, slept with them.

Her mother worked in the kitchen, and Candis had no work except "nursin' de babies." The white and black children often played in the woods together. They would make houses out of brown pine needles and "grass" out of the needles that were still green. Then they'd go over to the Missus' dairy and "steal anything we want an' tek it to our houses in de woods."

Candis used to play all sorts of pranks on "ole Massa Scott." At night, she said, everybody would be sitting around the big fireplace in the living room, including her. It would get late, and Mr. Scott would leave his chair to wind up his clock. Candis would slip up behind his chair, "an' quick sneak his cheer f'om un'er him." And when he finished with the clock and eased himself back down...there was no chair! And, "he set smack on de flo'."

Then there would be trouble—but not really. "'Doggone you lil cattin'. I gwan switch you,'" he'd threaten. "I jes' fly out de room. Won't scared though, 'cause I knows Massa wont goin' do nottin' to me."

Candis knew about slave whippings—elsewhere. Her Massa Scott, she said, allowed none of that on his place. "He say tain' right."

Nancy Williams of Norfolk, Virginia, on the other hand, had a "singing" uncle in the slave days—an uncle Jimmy who "usta sing an' pray all de time he wukin' in de fiel's" and who wasn't so fortunate. Her uncle Jimmy might have been born of God, she recalled in a 1930s interview, but like Jesus Christ Himself, Uncle Jimmy paid a high price for his devotion.

Her uncle lived and worked on a plantation next to her own, she related. He belonged to a master so mean he couldn't find overseers to "treat de niggers mean 'nough." None were so mean as the master himself. And all the time, there was her uncle Jimmy who sang and prayed as he worked the fields.

Most of the overseers who came and went at "Ole" Tom Covington's plantation didn't bother the singing slave man named Jimmy. But Covington eventually found an overseer who was mean enough. One day this "ole mean devil" was sitting on a stump as the blacks worked a field, Nancy Williams herself among them. Her uncle Jimmy as usual was "jes a-singin' an' praisin' his God." The new overseer didn't like that. He told the slave man to stop the singing; he said Uncle Jimmy wasn't working, he just was singing.

"Uncle Jimmy ain' said nottin'—jes' keep on plowin dat cawn an' a-singin'."

The overseer became obviously mad, but before doing anything about it, he went up to the main house to consult his boss, the master. Nancy Williams, who couldn't have been present there, too, but who possibly had sources, relates their conversation:

—I got a nigger down in the field who can't be working 'cause he's just singing all the time.
—Kill the nigger if he won't work. Go back down there and kill him! What's a nigger for if he won't work?

As the other slaves watched, the overseer returned to the cornfield, all right. He returned and took Uncle Jimmy across the field to a place near the fence. There he made the slave dig a hole in the ground with his bare hands. Then he had others put straw in the bottom of the hole, and then poured in some tar. And then the overseer "chained" Uncle Jimmy, threw him into the hole, and lit a match to the whole business. Nancy and unnamed others stood watching— "peepin' threw a crack in de fence."

And even as they watched the flames lick up, the fire didn't "stop" Uncle Jimmy. "Ise fixin' t' die to live agin' in Chris'," he said. And as the flames mounted and mounted, he began to preach and to pray. The flames grew hotter and hotter, and Uncle Jimmy sang. He sang:

God is de spring of all my joy.
De life of my delight.

And as the song faded away and the other slaves watched through the fence, Uncle Jimmy died.

Staggering Stats

CONSIDER THIS: THE AMERICAN CIVIL WAR ENCOMPASSED, BY BEST ESTIMATES, 10,455 battles, fights, engagements, actions, skirmishes, shooting affairs—whatever you wish to call them. By state, the leader far and away was Virginia, with 2,154 such military events recorded, while many states, chiefly in the North, had none.

Next to Virginia, the fratricidal war's most fought-over state was Tennessee, with 1,462 official "events." In descending order after Tennessee (and some of these may surprise) were: Missouri, with 1,162; Arkansas, with 771; West Virginia, with

632; Louisiana, with 566; Georgia, with 549; Kentucky, with 453; and Alabama, rounding out the top ten with 336. The famous "valley of humility between two mountains of conceit" did not make the top ten with her 313 combats, although North Carolina can be ranked as number 11 in this category, while her sister state, South Carolina, one of the two "mountains," ranked next with 239 combat affairs. Finishing out the eighteen states that hosted the most Civil War battles are Maryland, with 203; Florida, with 168; Texas, 90; Indian Territory, 89; California, 88; and the New Mexico Territory, last with 75. (Despite Gettysburg, Pennsylvania hardly ranked in the number of battles fought on its soil.)

Those are the statistics for the states as ranked and listed by historical compiler (and researcher for Bruce Catton) E. B. Long in his *The Civil War Day by Day, An Almanac 1861–1865*, which cites events of the war on a daily basis from start to finish. Consider also that the roster he cites is not really complete until you add odd, sporadic items such as the guerrilla actions in Kansas, John Hunt Morgan's raid into Ohio, or the Confederate bank robbery in a small Vermont town near the Canadian border.

Still, the stats of the war contribute much to our understanding of how and why it ended—had to end—the way it did. Consider horses, until the modern age an indispensable item for any army on the move (forward or backward). In horses alone, the North began the war with roughly 163 million to the South's 84 million.

More obvious, look at the navies. At the outset, the North had 90 ships. The South, none. Both forces soon ballooned, naturally. The Federals built or purchased 624 more vessels (not all of the original 90 were actually serviceable), while by the end of the war an estimated 500 vessels had served in the South's "Lost Cause."

Even more crucially, what about manpower? Just as the population of the North (an estimated 31.4 million) was greater than that of the South (an estimated 12.3 million), so were the sizes of their military forces disproportionate. Roughly 1.5 million to 2.2 million men served the Union as soldiers or sailors, to the South's 750,000.

Considering the country's centers of gravity in another way, of the nation's nine cities with more than 100,000 inhabitants (per the 1860 U.S. Census), only New Orleans was distinctly Southern, although Baltimore and St. Louis were divided in their loyalties. The two Confederate capitals—Montgomery, Alabama, and Richmond, Virginia—by contrast, could claim populations of only 36,000 and 38,000 respectively. Charleston, where the shooting really began, barely outdid those two with 40,578 folk.

And what about slavery, the divisive and evil institution that caused such heartache all around? Were there really that many slaves in the middle of the nineteenth century? The best estimate is that there were about four million, a sizable number. Oddly, though, while nearly all slaveowners were in the South, sixty-four slaves were counted as living in the North. Furthermore, the South's slaveowners included a handful who were themselves black, largely in New Orleans.

Not all blacks in the South were slaves, of course, but most of them were. Free blacks numbered an estimated 262,003 in the South—a few more than the 225,967 free blacks who lived in the North.

★ MIDDLES ★

Hello, Washington

THE WASHINGTON OF THE CIVIL WAR PERIOD WAS FAR REMOVED FROM THE beauteous city of today. In fact, it was distinctly primitive—even slovenly to look at—with an unfinished Capitol dome, a half-built Washington Monument, and even worse…

Even worse, in the words of Ohio's Representative Albert G. Riddle, it was "as unattractive, straggling, sodden a town, wandering up and down the left bank of the yellow [yellow!] Potomac, as fancy can sketch."

Perhaps Riddle exaggerated ever so slightly. But he offered factual observations, too. Pennsylvania Avenue, he later wrote, "twelve rods wide, stretched drearily over the mile between the unfinished Capitol and the unfinished Treasury building on Fifteenth Street, west, where it turned north for a square, and took its melancholy way to Georgetown."

Worse, "illy paved" with cobblestones, Pennsylvania Avenue "was the only paved street of the town," averred Mr. Riddle. "The other streets, which were long stretches of mud or deserts of dust and sand, with here and there clumps of poorly built residences with long gaps between them, passing little deserts of open lands, where their lines were lost, wandered from the highlands north towards the Potomac, and from the Eastern Branch (Anacostia) to Rock Creek."

Worst of all: "Not a sewer blessed the town, nor off of Pennsylvania Avenue was there a paved gutter."

It sounds unbelievable to us today, but Riddle very firmly stated: "Each house had an open drain from its rear, out across the sidewalk."

The result was of course not too pleasant for residents or visitors, to say little of the hygienic aspects. "As may be supposed the Capital of the Republic had more mal-odors than the poet Coleridge ascribed to ancient Cologne."

Just for added atmospheric color, Riddle also noted the open canal running from Rock Creek to the Anacostia River, a branch of the Chesapeake and Ohio and a breeding ground for tadpoles, mosquitoes and malaria.

In another vein, the Ohio Republican found that "politically, the city—the fixed population—was intensely Southern, as much so as Richmond or Baltimore." Indeed, "very few men of culture, and none below that grade, were Republicans at the advent of 'Lincoln and his Northern myrmidons,' as they were called in 1856–61."

The new political and social set, ushered into town by Lincoln's so-called advent, Riddle among them, changed all, it would seem. Fresh blood, heroic deeds, and the inspiration of men facing—and overcoming—hostile forces "excercized [sic] an irresistible influence upon the population, and at once and forever silenced the open utterance of sedition and rebellion."

Be that as it may, another visitor to the beleaguered capital city of the 1860s was James A. Garfield, a young Union officer and future congressman, and president of the reunited United States. In an outing with Kate Chase, daughter of Lincoln's treasury secretary Salmon P. Chase, in October 1862, Garfield saw that "the city is surrounded by a nearly complete circle of hills." They had a choice of spans over the Potomac River. "In crossing over into Virginia there are three famous bridges, the Long, the Aqueduct, and the Chain Bridge—the last being furthest upstream, and around which there have been many skirmishes during the past year. The great [Chesapeake and Ohio] canal which comes in here from the west, formerly crossed the Potomac and made its southern and eastern terminus at Alexandria. The water has been let off and it is now used as a bridge from Georgetown to Virginia. Hence the name [Aqueduct Bridge]."

The Union troops had been busy since their rout at First Bull Run. "The heights around Washington are all crowned with formidable fortifications, mostly heavy earthworks and are called Forts. We passed through Georgetown and over the Aqueduct Bridge and went via Arlington Heights, the home of Lee, the rebel General in Chief. He owns a large tract of land there and has a quaint old pillared residence on it with a touch of the Norman Castle style about it. He married a Custis, one of the Washington family."

So much for the grand Arlington House, it seems. "From there we went by Bailey's Cross-Roads to Fairfax Court House, about 18 miles through a country completely devastated, it having been in turn held by both armies several times during the last eighteen months. Fairfax is an old town built mainly of stone and brick, and seems to be nearly or quite one century old."

And from a tour later the same year, more Garfield observations on the future site of today's Arlington National Cemetery:

"We took the carriage and went across the Potomac to Arlington Heights, thence to Alexandria, then to Fairfax Seminary, back to Alexandria, drove the carriage on board a steamer and came back to Washington by water. General Lee's House at Arlington Heights was built by George Washington Custis whose daughter Lee married. It is a quaint old building, built in the castle style, and the walls of the main hall are ornamented with the skull and antlers of stags and

paintings of the chase, also several battle pictures of the Revolution. It is now the headquarters of General Heintzelman. [General Samuel P. Heintzelman, at the time commander of Union defenses in northern Virginia, across the Potomac from Washington proper.]"

No Panacea for Politicians

IMAGINE A MEMBER OF CONGRESS RIDING TO THE NATION'S CAPITAL IN AN unheated railroad boxcar, a national legislator wearing his unlaundered shirts and socks for days at a time and foregoing a Christmas recess. Imagine a capital where the seasonal turkey would cost $125 whole…where the legislative pay at any time of year barely covered the cost of a boarding house.

Imagine—but know that such were the experiences of Georgia's Warren Akin and other members of Congress during the Civil War—the Confederate Congress sitting in Richmond, that is.

The Confederate States of America enjoyed three Congresses in all: the Provisional Congress that first met in both Montgomery, Alabama, and Richmond, Virginia, to draw up the new Confederate government, plus two more Congresses meeting exclusively in Richmond. Members of the "Provisional" were selected at the secession conventions held by their respective states. This body was unicameral—one deliberative chamber only. The next two Congresses were bicameral with an elected membership.

The Provisional body, for the record, first convened in Montgomery on February 4, 1861. It assembled for five sessions over the next year, then dissolved itself with final adjournment in Richmond on February 17, 1862. The next day, the First Congress took over.

Meeting in Richmond, it held four sessions, then faded away in February 1864 to make room for the Second (and last) Confederate Congress, which met in two lengthy sessions from May 1864 to March 1865.

After that, it was all over. In fact, the last Southerner elected to the legislative body never assumed his seat. Nathaniel W. Townes of Texas had won the right to take the House seat of a deceased Confederate congressman, but Townes's special election of March 13, 1865, came too late—Appomattox was just weeks ahead.

Of the 267 other men who collectively made up the Confederate Congress, about one-third had been U.S. congressmen before the Civil War changed their lives and political careers. A clear majority, for that matter, had political experience on federal, state, or local levels.

Their lot in the more permanent Confederate capital of Richmond was not so enviable, noted history professor Bell Irvin Wiley in his book *Letters of Warren Akin: Confederate Congressman* (University of Georgia Press, 1959). The legislators were asked to do their job in a fragile house of glass in the midst of wide-ranging war against a powerful enemy. "The ultimate result," wrote Wiley, "was frustration and failure; and in the long time that intervened between the hopeful beginning and final defeat, most congressmen were subjected to considerable abuse by journalists, members of other departments of government, state authorities, constituents, and the public in general."

To make matters worse, their home districts were being overrun by the dreaded Yankees. Many a congressman's family "at home" no longer was at home—they were refugees living elsewhere, in exile. One member with exactly that problem was a former U.S. senator from Alabama, Clement C. Clay Jr. Now a Confederate senator, Clay was forced to flee from home base of Huntsville. As he plaintively wrote to a fellow senator: "My home & parents & most of my kindred [are] in the hands of the enemy & I an exile wandering about like a troubled spirit seeking rest." (Fortunately for the rest of the Confederacy, Clay's earlier efforts to have Huntsville picked as the permanent Confederate capital had been to no avail!)

House member Warren Akin's experience was strikingly similar. A lawyer and state legislator from Cassville in northern Georgia, Akin at first kept to a relatively normal course despite the outbreak of war in 1861. By early 1864, however, he and his family had moved to Oxford, southeast of Atlanta, in anticipation of Federal incursions. But they then had to beat a hasty retreat farther east to Elberton in his native Elbert County. The Yankees, meanwhile, burned down Akin's home and law office in Cassville in May 1864, then returned six months later to set fire to the rest of the town (except for three houses occupied by persons too infirm to flee). Atlanta, of course, fell to the invaders, and Akin himself was fortunate to escape capture by George Stoneman's cavalry raiders.

By this time—the summer of 1864—the fifty-two-year-old Akin was serving in the Second Confederate Congress that began its sessions in Richmond in May 1864. This meant Akin had to leave wife Mary Verdery, their seven small children (and six or seven slaves) on their own in a troubled, besieged land. Nor was he very well compensated for his lengthy absences from home and law practice. His monthly pay of $690 in Confederate money, he once wrote, would cover his boarding-house costs and other basic needs, with only "a little left to take home." And the $690-a-month sum did not even come until almost the end of the Civil War. At first, noted historian Wiley in his book of Akin letters, the Southern congressmen received only eight dollars a day and ten cents a mile as a travel allowance. An 1862 increase gave them $2,760 per annum in legislative salary, plus twenty cents a mile for official travel. Finally came the $690 a month—still no panacea.

Lodging and meals were high-cost items during congressional sessions, which customarily lasted for weeks at a time. "Some of the congressmen stayed in hotels," noted Wiley, "and a directory published in 1864 shows that the Exchange, the Ballard House, and the Spotswood were favorite places of abode. A few legislators bought or rented houses in the capital. But the majority of them lived in boarding houses or private homes."

And not always happily. A. M. Branch of Texas wrote home in May 1864 that he was paying six hundred dollars a month for his lodging and two meals a day, "which is pretty high board." Likewise, Missouri's Thomas A. Harris once lamented that his pay of ten to eleven dollars a day fell far short of his actual needs. "Board alone," he wrote in April 1864, "without washing, clothing or incidentals of any kind, is at hotels, $30 and at the most mediocre boarding houses from $8 to $12 per day. With my family, my absolute expenses average $50 per day & you know that I live plainly & with rigid economy."

Speaking of laundry, Akin often mentioned that subject and his enforced frugality. His letters reveal he wore his shirts for three or four days at a time and his socks for a week, to save laundry costs. He seemed always to be darning his own socks, and he once commented: "I carry and use my handkerchiefs until they are soiled so much I am ashamed to use them."

As the conflict wore down all elements of Southern society, Richmond became a dangerous place for the average citizen—even a legislator, it seems. One reason the Confederate House voted against extending its meeting time into the evening hours was the members' fear of muggings in the streets of the capital city.

By late 1864, various societal amenities—such as passenger train service— had deteriorated so much that Georgia Congressman Akin, once Speaker of the House in his own state legislature, had to travel in a railroad boxcar for the last leg of a trip back to Richmond. "I was just 9 ½ hours going from Greensboro, N.C., to Danville, Va.," he wrote, "a distance of 48 miles [I] travelled in a box car in the night and slept on some corn sacks, but as it was not very cold I made out pretty well."

Although he exhibited a cheerful and spartan attitude regarding his travel difficulties, Akin at the same time did despair over the larger portent of his plight—and that of the Confederacy. "I don't know how long I am to support my family, if this war continues long," he wrote to his wife. "Everything I have been working hard for so many years will be eaten up and in my old age myself, family and children will be left without the means of support."

The only answer, he added, was to trust in God—"and do the best I can."

Brave Deed Recorded

BEFORE THE UNION FLEET BULLED ITS WAY UPRIVER AND SET THE STAGE FOR THE fall of New Orleans, how were things ashore in the Big Easy? What were the local conditions after a year of War Between the States in this multicultural town?

In a word or two, pretty sad. A city of futile images and yet determined to go on.

George W. Cable—call him a young man or an old boy—was there, and he saw with keen eye. He saw at the Coliseum Place the daily dress parade of the Confederate guards. And so well turned out! "Long, spotless, gray, white-gloved ranks that stretched in such faultless alignment down the hard, harsh turf of our old ball-ground."

Except that these were not exactly frontline troops. Those fellows, the young men of the city, had long since passed on to distant fields. This was the home guard—"Gray heads, hoary heads, high heads, bald heads." These, bravely turned out as they might be, were "the merchants, bankers, underwriters, judges, real estate owners and capitalists of the Anglo-American part of the city."

Not that the Anglos held any monopoly on local patriotism, either. Elsewhere, down at the famous Levee (or steamboat landing) drilled "a superb body of Creoles in dark-blue uniforms." Their commands and their manual were in French.

Other ethnic groups were also vital, since, "as a gendarmerie they relieved just so many Confederate soldiers of police duty in a city under martial law, and enabled them to man forts and breastworks at short notice whenever that call should come."

The city had lost its normal bustle. People hid their valuables. "Gold and silver had long ago disappeared." Commerce slowed, and where business had been conducted or goods manufactured there now was armament...or nothing. For a short while after war began, even after the Union clamped on its blockade outside the mouth of the Mississippi, the Levee kept busy. But no longer. "Its stir and noise had gradually declined, faltered, turned into the commerce of war."

And even more of the young men had gone off to war. "The brave steady fellows," said Cable, "who at entry and shipping and cash and account desks could no longer keep a show of occupation, had laid down the pen, taken up the sword and musket and followed after the earlier and more eager volunteers."

From those early days, too, had come the sad and dismaying returns. The town "had never been really glad again after that awful day of Shiloh." They "had sent so many gallant fellows to help Beauregard, and some of them so young."

And now, in the spring of 1862, war was coming nearer and nearer. "For now even we, the uninformed, the lads and women…knew the enemy was closing down on upon us."

Still, was not every gray-haired man and boy ready to do his duty? Were not the fortifications ready? "But there was little laughter. Food was dear; the destitute poor were multiplying terribly…. The Mississippi was gnawing at the levees and threatening to plunge in on us. The city was believed to be full of spies."

Finally the day came that all had expected and feared. Heralded by alarm bells, the Union warships were moving up the river. Mobs gathered at the levees. They watched—and waited—as local firemen threw burning bales of cotton into the river, cast loose ships and boats of all kinds, and sent them burning into the jaws of the Federal monster.

To no avail, according to Cable. "'Are the Yankee ships in sight?,' I asked of an idler. He pointed out the tops of their naked masts as they showed up across the huge bend of the river…. Ah, me! I see them now as they come slowly round Slaughterhouse Point into full view, silent, grim, terrible; black with men, heavy with deadly portent; the long-banished Stars and Stripes flying against the frowning sky."

Not long after, Cable heard roars and shouts and curses outside the store he worked in. "Kill them!" were the shouts. "Hang them!" Or, "Hurrah for Jeff Davis!"

It was a mob, with a weapon in every third pair of hands. And in the center, two men—two officers of the United States Navy—strode on, undeviating, "never frowning, never flinching, while the mob screamed in their ears, shook cocked pistols in their faces, cursed and crowded, and gnashed upon them." And so, "through the gates of death," marched these two Union men to the City Hall to demand and receive the surrender of New Orleans, April 25, 1862. Just about the bravest deed our witness ever saw.

Complete Conquest Required

It was, said Ulysses S. Grant afterward, "the severest battle fought at the West during the war, and but few in the East equalled it for hard, determined fighting." He was recalling Shiloh. Bloody Shiloh.

It lasted two days, but that was enough. "I saw an open field, in our possession on the second day, over which the Confederates had made repeated charges the day before, so covered with dead that it would have been possible to walk across the clearing, in any direction, stepping on dead bodies, without a foot touching the ground."

Close to the Federal line, the Union and Confederate dead were "mingled together in about equal proportions." But sadly for the South, the rest of the field was *its* dead.

The battle took place in April 1862 on the western banks of the flooding Tennessee River, a place called Pittsburg Landing. A church stood nearby: the small Shiloh meetinghouse. Here in cold rain and mud, came the two armies for an early showdown—forty thousand Johnny Rebs under Albert S. Johnston come to fight forty-two thousand under Grant.

The fighting raged, and even some of the generals would not walk away unscathed. Johnston, for one, died after being wounded in the leg. He could have tended to it and lived. Instead, he stayed on his horse, kept his boots on, and bled to death. On the Union side, Grant's subordinate William Wallace was also mortally wounded.

Even Grant, before the shooting died down in the second day's fighting, survived a Confederate ball that plucked its way through the air to his very side, but struck his metal sword scabbard, "just below the hilt."

Not quite so fortunate—but a survivor—was Union General William Tecumseh Sherman. "A casualty to Sherman that would have taken him from the field on that day [Sunday, April 6] would have been a sad one for the troops engaged at Shiloh," wrote Grant later. "And how near we came to this! On the 6th Sherman was shot twice, once in the hand, once in the shoulder, the ball cutting his coat and making a slight wound, and a third ball passed through his hat. In addition to this he had several horses shot during the day."

A horse was the cause of Grant's own greatest physical discomfort at Shiloh—his mount had slipped on a muddy incline two days before and fallen, "with my leg under his body." Grant's ankle was so swollen afterward that his boot had to be cut off; he used crutches for the next two or three days.

The result was that the commander of Union forces at Shiloh spent the crucial night between the two days of fighting still in pain from the ankle injury and well aware that the Confederates had pushed back the Union line in the first day of fighting, capturing a Union general, Benjamin M. Prentiss, and 2,200 of his men in one fell swoop. That night, one would think, there was much to discourage U. S. Grant.

"During the night," he later related, "rain fell in torrents and our troops were exposed to the storm without shelter." Himself included: "I made my headquarters under a tree a few hundred yards back from the river bank. My ankle was so much swollen from the fall of my horse…and the bruise was so painful, that I could get no rest. The drenching rain would have precluded the possibility of sleep without this additional cause."

Sometime after midnight, Grant became so uncomfortable he sought shelter in a small log cabin nearby. But it had been turned into a field hospital, "and all night wounded men were being brought in, their wounds dressed, a leg or arm amputated, as the case might require, and everything being done to save life or alleviate suffering." In the end, Grant could stand it no more. "The sight was more unendurable than encountering the enemy's fire, and I returned to my tree in the rain."

The next day, Grant's anticipated reinforcements arrived, swelling the size of the Union force, and he counterattacked against the now-outnumbered and tiring Confederates. By mid-afternoon on April 7, they were in retreat. In Grant's view, that was what counted. Not who won the first day or phase of battle, but who won the final spasm in the battlefield.

In the harsh hours before the shooting died down, both sides experienced desertions from the front lines. Grant took a surprisingly forgiving and philosophical view of the "stragglers," as these men were called, even though they were enough of a problem for him to form his cavalry into a line at the rear to halt the runaways. "When there would be enough of them to make a show, and after they had recovered from their fright, they would be sent to reinforce some part of the line which needed support, without regard to their companies, regiments or brigades," he wrote in his memoirs.

He had had problems with stragglers earlier.

At one point in the first day's fighting, Grant found "as many as four or five thousand stragglers lying under cover of the river bluff, panic-stricken, most of whom would have been shot where they lay, without resistance, before they would have taken muskets and marched to the front to protect themselves."

Grant's fellow Union general, Don Carlos Buell, was furious with the malingerers. "I saw him berating them and trying to shame them into joining their regiments," wrote Grant. "He even threatened them with shells from the gun-boats near by."

Grant was not nearly so perturbed, even though Buell's tongue lashing had little effect. Said Grant: "Most of these men afterward proved themselves as gallant as any of those who saved the battle from which they deserted."

He asserted also that the Rebel stragglers at Shiloh were just as numerous, and the only difference was that they "left the field entirely" while "on the Union side, but few of the stragglers fell back further than the landing on the river, and many of these were in line for duty on the second day."

Indeed, one of the major positive results of the Union victory, in Grant's view, was the confidence it gave the largely green, inexperienced troops of his Army of the Tennessee. While the battle also gave the Union control of the middle Mississippi River line, it opened Grant's eyes to a central truth. "Up to the battle of Shiloh," he later said, "I, as well as thousands of other citizens, believed that the rebellion against the Government would collapse suddenly and soon, if a decisive victory could be gained over any of its armies." The fact is, Grant himself had already gained such a victory at Forts Donelson and Henry nearby, and still the Confederacy fielded its hard-fighting armies. It lost, if narrowly, at Shiloh, and still "not only attempted to hold the line farther south… but assumed the offensive and made…gallant effort to regain what had been lost." As a result, the Confederacy created a monster—its own nemesis—in the form of Grant, who now resolved the strategy by which he would lead the Union armies to ultimate victory just three years later. For Grant now "gave up all idea of saving the Union except by complete conquest."

Secession from Secession

AT ONE POINT DURING THE CIVIL WAR, WINSTON COUNTY IN NORTHERN Alabama (with Houston as its county seat) was so unhappy with events that it thought of seceding from the newly formed Confederacy. The populace here, often called "hill people," was not to be counted among the South's plantation owners or slaveowners. Far from either category, the Winstonites were so set against Alabama seceding from the Union, they sent a young schoolteacher named Chris Sheets to represent their point of view at the state's Secession Conference in Montgomery in January 1861.

A maverick among the fire-eaters and other secession-minded delegates to the convention, Sheets argued long and vociferously for the hill country's point of view. As cited in Alabama writer Drue Duke's anecdotal history, *Alabama Tales*, the hot debates in Montgomery led to name-calling and, for Sheets, even worse. "When Sheets refused to sign any papers of oath that the Secessionists offered him [after voting for secession], tempers flared more violently. 'I am an American,' Sheets declared, 'and an Alabamian, I don't need to sign anything to prove who I am.'" He might as well have spoken to the wind. "At that point, he and the remaining few who sided with him were seized and dragged off to jail," writes Duke. "A few of the non-secessionists were able to slip away and hide."

Naturally, news of their emissary's incarceration and other rough treatment "downstate" did not sit well with his fellow residents of Winston County. "The hill people grew more angry each time they heard it repeated," and "Sheets came to represent a real martyr to the people of Winston and the surrounding counties."

Nor did matters rest there. As the Confederacy and the Union came to actual blows, their respective loyalists in Winston were at odds, too. "Friends and neighbors who had known each other for years were now on opposite sides of the issue and weren't even speaking to each other. Church congregations, even denominations, split. Family members argued their conflicting beliefs, and young brothers left home to fight against each other."

Here in the deep South, the split rending the country was duplicated in microcosm. Some in Winston, though opposed to the idea in principle, wished to go along with Alabama's secession to keep the peace in their own community. Others, Sheets among them, weren't willing to let matters lie there. They issued a call for a "Neutrality Meeting" on July 4, Independence Day, and twenty-five hundred to three thousand persons, including "people from all over the South," turned out for the conference at Looney's Tavern. The talk soon turned to secession—secession from Alabama, that is! "The Free State of Winston" would be the result.

But secession from a state that had already left the Union, pointed out a speaker named J. L. Meeks, would mean that Winston had no representation in any governmental entity beyond the county borders. It would be "much wiser," he argued, "to declare ourselves neutral and ask that our rights as neutral citizens be recognized."

By Duke's account, those present were then asked to approve a declaration proposing "that the people continue to respect Old Glory and to…take up no arms against the flag." At the same time, the people of Winston would ask "both the Confederacy and the Union to respect their rights and leave them alone to settle their own affairs in their own way."

The declaration was approved by a loud and enthusiastic voice vote. And if no Free State of Winston ever emerged, "the hill people still proudly recall the day they took a strong stand in the face of great danger," wrote Duke.

Soldier A-Courting

HE HAD SMALL WHITE HANDS, AND HE ALWAYS LOOKED CLEAN. BUT HE WAS A BIG man, broad in the chest and proud in mein. He could be charming to the ladies, but he also knew what it was to hold firm—even to fight a duel. So when a man in his Kentucky hometown balked at taking his own wife and children to church, the preacher spoke with John Hunt Morgan, who then spoke with the recalcitrant husband.

The preacher had one way of speaking and Morgan another. He simply told the wayward soul, "I've come to give you a sound thrashing—if necessary." The offender became a regular churchgoer soon after.

Morgan came from Lexington in the bluegrass country, where cavalier attitudes and behavior were rife, where men (and women) thought with such independence that the town fed both the Confederate and the Union armies numerous hot-bloods intent on fighting for their respective beliefs. Here, for instance, three grandsons of Henry Clay cast their lot with the Union and four with the Confederacy. Among other citizens, Dr. Robert Breckinridge, himself a Union man, gave two sons to each side (and a son-in-law to the Southern cause), while U.S. Senator John J. Crittenden's two sons each became generals on opposing sides.

Indeed, this was Mary Todd Lincoln's home territory; her own half sister's husband, Benjamin H. Helm, was a Confederate general whose death at Chickamauga was sincerely mourned in the White House—the Union White House. No such splits, however, existed within John Hunt Morgan's family; all six of Morgan's "boys" joined the Confederate ranks.

One of them, John, soon became famous as a Confederate raider, a dashing war hero to rival Virginia's colorful icons "Jeb" Stuart and John Singleton

Mosby. Indeed, it is debatable whether either Stuart or Mosby inflicted as much damage overall on the enemy in personnel and materiel losses or had as great an impact on enemy strategy. It is absolutely nondebatable, of course, that only John Hunt Morgan took an invading force—raiding party, if one must be technical—as far north as a point in Ohio only one hundred miles south of Lake Erie.

It also can be argued that only the charming John Morgan would have courted an intended bride with quite the flourish he displayed when based for a time in Murfreesboro, Tennessee, home of the two Ready sisters, Alice and Martha (called Mattie). In one of his frequent visits to town, Morgan met their father, "Colonel" Ready, who promptly invited the cavalryman home for dinner, sending ahead a message: "Tell Mattie that Captain Morgan is a widower and a little sad. I want her to sing for him."

Mattie, it should be pointed out, was not an aging spinster or a callow country girl, but a winsome twenty-one-year-old who, as daughter of a former U.S. congressman, had lived in the Federal capital as a leading single socialite. And it was true—Morgan, a captain destined to become a general in just eight months' time, was a widower, his invalid wife, Rebecca, having died at the time of First Bull Run in July 1861.

After that first dinner at the Ready mansion in early 1862, Alice eagerly confided to her diary that their visitor was modest but pleasant and agreeable. He didn't look the part of "the daring reckless man he is." Before long John Morgan was spending his free time riding horseback with Mattie during frequent visits to the Ready household.

In February the Confederates pulled out of Murfreesboro (following a farewell dinner at the Ready home). Morgan and his men were left behind as a screening and scouting force. For his dashes and raids against the Federals, his daring "visits" inside Union-held Nashville, and other escapades, Morgan had by then achieved such a reputation that a crowd was known to collect outside the Ready door, a block from Courthouse Square, at word that Morgan was there.

His own division commander, William Hardee, warned Morgan to be more careful or risk being killed or captured. Said Morgan: "Sir, it would be an impossibility for them to catch me."

It seems his words were true, as seen by his escapades. While operating out of Murfreesboro, Morgan often sent challenging messages to pro-Union Louisville editor George D. Prentice by splicing into Union telegraph lines. And in March he set out one day to ambush and capture a Union general on the roads outside Nashville—the notion being that any general would do.

Morgan and his men soon rounded up eighty-five assorted prisoners, although no one was a general. He sent them to the rear and waited some more before bagging another eleven.

On the way back to Murfreesboro, some of the prisoners were lost to a pursuing Union detachment. So when Morgan was a bit late in making his reappearance, people began to worry. The two Ready sisters in particular were on pins and needles that Sunday morning. At church, though, they received word that Morgan and one of his officers were awaiting them with thirty-eight Yankee prisoners. As Morgan biographer Cecil Holland said in his book, *Morgan and His Raiders*, the two young women couldn't stay for church after that. "We felt it would be mockery to remain and pretend to hear the sermon," one of the sisters later explained.

Shortly, Morgan and his compatriot appeared in front of the Ready home with the prisoners and escorts, sixty to seventy horsemen in all. "Ladies," said the colorful raider, "we present you with your prisoners. What disposal should be made of them?"

And the reply, "You have performed your part so well we are willing to entrust it all to you."

Next, Morgan & Company were off to the Union-held railroad town of Gallatin, promising more trophies upon return, even though the Federals were moving ominously close to Murfreesboro itself.

At Gallatin, Morgan and his men performed their wrecking work on the rail facilities and obtained intelligence by approaching the telegraph operator in the guise of Federal officers. The operator accepted them at face value, then fool-ishly boasted that he was ready to face John Morgan if the Reb ever appeared in Gallatin. Morgan's companion of the moment couldn't resist: "Sir, let me introduce you to Captain Morgan."

Back in Murfreesboro, the Union Army had arrived at last, taking possession quietly but decisively. Fortunately, Morgan was warned before riding blithely back into town to visit his newfound love. Mattie, assuming she wouldn't see Morgan for a time, wrote him a farewell note to be sent by messenger. Then she received word he was at a village eight or ten miles away. Would it be safe for him to slip into town? The Union troops were encamped about eight miles out of town in another direction, so she sent back word to come ahead, then waited on tenterhooks, wondering if she had invited him to his doom.

Suddenly, he was there at the front door with a fellow officer and five prison-ers as more "trophies" for the ladies, who once again told Morgan to dispose of them as he knew best.

Morgan, in fact, stayed with the fair Mattie until dawn while his men and his prisoners waited. By Ready family tradition, that is the night they became engaged, although they would not see each other for another eight months, much less go ahead with marriage plans. But that ceremony—and a colorful, widely heralded one it was, too—did finally take place, by which time the young Morgan was a general.

Battery Disbanded

FEW, YESTERDAY OR TODAY, HAVE EVER HEARD OF THE 13TH INDEPENDENT Battery, Ohio Light Artillery, organized and mustered into the service of the Union Army at Camp Dennison, Ohio, on December 20, 1861, one year to the day after South Carolina seceded from the Union. Few at any time since the battery's first and only appearance in battle have heard of it because its furious division commander, Brigadier General Stephen A. Hurlbut, disbanded the unit, scattered its men, gave away its guns, and ordered its officers home, accusing all of cowardly performance in battle…even if it was their first combat experience.

By Hurlbut's angry account, the battery personnel ("ignorant of duty and drill") set up their guns on Sunday, April 6, 1862, and then—"A single shot from the enemy's batteries struck in [Captain John B.] Myers' 13th Ohio Battery, when officers, and men, with a common impulse of disgraceful cowardice, abandoned their entire battery, horses, caissons, and guns, and fled, and I saw no more of them until Tuesday."

The facts, as related by others, may have been somewhat less stinging. For instance, Thomas Jeffrey, a young enlisted man in the battery, later wrote that he and his companions spent most of the time after their unit's formation in December 1861 in marching drills, because only one practice cannon was available at their camp for the use of several artillery batteries.

On March 1, 1862, the battery at last received "guns and horses." Just four days later, the battery was ordered to the front. The front would be Pittsburg Landing on the Tennessee River; the battle awaiting Jeffrey and his comrades was Shiloh.

How did they get there from Ohio? They "marched to Cincinnati and by railroad to St. Louis, then by steamboat down to Cairo and up the Ohio and Tennessee Rivers to Pittsburg Landing."

The entire trip took nearly a month. Leaving on March 5, the 13th Ohio Battery arrived just six days before the fighting erupted on Sunday, April 6, near the Shiloh meetinghouse. "From the time of receiving their guns and horses to their arrival at Pittsburg," wrote Jeffrey later, "they had not had their horses hitched up more than a half dozen times."

On that "terrible first day," as he later called it, Jeffrey's artillery battery was "prompt to respond" as the fighting began, but had to wait for an hour or more in camp for orders. They came at last, carried by an aide to General Hurlbut: Move up to the front.

"After going forward a mile or more the Captain was ordered to place his battery in position in a narrow belt of timber to the right of an open field," wrote Jeffrey years later. Myers objected, saying he wanted to place his guns in the open field. "The staff officer peremptorily ordered him to place it in the timber."

It may be, too, as other accounts have it, that the inexperienced Myers mistakenly held back when his supporting infantry, four regiments under Brigadier General Jacob Lauman, dashed ahead. General Hurlbut later accused Myers of holding back, "either from ignorance or some other cause."

In the lines opposite, meanwhile, a very proficient artilleryman was preparing his own guns to support a Confederate charge against Lauman's position. This was Captain Felix H. Robertson, commander of an Alabama battery and a West Point graduate who had gone with the South. He had the 13th Ohio Battery in his sights.

As Jeffrey tells it: "As they [his battery] undertook to obey the order [to go into the trees], the enemy opened with both infantry and artillery which resulted in their becoming hopelessly entangled among the trees and logs, the horses shot down, the men in disorder. So complete was the destruction that but two of the team with one gun and its caisson escaped from the general disaster."

Said a friendly onlooker, Union Lieutenant Cuthbert W. Laing of the nearby 2nd Michigan Battery: "They had just got unlimbered when one of their caissons was shivered to pieces, and the horses on one of the guns took fright and ran through our lines. All then left the battery without firing a shot."

Other Union artillerymen, it seems, ran forward, cut loose the surviving horses, and spiked the guns left behind by the 13th Battery, which suffered one man killed and eight wounded.

The day wore on, with at least four Confederate assaults against Lauman's "Hornet's Nest" sector in the Federal line, which was gradually pushed back—but at horrendous cost to the attacking Rebels. Said an Indiana officer: "The advance was made up to within some 10 yards of my line and the slaughter among the enemy in its front was terrible." General Lauman recalled, as did U. S. Grant later: "The ground was literally covered with their dead."

Young Sergeant Jeffrey, meanwhile, wrote that his battery's one undamaged gun and "detached pieces of other batteries did efficient work in the repulse of the enemy on the evening of that terrible first day at Shiloh." Battery members, he wrote later, regrouped at "their old camp" after the battle ended the next day, "having recovered their guns and equipments except horses."

They were in for a shock. "A few days thereafter they were surprised by an order from General Hurlbut for the muster out of their officers and the assignment of the men to the Ninth, Tenth and Fourteenth Ohio batteries."

Even years later, Jeffrey could not understand Hurlbut's attitude. "Why this was done I do not know," he wrote. "No doubt General Hurlbut thought he had sufficient reason, but the only apparent reason was that the officers in attempting to obey orders had lost their battery."

According to Jeffrey, later an officer himself in the war, an official investigation by the Ohio Adjutant General's office "fully exonerated Captain Myers from blame," and further, according to Jeffrey, "The treatment of Captain Myers and his officers by General Hurlbut has been denounced as outrageous by all who knew of the affair."

In the meantime, though, the war continued. Jeffrey found himself assigned to the 14th Ohio Battery, which now took over the old 13th's remaining equipment. The 14th served honorably through the rest of the war—at Corinth, Mississippi, in the Atlanta Campaign, the Battle of Nashville, and the campaign against Mobile, Alabama.

At Resaca, Georgia, one day, the battery was asked to "knock out" some Confederate snipers in distant trees. "It took us but a short time to knock them out," Jeffrey reported, and the onlooking General James B. McPherson "remarked that in all his military experience it was the first time he had ever seen artillery used for the purpose of sharpshooting."

Another time, the battery marched so long through such completely stripped Confederate countryside in parts of Georgia and Alabama that its horses starved to death. Later still, the 14th Ohio covered 4,500 miles just in the final five months of the war.

If Jeffrey didn't see much of the war with the ill-fated 13th Ohio, he and a number of his old compatriots certainly did with the 14th Ohio.

"Granny" Lee

IT WAS A CRUCIAL BATTLE OUTSIDE RICHMOND. THE COMMANDER'S PREPARATIONS were not always the best, and the enemy's superiority in numbers was over-whelming. When the commander was suddenly wounded and incapacitated, the second in command was available to take over. He simply was not up to the job, though, and the enemy was virtually at the gates to Richmond.

Who to call in? Well, there was that deskbound fellow, that veteran of en-gineers. Why not him? Robert E. "Granny" Lee. Bring him forward to the rescue—if he can.

It is difficult to believe nowadays, but there was a time during the Civil War when the South's Robert E. Lee—now undoubtedly greatest icon of them all—was held in some contempt, was unknown to many, and was called "Granny" Lee by others for his supposedly slow, tentative ways.

Better-acquainted associates knew or suspected that he had strong fighting qualities…but not everyone knew. Not yet.

It was, in part, Lee's own fault for being so gentlemanly in manner. He had indeed begun his Civil War career as a deskbound planner rather than a field commander. While he had experience in combat during the Mexican War and had been in charge of the military unit that was sent pell-mell to arrest John Brown at Harpers Ferry in 1859, they were all small-unit actions, small potatoes in scope, however successful. Otherwise, his background largely was in engineering, defensive fortifications, and the like. A West Pointer himself, he had been superintendent of the academy for a time. But again, it was not the equivalent of major field command in war.

At the outset of the Civil War, Lee became commander of Virginia's forces, initiated their recruitment and training, and began gathering a coterie of bril-liant officers such as Thomas J. "Stonewall" Jackson. With First Bull Run in July 1861, the Confederate forces showed they could win battles. The resulting acclaim went to the two commanders with the troops: Pierre Gustav Toutant Beauregard and Joseph Johnston. Lee, chained to his desk in Richmond, was not on hand, although Jefferson Davis, president of the Confederacy, had gone up to Manassas to see things for himself. It was Lee's planning, in significant part, that positioned the Confederate forces and his training programs that pre-pared many of the troops for their first combat, but few were aware of these facts, and in all the excitement he did not receive public credit. And yet, when the Southern forces failed to chase the Union troops into Washington and perhaps lost the opportunity for a bold stroke to end the war, Lee was criticized for not seizing that opportunity.

The smoke had hardly cleared when Lee, as an aide and adviser to Jefferson Davis, was dispatched on a thankless errand that would not redound to his credit as a commander of men.

He was sent into the mountains of southwest Virginia to "iron out the differences between Generals Henry A. Wise and John B. Floyd, two temperamental former governors of the state, and General W. W. Loring," wrote Virginius Dabney in his *Virginia: The New Dominion*. Lee's charge was to achieve coordination among the three separate commands and to end the various rivalries among the three generals. And yet Lee did not have real authority over the "feuding prima donnas," adds Dabney. The gracious and genteel Lee was probably the wrong man to send on this errand—"What was needed was a knocking together of heads rather than attempts at tactful persuasion."

Unsurprisingly, he was unable to achieve the harmony needed among the three commanders. And "when many of Virginia's western counties went over to the enemy that winter, Lee got much of the blame."

And perhaps fairly so. "Lee's gentlemanliness, his humility, his unwillingness to be sharply categorical and critical in expressing his views, would plague him throughout much of the war." Now fully bearded for the first time, Lee returned to his Richmond desk job accompanied by "sneers from the press, which referred to him derisively as 'Granny' Lee and 'Evacuating' Lee."

His next assignment also lacked the color and sometime glory of combat command: He was sent south for the tedious work of developing fortifications for Charleston, Savannah, and the North Carolina coast, returning to Richmond once again in March 1862. By now, writes Dabney, "his reputation with the public was in tatters, and few could have foretold the future that awaited him."

The Union's George McClellan, meanwhile, had mounted his Peninsular campaign (between the James and York Rivers), intending to reach and seize the Confederate capital of Richmond. The slow-moving and overly cautious McClellan sparred for some weeks with Confederate field commander Joseph Johnston, but neither of the two found the bold stroke necessary to knock the other out of the contest.

McClellan, ironically enough, had seized upon White House Landing on the Pamunkey River, twenty miles east of Richmond, and turned it into a "small city of supply," in the words of Virginia historian Clifford Dowdey.

Circles within circles—the plantation here had once belonged to George Washington's wife, Martha Custis, and it now belonged by inheritance to Robert E. Lee's son "Rooney." When McClellan seized upon it as a supply depot and staging base, Lee's wife, Mary Custis Lee—a war refugee since being forced to leave her Arlington House to Federal troops the year before—was staying there. McClellan, though, graciously allowed her to pass through the lines with an officer escort to her own side—a relief for the distantly onlooking but helpless Lee.

A few weeks later, the McClellan-Johnston sparring finally led to the clash of giants—Johnston's sixty thousand men versus McClellan's one hundred thousand—at Fair Oaks, just a few miles east of Richmond. Johnston was twice wounded on the first day of battle, and Gustavus Smith, second in command, was not well enough to take over. Unshackled from his desk at last, Lee was sent forward to salvage the situation at the gates of Richmond.

What followed was Lee's surprisingly aggressive, often brilliant leadership in the Seven Days Battle that forced McClellan to give up his dream of seizing Richmond. Of necessity, Lee began his new stewardship by digging in; the result was that he picked up a new nickname: the "King of Spades."

By the end of the Seven Days, however, Robert E. Lee had acquired an entirely new image. Attacking again and again, albeit at great cost in human lives, he had saved Richmond. In the process, he had created his famous Army of Northern Virginia, which he would command for the rest of the war and take into Maryland, and even Pennsylvania, before it was all over.

In the meantime, various innovations made their appearance, including a Lee-inspired siege gun placed on a railroad flatcar that was brought into action under his subordinate John Magruder—"the first piece of railroad artillery ever used in warfare," according to historian Dowdey.

Observation balloons had already made their debut, and down in Hampton Roads the Confederacy's *Virginia* (originally the frigate *Merrimac*) and the Union's *Monitor* had traded blows (neither one greatly harmed) in history's first duel between ironclads. In like vein, the Confederacy would soon develop a submarine vessel, the belligerents would sow roads with "torpedoes" (early mines, actually), and the Gatling gun would just miss widespread use as an early "machine gun."

In sum, the new kind of warfare that was dawning added challenges for the gentlemanly Lee, whom Dowdey aptly named a product of "old America." Wrote Dowdey, too, of the watershed moment when Lee took command: "At the Seven Days, when the Army of Northern Virginia was born, the old

America died, and the Union [that] Lincoln and McClellan tried to restore became as lost in time as the traditional society [that] Lee sought to preserve."

Stirring Words Found

MINE EYES HAVE SEEN—IT WAS DARK AND BEFORE THE DAWN ONE MORNING IN Washington, D.C., just two city blocks from the Lincoln White House, when the New York–born woman in a hotel room took up pen and began to write down the words.

Mine eyes have seen the glory of the coming of the Lord.

For days she had struggled to find those words. For days she had seen the soldiers from her hotel window, had heard the tramp-tramp of marching feet, and had heard their old camp-meeting song, again and again. Only they called it "John Brown's Body" in reference to the crazed abolitionist who had tried to seize the U.S. Army arsenal at Harpers Ferry in 1859.

Now, in 1861, Julia Ward Howe hardly needed the Reverend James Freeman Clarke's urging to write fresh lyrics for the haunting tune that the soldiers obviously loved so well. "I have often prayed that I might," she told Clarke, who was with Julia and her husband, Dr. Samuel Gridley Howe, on a visit to Washington and the 12th Massachusetts Infantry Regiment. (The Howes were Boston residents, and Clarke was their pastor.)

The fact is, Dr. Howe was far better known at the time than his wife, Julia. A committed human rights activist, this proper Bostonian had spent time in a Prussian prison while attempting to help Polish refugees, had spent six years of his life as a fleet surgeon and even guerrilla fighter with Greeks fighting the Turks, and at home had taken up the cause of the insane and retarded, the blind and the deaf. It was only natural, then, that he would seek out and marry a woman who was a committed feminist, peace advocate, and abolitionist, becoming with her coeditor of the antislavery journal *The Commonwealth*. After taking up wife Julia's great cause, Samuel Howe plunged into activities such as opposing the forced return of escaped slaves, joining hands with the Free-Soilers of Kansas, and even developing vague ties with John Brown—ties close enough to force Howe to flee to Canada after the Harpers Ferry affair.

With the Civil War under way by 1861, however, he was back home and serving as a New England regional director of the U.S. Sanitary Commission, that good agency that sent doctors and nurses into Union-held battle zones to care for the wounded and injured of both sides. He had been dispatched to Washington by the governor of Massachusetts to make sure the Commonwealth's young soldiers were taken care of in proper and healthy fashion. Julia and the Reverend Clarke accompanied him, and it was from her Willard's Hotel window that she could see the Union campfires dotting the city environs every evening, could hear the tramp of many thousands of feet, could catch the strain of that song afloat in the air, again and again. Quite often it took the form of a march, thanks, it is said, to the adaption by the bandmaster of the 12th Massachusetts.

The tune cried for more acceptable, stirring words.

She awoke one of those tumultuous, early-in-the-war mornings in Washington, not far from where Lincoln slept. It was an hour or so before dawn, the room still dark, and the words suddenly had come! As a mother, she had learned beforehand how to write down her thoughts in the darkness of the children's nursery at home, and she now snatched up both pen and a piece of paper—stationery from her husband's Sanitary Commission. She scribbled rapidly before the words forming in her head, marching to the distant drumbeat, could fly away. She was successful, and soon her lyrics had flown across the country, soaring in a million hearts.

How far and wide did her song travel—how lasting was it? At Libby Prison in Richmond two years later in mid-1863, a black well-wisher slipped word to the Union prisoners held there of the great victory at Gettysburg. They sang in thankful jubilation Julia Ward Howe's "Battle Hymn of the Republic," its new words by now well known, repeatedly sung, and even published in the Atlantic for all to see, learn, or memorize. Not long after in Washington itself, a former prisoner from Libby Prison told an audience of that memorable and moving moment at the prison. The storyteller, a chaplain McCabe of the 122nd Ohio, then sang Julia Ward Howe's song before the Washington audience, a rendition so heartfelt that onlookers shouted, wept, sang with him, and burst into wild applause when it was over. President Lincoln was there, too, exclaiming, wrote Julia's daughters many years later, "Sing it again!" And "the tears rolled down his cheeks."

Jackson's Odd Failure

IT HAS NEVER BEEN FULLY EXPLAINED, AND MANY OF THOMAS J. "STONEWALL" Jackson's fellow Southern officers could not quite forgive him for his lethargy, delays, and downright nutty behavior when called to the aid of Robert E. Lee in defense of Richmond in June 1862. After all, here was the man labeled "Stonewall" for his forthright stand at First Bull Run hardly a year previous; here was the brilliant leader fresh from running rings around the Federal foe in the Shenandoah Valley campaign, probably just as famous among military men and historians today as Napoleon's First Italian campaign.

Here was the great, if eccentric, leader on his way to Lee's line-up for the first real counteroffensive against the massive Federal foe threatening from just six to ten miles outside of Richmond. And here was the genius of the Valley campaign, missing from Lee's lineup, even taking to a chair on a porch, reading a novel briefly, then going inside for a nap!

E. Porter Alexander, probably the leading artillerist of the Confederacy and a superb postwar memoir writer, stated the difficult-to-forgive case against Jackson most bluntly. "Lee's instructions to him were very brief and general, in supreme confidence that the Jackson of the Valley would win even brighter laurels on the Chickahominy River east of Richmond." Jackson's role was made easy for him, Alexander maintained. "The shortest route was assigned to him and the largest force was given him. Lee then took himself off to the farthest flank, as if generously to leave to Jackson the opportunity of the most brilliant victory of the war."

And what did Jackson do in response? He repeatedly turned up late for his assignments, or not at all. Alexander asserted: "His failure is not so much a military as a psychological phenomenon. He did not try and fail. He simply made no effort…. He spent the 29th of June 1862 in camp in disregard of Lee's instructions, and he spent the 30th in equal idleness at White Oak Swamp. His 25,000 infantry practically did not fire a shot in the two days."

Jackson's delays, naturally, were soon noticed by his companion command-ers in the field as Lee unfurled his battle plan to push George McClellan's great host away from Richmond in what became known as the Seven Days Battle. John Magruder, for instance, informed by Lee that Jackson would be crossing the Chickahominy alongside Magruder's own command, was stunned to hear from a subordinate, "I had hoped that Jackson would have cooperated with me on my left, but he sends me word that he cannot, as he has other important duty to perform."

Possibly, Alexander surmised, Jackson on one day was holding off because it was Sunday, the Sabbath, and Jackson was known to be fanatically religious. But in the past he had fought on Sundays.

As his part in Lee's plans to discourage McClellan from Richmond and its precincts, Jackson was expected to join in the battle opening the Seven

Days affair on June 26, his assignment to flank the Federal right and cut off McClellan's umbilical cord to the huge Union supply depot at White House Landing on the Pumunkey River near West Point, Virginia.

It was an extraordinary gamble that Lee had devised. With McClellan and his superior numbers obviously preparing to besiege Richmond and pound the city with huge guns that could only be moved up by rail or by barge, Lee would leave a token force demonstrating at his newly dug fortifications and attack the Federal left with the divisions headed by A. P. Hill, James Longstreet, and D. H. (Daniel Harvey) Hill. The risk was that McClellan might see through Lee's ruse and walk into Richmond past the defensive line with its small token force maintained by "Prince John" Magruder. In addition, Lee was willing to split his army and advance on either side of the Chickahominy, its swamps, and tributaries, a plan that made coordination difficult. Luckily for all, McClellan was so timorous that he never saw his great opportunity. Instead, in wailing tones he repeatedly asked Washington for more and more reinforcements and in the end predicted his far from irrevocable defeat.

But Jackson inexplicably did not appear at his assigned "jump-off" position on June 26, and A. P. Hill launched his portion of Lee's counteroffensive without waiting. That rash move dragged along Longstreet and D. H. Hill in support. Lee was thus committed to his plan without all his commanders in place.

Jackson at last arrived, twelve hours late. Fortunately, it appeared, he could still carry out his part of the attack the next morning. A. P. Hill's attack had been repulsed, but McClellan was alarmed enough to prepare for possible movement of his vulnerable supply base to Harrison's Landing on the James River below Richmond.

The next day, June 27, Jackson was again late in taking his position, but the Confederates at last mounted a more concerted advance and by nightfall had collapsed the Federal right as originally planned. That night McClellan made the fateful decision to retreat to the James. A long-tailed column of one hundred thousand or more men by this time, the Federal host began its rearward march the very next day, June 28, with the White House landing base left once again to the Rebs.

Here Lee was presented with an opportunity to pursue and strike a harsh blow, destroying the Union's greatest army on the spot—in the river swamps east of Richmond. But things kept going awry for the Confederacy's newly appointed field commander, even in the midst of a strategically great victory.

Lee briefly lost contact with McClellan's whereabouts, and it wasn't clear for some hours if the Federal commander had actually headed for the James.

Then, in mounting pursuit at last, Lee was frustrated by the mistakes of his subordinates (not only Jackson, but other subordinate commanders as well). As stated by historian Bruce Catton in his *Terrible Swift Sword*, "Magruder proved an inexpert tactician, [Benjamin] Huger moved much too slowly, and Jackson, most inexplicably, missed a crucial assignment."

And so, by July 1, "the head of the Federal column had reached Harrison's Landing and the protecting gunboats [out on the James River waters]." When Lee caught up at Malvern Hill, the Federal guns on the high ground were simply too much for the attacking Confederates—"that afternoon and evening saw one of the most tragic and hopeless attacks of the war, with Magruder's and D. H. Hill's divisions and elements from other commands trying heroically to do the impossible," added Catton.

Throughout the Seven Days, quite obviously from all accounts, Stonewall Jackson had not covered himself with glory. Years later, South Carolina's rough, tough cavalryman Wade Hampton would inform Porter Alexander of a visit to Jackson at a crucial point in the Seven Days to tell Jackson he had complied with orders to build a temporary infantry bridge over a small stream in their path. A key Federal force could be attacked just beyond.

Hampton said he found Jackson seated on a fallen pine and made his report. "He drew his cap down over his eyes, which were closed and after listening to me for some minutes, he rose without speaking."

Hampton's complaint was that if Jackson had proceeded, they might have defeated the Federal force just beyond, and thus the "Federal army would have been destroyed."

Jackson's own brother-in-law, D. H. Hill, on the other hand, sought to explain his "inaction" by blaming the exhausting rigors his troops had been through in their Valley campaign, his pity for his own men, and their reduced numbers. "He thought that the garrison of Richmond ought now to bear the brunt of the fighting."

To which Alexander retorted, in his *Military Memoir of a Confederate*, that the veterans of the long Peninsular campaign "had suffered just as many hardships and done even more severe fighting, as the casualties will attest."

Further, to show a natural pity or affection for one's own men "by shirking battle" was "no real kindness to them, apart from the tremendous consequences to the army and the nation." In sum, Jackson's failure was a "lapse of duty."

It wasn't long, though, before the "old Jackson" reasserted himself and fought with skill and bravery by Lee's side. It was his flanking movement at Chancellorsville a year later that won the battle but cost Jackson his own life when he was wounded by his own troops, who fired into the darkness as Jackson returned from a reconnaissance in front of them.

So what happened to the rightly vaunted Stonewall outside of Richmond in June of 1862?

Perhaps historian Clifford Dowdey was on the correct trail when, in the 1960s, he investigated the latest medical findings on the effects of stress. As he pointed out in his 1964 book *The Seven Days: The Emergence of Lee,* Jackson had been under extreme stress for the ten weeks of his whirlwind Shenandoah Valley campaign. When he led his forces to Richmond in response to Lee's call, "not only were his naturally limited physical powers extended…but his total organism [had been] exposed to the prolonged stress of danger, sustained alertness and the urgent need of constant decisions affecting the cause he represented as well as the lives of the men entrusted to him."

It did not help Jackson's condition that on his way to Richmond he left his marching columns to ride ahead by horseback. "He foolishly made the fourteen-hour night ride to Richmond from 1 a.m. to late afternoon on the 23rd, and then, without rest or food—taking only a glass of milk—made the return ride through a second night from about seven in the evening until mid-morning of the 24th."

All that was exhausting enough, but no doubt, as Dowdey adds, "his judgment had already been affected when he made the all-night rides on successive nights." In Dowdey's view, Jackson was the victim of stress exhaustion, his mental and physiological resources already depleted beforehand. Still, "in Stonewall Jackson's world, no general would have considered such an ailment as stress fatigue, even if he had been aware of the reactions to stress." While all certainly knew the effects of strain and loss of sleep, "a leader was supposed to be above the limitations of the flesh."

Obviously, not even a Stonewall Jackson could be that superhuman. Wrung out by his Valley exertions, he simply had been asked to resume the strain of march, command, and battle too soon…too soon again.

Hello, Richmond

For Richmond, these were giddy, crowded days. High drama side by side with everyday events. Real, classical tragedy together with the pathos and even the occasional human comedy. And all so tightly packed into such a short time frame.

One potentially bright moment in the capital of the Confederate States of America was the inauguration of Jefferson Davis as Permanent President, no longer provisional. But the event was not quite as gay as the prior ceremony held in Montgomery, Alabama, the previous year. For one thing, it was pouring down rain on this bleak twenty-second of February 1862 (George Washington's birthday, at that). The umbrellas of the assembled crowd struck the onlooking Constance Cary as "an immense mushroom bed." Wrote this teenage girl, "As the bishop and the President-elect came upon the stand, there was almost a painful hush in the crowd." They felt the gravity of the occasion, and although a shout went up when Davis "kissed the Book," the crowd quickly dispersed with no real show of elation.

And then there was that awful story about Mrs. Davis—Varina—on her way to the inauguration that day. Her coachman drove her carriage at "snail's pace," reported Constance Cary later, and escorting her were four black men, two to a side, all wearing white gloves and black clothing, all stepping slowly and somberly. It was just like a funeral procession, and indeed, the coachman said he thought that's what she wanted. "This is the way we do in Richmond at funerals and sich-like," he explained.

Earlier that winter, horrible weather had afflicted the Old Dominion, and in January scarlet fever had struck Richmond, a lethal threat to any child. Confederate General James Longstreet was in northern Virginia opposite the Federal lines when he received word to hurry to his family's side in Richmond. Wife Louise and their four children were staying with friends, and all four youngsters had come down with the fever.

Longstreet arrived in the capital in the final days of January just in time to see their twelve-month-old Mary Anne lose her battle with the disease. A day later, January 26, four-year-old James died. And after him, on February 1, six-year-old Augustus succumbed as well. Only thirteen-year-old Garland survived the fever's onslaught. The Longstreets were so devastated that Brigadier General George Pickett, later to lead Pickett's Charge at Gettysburg, had to make the funeral arrangements for them. They said that Longstreet was never the same again, and little wonder.

Soon Richmond itself heard the not-so-distant sound of guns. As May gave way to June and the weather turned fair, the Battle of Seven Pines (Fair Oaks) began. It was May 31, and "Every heart leaped as if deliverance were at hand," noted teenager Constance Cary. At the same time, she added, there "hardly" was "a family in the town whose father, son or brother was not part and parcel of the defending army."

For the city's civilians, its leaders, war planners, and soldiers alike, darkness brought a pause in the cannon fire, but they slept that night "lying down dressed upon beds." Early the next morning, "the whole town was on the street."

For now came the wounded, in from the great battle just beyond the city. "Ambulances, litters, carts, every vehicle that the city could produce went and came with a ghastly burden; those who could walk limped painfully home, in some cases so black with gunpowder they passed unrecognized." By afternoon, "the streets were one vast hospital." In homes and other buildings, hastily converted into temporary hospitals, mutilated men suffered or died—or both.

Several days after the "first flurry of distress," the young diarist saw "flitting about the streets" and hurrying to the hospitals from the homes of the affluent, "smiling, white-jacketed negroes, carrying silver trays with dishes of fine porcelain under napkins of thick white damask, containing soups, creams, jellies, thin bisquit [sic], eggs à la creme, broiled chicken, etc., surmounted by clusters of freshly gathered flowers."

Then, too, "day after day we were called to our windows by the wailing dirge of a military band preceding a soldier's funeral." Day after day. "One could not number those sad pageants: the coffin crowned with cap and sword and gloves, the riderless horse following with empty boots fixed in the stirrups...."

It wasn't always thus, of course. Only a year earlier, Richmond's beginnings as a new nation's wartime capital were heady, confusing, thrilling. "Noise of drums, tramps of marching regiments all day long, rattling of artillery wagons, bands of music, friends from every quarter coming in," wrote Mary Chesnut back in July 1861. "We ought to be miserable and anxious, and yet these are pleasant days. Perhaps we are unnaturally exhilarated and excited."

Perhaps so. "A young Carolinian with queer ideas of a joke rode his horse through the barroom of this hotel [the Spotswood]. How he scattered people and things right and left!"

Then, too, after news of the Federal defeat at First Manassas, Mary Chesnut could report: "Mrs. [Jefferson] Davis' drawing room last night was brilliant, and she was in great force. Outside a mob collected and called for the president. He did speak. He is an old war-horse—and scents the battlefields from afar. His enthusiasm was contagious."

And a few days after that: "At the fairgrounds today—such music and mustering and marching—such cheering and flying of flags. Such firing of guns and all that sort of thing. A gala day: double distilled 4th of July feeling." Only it was August 1, 1861, in the capital of the Confederacy. And soon, the glad excitement would give way more often to grim tidings, friends and relatives with wounds, others widowed or dead, depending upon their gender.

Mary Chesnut's fellow South Carolinian Frank Hampton died at Brandy Station, the largest cavalry engagement ever staged in North America. She and several other ladies visited their fallen soldier's open coffin at the State Capitol. "How I wished I had not looked! I remember him so well in all the pride of his magnificent manhood. He died of a saber cut across the face and head and was utterly disfigured."

In Richmond, too, despite the united war effort, not all was harmony among the principals. There came a moment of tension, for instance, between Longstreet and General Ambrose Powell Hill, both West Point graduates and among the generals responsible for the Confederate victory in the Seven Days campaign outside Richmond in June 1862. A Richmond newspaper editor, greatly impressed by the Virginia-born Hill, wrote a series of articles giving Hill exclusive credit for a major aspect of the Southern victory. Longstreet, outraged and feeling publicly humiliated, persuaded a more-than-willing aide to write to a rival paper pointing out the discrepancy.

Hill, upon that report's reaching the public, felt humiliated in his turn, and so the affair went, with Hill asking to be transferred out of Longstreet's command, then ignoring, then refusing a Longstreet order, then being placed under house arrest. He finally challenged fellow Confederate general Longstreet to a duel, but Robert E. Lee at last stepped into the dispute and ordered Hill transferred to Stonewall Jackson's command at Gordonsville.

That cooled the argument, but Hill naturally still visited Richmond from time to time. On one such occasion, he was called into the chamber of the Virginia House of Delegates to receive an official accolade from that body for his battlefield prowess. Another time, all Richmond was agog over the visit of a Confederate hero and brother-in-law to Hill who had recently escaped from Union custody—John Hunt Morgan, the cavalry raider revered for his breakout from the Ohio State Penitentiary.

Hill, accompanied by "Jeb" Stuart and Georgia's John B. Gordon, visited the Confederate capital in early January 1864 to greet the famous Kentuckian. They appeared at a public reception in front of the Richmond City Hall at noontime one day, and the next day Hill and Morgan visited Richmond's Libby Prison to chat with Union prisoners held there. They attended church with fellow Confederate officers on still the next day at St. Paul's Episcopal. Morgan next would pay a visit of his own to the Virginia legislature and appear at a ball held in the Ballard House.

Diarist Mary Chesnut mentioned the Morgan visit, which also included the former vice president of the United States, John Breckinridge, now a Confederate general and soon to be the Confederacy's secretary of war. She saw Richmond Mayor Joseph Mayo introduce Morgan at the City Hall affair. "These huge Kentuckians fill the town," she wrote. Shortly after, she added: "The City of Richmond entertains John Morgan. HQ is at free quarters. Tonight [January 12] there will be a great gathering of the Kentuckians. Morgan gives them a dinner."

She had known Morgan's wife, the former Mattie Ready, before the war. "A graceful girl and a Kentucky belle in Washington during the winter of 1859. We were glad to meet again once more under altered skies."

All was not so festive that same week in the Jefferson Davis household. Two slaves, a man and a woman, had fled. "The president's man Jim that he believed in, as we all believe in our own servants—'our own people' as we are apt to call them—and Betsy, Mrs. Davis' maid, decamped last night," wrote Mary Chesnut on January 9 or 10, 1864. Saying it was a miracle that the pair had resisted temptation so long, Chesnut added: "I do not think it had ever crossed Mrs. D's brain that these two would leave her." Richmond during the war was a city under siege, a city of visiting heroes and escaping slaves, of riderless horses and funeral dirges. Said Mary Chesnut's own maid (and slave) Molly, "I like Mrs. Davis, but Betsy did give herself such airs because she was Mrs. President's maid."

Loyalty Charge Dismissed

IT WAS "AN EVIL HOUR," JUSTICE GEORGE M. SAVAGE OF HENRICO COUNTY, Virginia, told the court in adjoining Richmond. An evil hour when, sorely tempted, he did "take the hated oath."

But then the circumstances had been mitigating to large degree, and perhaps his fellow Southerners could forgive and forget. He had succumbed to temptation at a moment of great duress involving not only himself but his family.

It all began, it seems, on Friday, May 23, 1862, the eve of the Battle of Fair Oaks that led to the Seven Days campaign, which in turn ended the Union Peninsular campaign.

Explained Henrico farmer-citizen-justice Savage: "Two Yankee pickets came to my door and enquired for milk and butter; I told them I had none to spare. They then enquired as to when our pickets left. I replied, I did not know exactly. One was very insolent, remarking that the rebels were cowards and would not stand. I replied that that was a matter on which we could not agree. They very soon left."

One thing led to another, as the Yankees very next day arrived in force, "some coming into the house and insulting me and my family."

After a skirmish took place about a mile away, the Northern visitors "appeared with their wounded." Savage told them they could not use his house as a hospital, but they were welcome to his barn.

On Sunday, May 25, Union Major General Erasmus D. Keyes (and staff) appeared as well. Keyes—polite—said he would like to use the house as his headquarters, and to this Savage did not object. "He then introduced the subject of this war. I replied that on this subject I did not care to converse, as I was sure we would not agree."

But Keyes insisted, and Savage then stated his pro-Southern views "frankly and fearlessly as I have over and over again expressed them among my own people."

Keyes was so impressed that he turned to his staff and declared, "This gentleman is an honest and candid man, and I wish you to see that his property is thoroughly protected." Unfortunately, Keyes soon left, only to be replaced by Union Major General Samuel P. Heinzelman.

Until now, the situation for Savage and his family had not been all bad. His crops and his property "were not much damaged," and the Union officers, "with some exceptions, were tolerably civil." At the same time, "I could not at any time go fifty yards from my house without being denounced by the men as a 'damned rebel and secesh.'"

Then came the Battle of Fair Oaks on May 31, when Joseph Johnston counterattacked the Union's George McClellan (with Johnston wounded and relieved of command in the process). The Yankee wounded now "came pouring in like an avalanche," recalled Savage. They just about took over the whole house, and when he appealed to the Union adjutant on the scene, that officer said, "he had no protection to give, nor did I deserve any." And, "I was a damned secessionist, and had been instrumental in bringing about this state of things and my head ought to be cut off, and the sooner I got away, the better."

With that warning, on Monday, June 2, Savage did send away his three children, and the next day his wife "had to leave," as well. By July 4, the day that Savage petitioned the court in Richmond to forgive him for taking the Union loyalty oath, his family had yet to return home, and the home was still in use as a hospital, although McClellan and his host of one hundred thousand or so had retreated from the Richmond area.

What had taken place on Savage's farm in the interim was close to indescribable. Starting with the night of May 31, he said, the Yankees "forced nearly every lock on the place and stole very nearly all my stores, together with crockery and innumerable articles of furniture, forced my corncribs and took all the corn, all long forage, ground and cut all my oats and wheat and hay, burned my enclosures of every description, destroyed my fruit trees, took the boards from my buildings for every use they could apply them, broke up and destroyed my farming implements, stole two horses, about 80 hogs, some sheep and cattle and appeared to try how much they could damage me."

Savage's wife was so distraught she twice was confined to bed, and on June 12 he himself was taken ill. He improved, however, and on June 16 returned home—a mistake, it transpired. "On the night of that day I was arrested on the order of General McClellan, taken to his headquarters, where I remained until the next day, without being able to learn what charge there was against me."

He was told on the seventeenth that he would be locked up at Fort Monroe, overlooking Hampton Roads. Savage asked to see his wife first, with Federal officers present, simply to let her know what was happening to him. Otherwise, he said, in her delicate health, his incarceration could have serious impact on her. When the Federals refused Savage's request, he caved in, "profoundly convinced that to be taken up under these circumstances would kill my wife." He took the Union oath, but "without kissing the Book" and while declaring his allegiance still lay with the South.

That apparently satisfied his Yankee tormentors (who had visited similar destruction upon the Henrico County farm of a free black woman named Isabella Adams), but he next had to defend himself before the court in Richmond against the charge of disloyalty to the Confederacy. In his court paper Savage earnestly and formally said: "I do here declare that I have not at any time up to this hour knowingly said or done anything the least prejudicial to the Southern cause, and that all my sympathies, interest and feelings, are today, as ever, with the South and I now hold myself ready and willing to do whatever the interests or laws of the Confederacy may require of me, and in conclusion I do hereby declare upon my honor and conscience that at the time of taking the [Union] oath I did not regard it, nor do I now regard it, as binding upon me, but laboring under a profound conviction that the life of my wife would be sacrificed, leaving three little children in the power of a merciless enemy, I was tempted in an evil hour to take the hated oath."

So be it, the charge of disloyalty to the Confederacy dismissed—by order of the court!

Poignant Moments in Battle

HERE WAS FIGHTING INDEED. IN THE STRATEGIC SENSE, THE CONFEDERATES WERE on the offensive, Union men on the defensive. But tactically, as the men actually did battle in the field, it was the men in blue who were on the attack. Small arms and artillery traded shots. The Confederate mounted infantry at one point climbed down from their steeds—some of them mules—to repel the Union infantry that had crossed the river between the two forces.

"As we were in the act of dismounting," wrote Virginia-born Alfred U. Peticolas, lawyer and future judge currently serving his "Victoria Invincibles" as sergeant, "[B. A.] Jones' horse was shot in the thigh, [Sergeant Charles A.] Wooapple's was crippled, and a ball tore a small peel of skin from my right thumb, which bled profusely." But Confederate Sergeant Peticolas hadn't seen anything yet.

This was war, and war truly is hell. The enemy had approached in strength just six hundred yards away from where Peticolas and his compatriots had taken position lying under the bank of the river. The men in blue were firing most rapidly. The shooting "began to play havoc with our horses." Sam Hyatt's went down, Louis J. Berkowitz's went down, and so did a number of others. And next came the men themselves. "One man on my left…was shot through the back, as he raised to load, by a flank fire, and fell with heart rending groans." Amazingly, though, the same man directed a companion to load his gun, then he "fired at them again, although he had a wound which proved mortal."

Peticolas himself was loading and shooting as fast as he could while taking careful aim at his quarry, though "their balls whistled with deadly intent around my head." Others nearby were hit. Corporal Al Field took a wound in the arm and exclaimed, "Oh, God, I'm shot." A man named S. Schmidt was struck in both upper legs by a single Minié ball. But by far the most grotesque casualty was William H. Onderdonk, who was struck in the mouth, "his tongue nearly shot out." The wounded Onderdonk certainly must have felt desperate. As Peticolas tells the story, "He pulled out a part of it [the mouth, the tongue, or other tissue] which was hanging ragged…and cut it off with his knife."

As Onderdonk was carried off the field, the fight went on. The Rebs were shooting with greater accuracy than their Yankee brothers, and soon the Blues were driven back across the river. The Confederate howitzers "opened upon their retiring column with killing effect, and they broke lines and ran back out of range."

One of the Confederate soldiers asked his captain's permission to go forward and kill a wounded Yank who was still shooting from behind a tree. Captain David Nunn assented, but the wounded Union man then "begged so hard" that he was merely disarmed.

The fight was not yet over. All around were dead and wounded horses. Sergeant Peticolas's own mule was shivering from the effects of a wound that proved fatal once the battle was over.

The Confederates now regrouped—both sides in fact spent considerable time simply maneuvering for position. The Confederates present numbered about two thousand, equalling the Union force. Around evening time, the Yankees crossed the river, artillery in tow, and advanced in strength. Their eight guns were heavier than the Confederate force's four six-pounders, and their small arms were longer-range pieces, too. "As long as we laid behind the sand banks our own lives were in comparative safety," wrote Peticolas in his journal, but "every few moments some one would be wounded or killed and our horses were being badly shot to pieces."

Soon six of the Union guns were brought up within "point blank range of us and began to play grape and shell upon us." In response, the Reb battery commanded by Captain Travonian Teel moved two guns to within ten yards of where Peticolas was lying and began firing back at the Union guns. "And now the battle was indeed hot."

Hot, and on the left the Confederates were slowly but surely being driven back. "In two minutes, a raking fire up our line on the side of the bank would slay the last man of us. The bombs and grape were bursting and flying all around us and [nearby] Colonel [Thomas] Green, and sweeping the trees and the bottom far behind us."

It was a critical moment, and Green, a regimental commander, realized it. "We must charge that battery, boys," he said, and when some of the men before him instead ran for their horses to flee, he chased after them while shouting: "Back, men, back! Would you disgrace yourself and your country here? Remember you are Texans!" (for most of the men there were).

With other officers sounding the same call to charge, about two hundred of the Johnny Rebs ("a mere handful," said Peticolas) responded. "[They] started up and with a wild yell dashed forward through the shower of Minié balls and grape toward the belching cannon and solid lines of infantry supporting them [the cannon]." Major Samuel A. Lockridge, "a heart of iron," led the Confederate charge, with three captains close behind brandishing their sabers and shouting, "Come on my boys, don't stop here."

The short-range Reb guns now were felling the Yankees at such pace that they wavered, then turned and ran, "and we poured in our deadly fire upon them."

Then came one of the most poignant moments of the battle. Major Lockridge, reaching a Union cannon, put his hand on it and exclaimed, "This is mine!"

"At that moment he was shot dead," wrote Peticolas later. "His last words were: 'Go on my boys, don't stop here!'"

The Yankees had a poignant moment of their own as they defended their artillery battery, "brave to the last," in the words of Peticolas. So brave were the men of Captain Alexander McRae's battery that one of them touched off the ammunition in a battery caisson just as the Rebs swept into the battery's position, sacrificing his own life in the process.

"Two guns were loaded when we took them," wrote Peticolas. "A gunner was just about to touch one off. One of our men, who had just killed one of the artillery men, was up on the caisson. He leveled his pistol at the gunner, who in an instant thrust his fuse into the caisson box, which blew up with a dread explosion."

By other accounts of the same action, McRae, himself Southern-born, saw and heard Major Lockridge and supposedly shouted at his Union troops, "Shoot the son of a bitch!" which someone quickly did. Then, too, a Union soldier from Colorado recalled the second part of the battery incident narrated by Peticolas: "When the battery was gone," wrote the Union survivor, "one of the battery boys sprang up on a magazine which was near, cried 'Victory or death' and then coolly fired his pistol into the ammunition. One long, loud crash and all was over for that brave boy."

So it went in the fighting of the Civil War, not only in the East or along the Mississippi and in adjoining states, but also in the far Southwest. For in the Battle of Valverde of February 21, 1862, the river in question was the Rio Grande, and the territory being fought over was New Mexico. There was no particular winner of this moment in the New Mexico campaign, mounted by the South's hard-drinking, blustering adventurer-general Henry H. Sibley. The losers, though, were the 170 killed and 310 wounded, casualties distributed about equally on each side.

Unnecessary Tragedies

★ MURDERS THREE ★

It was late September 1862, and in the Galt House hostelry in Louisville, Kentucky, a coterie of Federal flag rank officers was astir between seven and eight o'clock in the morning. Their overall commander, Don Carlos Buell, had not yet gone downstairs for breakfast, reported Roy Morris Jr. in his *Sheridan: The Life and Wars of General Phil Sheridan*. Among those staying at the Galt House was a longtime U.S. Navy officer turned Army general, William "Bull" Nelson, who had led a reinforcing division at Shiloh the previous spring. Another general on hand, brooding over running clashes with his superior, Nelson, was the lesser-ranking brigadier general Jefferson Columbus Davis.

"Bull" was an apt nickname for the hulking, sharp-tongued Nelson, described by Civil War historian Morris as "coarse, profane, and physically imposing." He could easily offend, it seems, "neither noticing nor caring what impression he left in his bullish wake."

The North's Jefferson Davis had also enjoyed a lengthy military career starting with the Mexican War of the 1840s, although at low rank for most of the time. He had been vaulted from lieutenant to colonel at the outset of the Civil War by his good friend in high office, Governor Oliver P. Morton of Indiana. Serving in the battles of Booneville, Missouri, and Pea Ridge, Arkansas, he then joined Buell's command in defense of Louisville—a series of confrontations with Bull Nelson soon followed. Their dispute had led Nelson to order Davis "out of town" toward the end of summer 1862, recalls Morris in his biography of their fellow Union officer Phil Sheridan (uninvolved in the unhappy affair).

But Davis was very much in town the early morning of September 29. "At the prompting of his close friend, the ubiquitous Governor Morton," writes Morris, "Davis had approached Nelson that morning and demanded an apology."

Nelson, although unarmed, was not to be cowed in the least. "Go away, you damned puppy," he bellowed. "I don't want anything to do with you." Davis reacted immediately. He had "nervously" been crumpling up a calling card in one hand, and now he "angrily flipped it into Nelson's face." Nelson reacted by smacking Davis in the face, sending his fellow general reeling backward.

"With the imprint of Nelson's hand still visible on his cheek, Davis borrowed a pistol from an obliging bystander and shot Nelson once in the chest."

For all his bulk and imposing physique (six feet five and more than three hundred pounds), Nelson was human: one bullet at close range was all that was needed to bring him down. "Tom," he said to another Union general, Thomas Crittenden, "I am murdered." These were his last words, and they were true.

Davis was placed under house arrest, but he won his release by Christmastime with the posting of a five-thousand-dollar bond in Louisville. As events turned out, Davis never would be tried for the slaying of fellow Union general Nelson, thanks to the intercession of his good friend Governor Morton and the press of wartime events. Davis went on to serve in the battles of Murfreesboro, Chickamauga, Atlanta, Savannah, and the Carolinas campaign as both a division and corps commander. He remained in the Army until his death in 1879 at age fifty-one.

★ MURDER TWO ★

The South, meanwhile, was in shock and consternation over a murder of its own—an elderly white woman in South Carolina murdered by her slaves. Betsey Witherspoon was her name, and by her family's accounts, she had long pampered and "indulged" her slaves.

In mid-1861, however, the Witherspoons discovered that while absent on a trip, her slaves had "borrowed" her china, linens, and silverware for a "ball" held some fifteen miles from her Society Hill plantation. Her son, John Witherspoon, visiting his mother one evening after her return, told her slave William that he would be back the next day, "and give every one of you a thrashing."

That night, his mother died in her bed—of natural causes, it first appeared. According to diarist Mary Boykin Chesnut, writing about her own second cousin Betsey, investigation—and the key confession of a slave—instead revealed a chilling scenario orchestrated by William.

In the middle of the night, long after the Widow Witherspoon had gone to sleep, William and Betsey's maid, Rhody, stole into Betsey's bedroom and smothered her with a bedspread. They thought it would appear she had simply died in her sleep, like her kinswoman Elizabeth not long before. The slaves then started to dress their victim in a clean nightgown—when she started up, conscious again!

Mary Boykin Chesnut does not say exactly how her cousin truly died, but she does say the unfortunate woman "begged them hard for life," and "she asked them what she had ever done that they should want to kill her. She promised before God never never to tell on them. Nobody should ever know. But Rhody stopped her mouth with the counterpane. William held her head and hands down. And the other two [slaves] sat on her legs."

Her children suspected foul play when they saw bruises on their mother's face and neck. They then found blood on a candlestick on her bedside table. They found bloody fingermarks on the underside of her bedspread. Further searching turned up bloody rags. Then they found that a trunk holding their mother's cache of gold pieces had been stolen. Finally, a detective called to the plantation home questioned a young, frightened-looking slave named Romeo, and he "told every particular from beginning to end."

There was talk of a lynching, but the murder victim's son John "will not allow anything wrong or violent to be done," wrote second cousin Mary Chesnut. The suspects would be "tried as the law directs." Oddly, she also noted, it was the maid Rhody who first pointed out the blood on the bed-spread. "They suppose she saw it, knew they would see it, and did it to avert suspicion from herself."

But Rhody seemed to want to call attention to herself. After the blood was found, the victim's daughter-in-law Mary Witherspoon wouldn't accept the obvious. "I wish they would not say such horrid things," she cried. "Poor soul, she died in peace with all the world. It is bad enough to find her dead. Nobody even touched a hair of her head. To think, any mortal could murder her. Never! I will not believe it."

To which Rhody looked "strangely" into Mary's eye and said, "Well done! Miss Mary. You stick to dat, my Missus. You stick to dat."

Postscript: The perpetrators were later convicted and hanged, Mary Chesnut reported in her diaries. And violence begat still more violence, as sometime after the trial a Captain W. H. Wingate, who had "stood by" the murderous slaves during their trial, shot and killed the victim's grandson, Captain George Williams, in cold blood, for reasons unclear. By Chesnut's account, the abolition-touting Wingate came up behind Williams as he sat in a chair at a railroad station waiting to leave with his troops and shot the young officer, "before the very faces of his soldiers." No surprise that "it was very hard to rescue Wingate from the hands of George's men, who wanted to shoot him instantly." In contrast to the earlier scenario, the jury convicting this murderer recommended mercy, and he was merely banished from South Carolina as his punishment.

★ MURDER THREE ★

"Oh, you coward!" How many times in the course of human affairs have such words led to violence, physical injury, and even death? So it was in Norfolk, Virginia, a city destined to be occupied by Federal troops from May 1862 until war's end. This was a difficult period for the port city's old-line, pro-Confederate white citizenry. Surely they winced at the parade of local blacks upon the effective date of Lincoln's Emancipation Proclamation (January 1, 1863). And no doubt they cringed at the sight of black women trampling the Confederate flag and at reports of Jefferson Davis being buried in effigy in a local cemetery.

Such events were close to mind the day a white Union lieutenant marched a company of black soldiers past the esteemed and widely loved physician David Minton Wright.

Here was a man dedicated to saving human life, a man "who had been heroic in his treatment of patients during the deadly yellow-fever epidemic of 1855," recalled Virginius Dabney in his *Virginia: The New Dominion, A History from 1607 to the Present.* And yet, at the sight of the Union officer and company of blacks something within the doctor snapped. Fists clenched, obviously agitated, he uttered those fateful words: "Oh, you coward!"

The accosted officer, Lieutenant A. L. Sanborn, immediately stopped. "You are under arrest," he said. "Whereupon Wright drew a pistol and fired twice at the Union officer, wounding him fatally. It was a rash and inexcusable act."

It was also one that would haunt Norfolk for months, even years. First, Dr. Wright underwent trial before a military commission. Next, he was convicted and sentenced to death. Then came the sensational moment when Wright's daughter Penelope visited him in his jail cell and exchanged clothing with her father and he briefly escaped.

But not for long. Discovered, he was returned to his cell and confined. Finally, in October 1863, a public hanging took place in the middle of the racetrack in the city's fairgrounds. "Thousands watched," reports Dabney, "as was the custom in those days, but 'few old citizens could be recognized,' since the 'better classes' were said to have stayed at home." Nor was that really the end of the affair, since "his death cast a pall over Norfolk for years."

Knights of the Realm

FEW IF ANY SCHOOLS OF THE NINETEENTH-CENTURY SOUTH WERE HELD IN SUCH high esteem as the University of Virginia in Charlottesville, founded by Thomas Jefferson within many a Southerner's own lifetime. Four decades later it had become a magnet for the elite of the Old South, the plantation South.

Let a university historian describe the students to be found on Thomas Jefferson's gorgeous campus at the outbreak of the war. Except for a small minority, wrote Professor Philip Alexander Bruce, the few hundred students at the university "were representative of the very best element of the Southern communities."

How so? According to Bruce's multivolume centennial history of the school (1818–1918), "They belonged to the widely known families which had always controlled the social and political destinies of that broad division of the country [the South]." Such prestigious background—good breeding, in effect—meant more, in his opinion, than mere social status. "Imbued to the fingertips with the free, virile, and chivalrous spirit which had been nurtured by the plantation system, they were at once democratic and aristocratic."

While that combination may seem unlikely to some, Bruce was probably correct when he noted that the young university scions came from a rural environment and were quite accustomed to manly pursuits such as riding horses, hunting, fishing, tramping in the countryside, and getting along in all kinds of weather.

They made good soldiers, not only because of these useful skills and a general self-reliance in the field, but also because of their "high sense of personal honor and unshakable devotion to country." It needs hardly be said that they held a special feeling for home and family tradition; they lived on or in properties passed down from colonial days. "The history of these houses—their heirlooms, their surroundings, their occupations, their atmosphere—had left a permanent impression on the spirit of the young men who went straight from these thresholds to be educated in the University of Virginia."

Therein, too, lay the explanation for their ultimate allegiance not to Union, but to home state. "Their loyalty to their respective states," wrote historian Bruce, "was a passion as ardent as that which the Swiss felt for their mountains, or the Highlanders for their glens."

When 515 university students joined the Confederate Army in 1861, only a handful of students remained at the school, which soon became a giant de facto

Confederate hospital. Of the school's nine thousand alumni as of 1865, more than a fourth "took an active part in the hostilities…about 500 of the university alumni perished in the service." Many more were wounded. Students in the later period of the Civil War, in fact, were recovered wounded—young men too maimed or disabled to fight again, but able to get around as students.

The conversion to a military hospital filled the school's dormitory rooms and even Jefferson's famous Rotunda, originally the school's library. In a dormitory room, at one point, a wounded Federal prisoner languished with two recuperating "Rebs."

"Hello," said a surprised visitor one day, "how did this Yank get in here?" Never mind, said the "Yank's" companions. "Leave him alone. We are brothers now through suffering."

While many of the university's casualties were twenty and over in age, quite a few were not: Sixteen were under twenty, eight under eighteen, nine under seventeen, and three under sixteen. Bruce's account reflects a romantic glow when mentioning the university's heroes, saying that all its sons "were equally unselfish, equally devoted, and equally brave," and all again, "with equal cheerfulness, offered up their lives upon the altars of their native commonwealths."

Despite his unabashed jingoism, Bruce did tell the stories of remarkable and inspiring young men. It is significant, though, how often the allusions to knights of old crop up—and not always in his words alone.

Take young Dabney Carr Harrison, who at nine "had read Hume's *History of England*"; who at fifteen had entered the sophomore class at Princeton; who had "a countenance classical"; who by nature "was at once frank, cordial, and fearless"; who in manners was "singularly gentle and refined"; who attended law school at the university for two years before becoming a minister; and who, at twenty-seven, as war broke out, was the University's chaplain.

He remained a man of God as the war's toll mounted, especially among the First Families of the South. "The war had now begun, and in a short time, the news arrived that two of his cousins, men of brilliant promise and graduates of the University, Holmes and Tucker Conrad of Winchester, had been killed. Then followed the announcement that a third cousin, Carter H. Harrison, had fallen, then that his own brother also had perished."

This news was too much for University Chaplain Harrison. "'I must take his place,' was his quiet response to this last sorrowful message."

As a soldier—a captain in fact—the young minister performed with courage but said, "I can fight for my country, but I cannot hate my enemy." It was reported that he never ordered his men forward—he led them from in front.

And the outcome? "He fell at last, shot through the lung, after three bullets had passed through his hat, and one across his temple, leaving a bloody streak in its course."

Dying, he said he was "content and happy, trusting in the merits of my Saviour, Jesus Christ." A "short, feverish sleep" silenced him for a while, but he then started up with a final cry. "Company K! You have no captain now, but never give up, never surrender."

A fellow minister, the Reverend J. M. Atkinson, held the same romantic viewpoint as that imbuing Bruce's history. Said Atkinson: "Among the deified heroes of ancient song, in the golden record of Grecian fame, in the stirring chronicles of the medieval knighthood, in the ranks of war, in the halls of learning, in the temple of religion, a nobler name is not registered than his, nor a nobler spirit mourned."

But Dabney Harrison was not alone. There was, for instance, Randolph Fairfax, "the grandson of the ninth Baron Fairfax, of Cameron...sprung from a family which had been conspicuous in England and America through eight centuries." A student who joined Virginia's Rockbridge Artillery, this martyr served so well and so conscientiously until his death in battle that Robert E. Lee wrote to the young man's mourning father, "I have watched his conduct from the commencement of the war, and have pointed with pride to the patriotism, self-denial, and manliness of character he has exhibited."

Another to be installed in the university's pantheon of heroes was a professor, Lewis M. Coleman, who taught ancient languages. An artillery major, he was fatally wounded at Fredericksburg.

Still another university hero was Cotesworth Pinckney Seabrook of South Carolina, who used to walk "many miles" into the mountains near the university to conduct religious services "for the mountaineers." Said a close friend from both college days and the soldierly ranks: "He seemed raised up from among the medieval dead and set in the midst of us, to give proof that the spirit of knightly courtesy, constancy, and valor had not departed from our times." This amazing young man, who hurried home to volunteer as soon as South Carolina seceded, managed to survive major battles of the war—Second Bull Run, Antietam, Fredericksburg among them—and the first clash at Cold Harbor. After that engagement, he wrote, almost unbelievably, "We had the satisfaction of charging through grape, canister, and bullets for half a mile."

He wrote to his mother to have no fear for him, since he had no fear for himself. The next day, at Chancellorsville, he was killed—another romanticized martyr from the ranks of those privileged by birth, background, and education to defend tradition, chivalry as they saw it, and a way of life they thought their right and responsibility.

Six-Year-Old's Flight

WHEN MARTHA HARPER WAS "ABOUT" SIX YEARS OLD, THERE LOOMED A GOOD night for her escape from the master's farm to rejoin her mother and father in Richmond. The white overseer's daughter was getting married, and all round the Ryland place in Saluda, Virginia, the white folks were getting ready for a big time. Who among them would be thinking about what the slaves were up to?

It was around 8:00 p.m. when a friendly slave named Bill crept up to a window in Martha's quarters and beckoned; the proverbial coast was clear. As instructed in advance, she ran out the door, and Bill handed her over a fence to her uncle Jack, who was waiting with another man.

The two men ran through the woods taking turns carrying the little girl on their shoulders. About midnight, however, four hours after their start, they heard the yelp of bloodhounds. Somebody was in pursuit after all!

The frightening sound was drawing steadily closer. The little girl knew the significance. "My poor heart started jumping as the sound neared and neared," she related many years later.

She was sure they'd all be caught any moment, but her uncle Jack reassured her. "Dem's Ryland's hounds," he said. He had outdistanced them before, and he would outdistance them this time.

The two men bent to it and ran faster and faster. They reached the Pamunkey River, where Uncle Jack took the child high on his shoulders and waded the deep stream. He just "ploughed" through the water to the other side. There the small party of fugitives paused under a brush for breath. They watched as the pack of hounds and their slave-hunting masters reached the shoreline left behind and the dogs muddled about in confusion over the lost scent. As the blacks held their breath, the white posse turned downstream. In minutes, the pursuers were gone.

The two men and the girl went on. Soon they found a place in the thick, hardly trammeled woods to hide out for the coming day. They did the rest of their traveling that way—rest and hide by day, travel by night—until the morning when they reached a farm in Hanover County, outside Richmond, where Martha's father had left his wagon for them. The two men placed

Martha under a pile of vegetables in the wagon and told her to be still while they proceeded toward nearby Richmond—and the two sets of military lines ahead of them.

"When they got to the Yankee lines, Uncle showed Father's pass, and they let us pass through the lines. Outside of Richmond, he had to show it to the Confederates, and they let him pass into the city because he was bringing provisions."

Soon the wagon turned down old Brook Road, and soon it turned into St. James Street. Martha's waiting mother at last saw the horse-drawn rig coming. "She screamed so loud that they must have heard her all over Richmond."

Davises Everywhere

So many people were involved in so many ways. All across America, from all across America, the Civil War sucked up many different people, pulled them into the maelstrom, and spit them out again, changed forever. Heroes, fools, rogues, knaves, and innocents were all affected, whether they wanted to be or not.

Take one common surname—the Davises.

There was Jefferson Davis, of course. President of the Confederacy and a mainstay of the history books. But how about the ten Davis men who won the Medal of Honor for their gallantry during the Civil War? They are hardly known today, except possibly among their descendants or by hometown historians, but all ten men—Union men, naturally—were visible enough to be decorated for their exploits.

Confederates named Davis (or otherwise) naturally did not qualify for Union decorations, and so few among us today will recall Private John Davis of the Confederacy's "Quitman Rifles," Kershaw's Brigade, at Chancellorsville on May 3, 1863. A compatriot, Dr. Augustus Dickert, called this particular Davis "one of the bravest men in our regiment." Said Dickert: "He was reckless beyond all reason. He loved danger for danger's sake. Stepping behind a tree to load—he was on the skirmish line—he would pass out from this cover in plain view, take deliberate aim, and fire. Again and again he was entreated and urged by his comrades to shield himself, but in vain."

Finally, a Union sharpshooter's bullet found the little-known John Davis.

Others by the same name were better known in their day, though none quite on the scale of Jefferson Davis. Not even the Union's own Jefferson Davis—the

U.S. Army brigadier and Mexican War veteran who, in September 1862, shot and killed fellow Union general William Nelson at the Galt House hostelry in Louisville, Kentucky, as the climax to a personal quarrel.

Among other Davis nameholders who achieved notice during the Civil War was Confederate President Jefferson Davis's nephew, Mississippi State Senator and lawyer Joseph Robert Davis, who led a brigade in Pickett's Charge at Gettysburg and served later at the Wilderness, Spotsylvania, Cold Harbor, and Petersburg, surviving all before returning to more normal life as an attorney. This Davis at first encountered difficulty winning confirmation from the Confederate Congress for his nomination to brigadier general. Opponents charged his uncle Jefferson with nepotism. It was true that he had served his uncle in Richmond as an aide-de-camp for about a year.

Two Davis men named George served in the war—on opposite sides. George Davis of North Carolina at first opposed secession, but then served in the Confederate Congress as a state senator. He later served the Confederacy as its last attorney general (appointed by Jefferson Davis), and he was in the party of high government officials who had to flee Richmond when their capital fell to the invading Union Army in April 1865. George Davis, later separated from the Jefferson Davis entourage, was captured at Key West, Florida, spent a year as a Federal prisoner, then resumed his law practice, later declining an appointment to North Carolina's supreme court. (It didn't pay enough.)

The other George Davis, a Vermonter and thus a Union man, was one of those ten Medal of Honor winners mentioned earlier. His was earned at the Monocacy River, Maryland, where in July 1864 he helped to hold off Jubal Early's Washington-bound force at a pair of bridges. Davis was the last man to hurry across a key rail bridge, stepping gingerly on the cross ties under heavy fire as his small delaying force withdrew. He had begun the war as an enlisted man, and he left it as an officer after suffering severe injury from the collapse of a log cabin during the siege of Petersburg.

Two more Union men, both fine cavalry officers and combat standouts, were Hasbrouck and Benjamin F. "Grimes" Davis—the second a native of Alabama. In September of 1862, just before the Battle of Antietam, both were at Harpers Ferry as Stonewall Jackson enveloped the town and placed it under siege. Coordinating their efforts, they formulated and led a bold breakout by the Union cavalry under the darkness of night, a long file that snaked across the Potomac and into the Maryland heights beyond. In the process they came upon Confederate General James Longstreet's reserve ammunition train of ninety-seven wagons—opportunity enough for Grimes Davis! Using his Southern accent (and hoping that his uniform couldn't be discerned in the dark), he ordered Longstreet's teamsters to fall in with the silent column of horsemen headed north. They did, and in the morning's light they discovered they were prisoners of the two Davises—Union men!

Both later served at Chancellorsville, among other engagements of the Civil War. Grimes Davis, unfortunately, did not survive the subsequent cavalry battle of Brandy Station, where he had led a brigade; his Harpers Ferry sidekick Hasbrouck, also a brigade commander before war's end, did survive the conflict, but disappeared at sea in 1870.

Let us not overlook still more Davises of Civil War fame. Sam Davis, for instance—Confederate spy and heroic figure who, like Nathan Hale of another day, refused upon capture to divulge what he knew about his Confederates— and was hanged for his efforts.

Or naval officer Charles Henry Davis, who led the Union forces on the upper Mississippi that captured Memphis. He was a founder of the National Academy of Sciences and a career naval officer until his death in 1877 as a rear admiral.

Or Florida native Edmund J. Davis. This Texas lawyer and judge, who raised a "Texas" cavalry regiment in Mexico, fought for the Union throughout the war and later became a Reconstruction governor of Texas.

Or a politician, Abraham Lincoln's fellow Illinois attorney, presidential campaign manager, and later U.S. Supreme Court appointee, David Davis. Ironically, this Davis could have wound up president himself. In 1877 he left the bench and entered the U.S. Senate, where he eventually became the body's president pro tempore. He held that post when Chester Arthur, as vice president, succeeded the assassinated Civil War veteran James Garfield as president. With no vice president actually in place during the time that Arthur served in the White House, David Davis would have been next in line if Chester Arthur died. As it happened, and as yet unknown to most, Arthur suffered from a terminal kidney disease, but he served out his term and died a year later (1886) at the age of fifty-six.

Capitalism at Andersonville

"WE HAD NOT LONG BEEN PRISONERS," WROTE A SURVIVOR OF THE NOTORIOUS Confederate prison called Andersonville. Not long at all, he later said, in those conditions of deprivation and near-starvation before he discovered a remarkable fact of prison life: Free enterprise flourished, even in an appalling prison!

"We had not long been prisoners before we discovered that men here, as in other conditions of life, in order to 'get on' and preserve life, must adopt some trade or business," wrote Warren Lee Cross. Business? Trade! Yes, indeed. Even in a prison so bad that ration time was like a gathering of wolves. "These rations consisted of Indian meal, and sometimes of bacon. As a whole there was a large quantity, but when subdivided among 20,000 or 30,000 men it gave to each one but a small quantity."

The rations arrived via the North Gate. "A street or path, to which was given the name of Broadway, led from the gate through the stockade from east to west. Here, at ration time, was gathered a motley crowd. With eager, hungry eyes, they watched each division of the food, the sight of which seemed to have a strange fascination for the hungry wretches, long unused to full stomachs. They crowded to the wagons to get a sight of each bag of meal or piece of meat."

These were searing scenes, hard ever to forget. "The attempt to grasp a morsel which sometimes fell from the wagon, the piteous expression of disappointment on their pinched and unwashed faces if they failed, the involuntary exclamations, and the wistful hungry look, had in them a pathos not easily described."

Then came the moment of trade. "After the drawing of rations, a dense throng of prisoners always gathered near the North Gate to trade. One with tobacco cut in pieces not larger than dice might be seen trying to trade it for rations. Another could be heard crying out, 'Who will trade a soup-bone for Indian meal?,' 'Who'll trade cooked rations for raw?' 'Who'll trade beans for wood?' While others with small pieces of dirty bacon an inch or two in size, held on a sharpened stick, would drive a sharp trade with someone whose mouth was watering for its possession. But for its misery, the scene would often have been intensely comical."

It was far from comical, naturally. But the fact is that trade—business, if you wish—apparently did flourish. Necessity, wrote Gross, produced ingenuity, which produced amazing adaptation: "Some [men] set up as bakers, and bought flour, and baked biscuits which they sold to such as had money to buy. The ovens which were built showed such ingenuity as to extort expressions of surprise from the Confederates who occasionally visited us. The soil contained a red precipitate of iron, which was very adhesive. This was made into rude bricks by mixing the earth with water, and the oven was built of these over a mould of sand. After being left to harden in the sun for a few days, the sand was removed, a fire was kindled, and the oven was ready for use."

Other entrepreneurs made wooden buckets to hold water, "whittling out the staves and making the hoops with a jackknife." Still others managed to obtain from mysterious "outside parties" sheet tin, "generally taken from the roofs of railway cars, and, with a railway spike and a stone for tools, made small camp kettles, without solder, by bending the pieces ingeniously together." These remarkable containers were popular with "those who had money." And they were badly needed. "As no cooking utensils were possessed by the prisoners, except such as they brought into prison with them, these tinmen were benefactors."

Some prisoners tinkered with broken-down watches, "the object of their owners being simply to make them 'go' long enough to effect a trade [often with the purchaser a Confederate]."

Then there was the crowd who "fried flapjacks of Indian meal, and sold them hot from the griddle for ten cents each." One real success story—call it survival—came from "the camp beer made of Indian meal soured in water." The beer, "proclaimed by the vendors to be a cure for scurvy," was considered a refreshing drink. As for that success story, "a certain enterprising prisoner added ginger and molasses to the compound, and made, as he termed his success, a 'boom' by selling it. He became so rich as to buy food, and so regained his health and strength."

Not many were so fortunate at Andersonville, where many Union prisoners met their death.

Jaws of Death

HIS COMMANDING OFFICER, BRAXTON BRAGG, HAD ORDERED IT DONE, AND SO the division commander led his men into the jaws of death. It was the Charge of the Light Brigade all over again, but this advance was at the Stones River outside Murfreesboro, Tennessee, and the guns on the high bluff opposite were Union.

On foot, John Cabell Breckinridge's division, "with guns loaded and bayonets fixed, marched with steady step to the assault," wrote a perceptive Northern onlooker.

A proud Confederate agreed. "A more imposing and thoroughly disciplined line of soldiers never moved to the attack of an enemy than responded to the signal gun stationed immediately to our rear."

On the high bluff on the west side of the river, Union artillerymen stiffened behind their fifty-eight guns.

On the eastern ground opposite, the advance continued. "Every man vied with his fellow man in steadiness of step and correct alignment," recalled the Confederate participant, "with the officers giving low and cautionary commands, many knowing that it was their last hour on earth."

Then came the explosions. "Suddenly the ground shook as if rocked by a fearful earthquake, and the fifty-eight cannons emptied their double-shotted contents on this living human mass in front of them; but a few seconds intervened, and again and again the fifty-eight cannons spread death into Breckinridge's men."

It was too much, and in minutes the Rebels were streaming back in rout.

Before his assault of January 2, 1863, Breckinridge had argued in vain with his commander, Bragg, that they faced a trap. Moments before the assault, the Kentuckian told a fellow general that the attack was being made "'gainst my judgment." He asked that if he should be killed, "I want you to do justice to my memory and tell the people that I believed this attack to be very unwise, and tried to prevent it."

Now, with the assault over, riding to the rear past the dead and the dying, many from his native Kentucky's "Orphan Brigade," "with tears falling from his eyes, he was heard to say in tones of anguish, 'My poor Orphans! My poor Orphans!'"

This was John Cabell Breckinridge in an hour of agony outside of Murfreesboro, Tennessee. The same officer who hated committing the youthful cadets of the Virginia Military Institute to the Battle of New Market. In triumph or tragedy, such a unique soldier there hardly was, even in the fratricidal American Civil War.

Stones River came as 1862 passed into 1863. Only a few months earlier Breckinridge had served the Union as vice president under James Buchanan. He ran for president against Abraham Lincoln in 1860 as the nominee of the Southern Democrats. He then took his seat as a U.S. senator from Kentucky, but after joining the Confederacy was expelled, posthaste, from the Senate.

His gallantry, however, rarely failed him or his men, and few generals of either side attended so many of the war's major battles—Shiloh, the defense of Vicksburg, Chickamauga, Baton Rouge, Chattanooga-Missionary Ridge, Cold Harbor. In most, as at Stones River, he appeared in a subordinate command role. But as an overall commander, he prevailed over the enemy at New Market, at the second Battle of Kernstown, and again in Virginia at Lynchburg.

Later, as secretary of war, he was a mainstay for the Confederacy in its dying hours, helping to direct the evacuation of Richmond and to organize Jefferson

Davis's flight south. Davis was captured, but Breckinridge made his way to Florida and escaped to Cuba in an open boat.

He returned to America from England under amnesty in 1868—still and well remembered for the fairness with which he had presided over the Senate in those difficult years just before the Civil War.

Bride Left Behind

THE BRIDE WORE LACE, AND THE GROOM WORE HIS GENERAL'S UNIFORM, AS DID the clergyman performing the wedding ceremony in Murfreesboro, Tennessee, in December 1862. Actually, the clergyman, one Leonidas Polk, also wore his Episcopal bishop's vestments, with his own general's uniform peeping out from beneath.

Standing by as the groom's very proper groomsmen were a corps of Confederate generals—Braxton Bragg, William Hardee, John C. Breckinridge, and Benjamin Cheatham—while many other officers and two regimental bands filled the bride's happily bedecked home. Outside, hundreds of soldiers filled the streets, built bonfires, sang, and cheered.

The bride's father, a former U.S. congressman fresh from a prison cell in Nashville, held nothing back in providing a memorable wartime affair for his daughter and her guests. Their supper ranged from turkey to ham, chicken, duck, and various delicacies, plus plentiful bottles of wine for toasts to the happy couple.

For cavalry raider John Hunt Morgan, his marriage to Mattie Ready was the culmination of a heady week that had begun with his signal victory over a large Federal force at Hartsville, Tennessee, followed by his award of a brigadier's star from President Jefferson Davis in person, and an unusually warm commendation from the usually reserved Bragg. "To the brave officers and men composing the expedition the General tenders his cordial thanks and congratulations," Bragg's official orders had read. "He is proud of them and hails the success achieved by their valor as but the precursor of still greater victories."

The site of Morgan's wedding, Murfreesboro was in the eye of a storm that swept back and forth—buffeted by Confederate, then Union, then Confederate forces. (The townspeople were largely Southern in their loyalties.) Just eight months earlier, Morgan had been forced by Yankee occupation to quit his courting of Mattie Ready in person. Now he and his fellow Rebs were back, but who could tell for how long? Whatever the case, he would marry her while he could.

In his absence of eight months, Morgan's future father-in-law, Colonel Ready, once a member of the U.S. House in Washington, had been imprisoned for refusing to take the Federal oath of allegiance. Now he was free again, and the Rebs were in town. On December 14 they had themselves a spectacular wedding as Morgan and Mattie became man and wife to the words intoned by Confederate Lieutenant General Polk, an Episcopal bishop in civilian life.

The circumstances allowed no time to linger. War still called, and in six days Morgan was off again on his Christmas Raid of 1862-63. It lasted for fourteen days and covered more than five hundred miles of snow—four engagements and countless skirmishes. In total, two thousand Union prisoners were taken, and four bridges, twenty-five miles of railroad tracks, and five million dollars in Federal stores were destroyed.

As one result of this excursion, however, Morgan missed the big Battle of Stones River at Murfreesboro over New Year's—a defeat that meant Bragg's Rebels must move out as William S. Rosecrans and his Union legions moved in.

While Mattie persevered under the Federal occupation that now resumed for the better part of a year, Morgan was kept busy fighting the war in other quarters. His most spectacular foray of all was about to take place: his famous (and unauthorized) summertime raid of 1863 into Ohio, an incursion that took Morgan and a steadily dwindling band to a point one hundred miles south of Lake Erie, with the Federals in hot pursuit.

He was captured subsequently, but the story didn't stop there. A few months later, he and a handful of his men further electrified an admiring public in the South by escaping from their confines in the Ohio State Penitentiary. Morgan then worked his way back to Confederate territory and to his anxious Mattie, still more a bride than a wife.

Audible, Not Visible

Was there ever a storm like that at Stones River, near Murfreesboro, Tennessee? From the accounts of those who survived, you could wonder.

Acting as his unit's sergeant major, for instance, was Union Private Henry A. Castle, deployed for the moment with his regiment—the afternoon of December 31, 1862—in a railroad cut oblique to the front line. He saw a

Confederate officer spot exactly where Castle and his compatriots were located "and then gallop off" to fetch his artillery. Sure enough, in short time a Rebel battery came within Castle's view.

It would not be long before the Rebel guns began firing down his rail cut; so Castle, as acting sergeant major, hastened off to notify his regiment's commander, a major. But the major had been wounded and carried off the field. Castle then sought out his next in command, the adjutant, but he, too, had been carried off.

With no one to give him orders for the moment, Private Castle then marched his company "double quick out of the defile, trusting the rest to follow." They did, and just in time, "as just then the shells came shrieking through the straight and narrow gorge with a venom that would have left few unscathed in five minutes more."

Castle's next step was to tell the four captains still with his regiment that they had no overall commander. In response, they dispatched him to the brigade commander, clearly visible on his horse just two hundred yards away. Castle started out on the errand to settle the matter of seniority among the captains, "but before I had made half the distance, he, the last of our brigade commanders, was shot before my eyes and fell to the ground a corpse."

Another Union private, George H. Daggett, found himself during the same battle in a strange wood.

It was a patch of cedars, about two hundred acres, with the ground covered with rock—all slabs, boulders, and fissures. There was no soil, and the tree trunks were so thick and close they were almost impenetrable—"so near together that the sunlight was obscured and the vision extended but a short distance horizontally."

The Union men who retreated into this shelter at one point had no idea what was going on just outside the cedar woods. All they knew came from "avalanches of sound which assailed us from every direction."

The Confederate enemy poured artillery and musket fire into the wooded patch, while close by other Union forces fought off other Rebel forces. "Thus on all sides we were stormed at and stunned by the conglomeration of fiendish noises that came seemingly from every point of the compass."

Then, too, "not the least terrible of these sounds was an occasional explosion of the hot, fierce, indescribable Rebel yell."

Echoing Daggett's impressions, an onlooking Union officer was aware that the Confederate left was desperate to overrun the cedar woods and reach the Nashville Turnpike beyond, thus to cut off the Union force there. Union

General William S. Rosecrans rushed forward some reinforcements into the woods, but under the pressure of the determined Confederates, they were inadequate. The Union officer could not see into the woods and estimate what was happening. All he knew was that "nearer and nearer came the storm; louder and louder the tumult of battle."

Luckily, Rosecrans had massed more men along the turnpike, for quite suddenly, "10,000 fugitives [Union troops] burst from the cedar thickets and rushed into the open space between them and the turnpike."

Many of the fleeing men fell to the fire of their Rebel pursuers from behind, but "fresh crowds...burst from the thickets" to replace the fallen—to overrun their prone forms in the field. For long moments it appeared the routed regiments would even overrun the Union line formed along the turnpike.

Indeed, "it was with the greatest difficulty that some of the regiments, which had been massed together as sort of a forlorn hope, could prevent their ranks from being crushed by the mass of fugitives." And the pursuers? Previously hidden from sight in the deep deep woods, they suddenly burst forth: "At last the long lines of the enemy emerged from the woods with a demoniac yell, intended to strike terror into the souls of the 'Yankees.'"

From the awaiting Union line there came a "dazzling sheet of flame." In that response, "an awful roar shook the earth; a crash rent the atmosphere." The advance ranks of the Rebel charge "seemed to melt away like snowflakes before a flame." In seconds, a vast cloud covered the field—"smoke which hid everything from the eye."

While in one quarter the Union men still fled, in this covered field a fierce battle ensued before the onlookers. Yet it remained invisible to them. "The combat under that great cloud of smoke was somewhat similar to that in the woods. No one knows exactly what occurred. There was a shout, a charge, a rush of fire, a recoil, and then all for a time disappeared." Yet there was no doubting what was happening inside the obscuring vapors. "For 10 minutes the thunder of battle burst forth from the cloud."

Finally, the battalion of the officer who had been observing the battle was able to advance. His men found "no Rebels between the woods and the turnpike except the dead, dying, and disabled." Those there were in the hundreds, on ground soaked and reddened with blood. "Since the annihilation of the 'Old Guard' in their charge at Waterloo, there has probably been no instance of so great a slaughter in so short a time as during this repulse of the Reb left at Murfreesboro."

The left was certainly key to the entire day's events, since each of the warring sides had decided in advance to employ his own left against the enemy's right.

In theory this would have produced a revolving-door effect. The Confederates, however, under Commander Braxton Bragg, gained the initial advantage by beginning battle an hour ahead of the Union timetable.

On the Union left that morning, breakfast was still a very recent memory, and the troops had barely begun to cross the Stones River with the town of Murfreesboro as their goal when, reported Union officer William D. Birckham, "some firing" was heard on the right, "but not enough to indicate a battle."

Not for long, for suddenly, "all hearts were thrilled by a sound sweeping from the right like a strong wind sweeping through a forest." The Rebel left had hurled itself against the Union right.

The sound was the "din of battle," swelling up rapidly. Then came a tide of fugitives from the thickets. "You have seen cinders from burning buildings flying when the conflagration was still invisible. You could hear the roaring flames and crackling beams. Seeing the cinders, you would say, 'There is a fire.' You had not yet felt the blast, but its avant-couriers were unmistakable. These teamsters [wagon crews] Negroes, soldiers, flying before it were cinders from the flames of battle."

That early development, of course, spoiled the Union plan to advance with the left, since the Union right already was giving way to the Rebel left. Later, after the charge through the cedars and the equally invisible battle under the cloud of smoke, the trend again reversed itself, and the Rebel left was beaten back, all at great cost to both sides.

In the midst of that day, good Kentucky men on the Rebel side at one point met good Kentucky men on the Union side—many of them old friends and neighbors from the same county. "As soon as they came near enough for recognition," related Union Colonel Charles S. Greene later, "they ceased firing, and began abusing, and cursing, and swearing at each other, calling each other the most outlandish names."

For a time the Kentuckians paid no attention to the violent battle all around them, but that couldn't last. "By mutual consent they finally ceased swearing, and charged into each other with the most unearthly yell ever heard. The muskets were thrown away, and at it they went, pulling and gouging." And why not? At least pulling, gouging, yelling, and cussing was not killing each other.

The Confederate 3rd Kentucky was "getting the best of it" when the outsider 9th Ohio intervened and took many of the Confederates prisoner. "As the late belligerents were conducted to the rear, they were on the best terms with their captors, laughing and chatting and joking; and they all became jolly as possible."

Spank the Boys

INTREPIDLY HE PUSHED ON AND ON. "SEVERELY WOUNDED," IT SAYS IN HIS CITATION for the Congressional Medal of Honor, "and exposed to a heavy fire from the enemy, he persistently remained upon the field of battle until he had reported to…[General William Tecumseh] Sherman the necessity of supplying cartridges for the use of troops under command of Colonel Malmborg [Company C, 55th Illinois Infantry]."

Many a man performed similar brave duty when called upon, rather than fail his comrades in battle. After all, it is every soldier's duty to ignore the storm of shot and shell and to press on.

Every man's duty, even when struck in the leg by a Minié bullet while on the way with a crucial message for General Sherman. Such was the case that day in May 1863 at Vicksburg for Orion P. Howe, native of Portage County, Ohio.

He was no average Union soldier, and not even a man. Not yet, anyway. At age fourteen, he was his Illinois company's drummer boy, one of thousands, perhaps even forty thousand or more, of mere boys who marched off to war with the Union and Confederate armies.

In the Union forces alone, an estimated three hundred such youths served at the age of thirteen or even younger. Indeed, by another reliable estimate, a startling twenty-five children began their Army tours at the age of ten or less! One was the redoubtable Johnny Clem, also known as "Johnny Shiloh" after his drum was knocked to pieces by a shell at Shiloh. Only nine when he "joined up" (a bit unofficially, it seems), Johnny not only became a lance sergeant by the time he was twelve, but he didn't muster out of service for fifty-five years! It was 1916 before he finally retired, by that time a major general and the last Civil War combat veteran still in active service in the U.S. Army.

Many such youngsters slipped into Civil War units by the wink of someone's eye or by one sort of chicanery or another. Most were drummer boys, buglers, musicians.

In young Clem's case, the recruiters visiting his home of Newark, Ohio, in 1861 turned aside the small lad who tried to join their 3rd Ohio Regiment. One even said, "We can't use infants here." As David Mallinson reported in the magazine *America's Civil War*, however, Clem hid in the baggage car of the train carrying the 3rd Ohio to camp at Covington, Kentucky. "Once there, he attached himself to the 22nd Michigan and became the drummer for Company C."

At Shiloh in April 1862, his drum was hit as he tapped the advance for Company C. But there was more to come. "Drumless, Clem went into the battle of Chickamauga carrying a musket cut down to size." Left alone at one point, he used the weapon to wound a Confederate colonel who "rode up and yelled for Johnny to surrender."

After that they called him "the Drummer Boy of Chickamauga." Taken prisoner just three weeks later and released in a few more weeks, he was able to serve as an orderly in the headquarters of Union Major General George H. Thomas and carry dispatches for Thomas in the Atlanta campaign, during which the youngster's horse was shot down beneath him.

Rejected by West Point after the war for his lack of schooling, the young veteran appealed to President Ulysses S. Grant, the youth's commander at Shiloh. Grant relented, and Clem was allowed a commission as a second lieutenant in the Regular Army.

It should be noted that other youths managed to gain entrance to the military academies. One was Orion Howe, the fourteen-year-old given the Medal of Honor for his bravery at Vicksburg. Sherman recalled the wounded youth's message so well, he gladly appointed him to Annapolis, but Howe struggled with the books and bowed out after two years.

Another appointee received his boost from none other than Abe Lincoln, who often showed interest in the welfare of the Union's drummer boys. Young Robert Henry Henderson, also of a Michigan regiment (the 8th), came to Lincoln's attention as "the Drummer Boy of the Rappahannock," a sobriquet given after the teenager crossed the icy Rappahannock River at the Battle of Fredericksburg on December 11, 1862, by hanging on to a boat carrying Union soldiers across under heavy Confederate fire. Losing his drum to a piece of flying shrapnel on the far side, he took up a musket, found a Reb soldier, and took him prisoner.

After the boy's discharge, Lincoln asked War Secretary Edwin Stanton to find a job for "the gallant drummer-boy Robert H. Henderson." The result was a messenger's berth in the U.S. treasurer's office. Later still, Lincoln endorsed Treasurer Francis E. Spinner's recommendation of Henderson for appointment to the U.S. Military Academy at West Point. At that time, Lincoln wrote: "I know something of this boy, and believe he is brave, manly and worthy."

The U.S. Congress late in the war acted upon the reservations of many who felt mere children should not be thrown into war; as might be expected, the boys did not always live to become men. Congress acted in March 1864 to prohibit the enlistment of anyone under sixteen—action finally taken after a young Cincinnati boy was killed in battle at Resaca, Georgia.

Most men in the Union armies—all but 1.5 percent—fell into the age bracket of eighteen to forty-six, with an average age of 25.8 years at the time of enlistment. Only hundreds served at age fifteen or less, although the numbers began to jump into the thousands for consecutive ages. At age sixteen for instance, 2,758; at age seventeen, 6,425; at age eighteen, 133,475—the largest age group among all Union soldiers.

The real youngsters not only served as musicians (and mascots) but as "gofers," too. They were seen in camp as barbers and water carriers, and on the battlefield, they tended to the wounded—or even took a wounded man's place in the line.

If the enemy didn't kill or wound such a youngster, his own compatriots might! Some boys were sentenced to death for desertion. Lincoln once took up the cause of such a youth the day before his scheduled execution. "I am unwilling," wrote the president, "for any boy under 18 to be shot; and his father affirms that he is yet under 16." Another time, informed of a fourteen-year-old facing the firing squad for desertion, Lincoln wrote to War Secretary Edwin Stanton: "Hadn't we better spank this drummer boy and send him home?"

Perhaps Lincoln on such occasions was thinking of home life in the White House itself, where son Tad sometimes wore a Union officer's uniform tailored to fit his diminutive stature, where Tad and brother Willie subjected an unfortunate toy soldier named Jack to occasional "execution," and where a playful Lincoln once wrote a pardon sparing Jack from still another firing squad. Perhaps Lincoln's obvious empathy for the boys in service reflected the fact that his beloved Willie died of fever in early 1862, long before the war ended.

Injury Added to Insult

On the morning of July 2, 1863, disputing Confederate officers George Moody of a Louisiana artillery battery and Pichegru Woolfolk of a Virginia artillery battery were scheduled to duel with rifles at ten paces—except that this was Gettysburg, and events overtook their disagreement and postponed their duel forever.

A Confederate legislator, Henry Cousins Chambers, did attend a duel, however—in his case, rifles at fifty paces. He killed his political rival William Lake in the process. Chambers then took his seat in the Confederate Congress—and no one rose to oppose him in the next election.

It was a violent period, with people often killed over insult, honor, politics, and the slavery issue even for years before the Civil War broke out. Abraham Lincoln once came close to a dual by broadsword, but it was called off at the last moment by mutual agreement. Even during the Civil War, not all the passion and violence were directed at the enemy.

Nathan Bedford Forrest, preeminent as a cavalry leader for the South, was a notoriously violent man. Well known among Civil War buffs and historians even today is his angry threat directed at Braxton Bragg, a senior Confederate general. Face to face and very personal indeed, Forrest called Bragg "a damned scoundrel" and said, "If you ever again try to interfere with me or cross my path, it will be at the peril of your life."

Not so well known is the time Forrest and a fellow officer in the Confederate Army came to blows, with a truly dismal result. The scenario began when a youthful artillery officer was placed in charge of two recently captured Union artillery pieces. The young lieutenant, Andrew Willis Gould, first served with his cousin Colonel Alonzo Napier's Tennessee Cavalry Battalion, and next with Morton's Tennessee Battery.

Then came a firefight on April 30, 1863, at Sand Mountain, Alabama. Gould had to withdraw too quickly to take his two guns, but he spiked them, at considerable personal risk. All that Forrest heard, unfortunately, was that Gould had lost the two precious guns. A pending command slot went to another officer, and Forrest questioned Gould's courage.

The unfairly maligned young man confronted Forrest at Columbia, Tennessee, on June 13, 1863, and a heated argument followed in the hallway of the Masonic Building. Gould suddenly struggled to pull his pistol out of the pocket of his lengthy coat of linen, while Forrest, anticipating trouble, reached into his own pocket for his penknife.

Gould was unable to free his weapon, which suddenly discharged. At almost the same moment, Forrest was opening the penknife wih his teeth and lunging at Gould. The pistol ball lodged in Forrest's left hip with a painful impact that produced a visible reaction. With one hand, Forrest managed to grab Gould's hand, which now held the freed pistol, and pushed it up into the air while at the same moment, with the other hand, plunging the penknife into the younger officer's rib cage.

The next few minutes were filled with pandemonium. Gould ran from the building into the street. Other officers rushed Forrest, stunned, into a nearby doctor's office. Two more doctors, one of them a relative, saw Gould staggering in the street and pushed him into a nearby tailor's shop.

In his haste the doctor treating Forrest made the mistake of blurting out that the hip wound could be fatal. Forrest was enraged. "No damned man shall kill me and live," he shouted, jumping to his feet and taking to the street in search of Gould.

In the tailor's shop, Gould looked well enough—he could stand and could talk—but blood squeezed out of his puncture wound with every breath. One doctor tried to help him while the other hurried off for his surgical instruments.

In the street Forrest still raged. "By God, he has mortally wounded me and I'll kill him dead before I die," he roared again. One officer told Forrest "that damned scoundrel is not much hurt," but a local citizen said Gould was "bleeding profusely" and likely to die.

Forrest told the citizen to get out of his way. By now Forrest had taken a pistol from the saddle gear of a horse tethered nearby and had somehow found another. He burst into the tailor's shop brandishing both weapons wildly and cursing. As Gould dashed into a back alley, one pistol went off, the bullet striking a bystander in the leg (a minor injury, as it turned out). Pursuing Gould, Forrest found him supine in a clump of weeds, pushed at him with a foot, and turned away. After commandeering Gould's two doctors, Forrest then learned that his own wound would not be fatal after all.

With that welcome news, he suddenly told the doctors to hasten to Gould's aid and "spare nothing to save him." It is still unclear whether Forrest later visited Gould and granted him forgiveness, as some accounts report, but it is absolutely clear that in the aftermath it was Forrest who soon rode off into battle again. Young Gould died just days after the ugly incident.

Family Affair

ELLET, ELLET, ELLET, AND ELLET SOUNDS LIKE A FIRM OF BARRISTERS OR SOLICITORS out of a Charles Dickens novel. But no, these Ellets more accurately can be associated with operations on the Mississippi River during the Civil War.

All four Ellets, a father and son, a brother of the father, and a nephew, were associated, more precisely, with the Union's ram fleet on the Mississippi. Their tale begins with the birth of the first Ellet, Charles, in Bucks County, Pennsylvania, in 1810. Called Charles Ellet Jr., he grew up to be an engineer, railroader, inventor, and bridge-builder. As one engineering feat, for instance, he built the first wire-suspension bridge in the United States—across the Schuylkill River at Fairmount, Pennsylvania. He then spanned the Niagara River (below the famous falls), and at Wheeling, Ohio, in 1849, he erected a bridge of 1,010 feet over the Ohio River—at that time the world's longest single-span bridge.

While helping to build a Virginia rail line across the Blue Ridge in the 1850s, he also had on his mind an odd naval vessel—sort of an ironclad ram. No one in the United States seemed interested until the Confederacy produced the ironclad *Virginia* in 1862 (previously the *Merrimac*) along lines suggested in Ellet's published proposals.

Suddenly Washington and the Lincoln administration awoke to the possibilities of Ellet's design. In short time he was dispatched by Secretary of War Edwin Stanton to the Mississippi River (where he had worked before on flood control projects) to establish a fleet of rams. This he did by fitting out nine steam vessels with armor and rams, then moving them down the Ohio River to join the Union Navy's Captain Charles H. Davis and his Mississippi Flotilla.

Ellet managed to skim safely by Fort Pillow on June 5, 1862. The next day he took on eight Confederate vessels guarding Memphis, Tennessee. Four of them were sunk by the Union rams, with Ellet's own *Queen of the West* ramming and sinking the enemy's *General Lowell*. The remaining Rebel vessels fled downriver with the Union craft in close pursuit. Ellet's ships managed to sink another of the Rebel vessels and capture two more, a total of seven Confederate ships eliminated in one fell swoop.

The Union that day suffered but one casualty—a mortal wound inflicted upon the man behind the Union rams, Charles Ellet Jr. He died on June 21.

The Ellet name, however, did not die with him. Far from it!

The inventor's son, Charles Rivers Ellet, a medical student at Georgetown when the Civil War erupted, had just joined his father in time to bypass the Rebel batteries at Fort Pillow and was with him for the river battle at Memphis the next day. In fact, the elder Ellet had dispatched son Charles, officially a medical cadet, and two fellow Union men on the dangerous mission of going ashore in Memphis and demanding the city's surrender. They faced an angry mob (but no Confederate soldiers) and had to ignore hurled bricks and even stray shots, but they did it. They marched to the post office, took down the Confederate flag, and raised the U.S. flag in its place.

The younger Ellet would soon risk his life again by crossing disputed territory on foot outside besieged Vicksburg on his way to inform Admiral David G. Farragut that Memphis had fallen into Union hands. Soon, too, the younger

Ellet had been raised to colonel's rank and placed in command of his late father's ram fleet.

As a riverboat commander, he didn't do so badly. Four times in the next four months he ran the Vicksburg batteries. On the fourth such excursion—February 2, 1863—he attacked and rammed the Rebel *Vicksburg* at the city's south landing. The next day he and the redoubtable *Queen* captured three Confederate supply vessels at the mouth of the Red River.

It was on another occasion at the Red River, however, that the younger Ellet ran into misfortune. Ascending the river, the *Queen of the West* ran aground and came under fire by a hidden shore battery, and he and the crew had to abandon their ram. Worse, he had gone ahead of his supporting gunboat, *Indianola*. When it appeared, the Rebels turned the *Queen*'s own guns on Indianola, which also became a casualty of the day's activities. Ellet had to escape on board the accompanying *De Sota*.

Although this young and relatively untried "sailor" had been promoted to the rank of colonel, he was not really a sailor (neither was his late father) but was an Army officer. Technically, he was commander of the Mississippi Marine Brigade. The Red River incident only inflamed Army-Navy rivalries over control of the small ram fleet and the Marines.

That odd situation also involved the younger Ellet's uncle. The brother of the late Charles Jr., Alfred Washington Ellet was a brigadier general of volunteers who had been second to his brother in command of the ram fleet. He had been present for the Memphis battle and had taken command after his brother was mortally wounded. He was briefly in command of the Marine Brigade itself, but after a time he was sent with brigade infantry elements to join Union General William Rosecrans on the Tennessee River.

Adding to the not-always-so-clear muddle was a fourth Ellet who served on the Mississippi, John A. Ellet, a nephew to both older Ellets and cousin to the younger Charles. This younger Ellet, often in conflict with naval authorities, was also an Army officer. He served as second in command to Cousin Charles with the Marine Brigade. He had lost the ram *Lancaster*, and eventually he would command the Union *Switzerland*, which Cousin Charles had taken over for a time after the *Queen* had been lost.

Soon John Ellet ran afoul of Union Admiral David Porter. When Porter gave him orders, Ellet would not obey them without first checking with his Army uncle, General Alfred Ellet. Young John avoided Porter's threats of arrest and court-martial by joining Farragut downriver and strictly obeying the latter officer's dictates.

Meanwhile, young Charles, replaced earlier by Cousin John in command of the *Switzerland*, went with the Marine Brigade's infantrymen to join Rosecrans. He then became ill, retired to his uncle Alfred's farm in Illinois, and died in the fall of 1863, at age twenty or twenty-one.

Miss Kate's Brief Run

SHE WAS YOUNG, VIVACIOUS—THE BELLE OF THE BALL AMONG WASHINGTON society during the Civil War. Kate Chase, daughter and official hostess for the widowed secretary of the treasury, Salmon P. Chase. Poor, star-crossed Kate Chase Sprague, as events later turned out.

With the eruption of the war and the departure of so many prominent political figures hailing from the South, the Federal capital lost the prime movers of its social circles. For years Washington society had been Southern-tilted, peopled by luminaries such as Varina Davis, wife of the new Confederate president now ensconced in Richmond. In the past four decades, in fact, a majority of presidents had been Southern-born slaveowners. As recently as the Zachary Taylor administration (he died in office in 1850), the White House itself had been home to slaves. In his case, the slaves were sequestered in the attic rooms and kept to the private family quarters to avoid ruffling ever-more-sensitive feelings in Washington.

Under Lincoln, with the Union split in two, the social order was far different. As Union officer James A. Garfield (destined, himself, to be a future White House occupant) wrote in 1862: "This is the transition period between the old, slaveholding, aristocratic social dynasty and the New Republican one." It was a leap from one social order to the next, he added in a letter to his wife, Lucretia. Further, "The old social dynasty has been one of the most powerful political elements in Washington and is the secret of a great many successes for the South. From the days of General [Andrew] Jackson…it has been a great power."

Where was Garfield when he wrote that thought in the fall of 1862? At the home of fellow Ohioans Salmon P. Chase and daughter Kate. They were a perfect match, too, since the Chase duo and Garfield were all politically ambitious. (Garfield soon would be serving the first of nine terms as a member of the U.S. House of Representatives.) "Mr. Chase and his daughter Kate," wrote Garfield to his wife on September 27, 1862, "have insisted that I shall stay with them while I remain in Washington, and so I came here this evening with all my luggage."

Garfield had previously stayed at Willard's Hotel, progenitor to today's Willard at the same site, just two blocks from the White House. After leading his regiment, the 42nd Ohio Infantry, in battle, the young colonel was in Washington in hopes of securing a new command that would advance his political agenda after the war—if, as he himself wrote, he didn't get killed in the meantime.

Soon, Garfield and Kate were taking "sightseeing" sojourns into the war-torn Virginia countryside, as well as enjoying the social gatherings that took place in the Chase home on many an evening, with the high and mighty of wartime Washington much in evidence. One Friday early in October they set out to visit Union troops quartered near Fairfax Court House and to view the site of the Second Battle of Bull Run. "On Friday last," Garfield wrote to his brother Harry, "Miss Kate Chase and I took their carriage and pompous liveried driver and, allowing him to change his tall plug for a comfortable slouch, we set out for General [Franz] Siegel's headquarters at Fairfax Courthouse. Miss Chase had prepared two large baskets of provisions, partly for a present to the General and partly for our use if we should go on to the battlefield."

On Sunday morning the outing continued, with Garfield riding a borrowed horse in borrowed boots and Kate traveling in a carriage with another German general's wife, Mrs. Carl Schurz. Another foreign general, Hungarian-born Julius Stahel, quartered in nearby Centreville, Virginia, furnished a cavalry troop "to see that the country was clear and safe for us to go to the battlefield."

What the visitors found there, almost within earshot of Washington and just a month after the second Union debacle at Bull Run, was no pretty sight.

"We went on," wrote Garfield, "across Bull Run to the limit of the late battle for about five miles beyond Centreville…and General Schurz, who was in the engagement, gave us a fine description of the whole two days' work and the shameful and unnecessary retreat which followed. We saw hundreds of graves, or rather, heaps of earth piled upon the bodies where they lay. Scores of heads, hands and feet were protruding, and so rapid had been the decomposition of 34 days that naked, eyeless skulls grinned at us as if the corpses had lifted their heads from their deathbeds to leer at us as we passed by. Shells and round shot lay scattered all over the field and broken muskets and dismantled gun carriages were very plenty. Hats, caps, coats, equipment, letters, and all that lately belonged to life were scattered around.

"I picked up a joint promissory note of $1,000, which would probably be valuable to the heirs of some poor skeleton. 'Your loving wife til death' was the conclusion of a letter which lay near the bones of a skeleton arm which reached through the side of its grave, and had doubtless one day not long ago clasped the loving wife, but now the 'til death' has opened for him the portal of the world where 'there is neither marrying nor giving in the grave.'

"We followed the path of where the fierce giants struggled and saw their battle tracks thick with graves. At last we stopped and took a glass of milk with the old Negro who lives on the eastern marge of the field on the bank of Bull Run (to be a sadly famous stream hereafter) and who saw both battles—of 1861 and 1862. All along the road from the Run to Centreville, and even far this side toward Fairfax, are wrecks of burned wagons and artillery carriages."

Garfield and Miss Kate returned to the capital the next day, crossing the Potomac by way of the Chain Bridge, but not before enjoying another night as guests of the German officers and a rousing sing-song with them and Mrs. Schurz. The day before Garfield also saw the "formidable" fortifications that Confederate General Beauregard had built on a "lofty ridge" at Centreville as well as "the thousands of log huts [previously] built and occupied by the rebels...."

After writing about such adventures with the popular Miss Kate, Garfield soon heard a plaintive response from a piqued Mrs. Garfield back in Ohio. "From your letters to others," she wrote, "I learn that you and Miss Kate are taking dinners out, visiting camps, etc., and I have a good deal of woman's curiosity to hear about some of those doings; and is Miss Kate a very charming, interesting young lady?"

To which Garfield hastily replied that his socialite hostess Kate Chase "is a woman of good sense and pretty good culture, has a good form but not a pretty face, its beauty being marred by a nose slightly inclined to pug." Nonetheless, Garfield added, "She has probably more social influence and makes a better impression generally than any other Cabinet lady."

Garfield soon departed from the Washington scene for a time to become chief of staff to General William S. Rosecrans. He would become a hero, it also would transpire, at the Battle of Chickamauga, even though it was a defeat for Rosecrans and his Union forces.

After Garfield's leave-taking, Kate Chase continued her heady social life. A major figure in that unfolding drama was William Sprague, the thirty-one-year-old governor of Rhode Island who had come to Washington to fight as a militia colonel. He had allegedly irritated his Regular Army colleagues for his inexperienced blundering at First Bull Run, and he also had taken part in a minor way in the ill-fated Peninsular campaign against Richmond. He apparently preferred the nation's capital to his own state capital, since he officially left his governorship behind to serve in the U.S. Senate as of March 1863, a Democrat considered supportive of the Lincoln administration. One reason for such support on his part may have been his relationship with Cabinet member Salmon Chase's daughter Kate, whom he married in the fall of 1863.

With his money—he had considerable—her father's prestige, and Kate's reputation as a vivacious Washington hostess, it should have been a marriage made in heaven, at least for the politically ambitious. But it wasn't.

Secretary Chase, allied with the Radical Republicans, was briefly considered a possible rival to Lincoln himself for the 1864 Republican presidential nomination, just as he had been in 1860. Chase left the Cabinet in June 1864, only to receive a surprise appointment from Lincoln at year's end as Chief Justice of the Supreme Court. There he was considered a Lincoln ally, ironic in light of their earlier rivalry.

Daughter Kate weathered the intrigues of the Civil War period as the socialite whose marriage in late 1863 had been a high point of that winter's social season. Five years later she was still active on her father's behalf in stirrings aimed at giving him the party's presidential nomination for 1868, but to no avail.

Her husband, meanwhile, had become too fond of the bottle, it is said. In time, Kate was linked by capital whispers to another Senate member. Her fourth child was mentally disabled, and her husband lost his fortune. Her father died, and by 1882 she was a divorced woman with little to show for all the glamour and glitter she once had known. Even her family's old friend Garfield, nine times a congressman and then president, could be of no help since he had been assassinated shortly after taking office as president in 1881.

At the end of her life (1899) Kate Chase Sprague was managing her own small dairy and poultry farm. Her onetime husband, Sprague, lived longer. A two-term senator, he lived to the age of eighty-five; at the time of his death in Paris, France, in 1915, he was the last governor of the Civil War era still surviving.

Escape from Success

THE ENEMY'S FIRE, SAID COMMANDER WILLIAM B. CUSHING LATER, "WAS VERY severe," so severe that in one instance, "the whole back of my coat was torn out by buckshot, and the sole of my shoe was carried away." And in another:

"My clothing was perforated with bullets as I stood in the bow, the heel-jigger in my right hand and the exploding-line in the left."

In seconds, though, he had placed his torpedo device, primitive by today's standards, and set it off. "The explosion took place at the same instant that 100 pounds of grape [grapeshot], at 10 feet range, crashed among us, and the dense mass of water thrown out by the torpedo came down with choking weight upon us."

Cushing, a daring young officer of the Union Navy, had achieved his aim of delivering a mortal blow to the last of the Confederate ironclads, the CSS *Albemarle*. To accomplish the feat, he and his volunteer crew ran a steam launch eight miles up the Roanoke River in North Carolina to Plymouth, a hotbed town of Rebel soldiery and sailors.

The Union men came at night, of course, late on October 16, 1864, and they weren't spotted until close to the "dark mountain of iron" looming in front of them. Once Cushing and his men were seen, however, it seemed every gun in the world was shooting at them. At this point, too, Cushing discovered his target was surrounded at its mooring by a ring of logs meant to keep away intruders like himself.

Undeterred and still under fire, Cushing slowed his launch to a full stop, backed off to give himself room to make speed, then went at the log booms head-on, "trusting to their having been long enough in the water to have become slimy—in which case my boat, under full headway, would bump up against them and slip over into the pen with the ram."

And that's exactly what Cushing managed to do, blowing up the *Albemarle* at the end of his scoot over the logs. It was quite a feat of dexterity, to say nothing of coolness under fire, since Cushing in his standing position at the bow had his boat to control, his spar torpedo to place, and his lines to yank and pull in order to detach and then trigger the torpedo. And it was accomplished with a dangerous penalty: Once his craft vaulted the log boom, Cushing knew that while he might succeed in blowing up the enemy ship, his steam launch "would never get out again."

The huge explosion that rent the *Albemarle* resolved any doubts. Cushing's Union vessel was instantly swamped and began to sink. And at this time of year the water was cold.

Cushing shouted to his men to save themselves, then struck out in the water for the opposite shore. "The whole surface of the stream was plowed up by grape and musketry, and my nearest friends, the [Union] fleet, were 12 miles away."

Nearby, with a "great, gurgling yell," Cushing's fireman Samuel Higgins went under and disappeared. Nearby, too, the Confederates soon were out on the water in their own boats, picking up other members of the Union raiding party.

Cushing, his strength fast ebbing in the chill water, swam onward in the dark. He tried to help another crewman he heard splashing just behind, but that man also "sank like a stone."

Cushing then forced himself to keep moving, keep stroking, in the direction of the town side of the river. "At last, and not a moment too soon," he wrote later, "I touched the soft mud and in the excitement of the first shock I half raised my body and made one step forward; then fell, and remained half in the mud and half in the water until daylight, unable to even crawl on hands and knees, nearly frozen with my brain in a whirl, but with one thing strong in me—the fixed determination to escape."

The growing light disclosed that he was at one end of a swamp on the edge of Plymouth—"not 40 yards from one of the forts." Daylight showed the rebel town to be "swarming" with excited, angry soldiers and sailors. "It was a source of satisfaction to me to know that I had pulled the wire that set all these figures moving, but as I had no desire of being discovered, my first object was to get into a dry fringe of rushes that edged the swamp."

First he would have to cross a belt of open ground thirty or forty feet in width without alarming the sentry pacing back and forth on a nearby Confederate parapet. Cushing waited until the man turned, dashed for half the distance and then threw himself flat as the sentry turned once more. The dash had placed Cushing between two paths—and with little cover except the river mud that covered him from head to toe. "Soon a party of four men came down the path at my right, two of them being officers, and passed so close to me as almost to tread upon my arm."

To Cushing's great relief, they moved on. He resumed his journey to the swamp, crawling "inch by inch, toward it." Once there and out of sight, he rose to his feet and struggled ahead for about five hours before he came to solid ground. His path then took him alternately through thickets of thorns and briars "that cut into the flesh at every step like knives" or through mire so soft under his weight that he was forced to throw his body upon it at length, and haul himself along by the arms.

"Hands and feet raw from the ordeal" and thoroughly exhausted, Cushing found more trouble ahead—a party of Confederate soldiers busy sinking schooners in the river channel to block it. He circled behind them in a cornfield, then plunged into a woods, where he found an old black man and paid him $20 to go into town and find out what had happened to the Rebel ironclad the night before. While awaiting the report, Cushing was able to rest.

The old man returned with welcome news—the *Albemarle* had "gone down." Happy, Cushing resumed his escape journey. He was soon in more swamp with thick underbrush, thrashing around until he hit a road, a stream, and a Confederate picket party of seven soldiers. More important, he found their small, flat-bottomed skiff tied to the root of a cypress tree.

The pickets were eating, and as they did so, Cushing braved chill waters one more time to cast loose the skiff, push it along for thirty yards to the first bend in the stream, then squirm aboard. He then paddled away furiously—"as only a man could whose liberty was at stake."

Rowing unceasingly for hours, he finally reached the mouth of the Roanoke River, the sound beyond, and at last the first ships of his own Union fleet on blockade station. With a cry to the nearest vessel of "Ship ahoy," he fell, now totally exhausted, into the water in the bottom of the skiff. "I had paddled every minute for ten successive hours, and for four my body had been 'asleep' with the exception of my arms and brain."

The Union sailors of the picket ship *Valley City* pulled the remarkable Commander Cushing aboard, and soon "rockets were thrown up and all hands...called to cheer ship" at news of his safe return.

Faces in the Crowd

A SECRET AGENT SO SECRET NOT EVEN HIS OWN SIDE KNEW OF HIS EXISTENCE! THAT was smalltime publisher William A. Lloyd's precarious situation the moment that Abraham Lincoln was shot. Only the late president, it seems, had been aware that Lloyd did a bit more than simply publish railroad and steamship guides for Southern consumption. It was in that guise, though, that Lloyd had been allowed to reenter the break-away territory, live there, and travel widely while ostensibly gathering material for his guidebooks.

By prior, personal arrangement with Abe Lincoln, Lloyd was also gathering information on forts and troop dispositions, along with any other useful intelligence to be gleaned in his travels throughout the South. In short, he was spying.

The oddity was that he was spying for Lincoln, and Lincoln alone. He was, by contract signed with Lincoln, the president's own man in the Confederacy. He was paid two hundred dollars a month and expenses for his services.

The trouble was, only two of Lloyd's employees (and possibly his wife) knew of the arrangement. When Lloyd returned to Washington at war's end, after four years spent in the Confederacy, Secretary of War Edwin Stanton was willing to reimburse him for expenses ($2,380) but balked at paying the two hundred dollars a month retroactively. After Lloyd's own death just three years later, his estate sued the government for his back pay. Like Stanton, the U.S. Supreme Court raised a central question: Where's the contract signed with Lincoln? Unfortunately, at one time, faced with arrest in the South and the contract in his hat, Lloyd had destroyed it. Sorry, plaintiff denied.

★★★

Boston Corbett was a mystery man. A sergeant in the 16th New York Cavalry who survived five years as a prisoner at Andersonville, in April 1865 he joined in the pursuit of John Wilkes Booth and was present when the barn in which Booth was trapped was set on fire. When Booth was shot and wounded fatally, people asked who fired the shot. I did, Boston Corbett replied. God told me to.

Perhaps Booth shot himself, perhaps not, perhaps Corbett shot him—but some say Booth's pistol-ball wound could not have been caused by Corbett's carbine. In any case, Corbett accepted accolades (and reward money) from Secretary of War Stanton, then stumped the country as the "Avenger of Blood." With Corbett, it should be explained, anything was possible. Before the war, he castrated himself. Later, hired as a doorkeeper for the Kansas state legislature, he fired two pistols indoors one day in 1886. No one was killed, but he was sent to an insane asylum. Eventually he escaped and was never seen publicly again.

★★★

A mystery man of another sort was Confederate officer John D. Kennedy of South Carolina, who somehow survived being wounded six times and being struck by fifteen spent balls. An attorney in civilian life, he watched the shelling of Fort Sumter, then appeared at First Bull Run, Yorktown, Fair Oaks and Seven Days, Savage's Station, Antietam, Chancellorsville, Fredericksburg, Gettysburg, Knoxville, Petersburg, Shenandoah Valley, and even Bentonville at the war's eleventh hour. After all this action, he then returned to his lawyering but only lived to age fifty-six.

★★★

This captain of Confederate cavalry was probably unique. Not because the captain ran a hospital in Richmond and never rode a horse into combat, but because she was a woman—Captain Sally Tompkins. A single, still young and wealthy woman when the war began, she arranged to use a recently vacated home in Richmond as an emergency medical facility when the wounded from First Manassas began to flow back from the front lines. The city was overwhelmed, and Judge John Robertson was more than happy to lend his Richmond home at Third and Main Streets for use as a twenty-five-bed medical facility, since he and his family were moving to the country. In short order, and for some time after that battle, Sally Tompkins ran Robertson Hospital with a better survival record for its patients than most, if not all, other Confederate hospitals—thanks in large part to her obsession with cleanliness. When the government insisted a few months later upon closing all such private hospitals to centralize the management of scarce medical supplies (and keep track of the soldier-patients), she appealed to Jefferson Davis. Impressed, he appointed her a captain in the Confederate Army. "In that way, your hospital can be saved," he said. With her close companion and faithful worker, a slave woman named Phoebe, Sally Tompkins kept her hospital going until war's end. Her astounding record was only seventy-three deaths among her 1,333 patients.

★★★

Both grandsons of Revolutionary War icon Paul Revere, Joseph Warren Revere and Paul Joseph Revere carved out entirely contradictory careers as Civil War soldiers. Only one of them survived. Joseph, the older of the pair, had served in the U.S. Navy and in the Mexican Army prior to the Civil War. Twenty years younger, Paul was far less experienced in military matters. Both served in the Union Army, and both appeared at one or more of the war's major battles in the East—Joe at Chancellorsville, Paul at Ball's Bluff and Antietam, among others. Joseph, however, didn't fare so well as a temporary division commander at Chancellorsville. He was court-martialed for withdrawing his command without orders to do so. The sentence was outright dismissal from the Army, but President Lincoln allowed him to resign instead.

In the meantime, young Paul had been wounded and captured at Ball's Bluff. He was held as a hostage, guaranteeing the safety of Confederate privateers detained by Union authorities. Released at last, he was wounded again at

Antietam. Once more recovered from his wounds, he led the 20th Massachusetts at Gettysburg, where he was wounded again, this time fatally. Paul died two days after his wounding the second day of battle at Gettysburg. Joseph Revere lived until 1880, publishing a memoir of his career and traveling widely in the postwar period.

★★★

You don't hear much about Jay Cooke, a high school dropout, but where would the Union Army have found its funding without his success in selling government bond issues? Arriving in Washington as a financial adviser to Secretary of the Treasury Salmon P. Chase, Cooke wasted no time in obtaining loan guarantees from Northern banks. His Jay Cooke and Company, as the Federal government's exclusive agent, then sold more than $850 million in bonds during the early months of the war. "This money kept the army in the field," said Stewart Sifakis in his compendium *Who Was Who in the Civil War*. Some in Congress, Sifakis also said, gave vent to their uneasiness over allowing the Ohioan what amounted to a monopoly, but Cooke nevertheless proved himself a wizard with money and "has been credited with doing as much to win the war as the armies in the field." Toward war's end, he even advanced personal and company millions "to stabilize the market, which, due to the actions of speculators, was facing a panic." All this from a man who left school at the age of fourteen.

★★★

If Jefferson Davis, future president of the Confederacy, was one of Mississippi's two U.S. senators at the time of secession, who was the other, and what became of him? Meet, please, Albert Gallatin Brown, South Carolina–born antebellum attorney and militia general in Mississippi after moving there as a child. A successful—indeed, outstanding—politician, he served in the state legislature and in the U.S. House, and then became governor of Mississippi. Brown had been in the U.S. Senate for nearly ten years at the time he and Davis resigned their seats on January 12, 1861. Brown then went home, gathered together an infantry company, and, as a captain with the 18th Mississippi, saw action at First Bull Run and Ball's Bluff. He returned to the legislative forum as an appointed member of the Senate in the First Confederate Congress (February 1862). There, as chairman of the Naval Affairs Committee, he argued that the legislature should have greater control over the war effort, even at the expense of some civil liberties. If that were not enough to explain his split with fellow Mississippian Jefferson Davis, Brown also urged the emancipation and arming of the South's slaves, an expanded draft, and using the Confederacy's moneymaking cotton fields to produce vitally needed food crops. At war's end, he urged the South to "shake hands" with the North and adopt a cooperative attitude during Reconstruction. For this, he was branded a "submissionist."

★★★

He was black, a freed slave, and he sang a number of Scottish songs with an authentic Scottish "burr," thanks to his onetime master, a Virginian of Scottish descent. For a time John Scobell traveled with Union spymaster Allan Pinkerton's agent Hattie Lawson (white and female), as her servant. When she was arrested in Richmond in March 1862, her "manservant" Scobell was allowed to walk away—no interrogation, no suspicion attached. He spent the entire war as a spy for the Union, protected in large part by the fact he was a black man. Thus he worked at different places—as a laborer helping to build earthworks, even as a vendor visiting Southern encampments. Said Pinkerton one time: "He had only to assume the role of a light-hearted darky, and no one would suspect his real role." Helpful in Scobell's spying career, too, was the fact that his equally "invisible" wife stayed in Richmond, the Confederate capital, as a cook—presumably feeding valuable information, knowingly or unknowingly, to her spy husband. With the war's end, though, there were no medals, no hoopla—the pair simply disappeared from the pages of history.

Red Shirt, White Shirt

IN THE UNION CAMP HARD BY THE RAPPAHANNOCK RIVER, FEW OF THE MEN IN blue gave much thought to the new black man Dabney, hired to serve as cook and body servant. This was at "Fighting Joe" Hooker's headquarters in early 1863, after Fredericksburg and before Chancellorsville.

Few thought it odd when the free black from a farm across the river offered to share his knowledge of the local terrain. Nor did it seem unusual when he showed a lively interest in the Union Army's signals system and picked up on the various signals, remembering them quite easily.

One day his wife, having arrived in camp with him, announced that she would like to go back across the river because, it was explained, she had opportunity to work as a servant over there for a "secesh woman." Neither Hooker nor his staff made any real objection.

Life went on with Dabney home at Union headquarters and his wife gone across the river.

Perhaps her job wasn't quite what it first seemed, since it soon turned out that she was really a laundress at a Confederate Army headquarters. If such a situation really existed—a husband at one headquarters and his wife at the opposing army's headquarters—it does seem surprising to us today that the arrangement would have been allowed by either headquarters to continue, had either set of officers really known.

At Hooker's headquarters, people began to realize that Dabney knew amazing things about Confederate plans and movements, yet he never left the Union encampment. He was too busy as a cook and body servant. Hooker had his reliable scouts and other intelligence sources, but as time went on, few of them could match the stream of accurate information that Dabney seemed to pick up daily.

How did he do it? One day he agreed to explain the mystery to one of the Union officers. He took the officer to a nearby spot with a view across the river on the outskirts of Fredericksburg. He told his listener to take note of a cabin close to the river on the opposite side—to look at its clothesline.

Here's what he allegedly said: "Well, that clothesline tells me in a half an hour just what goes on at Lee's headquarters. You see my wife over there? She washes for the officers, cooks, and waits around, and as soon as she hears about any movement or anything going on she comes down and moves the clothes on that line so I can understand in a minute." In sum, Dabney's tutelage in Union signals had come home to roost. He and his wife had worked out a system of communication that wasn't exactly from the manual but, like a baseball manager's signals to his pitcher, worked very effectively.

"That there gray shirt," explained Dabney to his dumbfounded listener, "is Longstreet; and when she takes it off it means he's gone down about Richmond."

There were other shirts, too. "That white shirt means [A. P.] Hill; and when she moves it down to the west end of the line, Hill's corps has moved upstream. That red one is Stonewall Jackson. He's down on the right now, and if he moves, she'll move that red shirt."

Dabney was able to point out a clothesline signal being sent even as they gazed across the river. See the two blankets pinned together at the bottom? he asked his companion. "Why that's her way of making a fish trap; and when she pins the clothes together that way, it means that Lee is only trying to draw us into his fish-trap."

Who knows? Perhaps a "fish trap" was in Lee's mind not long after when he engaged Hooker at Chancellorsville on May 1 and sent "Red Shirt" Jackson on a fourteen-mile loop to strike Hooker's forces at their western flank. Except that in carrying out the maneuver, Stonewall Jackson was mortally wounded by his own men. He died shortly afterward, and A. P. Hill (Dabney's "White Shirt") was one of the last names he mentioned.

More Than a Few Ghosts

YOU MAY BELIEVE THEM OR NOT, BUT QUITE A FEW GHOSTLY STORIES CAME OUT OF the Civil War era…such as the repeated sightings over the years of a phantom train plying the rails of upstate New York, its headlight stabbing through the night. Abe Lincoln's funeral train, it is alleged.

Or Lincoln's very own story—a lengthy, detailed statement—that he dreamed of a person lying dead in a casket, surrounded by mourners, in the East Room of the White House. In his dream, Lincoln approached a soldier guarding the catafalque bearing the body that was lying in state. The dead man's face was covered up.

"Who is dead in the White House?" Lincoln demanded to know in his dream. "The president," came the horrifying reply. "He was killed by an assassin."

A haunting dream indeed! "I slept no more that night," said Lincoln later, "and although it was only a dream, I have been strangely annoyed by it ever since." It was shortly afterward that Lincoln was killed by assassin John Wilkes Booth and himself lay in state in the same East Room of the White House.

It would have been quite natural for Lincoln, a constant target of hate mail, vilification, and death threats, to fear assassination on some inner level. Outwardly, he usually appeared calm and unafraid, but he would have been less than human not to have had worries, and they easily could have manifested themselves in a nightmarish dream. Mary Todd Lincoln, however, saw it differently. Hysterical in the aftermath of his fatal shooting, she quickly claimed, "His dream was prophetic."

For that matter, another somber moment in the Lincoln White House came with the death of their young son Willie in the winter of 1862 from a severe fever. The boy's mother went to bed and screamed until exhaustion overtook her and she fell asleep. Lincoln, in the meantime, went to his secretary John Nicolay's office, the "Lincoln Sitting Room" of today, and sobbed and wept.

During the funeral five days later, it is said, a fierce wind springing up under black skies rolled up tin roofs all over Washington, toppled chimneys, and upset church steeples.

A half century later, President William Howard Taft was quite annoyed one day when told that a kitchen worker was quitting and other servants might do the same because of a White House ghost. Maids and housemen, it was alleged, had been frightened by sightings of a gossamer figure, even the cold touch of an invisible hand. Nonsense! exploded Taft. But...he did ask whose ghost it was and was told it was the pathetic Willie Lincoln, who had died in the second-floor Prince of Wales Room—the same chamber where his slain father's body would be embalmed three years later.

Taft still didn't think much of such mewlings: He told his staff never to discuss such happenings again.

Even so, ghost stories persisted at the White House, and many other odd and ghostly tales related to the Civil War have also emerged from widely scattered sites over the years.

At Virginia Military Institute, for instance, home of the young cadets who fought the Battle of New Market against heavy odds, they say that Civil War sculptor Sir Moses Ezekiel's statue of Virginia Mourning Her Dead has been known to moan in grief on some evenings, even to show tears on her finely chiseled face.

Not far away from VMI's home in Lexington, Virginia, stands a twenty-room mansion with thirteen fireplaces (one with no accompanying chimney) called "Selma." The story is that a young Confederate soldier was chased into the Shenandoah Valley home one day by a Union cavalryman and killed in front of its fireplace in the dining room. A bloodstain remained there for years.

So, it seems, did his ghost. Visitors often asked the owners of the house about the mysterious stranger they had encountered, while servants repeatedly told of a "soldier gentleman" they had seen. According to L. B. Taylor Jr., author of a series of books about Virginia ghosts, no one other than the immediate family was in the house at those odd moments. "Although ownership of the mansion passed through several hands over the years, the apparitional soldier stayed on." Also according to Taylor, Phyllis Atwater of Charlottesville, Virginia, who said she was "very sensitive" to psychic phenomena, conducted a "release ceremony" at Selma in which she counseled the soldierly ghost to leave the house and find his final peace. He did.

Another site of "haunted" visitation, writes Taylor, is the Lee family's ancestral home of Stratford Hall in Westmoreland County, east of Fredericksburg, Virginia. This was the magnificent home built by L. Thomas Lee in the 1730s, later to be home to "Lighthorse Harry" Lee, father of Robert E. Lee, and, briefly, for young Robert, too. The ghosts allegedly seen in and about Stratford Hall and its various outbuildings are associated with earlier family members rather than Civil War figures, but there also have been reports of a ghostly boy and dog seen at the brick home in Alexandria, Virginia, where Robert spent most of his boyhood.

More grim are the visions at sites associated with Mary Surratt, the boarding-house owner convicted of taking part in the assassination plot against Abraham Lincoln and hanged in the yard at Washington Arsenal Prison (the first woman ever executed for murder in the United States, noted writer Taylor). The old prison site is now Fort Leslie J. McNair, and here a ghostly middle-aged woman dressed in black has been seen "floating through the hallways," by one officer's account. Here, too, are heard strange voices, and touchings by unseen hands are alleged. Similar sightings were reported years earlier at the H Street site in Washington where Mary Surratt once operated her boarding house.

Do people respond to such stories of the macabre? Indeed. So many people wanted to see the reappearing bloodstains on the farm porch near Port Royal, Virginia, where the fatally wounded John Wilkes Booth died, that the owners "finally had to remove the boards and refloor the porch," reported Taylor.

Likewise, when Mary Surratt's specter was reported at the H Street house in Washington, "crowds gathered outside the house daily." Her daughter sold the house, "but the purchaser was driven away within six weeks because 'his nervous system was reputedly shattered by what he had seen and heard.'" The Boston Post followed the story and said other proprietors came and went in "swift succession, swearing that in the dead of night Mrs. Surratt walked the hallways clad in her robe of death." Then, too, Mrs. Lincoln once said that her two dead sons, Willie and Eddie, appeared at the foot of her bed every night! Yours to believe—or not.

"Shot for You"

TRULY NOW, HOW BAD WAS IT? SURELY WARFARE IN THAT DISTANT DAY AND AGE was archaic, mere child's play by today's grim standards. So, truly, what was it like? When those old-timers fired a gun or a cannon, a fellow could duck, right?

Well, on occasion, perhaps a fellow could see it coming. James Longstreet, Confederate general of considerable note, once recalled the time at Antietam Creek—Sharpsburg, Maryland—when he, Robert E. Lee, and fellow general D. H. Hill started up a ridge to reconnoiter and Hill insisted on staying on his horse while the other two more wisely dismounted.

Perhaps jokingly—but prophetically, as it turned out—Longstreet warned Hill he would draw Union fire and added, "Give us a little interval so that we may not be in the line of fire when they open up on you."

Minutes later, at the top of the crest with his companions, Longstreet saw a particular puff of smoke from the cannons on the Federal left. The gunner had to be a mile distant, but Longstreet told Hill, still on his horse, "There is a shot for you."

Sure enough, seconds later, the cannon shot "came whisking through the air" toward the very spot where the three men waited. It sheared off the front legs of General Hill's horse…without harming the rider.

It was rare, however, that a battlefield victim "saw it coming" or could duck away. In the same battle on the same day, in a suicidal charge like Pickett's at Gettysburg, an overwhelming wedge of bluecoats advanced on the center of Lee's line—advanced, more specifically, on Confederate General John Gordon of Georgia and his men, with bayonets at the ready. "As I saw this solid mass of men moving upon me with determined step and front of steel," said Gordon later, "every conceivable plan of meeting and repelling was rapidly considered. To oppose man against man and strength against strength was impossible, for there were four lines of blue to my one of gray."

Gordon's first thought was to open fire the moment the Union men came into range, but he just as quickly realized that would not be enough. "I could not hope to kill and disable a sufficient number of the enemy to reduce his strength to an equality of mine."

At the same time, he knew from all visible signs that his Union counterpart ("superbly mounted") would have ordered the bluecoats to advance with unloaded guns, a familiar battlefield tactic intended to keep a few men from stopping to aim and fire. A scattered few doing so in the front ranks obviously would stop others behind and disturb the solid wall of men assembled to advance en masse. As Gordon could see, it was the Union's intent "to break through Lee's center by the crushing weight and momentum of his solid column."

The only thought that appealed to Gordon in the few minutes he had to form a battle plan—and stop the Union tide—was one he had never tried but could trust to have terrible effect. "It was to hold my fire until the advancing Federals were almost upon my lines, and then turn loose a sheet of flame and lead into their faces. I did not believe that any troops on earth, with empty guns in their hands, could withstand so sudden a shock and withering a fire."

And so it was. With difficulty to be sure, Gordon restrained his own men from firing, even when they could see the eagles on the buttons of the blue uniforms, until finally "it would not do to wait another second," and Gordon shouted with all conceivable lung power, "Fire!"

At that, "My rifles flamed and roared in the Federals' faces like a blinding blaze of lightning accompanied by the quick and deadly thunderbolt."

No Union man in that front line could have ducked, surely. None who survived would ever say, if alive today, that the firepower of the 1860s was any less frightening than that of today.

"The entire front line," related Gordon in his later account, "with few exceptions, went down in the consuming blast." Gordon, himself, considered the effect of his tactic "appalling."

The Union commander, he noted, went down, too, but the victim in this case was only the horse, "the rider unhurt."

The sudden and massive volley saved Lee's center for the moment; the blue ranks had to fall back as the Rebels continued to fire into the Union mass. But the unhorsed Union commander was not yet through for the day. "Beyond the range of my rifles he reformed his men into three lines, and on foot led them to the second charge, still with unloaded guns."

But again they were repulsed. After that, yet again, four successive charges in all, "in the fruitless effort to break through my lines with the bayonet."

At last the Union men loaded their own weapons, drew up in close ranks and within easy range opened a "galling" fire of their own. From that point the battle between "these hostile American lines" waxed "furious and deadly" for some time after. "The list of the slain was lengthened with each passing moment."

Indeed, Antietam went down in history as the bloodiest single day of the Civil War, with nearly twenty-six thousand men on both sides counted as casualties. The five thousand or so killed outright obviously didn't, and couldn't, duck the fire.

No Whizz, Bang Heard

FAR FROM "DUCKING" THE SHOT AND SHELL OF THE CIVIL WAR, THE WAR'S fighting men often couldn't get away from all the shooting, of all shapes and sizes. One who could later tell you was Prussian-born Heros von Borcke, a staff aide to Confederate cavalry General "Jeb" Stuart. He was placed in a doctor's home in Sharpsburg, Maryland (Battle of Antietam Creek), the morning of September 16, 1862, with about ten couriers while Stuart rode on a reconnaissance mission up the nearby Potomac River. Von Borcke's job was to look over the incoming reports and "forward any important information" to Generals Lee, Longstreet, or "Stonewall" Jackson, who was just then approaching from freshly seized Harpers Ferry.

The Union artillery began to find the range about eleven o'clock in the morning, with a nearby church steeple an obvious reference point. Outside the doctor's house, the streets of the small village had been full of wagon trains, artillery, ambulances, and galloping riders, but now no one indoors or out could be considered safe. Indeed, as von Borcke sat there, a shell "fell with a terrific crash through the top of the building."

About noon, the shelling "became really appalling, and the explosion of innumerable projectiles stunned the ear."

Von Borcke remained on a sofa on the first floor to be available as Stuart's headquarters contact. He was sitting there, writing in his journal, "when a shell, piercing the wall of the room a few feet above my head, covered me with debris, and, exploding, scattered furniture in every direction." Simultaneously, "another missile, entering the upper part of the house and passing directly through, burst in the courtyard, killing one of our horses and rendering the others frantic with terror."

Von Borcke and his couriers hurriedly left the house at last, but the Prussian had a difficult time calming his horse long enough to climb into the saddle for a fast retreat. The streets were now filled with dead and wounded men, overturned wagons and ambulances, and in the village "cannonballs whizzed incessantly through the air, and pieces of bursting shells, splinters of wood, and scattered fragments of brick were whirled about in a dense cloud of powder smoke that enveloped all things."

Von Borcke escaped personal harm after leaving the village in "an exciting ride," but his horse was pinked on a hind leg by a shell fragment.

Others engaged in the Battles of Antietam and its preliminary at South Mountain often never knew what hit them. Death, maiming, or recoverable injury struck with no warning whatsoever.

George Smith, a minister from Georgia, was at South Mountain with the Phillips Legion, a regiment commanded by Colonel William Phillips. Smith and his fellows soon encountered the bluecoats while charging into the woods.

"I saw a poor fellow fall and heard him say, 'Lord Jesus, receive my spirit.' I went to him and said, 'My friend, that's a good prayer; I hope you feel it.' He answered, 'Stranger, I am not afraid to die; I made my peace with God over thirty years ago.'"

If Smith found that response surprising, he didn't have long to ponder it. The bluecoats suddenly appeared on all sides of the Georgians, who were forced into retreat. "Just then I felt a strange dizziness, and fell, my arm dropping lifeless by my side." Worse, "blood was gurgling from my throat."

Smith thought he was mortally wounded—and was close to correct, since the ball had "entered my neck, and, ranging downward, came out near my spine, paralyzing my arm." The men with Smith were not overly encouraging. "'Yes, parson,' they said, 'it's all up with you.'" Obviously, they were incorrect, and he lived to tell the tale.

Likewise, Union Sergeant A. F. Hill witnessed—and soon enough felt—the random danger of the battlefield. Marching with George Meade's division, Hill and his men came under Rebel artillery fire. At the command to lie down, Hill instead took a seat on a stump. Just then "a large ragged fragment of a shell whizzed savagely past the top of my head and struck the ground a few paces in [the] rear with a fierce splat. It must have struck my head had I been a moment later in sitting down."

Moments later, another shell—"Whizz, bang!"—burst ten or fifteen feet above Hill and his comrades, but with no apparent ill effect. The next day, though, Hill ran into more Rebel fire—this time, "a regiment of rebels who had lain concealed among the tall corn arose and poured on us the most withering volley we had ever felt." And then another and another. "The slaughter was fearful. I never saw men fall so fast. I was obliged to step over them at every step."

Minutes later, Hill saw a pair of Rebels helping a wounded comrade from the field, their backs turned to him. "I was going to fire, but…I could not. I sought another mark; and seeing a rebel in the act of loading his gun just at the edge of the cornfield, I fired at him."

There was no mention of the outcome, but the battle continued to rage in any case. Minutes later, Sergeant Hill had organized his men, and all opened fire at a line of Confederates. Hill tried to bring down the enemy's color-bearer. "I aimed every shot at the point over which the flag waved. At every fire I looked eagerly to see it fall."

Someone was apparently looking at Hill. "I had fired a dozen rounds at the rebel flag when I suddenly became conscious of a most singular and unpleasant feeling in my left leg. I was in the act of ramming down a ball at the time, and I would have finished, but my left foot, of its own accord, raised from the ground, a benumbing sensation ran through my leg, and I felt the hot blood streaming down my thigh. The truth flashed upon me—I was wounded."

That's often how it happened—out of the blue; not even a whizz, bang. And that was the end of the war for Hill, who was carried from the front by his comrades, then trundled over a rough cornfield in a wagon. Soon he was told the bad news. The bone in his upper thigh was "all smashed," and the leg would have to come off. He protested, but the doctors were firm.

He had been left with other wounded men outside a small schoolhouse serving as a field hospital. "It was evening when my turn came. I had lain during the whole afternoon…listening to the horrible screams which came from within and occasionally, to kill time, gazing upon a heap of men's arms and legs which lay piled up against the side of the house. The sound of battle could still be heard."

Then he was carried inside, and again he asked if his leg absolutely had to be taken off. The doctor "coolly thrust his finger into the wound and felt the pieces of shattered bone. 'That bone,' said he, 'is shivered all to pieces, and if you value your life—'

"'Can my life be saved only by—?'

"'Yes, and even then I doubt—I—' He hesitated.

"'You think it a doubtful case, even then?'

"'Yes.'

"I said no more. Chloroform was administered. I sank into unconsciousness, and when I awoke—it was all over." So it was over—except that Hill was another one who survived to tell the tale, in a book published nearly thirty years later. He had been fortunate after all.

Women of the Times

HERE ARE STORIES OF A FEW WOMEN OF THE TIMES.

Not all were like Bridget Fury, born in Cincinnati under the name Delia Swift, but long since removed to New Orleans as a prostitute, pickpocket, mugger, and murderess. She moved on to become a madam after being freed from prison by the Federal authorities occupying the city in 1862. Born in 1837, she would have been in her late twenties during most of the Civil War. She had her own street gang at one time. After her release from prison under a general Union pardon, she again had to serve behind prison walls, this time for robbery. It is believed she died at age thirty-five or thirty-six, unsung by decent folk but thoroughly notorious in the South for her life of crime.

★★★

Rose O'Neal Greenhow reveled in rubbing elbows with antebellum Washington society, meeting high and mighty figures such as President James Buchanan and South Carolina's famous John C. Calhoun. She would be a remarkable heroine of the war, too—as a spy for the Confederate cause. It was her information, quite likely, that alerted Southern forces to the approach of Union General Irvin McDowell at the time of First Bull Run in 1861, a significant Confederate victory.

Rose Greenhow did not travel among the high and mighty of wartime Washington for very long. Once her spying activities came to light, she first was placed under house arrest, then was held in the Old Capitol Prison. Amazingly, she still sent out her information, and at last she was forced to leave town— deported South. Then, leaving her safe place among her compatriots of the Confederacy, the Maryland-born widow traveled to England and France in 1863 to win friends and influence Europeans on behalf of the South. She also published an account of her detention in Washington under the Lincoln administration called *My Imprisonment and the First Year of Abolition Rule at Washington.*

In 1864 she returned to her native land and met a tragic end off the coast of North Carolina. Her small boat was swamped as she tried to reach the shore during a storm that roiled the waters. Weighted down by a money belt filled with gold for her beloved Confederacy, she was drowned on the spot.

★★★

Private Franklin Thompson of Company F, 2nd Michigan Infantry, born in Canada in 1841, would go down in history as the only female member of the postwar Union veterans' organization, the Grand Army of the Republic. Startling, yes, but fitting, since Private "Franklin" was really a young woman in soldier's uniform whose real name was Sarah Emma Edmonds. It seems she had worked on her father's farm in boy's clothes as a child, had run off from an "arranged" marriage, had sold Bibles in the United States under the name Franklin Thompson, and subsequently joined the Union army, at first serving as a field nurse.

She then operated as a spy, passing through enemy lines in Virginia in both male and female guises, as both black and white. When she eventually contracted malaria, she deserted for fear of being exposed as a woman while ill. As a woman once more, she became a civilian nurse for a religious organization. After the war, she married—and shocked her old comrades of the 2nd Michigan by appearing at a reunion as herself, a woman. She joined the Grand Army and also successfully petitioned Congress to forgive her desertion by official action. Most amazing of all, perhaps, she now reported that at the Battle of Antietam she had buried a Union soldier who was a woman! Incidentally, in 1934 another woman's remains were found in a common grave for nine soldiers killed at Shiloh, all Union.

★★★

Louisa May Alcott, yet to write *Little Women*, spent time during the Civil War working as a nurse at a Georgetown hospital—the basis for her *Hospital Sketches* of 1863. Her first novel, *Moods*, would appear the next year, with her best-known work, *Little Women*, emerging soon after the war in 1868.

★★★

The idea of Margaret Anna Parker Knobeloch won informal approval from the Union's secretary of war, Edwin Stanton, usually an implacable enemy of anything Confederate. Please, proposed this Northern-born, Southern-raised woman, allow her to provide aid for Confederate prisoners held near her home in Philadelphia, the money to be provided by Southerners then living in Europe. Married to a German, John Knobeloch, who had returned home to avoid the Northern draft, Margaret could make the necessary funding arrangements through their European contacts. Stanton allowed her work to go forward in exactly that manner from 1862 through the end of the war. Margaret did her Good Samaritan work among the prisoners held at hospitals in Philadelphia, where she had been born, and at Fort Delaware nearby.

★★★

This next woman's dream began during the Civil War but would not reach fruition until a tragic anticlimax, the assassination of Abraham Lincoln. As an apprentice to the famous sculptor Clark Mills, Vinnie Ream, not yet twenty, was determined some day to render Lincoln in stone. He agreed to sit for the young woman in late 1864. After he was killed a few months later on April 14, 1865, Vinnie Ream was among the artists who competed for the honor of producing a congressionally commissioned life-size, full-length statue of the martyred president. As the first woman ever given a congressional sculpting commission, she won the ten-thousand-dollar contract. Her work, completed in 1870, went into the Statuary Hall at the U.S. Capitol, where it still may be seen today.

★★★

Harriet Tubman's name before she escaped slavery in 1849 was Araminta. Once safe in the North, she could have stayed inactive. But even before the Civil War began, she repeatedly risked recapture to travel south and help guide other runaway slaves to freedom—possibly as many as three hundred, among them her own parents. When war erupted, she again could have remained inactive, her self-appointed duty largely done. But again risking her freedom, and even her life, she joined Union forces on the South Carolina coast as a cook, nurse, and laundress—and perhaps as a spy, too. She was well able, because of her black skin and knowledge of slave life, to operate behind the Confederate lines unsuspected of what she really was—an enemy of all that smacked of slavery.

★★★

A female doctor of the nineteenth century, a suffragette, a divorcée, and a winner of the Medal of Honor, Mary Edwards Walker was thirty years old when the Civil War began. How could all that be? It seems that she graduated from a New York medical school in 1855, but soon found it difficult to build a practice as a recently divorced woman. Along came the Civil War and a post at the Patent Office Hospital in Washington as an army surgeon. But that was not enough for this young woman. She soon had arranged for a field post as an assistant surgeon in an Ohio regiment, the 52nd. She was captured while tending to civilians outside her unit's encampment and was held prisoner in Richmond for four months. Exchanged, she returned to her Army duties, but no longer operated "in the field."

A few months after the war's end, she was awarded the Medal of Honor for her wartime performance, and she became an active suffragette and reformer, traveling and lecturing, often in male clothing. She didn't get along with her fellow reformers; she was later fired from a government job for insubordination and wound up making appearances in carnival sideshows. In 1917 Mary Edwards was told to return her Medal of Honor, in accord with new government policy stating that it could only be given for bravery in combat, rather than for meritorious service. She ignored the request, and when she died at eighty-seven, she still had her medal.

Woman at the Lead

WHEN ALL IS SAID AND DONE IN RESPECT TO THE BATTLE OF BRANDY STATION, Virginia (often noted as the largest cavalry engagement in American history), one more thing might be said of the hulking German horseman who fought on one side and of the dashing Frenchman who rode for the opposite side.

Both officers had earned their epaulets in the armies of Europe. They were among the thousands of foreign-born immigrants (or passing visitors) who took sides for either the Union or the Confederacy. At the time they were among the handful of "furriners" who rose to high rank, created legends, or both.

For instance, the Confederacy's brave and esteemed General Patrick Cleburne was a product of County Cork, Ireland. Here was an immigrant who arrived on these shores as a young man and became one of the South's most astute and beloved generals before he fell in battle at Franklin, Tennessee.

At Brandy Station, much earlier, the German fighting for the Confederates was Major Johann August Heinrich Heros von Borcke, a staff officer and aide to "Jeb" Stuart of cavalry fame. Easily noticed, Borcke was once described by a Northern journalist as a "giant, mounted on a tremendous horse, and brandishing wildly over his head a sword as long and big as a fence rail."

The dashing Frenchman riding opposite the Prussian-born giant at Brandy Station was named Alfred Napoleon Alexander Duffié. A graduate of the St. Cyr military academy and a veteran of the Crimean War, "Nattie," as friends and comrades called him, was at Brandy Station in command of a Union division.

Among others, Prussian-born Carl Schurz was an immigrant and a Lincoln political disciple appointed general. He was a division commander at both Second Bull Run in 1862 and at Gettysburg. He was in the lines opposite the Irish-born Cleburne at Chattanooga as well.

Another German-born general with political clout was the less fortunate Franz Sigel, who sported an impressive array of battle stars, only to ruin it all by emerging the loser in the Battle of New Market despite the superior force he had wheeled up against the Rebels and their VMI cadets.

Hungarian-born Julius Stahel began his adult life by rising from private to lieutenant in the Austrian army. He turned European revolutionary, then fled to America as a journalist and educator. Here he became, in time, a Union general, a veteran of both Bull Run battles, and winner of the Medal of Honor.

Perhaps the most romantic of all the immigrant figures who appeared in the ranks of Civil War soldiers, however, was a Russian named Turchin. This, however, was not the *Ivan* Turchininoff who graduated from the Imperial Military School of St. Petersburg and served on the staff of future Czar Alexander II before renaming himself John Basil Turchin and emigrating to America to become the Union colonel notorious for allowing—indeed, encouraging—his men to sack and pillage Athens, Alabama.

Not John Turchin, but rather his Russian-born wife. Mrs. Turchininoff— Turchin, that is—allegedly took command of her husband's regiment for several days while he was ill, and may have led that same regiment in battle (minor though it was) one day in Tennessee. She is also credited with rushing to Washington, gaining entrance to the White House, and persuading Abe Lincoln to void the court-martial verdict against her husband for the rape of Athens—and even to promote him to brigadier general.

Road to Gettysburg

SEEN AND HEARD ON THE ROAD TO GETTYSBURG—AT THE POTOMAC RIVER on June 23, 1863, Colonel Abner Perrin of the 14th South Carolina Infantry Regiment: "I do not suppose that any army ever marched into an enemies' [sic] country with greater confidence in its ability…and with more reasonable grounds for that confidence." Likewise, British Lieutenant Colonel Arthur Freemantle, a friendly, self-appointed observer traveling with Robert E. Lee's northbound columns, was moved to call the troops marching before him "a remarkably fine body of men…[who] looked quite seasoned and ready for any work."

The next day, on the Maryland side of the Potomac, a famous Confederate threesome gathered at Robert E. Lee's tent for a conference: Lee himself and A. P. Hill and James Longstreet, his two corps commanders. In came a young- ster named Leighton Parks, an acquaintance from Lee's invasion of Maryland the previous year. The small boy appeared this time with a bucket of raspberries for Lee, who picked him up, kissed him, and invited him to stay for lunch. The child then took turns on the great commander's knee, on Longstreet's knee, and on a horse ordered forward by A. P. Hill.

Soon after, Lee's march northward resumed.

Seen and heard on the road to Gettysburg as the Maryland countryside fell behind—British observer Freemantle on the Pennsylvania Dutch: "They are the most unpatriotic people I ever saw, and openly state that they don't care which side wins, provided they are left alone. They abuse Lincoln tremendously."

Confederate division commander Dorsey Pender, in a letter to his wife on June 28: "I never saw troops march as ours do; they will go 15 or 20 miles a day without leaving a straggler and hoop and yell on all occasions."

Also seen and heard—*Cincinnati Gazette* reporter Whitelaw Reid wrote that the Union Army "had done surprisingly little damage to property along their route." Breaking off the fruit-laden boughs of cherry trees was the army's worst offense. But Yankee stragglers and drunks were another matter altogether. Approaching Gettysburg on July 1, the first day of the watershed battle, Reid found "drunken loafers in uniform" in every farmhouse. "They swarmed about the stables, stealing horses at every opportunity and compelling farmers to keep up a constant watch." Further, "In the fence corners groups of them lay, too drunk to get on at all."

Back with the invading Confederate force, British observer Freemantle, on the other hand, was impressed by the lack of Rebel stragglers and the order from on high forbidding indiscriminate foraging in the enemy country. Even so, "in such a large army as this there must be many instances of bad characters, who are always ready to plunder and pillage whenever they can do so without being caught." Stragglers left behind no doubt would do their harm, thought Freemantle. "It is impossible to prevent this," he later wrote, "but every thing that can be done is done to protect private property and non–combatants, and I can say, from my own observation, with wonderful success."

At Chambersburg, Pennsylvania, he also noted, some Texans were ordered to break up a few barrels of whiskey "liberated" in or near the town. The order was a "pretty good trial for their discipline…[but] they did their duty like good soldiers."

Freemantle, like Pender, was impressed by the good marching order of the Rebel soldiery. As the Confederates closest to the Brit drew near Gettysburg on July 1, they heard firing ahead and began to see the wounded carried back from up front, stripped "nearly naked" and displaying "very bad wounds." Even so, the men moving forward did not flinch.

"This spectacle, so revolting to a person unaccustomed to such sights, produced no impression whatever upon the advancing troops, who certainly go under fire with the most perfect nonchalance," wrote Freemantle. "They show no enthusiasm or excitement, but the most complete indifference. This is the effect of two years' almost uninterrupted fighting."

Also on July 1, Northern reporter Reid reached the village of Taneytown, Maryland, just eighteen miles from Gettysburg. Here, he was clear at last of the stragglers and drunks seen earlier. Here, all was abustle. "Army trains blocked up the streets; a group of quartermasters and commissaries were bustling about the principal corner; across on the hills and along the road to the left, far as the eye could reach, rose the glitter from the swaying points of bayonets as with steady tramp the columns of our Second and Third Corps were marching northward."

Robert E. Lee, meanwhile, had learned on June 29 of George Meade's ascension to command of the Union Army that was catching up to Lee's own Confederate force. The distinguished Rebel commander saw that events were leading him to a small town to the east, just above the Maryland-Pennsylvania line. "Tomorrow, gentlemen," he told a group of officers taking a walk with him, "we will not move to Harrisburg, as we expected, but will go over to Gettysburg and see what General Meade is after."

As for Meade's possible actions: "General Meade will commit no blunder in my front, and if I make one he will make haste to take advantage of it."

For that matter, how did either of the two commanders drawing close to Gettysburg strike the unacquainted observer? Freemantle first met Lee the morning of June 30 and was most impressed. "General Lee is almost without exception the handsomest man of his age I ever saw. He is 56 years old, tall, broad-shouldered, very well made, well set-up—a thorough soldier in appearance; and his manners are most courteous and full of dignity. He is a perfect gentleman in every respect."

The Southern commander didn't smoke, drink, chew tobacco, or swear. He usually wore a "high black hat," along with his lengthy gray uniform jacket, blue trousers, and Wellington boots. Neat in dress, "in the most arduous marches he always looks smart and clean."

Whitelaw Reid, meanwhile, found Union commander Meade early on July 1 at a headquarters half a mile east of Taneytown (named for U.S. Chief Justice Roger Brooke Taney, who wrote the majority opinion in the famous Dred Scott case). "In a plain little wall tent, just like the rest, pen in hand, seated on a campstool and bending over a map is the new 'General Commanding' of the Army of the Potomac," wrote Reid later. Meade, the correspondent also noted, was a slender, dark-haired, bearded man of middle age, neither handsome nor graceful, "who impresses you rather as a thoughtful student than a dashing soldier."

While Reid was at Meade's headquarters, another reporter, Lorenzo Crounze of the *New York Times*, galloped up with news of a fight developing to the west, near Gettysburg. "Mount and spur for Gettysburg is, of course, the word," wrote Reid later.

A little earlier Robert E. Lee had heard the distant thunder of artillery. His advance elements obviously had found the enemy, but how many—how serious was the meeting? Lee hurried to Cashtown, just west of Gettysburg, to confer with his Third Corps commander, A. P. Hill, who looked pale and ill. He didn't know much yet, and Lee rushed on blindly toward the sound of the guns, until he reached Dorsey Pender's division, three miles outside of Gettysburg. From there, with open country lying before him, he could see the action ahead through his binoculars. The battle had been joined.

Love Story

HARRY AND BOB WERE PALS IN COLLEGE, AND NOW EACH WAS A SOLDIER. AND Bess Marl was the love of Harry's life.

And also the love of Bob's life!

Bess lived on a farm outside Gettysburg, where the two young men went to school. Before the war, Bob used to pay calls on pretty young Bess, but he didn't always tell everybody back at the school. They might kid him too much.

Harry was smitten, too. He kept up with the young woman's family. He knew that her father and brothers had joined the Union Army once the war broke out. And so did he.

Bob also joined the army—the Confederate Army.

With the menfolk all scattered, Bess and her mother stayed at the farm outside Gettysburg.

In early July of 1863, the war suddenly turned and came right at them—like a tornado touching down, with their farm in its path. That July 1 a young Confederate officer on horseback emerged from a thicket outside Gettysburg, dismounted, and climbed to the top of a rise to scan the terrain ahead with his field glasses. It was Bob.

A low voice behind said: "Surrender or die!"

But there was laughter in his voice, according to the Gettysburg College *Mercury* of April 1899. It was a young Union officer speaking—Harry!

Startled, Bob at first had whirled and reached for his revolver, but then he saw who it was, and the two old pals from college days joyously embraced. "For a while the grim business on which they were engaged was forgotten, and they fairly overwhelmed each other with questions," recalled the *Mercury*.

Harry suddenly mentioned Bess. That was when Bob confessed he used to visit Bess quite frequently. Now Harry was startled.

"Don't you remember?" queried Bob.

"No, I don't," Harry replied stiffly.

"Well, perhaps I didn't tell you where I went. We used to keep such things quiet at college, but that is where I made the calls you and the other fellows used to jolly me so much about."

Bob had a question. "How is she?"

For two or more years, Bess and family had lived within Union perimeters, and Harry, of course, as a Union officer, was on that side of the Civil War's dividing line. Bob was not.

But now Bob was close to her home, a scout for Robert E. Lee's invading army. He was so close and he was burning to know about her.

Harry provided a reply—and a question of his own. "Her father and brothers are all enlisted in the Northern army, and she and her mother, as they remained on the place, are right in your line of attack. But Bob, how come you are so interested?"

The truth was out. Bob's face turned red, and Harry's then darkened with anger. Both Bob Lancy and Harry Sinclair loved Bess Marl.

They acknowledged the fact with some difficulty. After a while Harry urged Bob to shield her while the farm remained within Confederate lines, and Bob agreed that someday they would let Bess decide between them. "Then the two men pledged each other to shield and protect the girl for whom they would both have given their lives." They shook hands on it, with Bob warning they might not meet again. And so, good-bye.

It was late afternoon now. Two women stood on the plain below the onlooking sky, tiny figures in the scheme of the ages, hurriedly packing their goods into a wagon with the help of a servant. Bess and her mother were fleeing their home because it was in the line of battle, caught between forces and likely to be blown to pieces the next day.

Down the road they trundled until from the adjoining woods came a Reb horseman.

Horseman and wagon-riders drew closer to one another until at last there was full realization. Bob recognized them, and they Bob. "Why, Miss Bess," he said, "I am in luck."

After informing them the road ahead was clear, Bob acknowledged he must ride off to his duties of war. And yet—"Not before he had looked deep into Bess Marl's eyes," we are told. And hers did frankly meet his, we are informed as well, "then dropped as he inquired where he might see them [Bess and her mother], if he lived."

Lived? With that frightening statement, "Miss Marl had looked up quickly and then had bent to arrange something in the wagon and he saw her lips trembling; then with a lingering hand clasp he was gone."

Bob was gone, but not Harry. In the woods nearby he had been the silent spectator. He surely did not mean to spy. He himself had been "about to ride up to the wagon," the *Mercury* divined, but Bob had appeared too soon, too quickly.

Now, in what pain did Harry ride away?

We'll never know.

All we know is that during the grim battle the next day, Bob and Harry "clashed in hand to hand combat." Sabers "flashed." A stray shot coursed through the air. One of Bess Marl's two young men went down.

His old friend and college chum was by his side at the last. Tell her, said the stricken suitor, "Tell—Bess—I—knew she—loved you and so I didn't—"

Didn't what?—Approach at the same moment?

We'll never know what else he might have told his old college pal. Mumbling something also about his mother, he pointed to his coat pocket and said, "Give—Mother—"

And said no more. Harry. Oh, Harry!

Coincidences at Gettysburg

INCREDIBLE THINGS HAPPENED AT GETTYSBURG. IT WAS A DECISIVE CONFLICT, A great sprawling battle for more than 165,000 men and for hundreds of awed, terrified civilians. More artillery shells hurled from one side to the other than those sent arcing their deadly way through all of Napoleon's battles. A microcosm of the American Civil War, it was full of ironic encounters and downright oddities.

Here, at Gettysburg, for instance, Robert E. Lee's invading Army of Northern Virginia had achieved an initial victory in the first day of the three-day battle. Far to the west, Ulysses S. Grant was at the same time still drawing tight the noose he had placed around Vicksburg. At Gettysburg early the afternoon of that July 1, a wounded officer from Georgia lay near death in a Gettysburg home turned into a field hospital. Just before he died, he was heard to say: "There now, there now, Vicksburg has fallen, General Lee is retreating and the South is whipped."

So it was...three days later. Both the Gettysburg and Vicksburg battles were lost by July 4, and the decline of Confederate fortunes was now inevitable.

On the way to Gettysburg on June 30 a New York cavalryman named Abraham Folger had been captured by Lieutenant Colonel William H. Paine's 2nd North Carolina Cavalry. Passing a tannery while being escorted to the Confederate rear, Folger saw a discarded carbine lying on the ground. He seized it and immediately shot his captor's horse. The stricken animal inadvertently threw its rider, Colonel Paine, into one of the tanning vats.

Turning the carbine on the officer's orderly, Folger ordered him to help Paine out of the vat, then marched them both to his own lines, not far away. The Confederate officer had been completely submerged in the foul tanning liquid. "His gray uniform with its white velvet facing, his white gauntlet gloves, face and hair, had all become completely stained so that he presented a most laughable sight," wrote Folger later.

For Folger, in fact, there were double and triple laughs. The carbine that subdued both Rebel prisoners had held only one round—the one he used to kill the unfortunate horse. His two prisoners could have run or turned on him with impunity, if only they had known. More amazing, though, Folger had been captured once before during the Civil War—by the same Colonel Paine's 2nd North Carolina Cavalry. It had been the winter before, recalled Folger later, "and you can just believe that I was glad to return the compliment with interest."

Sometimes the events seemed like more than coincidences. On June 28, advancing elements of Lee's army stayed overnight in tiny Wrightsville, Pennsylvania, not far from Gettysburg. One house occupied so briefly by the Southerners belonged to Mr. and Mrs. Samuel Smith. Their son Silas, carrying a pocket Bible, had gone off to war with the Union Army months earlier. Wounded and captured, he died of his wounds in a Confederate hospital far from home.

When the Rebels left Wrightsville and the Smiths returned to their home on Locust Street, across from a church, their son's pocket Bible was lying on a table, his name and address still written on the flyleaf. Someone had left it, but who?

The Southern troops quartered in Wrightsville had been led, incidentally, by John B. Gordon of Georgia, destined himself for a thought-provoking coincidence in connection with Gettysburg. It came during the heat of battle on July 1 as Brigadier General Gordon, in command of a brigade under Jubal Early, fought Union troops for control of a hill north of Gettysburg. The Union troops were also led by a brigadier, Francis C. Barlow of New York. When Barlow fell gravely wounded, his men had to leave him behind as they retreated before the fired-up Rebels.

Gordon came along on his horse, saw his stricken counterpart, and dismounted to ask if he could do anything for him. Both men thought Barlow surely must die from his terrible wound, and Gordon made arrangements at Barlow's request for the latter's wife, a Union nurse, to pass through the lines to be by her husband's side in his final hours.

Gordon went on his way, assuming that Barlow would die. But he didn't. He survived to fight another day, to prosper later as an attorney and to rise to the post of attorney general of New York. In the meantime, he heard that a General Gordon had died in battle the year after Gettysburg.

But John Gordon had also survived the war, and he became governor of Georgia and a U.S. senator. Years later, at a political dinner in Washington, D.C., each was startled and gratified to meet the man each had thought dead all those years.

Nor were those two the only soldiers at Gettysburg destined for high achievement in later life or descended from historically significant luminaries. In the latter category were a great-grandson of Patrick Henry, the 53rd Virginia Infantry's Colonel W. R. Aylett (wounded); a grandson of former President John Tyler, the same 53rd Virginia's color-bearer, Robert Tyler Jones (badly wounded); Harriet Beecher Stowe's son Federick, a Union staff officer; African explorer-missionary Dr. David Livingstone's son Robert, a Union soldier (wounded, captured, died in prison camp).

As for those with future portent, Chaplain (Father) William Corby of the Irish Brigade (New York, Massachusetts, and Pennsylvania) would later be president of Notre Dame University; Captain Emil Frey of the 82nd Illinois Infantry, a Swiss-born immigrant, would later be president of Switzerland (even after his capture at Gettysburg and subsequent eighteen-month imprisonment at Libby Prison in Richmond). Lewis T. Powell, a private in the 2nd Florida Infantry, would later, under the name Lewis Paine, join John Wilkes Booth's conspiracy and hang for the assassination of Abraham Lincoln (at Gettysburg, Powell was wounded and captured; he soon would escape and change his name). Finally, there was one George Nixon, whose grandson would be father of future U.S. president Richard M. Nixon. Forebear George was a private with Ohio's 73rd Infantry. Fortunately for descendant Richard, George's nine children had already been born; they were left fatherless when the forty-three-year-old George was mortally wounded in the second day of battle at Gettysburg.

Many of the wounded, Union and Confederate, were taken to a field hospital a mile east of Gettysburg. There they began the road to recovery—or often death. It was at this giant hospital that Union soldier Frank Stokes one day saw two nurses and a "wardmaster" carrying a recumbent Confederate soldier on a stretcher to the "dead house" to await burial. "After they passed me a few steps, the supposed dead man partly raised himself up on the stretcher and asked what they intended to do with him." With a "hearty laugh," the hospital workers turned and carried their patient back to the wards.

In a similar incident, Private Luther White of the 20th Massachusetts was himself trundled to the very edge of an open grave. The men carrying him on an "army couch" dropped it with such a jolt, the supposedly deceased young man awoke, raised his head, and said, "Boys, what are you doing?" He, too, was spared a premature burial.

Also at Gettysburg was a badly wounded officer from Georgia who had been captured. He and his companions were to be escorted to prison camps in the North, but the Union surgeons said this man, Henry D. McDaniel, could not possibly survive the rigors of such a trip. His friends came to say good-bye, but McDaniel said he would not stay behind. Either put me on a litter and take me with you, or I'll start walking until I drop dead, he said.

The doctors then gave in, and the difficult march began. But the patient on the litter grew steadily weaker, so the group stopped at a small Pennsylvania town for a rest. The curious townspeople gathered to stare; McDaniel appeared all but gone. A friend, a Colonel Nesbit, drew close to see if he indeed might really be dead, but McDaniel's eyes suddenly flew open and he motioned Nesbit to come close. When Nesbit did, the wounded man grabbed his friend's coat and pulled him still closer to impart what might be his final words.

"Nesbit," he whispered. "Nesbit, old fellow. Did you ever see such an ungodly pair of ankles as that Dutch woman on that porch has got?"

Needless to say, McDaniel was not yet ready to die. In fact, he recovered, returned to the South, and some time later was reincarnated as the governor of Georgia.

Old White Oak

THE OLD WHITE OAK, WROTE GETTYSBURG HISTORIAN GREGORY A. COCO, STOOD solitary in its open field for probably 150 years. The field was part of the Bliss Farm at Gettysburg, once the home of Adelina and Williams Bliss.

No buildings from the Civil War era remain there today, thanks largely to one of the many thousands of incidents that comprised the three days of deadly battle at Gettysburg—July 1 through July 3 of 1863—between those two armies of 165,000 men in all.

With Confederate sharpshooters picking at his men from buildings on the Bliss farm, Union General Alexander Hays on the third day of battle finally decided he must order the barn and house of his Yankee countryman burned down, thus denying the Rebel marksmen their sanctuary. The man who volunteered to carry out the mission had to zigzag right up to the buildings where the enemy was sheltered and set them afire.

That volunteer was Sergeant Charles A. Hitchcock of the 111th New York Infantry, reported National Park Service Ranger Historian Coco in his book *On the Bloodstained Field II*. Even though Hitchcock suffered a serious wound in the arm in the process, he accomplished the task—house and barn soon were brightly ablaze.

The aforementioned white oak reared its lovely head in an empty field not far away. It, too, was a haven for Rebel sharpshooters harassing the Union lines. On the third day of battle, wrote Lieutenant Tom Galwey, 8th Ohio Infantry, he was again confounded by Rebel marksmen shooting at his company from beneath the solitary tree, not thirty yards in front of the Union men.

To the surprise of the Yankees at one point, however, came a pause as one of the Rebs hidden behind the old oak cried out, "Don't fire, Yanks!"

Not knowing what to expect, the Ohioans complied, curious to see what would happen next.

"A man with his gun slung across his shoulder came out from the tree," recalled Galwey. Some of the Union men, angry and grieving over comrades already struck down by the Confederate shooters, took quick aim at this bold enemy, "but the others checked them, to see what would follow."

The Yankees could see that their Reb enemy carried a canteen in his hand as he made his way halfway to the Union line. He stopped then, kneeled, and gently gave a wounded man a drink from the canteen—a wounded Yank!

"Of course, we cheered the Reb," wrote Galwey. Indeed, the Union men by now had risen to their feet, and the Rebs behind their Good Samaritan had stopped firing, too, and were standing in full view. Everybody was now an easy target for their opponents; it was a scenario that could not, and would not, last.

"As soon as the sharpshooter had finished his generous work, he turned and went back to the tree, and then at the top of his voice shouted, 'Down Yanks, we're going to fire.' And down we lay again."

Their battle at the foot of the old white oak resumed, and the next day, with Lee's army now in retreat, "a heap of Confederates was found under that tree," said Galwey. "Whether the hero of the day before was one of the ghastly dead will probably never be known."

Indeed, only the oak could ever have told, but the tree maintained its silent vigil for more than a century until on June 20, 1987, a severe windstorm blew it down.

Black Faces in the Crowd

ROBERT MORROW WENT TO WEST POINT—AS A BODY SERVANT TO CADET JAMES J. Pettigrew of North Carolina. Pettigrew went on to become a Confederate general and to suffer a mortal wound while leading a division in Pickett's Charge at Gettysburg. Morrow, on the other hand, sought refuge in Union-held New Bern, North Carolina, early in the war.

There he became a teacher in schools formed to educate the newly freed blacks in the state's federally held territory. He was a favorite of Horace James, a Northern minister and former Union Army chaplain appointed Superintendent of Negro Affairs in North Carolina. Morrow was a Union soldier himself, a sergeant in the newly formed 1st North Carolina Heavy Artillery, one of the all-black military units manned by escaped slaves—and freed blacks—who wanted to fight for the Union. He had been "for many years a body servant of the rebel General Pettigrew, whom he deserted for liberty and Union," wrote James in 1864. Morrow was "an enthusiastic and excellent teacher," added James.

Sadly, though, Morrow contracted yellow fever while recruiting additional black troops on Roanoke Island and died suddenly in his bed one night. "It matters little to him that he left the world without warning," wrote minister James also, "for he daily walked with God."

★★★

The obituaries of 1915 told this man's rare story—born a slave in South Carolina and later a member of Congress from South Carolina. In between, he organized a spectacular escape from slavery for himself and sixteen fellow blacks, with five women and three children among them.

Early in the Civil War, Robert Small was a pilot aboard the Confederate Army supply steamer Planter, often plying the waters of Charleston Harbor. On the night of May 13, 1862, the vessel's captain went ashore, and Small made his move—taking over the Planter and steaming, hell-bent, for the Union warships blockading the harbor. After saluting the Confederate forts on his way toward the open sea, Small delivered himself and his escaping party to the Federal naval authorities, who then benefited from his knowledge of the area's waters and the Charleston defenses. He spent the rest of the war as a Union pilot. During Reconstruction after the war, he served as a South Carolina lawmaker and member of the House of Representatives in Washington. In his early twenties at the time of his escape, he lived to the age of seventy-six before his death in 1915.

★★★

They came forth in droves to greet, to follow, to help, to entreat the Union conquerors. Especially the highly visible William Tecumseh Sherman in his march not only to the sea, but later northward from Savannah into North Carolina with the intention of meeting Grant's great army at the gates of Richmond.

The march had originally begun in Atlanta, as Sherman's subordinate Major General Henry W. Slocum later recalled: "We were dependent upon the country for our supplies of food and forage, and every one not connected with the army was a source of weakness to us." And so, "on several occasions... we had been compelled to drive thousands of colored people back, not from lack of sympathy with them, but simply as a matter of safety to the army. The refugee-train following in the rear of the army was one of the most singular features of the march."

Somehow, by underground communication all their own, slaves and former slaves, escapees, blacks of all stations in life—Southern life—for miles and miles in advance knew the Union column was on its way. "It was natural," wrote Slocum, "that these poor creatures, seeking a place of safety, should flee to the army, and endeavor to keep in sight of it. Every day, as we marched on we could see, on each side of our line of march, crowds of these people coming to us through roads and across the fields, bringing with them all their earthly goods, and many goods which were not theirs. Horses, mules, cows, dogs, old family carriages, carts, and whatever they thought might be of use to them were seized upon and brought to us."

Allowing the black refugees to follow behind the blue-clad line, the Union troops found "at times they were almost equal in numbers to the army they were following." And so, the two columns moved on—the soldiers in front, their liberated followers close behind. "Old stages, family carriages, carts and lumber wagons filled with bedding, cooking-utensils and 'traps' of all kinds, with men, women, and children loaded with bundles, made up the balance of the refugee-train which followed in our rear." And where they all wound up, only their scattered descendants of today may know.

★★★

Not so fortunate was a runaway slave named Jake from A. M. Reed's Mulberry Grove plantation below Jacksonville, Florida. When a group of Reed's slaves organized a mass escape in hopes of fleeing to nearby Union forces, one of them was shot in the legs and the exodus was halted in its tracks. Two of the men did manage to flee, however, and slaveowner Reed himself made note of the event in a diary: "About 12 p.m. found my negroes preparing to leave. In the melee, Jake and Dave escaped carrying off my boat, the *Laura Shaw*."

The two escapees reached friendly Northern shelter in the form of a gunboat, and two days later the Yankees steamed up to Reed's wharf with the runaway Jake, "to get his family and things," wrote Reed in an added diary entry. Unfortunately, after the mass escape attempt Reed had acted promptly and began moving his slaves into the "interior," far from Yankee gunboats and soldiers. Jake's wife, Etta, was among them.

A bitter Jake could only leave again with his newfound friends, going with them to federally held Jacksonville. When the Yankees temporarily pulled out of Jacksonville that fall of 1862, Jake was among the 276 blacks who went with them for protection. After a second occupation and evacuation by the Federals, Jacksonville again fell to the Union in March 1863—to the all-black First South Carolina Volunteers (many of its soldiers runaways from North Florida), without a shot being fired.

According to History Professor Daniel L. Schafer of the University of North Florida, most of the five hundred civilians living in Jacksonville at the time were whites "who regarded this third occupation by their former slaves to be the 'last crowning humiliation' in their wartime experience." As one result, even the "ladies of the town" insulted and cursed the black soldiers.

Among others, Jake was back, and he wasted no time in searching for planter-banker A. M. Reed, openly "threatening to take vengeance on him." According to Reed's daughter Hattie, Jake hoped "to meet Pa face to face to teach him what it is to part man and wife." Frightened now, Reed wouldn't stay alone at night at his plantation. Hattie reported, "We are moving away as many things as possible."

The "bold soldier boy," as she sneeringly called Jake, was known to have put a gun to the head of one man who had helped thwart the mass escape of Reed's slaves months earlier, said historian Schafer in the book *Civil War Times in St. Augustine.* Now, poor embittered Jake went too far: After threatening to burn down Reed's home, "he was arrested and confined for the duration of the Union occupation." As for his unfortunate wife, Etta had been sold to new owners "somewhere in Georgia."

Gettysburg Facts, Stats

WHERE MORE THAN THIRTEEN HUNDRED MEMORIALS AND COMMEMORATIVE markers now stand in one central area, the Union fielded 246 infantry regiments for the famous Battle of Gettysburg, along with thirty-eight cavalry regiments and sixty-eight artillery batteries. Drawn up in opposition on the Confederate side were 167 infantry regiments (plus two small batteries), twenty-eight cavalry regiments (and again a battalion), and sixty-seven artillery batteries.

The Union men came from units representing eighteen states, including Maryland, in addition to the ranks of the Nation's Regular Army. The Confederate units hailed from twelve states, again including Maryland, whose people were divided in their loyalties.

Accessible to visitors today is a federally owned and maintained national park of 3,874 acres, including the twenty-two-acre national cemetery that Abe Lincoln dedicated with a short speech only a few months after the battle took place. For it, of course, was here that he delivered the Gettysburg Address.

Also heavily trodden—and bloodied, too—during the three-day battle of July 1863 were twelve thousand adjoining acres. Next door to the military park and cemetery is the Eisenhower National Historic Site, the farm to which "Ike" (also of military and battle fame) retired after his twentieth-century presidency.

Thirty miles of paved roads wind through the park among the thirteen hundred–plus markers and memorials, past dozens of Civil War cannons and forty-five historic structures predating the battle. At one end, also maintained by the National Park Service as a "living history" project, is John Slyder's "Granite Farm" of Civil War vintage.

After Lincoln's dedicatory remarks in November of 1863, the new national cemetery was available for the reburial of Union men who had fallen in the battle itself. Nearly thirty-six hundred bodies from the battlefields were reinterred in sections set aside by states (with space for the Regular Army men and 979 "unknowns" as well). By far the most "populous" state section in the cemetery holding those early burials was New York's, with 867 bodies reburied. The smallest such grouping was that of Abe Lincoln's home state, Illinois, with only six bodies dug up and reinterred.

From its Confederate Avenue to the many Confederate monuments scattered about, the battlefield park also includes tributes to the Confederacy. "Alabamians!" says one of the Confederate memorials, "Your names are inscribed on fame's immortal scroll."

Union General Samuel W. Crawford, who had begun the war as an army surgeon posted at Fort Sumter, contributed to the great memorial park by purchasing the terrain where his men of the Pennsylvania Reserves had fought in defense of the Round Top. He held and preserved that ground until it could become a part of the magnificent park that developed adjacent to the original national cemetery.

It was a Pennsylvania outfit, incidentally, the 56th Infantry Regiment, that fired the first volley against Robert E. Lee's invaders from the South in the opening engagement of the battle, July 1, 1863. So extensive was the aftermath over the next three days that Union men later retrieved nearly twenty-five thousand firearms left on the battleground, plus more than ten thousand abandoned bayonets and 350 sabers.

Still another statistic explains why the nine-hundred-man 151st Pennsylvania Infantry was called the "Schoolteacher Regiment"—113 of those nine hundred had been schoolteachers before the onset of the war.

Pickett's ill-fated charge on the third day virtually ended the Battle of Gettysburg, with absolutely dismaying, sad loss of life and widespread bodily mayhem even among the living. One wounded general, Lewis Armistead, a brigade commander under Pickett, did not die of his injuries. His death was attributed to just plain exhaustion.

Lee Family Saga, Continued

LYING ABED FROM HIS BATTLE WOUNDS WAS WILLIAM HENRY FITZHUGH LEE, second son of Robert E. Lee. In two years of wartime service, "Rooney" Lee, a Harvard graduate in his mid-twenties, had accumulated an impressive list of battle stars. He had led the 9th Virginia Cavalry during "Jeb" Stuart's famous "ride around McClellan" on the Virginia Peninsula between the York and James Rivers. Rooney had served in the Seven Days battles of 1862 that were a part of the Peninsular campaign; he was at Second Bull Run, Antietam, and Fredericksburg, followed by Chancellorsville. Then, in June of 1863, he was wounded at the great cavalry battle known as Brandy Station and was forced out of action for a time.

One day not long afterward, Union gunboats stole up the Pamunkey River, an offshoot of the York near West Point, Virginia. Rooney Lee was convalescing at his wife Charlotte's family home—Hickory Hill in Hanover County. To the northwest, his famous father was on his way to destiny at a place called Gettysburg.

Disembarking at young Lee's own White House plantation on the Pamunkey River June 25 were one thousand Union cavalrymen who quickly mounted up and rode for the Virginia Central Railroad bridge across the South Anna River, thirty miles from White House. Their raid resulted in the destruction of the bridge and the capture of 360 horses and mules, plus one hundred Johnny Rebs, with only eight Union casualties: overall, it was a success. The real goal, though, turned out to be Rooney Lee, who was surprised and captured at Charlotte Wickham Lee's nearby Hickory Hill home.

Rooney was carried off on his mattress before the eyes of his remonstrating mother and his frail, pregnant wife. The Federal raiders also took his father-in-law's carriage and horses—used to convey the prized prisoner back to their own lines. He was taken to Fort Monroe, Virginia, a hostage held as counter to Confederate threats to execute two Union officers.

His capture was a blow to his arthritis-stricken mother and to his wife, Charlotte. It was decided that both women should seek the quiet solace of a spa in Hot Springs, Virginia. But with the elder Mrs. Lee confined to crutches and any travel subject to the vicissitudes of war, the journey to the western part of Virginia wouldn't be easy. The solution arrived at was a slow train, with the women traveling in a freight car outfitted like a bedroom. The train traveled so slowly the ladies could leave the big sliding door open and enjoy the scenery passing them by.

At Hot Springs, however, Charlotte's health didn't improve, and so they moved on to nearby Warm Springs. There, Mrs. Lee Sr. wrote, they settled into "a delightful cottage with a portico all around, covered with beautiful vines & roses & looking upon a meadow full of haycocks & a clear stream running thro it & very near the bath…mountains all around."

They had taken the cottage for a month, and soon Robert E. Lee's wife was happy to hear that her prisoner-son Rooney was on his feet and beginning to use crutches as he continued to recover from his wounds. She wrote his sister Mildred that she hoped his prospects for exchange could be considered real, since Charlotte's health was "very delicate."

By October 1863—long after General Lee's defeat at Gettysburg in July and with his son still held as a prisoner—the Lee ladies had returned to Richmond. There Mrs. Lee Sr. and her two daughters, Agnes and Mildred, moved into a small house on Leigh Street—too small, it is said, to accommodate Charlotte as well.

Rooney's wife found quarters some distance away, and General Lee soon wrote that he was "sorry" the Leigh Street abode wasn't large enough to include Charlotte. "It takes from me half the pleasure of your accommodation," he wrote to his wife, Mary Custis Lee, "as I wish to think of you all together; and in her feeble condition and separation from her Fitzhugh, none can sympathize or attend to her as yourself."

One comfort for the family during this period was the presence of eldest son George Washington Custis Lee, an 1854 West Point graduate serving as an aide-de-camp to Confederate President (and fellow West Pointer) Jefferson Davis. Like many other deskbound soldiers, however, Custis was unhappy at being kept away from the battlefield by his posting in the capital. Diarist Mary Chesnut wrote that he earlier "offered himself to the Yankees in place of his brother, as he was a single man with no wife and children to be hurt by his imprisonment or made miserable by his danger." The Yankees, though, "preferred Rooney."

Soon came the Christmas season, and Rooney was still in captivity. Some onlookers, such as diarist Mary Chesnut, complained that Charlotte had been foolish to take Rooney so close to Union lines for his recuperation rather than to the comparative safety of Richmond. Still, all were saddened on her behalf to know she had lost the child she was carrying.

General Lee, meanwhile, was able to visit at the Leigh Street house for a short time, but Mary Lee was shocked by his appearance—his hair and beard had turned white. She also worried over the severe pain he occasionally suffered in his left side.

By now it was clear that the Lee family had lost the magnificent Arlington House. Under a Federal law passed by Congress the previous year, the government imposed real estate taxes on property in "insurrectionary districts." It could—and would—confiscate said properties when the said taxes went unpaid. The added catch was that the taxes had to be paid in person by the property owner or owners.

In the case of Robert and Mary Lee, that was impossible. General Lee obviously couldn't pass through the Federal lines outside Washington to pay the tax for his wife, rightful owner of the estate. Nor was she physically able to try passing through those lines herself, although she did consider the attempt. Instead a cousin went on her behalf and tried to pay the real estate tax levied on the Arlington property. Federal officers rejected the cousin, and the government then "legally" confiscated Arlington House, its grounds now destined to be a mass burial ground.

General Lee was able to repeat his Richmond visits almost until Christmas Day of 1863, but he returned to his troops for Christmas Day itself. Rooney was still a prisoner, not to be released until an exchange was finally arranged in March 1864. On the day after Christmas 1863, Charlotte Wickham Lee, not yet twenty-three, died.

Three Generals Named Winfield

TWO GENERALS NAMED WINFIELD SCOTT SIMULTANEOUSLY TOOK TO THE FIELD— on opposite sides—for at least two of the Civil War's major campaigns. Neither one was "Ole Fuss and Feathers" himself. That one, the original Winfield Scott—Mexican War hero, general in chief of the U.S. Army, and the country's military idol for the past two decades—was in his mid-seventies and too corpulent to mount his horse when the Civil War broke out. Not yet disposed to step aside entirely, he realized he was not physically able to lead in the field; thus, it was probably Winfield Scott's idea to offer field command of the Union armies to his chief of staff and fellow Virginian, Robert E. Lee.

After Lee declined and remained loyal to his seceding native state, Scott remained on duty and directed Union forces from Washington until shortly after the embarrassing Union defeat at First Bull Run, virtually on the doorstep of the capital. With George "Little Mac" McClellan, then brought to the fore and reporting directly to President Lincoln, Scott saw his duty and retired—with full pay and rank.

Out in the field, two far younger men, both born in the 1820s and both named for the hero of the War of 1812 (even before his feats of the Mexican War in the 1840s), were leading their troops against each other's forces. One of them, Confederate Winfield Scott Featherston, was at First Bull Run with his 17th Mississippi in the summer of 1861.

By spring of the following year, both Featherston and his Union counterpart, Winfield Scott Hancock, were commanding troops in the Peninsular campaign, George McClellan's abortive drive against Richmond. Both brigadiers commanded brigades at the Battle of Williamsburg, where Hancock earned his first plaudits of the war by leading a vital flank attack against the Rebels.

Both men appeared at Fredericksburg in late 1862, with Hancock now leading a division. After that, their wartime careers took them on widely divergent paths.

Confederate General Featherston soon moved into the western theater to appear at Champion Hill in Mississippi and in the Vicksburg campaign, in which he served as a brigade commander under William "Old Blizzards" Loring, the one-armed Mexican War veteran who led his troops into battle with the cry, "Give them blizzards, boys!"

Featherston also took part in the defense of Atlanta under Joseph E. Johnston's overall command before serving under John Bell Hood as the latter moved into Tennessee for his sequential disasters at Franklin and Nashville. Not yet bowed, Featherston was with Johnston again in the final days in North Carolina, surrendering finally at Greensboro.

The war's other Winfield Scott—Hancock, that is—carved out an illustrious career after commanding a Union division at Fredericksburg, a debacle for the North. As 2nd Corps commander, Hancock appeared at Chancellorsville and at Gettysburg in 1863. He then served as a major general under Ulysses S. Grant during Grant's final drive on Richmond and Petersburg in 1864. Hancock led his troops at the high-casualty battles of the Wilderness, Spotsylvania, and Cold Harbor.

His contribution at Spotsylvania was vital to Grant's victory there, but his corps took significant losses at Cold Harbor. During the siege of Petersburg, Hancock was embarrassed at the minor clash known as Reams Station, where Confederate Generals A. P. Hill and Wade Hampton exacted twenty-four hundred casualties among the eight thousand in Hancock's command.

Both of the Winfield Scotts serving in the field during the Civil War suffered combat wounds—the Confederate Featherston at Glendale during the Seven Days campaign outside Richmond in 1862, and Union officer Hancock at Gettysburg. Both also had political interests. Featherston, a Tennessee native and an attorney in Mississippi before the war, had served two terms in the U.S. House in the 1840s and 1850s. After the war, he served in the Mississippi legislature. He lived until 1891.

Alter ego Hancock aired his political ambitions fifteen years after the Civil War. He was the Democratic Party's nominee for president in 1880, but he lost the general election that fall to another former Union officer, James A. Garfield. Hancock remained in the Army for the next six years, until his death in 1886.

Ironically, the original Winfield Scott had also dallied in politics: In 1852, the hero of the Mexican War had run for president as the Whig Party's nominee, only to be defeated by Franklin Pierce, a very junior and undistinguished officer under Scott's command in Mexico fifteen years earlier. Jefferson Davis, incidentally, served as Pierce's secretary of war.

The venerable General in Chief Scott survived his retirement through the Civil War years, living until 1866. While chafing at his inactive seat on the sidelines, Scott nonetheless could take pride in seeing his Anaconda Plan pretty much followed by the Union to ultimate, albeit costly, triumph. That strategy called for Union control of the Mississippi Valley (thus splitting the Confederacy in two), coupled with a suffocating naval blockade of the South's Atlantic ports. Scott lived long enough to write his memoirs and to send a copy to Grant, also once a junior officer with Scott in Mexico. The book was inscribed in touching terms by "Ole Fuss and Feathers." His personal note to Grant was, "From the oldest general to the greatest general."

Cat Parties Ended

A TALE PAINFUL TO RELATE, BUT NECESSARY TO COMPLETE THE RECORD IN ANY case, is that of the unnamed cat that paid a visit one day to Captain Isaac Coles of Virginia while he was sitting on his bunk and conversing with a compatriot from Kentucky. It was the fall of 1864, and Coles and his partner were prisoners.

Their quarters, located at Hilton Head, South Carolina, consisted of a long structure with rows of bunks on each side and plank tables set up in the middle aisle for meals. Rations had been short and unappealing in their Yankee-operated prison camp, and the two men were discussing the food and the long time—forty or fifty days at least—since they had had a decent meal. They were speaking rather pathetically of "our reduced state and of our longings to satisfy the very humble cravings of the inner man."

And then along came General John Foster's cat (it was presumably the Union commandant's cat since the next day he issued orders to lock up any and all other pets within sight or hearing).

Coles later wrote in good humor of his wartime adventures, his account appearing in *War Recollections of Confederate Veterans of Pittsylvania County* (Virginia). On this particular occasion, "We were nearly desperate," he recalled, and "anything would have been joyfully tried that looked like meat." Their stomachs were "gnawing and begging" and were by no means to be ignored when, he said, "like an answer to prayer," along came this "big, fat cat" into the barracks, "daintily tripping in, straight up to us, fawning at our feet."

The rest would be history—cat history. The starving prisoners reacted immediately: "My boyish antagonism to the feline kind vanished, and I hailed her as Manna from heaven, or quail, or what you will—it certainly looked like Providence to me as surely providing for us as for His other children in the wilderness."

The two men glanced one to another—"He, too, had a look of inspiration—and so from common impulse we acted."

Perhaps "the fair visitoress" never quite knew exactly what hit her. We can hope that her end was mercifully quick. She certainly never knew the indignities that came next. "How joyously we skinned and dressed her! We surmised she was General Foster's pet. We hoped so!"

No time was wasted: "We parboiled and stewed her up, no pepper nor salt. She was deliciously fat, she must have been a notoriously fine mouser."

The entire culinary event unfolded without a hitch. "She required no grease, we baked our corn meal and could scarcely contain ourselves until the feast was ready. And it was a king's dish indeed, a whole pan full, two whole yawning stomach fulls and to spare! We invited several to dine with us."

Not a scrap was left, and afterward Coles and his partners were quite ready to declare "the cat as an article of food was misunderstood, that it was wholesome and delicious."

The only regret was when General Foster ordered "all dogs and cats locked up next day." There went any hopes for "another cat party."

The Fighting McCooks

SEVENTEEN OF THE MENFOLK OF THE AMAZING McCOOKS OF OHIO SERVED THE Union, all but one as Army men and five as generals. Patriarch of the clan was Daniel McCook, born in 1798 in Pennsylvania and later removed to Carrollton, Ohio. In his sixties by the time of the Civil War, he saw eight sons, a brother, and six nephews step forward to serve the Union cause. Three of his sons were killed—as was Daniel McCook himself.

Considered too old for duty in the field, the eager volunteer Major Daniel McCook had been allowed to serve as a paymaster of volunteers far behind normal Union lines. But even homebound troops were called out to oppose John Hunt Morgan's raid into Ohio in midsummer of 1863. In the running clashes that ensued, the eldest of all the "Fighting McCooks" was mortally wounded July 20, 1863 near Buffington Island, Ohio. He died the next day.

His son Daniel Jr., a law partner to William Tecumseh Sherman in civilian life, became a brigade commander—one of three McCook brothers to reach general's rank. He fought at Chickamauga and Chattanooga, among other battles, then in the Atlanta campaign suffered a fatal wound of his own as his brigade led a costly charge ordered by General Sherman at Kennesaw Mountain. This Dan McCook received his brigadier's star on July 16, 1864, and died the next day.

His two brothers also reached general's rank. Both Alexander and Robert were veterans of the fighting in the war's western theater.

Alexander survived the war, served in the U.S. Army until 1895, and retired as a major general, although his Civil War reputation was tarnished by the Union defeat at Chickamauga. There he and his command had joined overall Union commander William S. Rosecrans in retreat from the battlefield.

Robert L. McCook, Alexander's brother, was not fortunate enough to survive the fighting, dying a controversial death. Laid low by illness, he nonetheless was on a scouting foray in a horse-drawn ambulance when, accosted by a band of Southern irregulars near Decherd, Tennessee, he was shot while on his sick bed, it is said. Fatally injured, he died the next day. Many of his Northern countrymen felt his death was outright murder rather than an act of war.

Others among the Fighting McCooks of Ohio included Cousin Edward, fourth Union general in the clan and still another veteran of service with Sherman and U. S. Grant in the war's west. Also an attorney before the war,

Edward McCook took part in George Stoneman's raid into the Atlanta area, his command taking significant casualties before returning to Union lines. He also joined in James Wilson's 1864 raid into Georgia and Alabama that resulted in the capture of Selma.

A war survivor, Edward McCook later served as governor of the Colorado Territory and as an envoy to the future state of Hawaii. He built a postwar fortune in business ventures that included "telephone companies in Europe," noted Stewart Sifakis in his *Who Was Who in the Civil War*.

There also was Cousin Anson—a brigadier general as well. As an officer in the 2nd Ohio, he traveled east to fight at First Bull Run (a battle proving fatal to another cousin in the same regiment, probably Private David McCook, a hospital guard), then returned to the western theater, where he served quite honorably at Perryville, Murfreesboro, Tullahoma, Chattanooga, and Atlanta. Late in the war he commanded a newly formed regiment back east in Virginia's Shenandoah Valley. A war survivor also, he returned to the practice of law and served as a Republican congressman.

The only known sailor among all the McCooks of Ohio was Roderick, born in 1839 and an Annapolis graduate. He served as a line officer in the Atlantic Blockading Squadron and commanded a battery in the naval assault of 1862 against New Bern, North Carolina. Near war's end, he also took part in the Union's amphibious operations against Fort Fisher at the mouth of the Cape Fear River in North Carolina. Illness then forced him to accept a postwar naval career of lighthouse duty.

Sidling Down to Richmond

"I FEEL AS CERTAIN OF CRUSHING LEE AS I DO OF DYING," ULYSSES S. GRANT IS SAID to have declared in those dark days of 1864 when his strategy of bludgeoning Robert E. Lee into submission was taking terrible toll of Grant's own forces.

Not only were the casualties cause for vilification in the North, behind Grant's back, but in Lee he faced a legend pumped larger than life by even the Northern press. And yet the dogged, newly emplaced commander of the Union armies was undismayed.

As a fellow West Point graduate and veteran of the Mexican War, Grant felt it was to his advantage to have known Lee the man and U.S. Army officer before they were fated to become enemies locked in titanic struggle.

"The natural disposition of most people," wrote Grant later, "is to clothe a commander of a large army whom they do not know with almost superhuman abilities. A large part of the National army, for instance, and most of the press of the country clothed General Lee with just such qualities, but I had known him personally, and knew that he was mortal; and it was just as well that I felt this."

Refusing to bow to Lee the legend, Grant slipped and sidled in one lateral move after another in the spring of 1864, from one costly battle to another—from the Wilderness to Spotsylvania to Cold Harbor, and finally to Petersburg. "I propose to fight it out on this line if it takes all summer," he said at one point. He settled in the end for his siege of Petersburg, the vital rail hub just below Richmond, a siege that lasted until early 1865—followed quickly by Lee's surrender at Appomattox.

If Grant thought Lee was "mortal," he also viewed the Confederate strategist as "a large, austere man, and I judge difficult of approach to his subordinates." In the "sidling" campaign of 1864 marked by staggering Union casualties, Grant felt his "austere" opponent actually enjoyed certain advantages.

The Union might have had superior numbers, but Lee was defending a familiar countryside: "Every stream, every road, every obstacle to the movement of troops and every natural defense was familiar to him and his army." Lee also had the support of local citizens who furnished "accurate reports of our every move." And Lee had "a railroad at his back" and needed no rear guard.

So towering was Lee's reputation when Grant came from the West to take over the war effort, Grant noted also, "It was not an uncommon thing for my staff officers to hear from Eastern officers, 'Well, Grant has never met Bobby Lee yet.'"

But then Grant did, and even the ordinary soldier of the South could see the difference.

"Surprise and disappointment were the prevailing emotions," recalled one Confederate veteran of Grant's "sidling" campaign in 1864, "when we discovered after the contest in the Wilderness, that General Grant was not going to retire behind the river and permit General Lee to carry on a campaign against Washington the usual way, but was moving to the Spotsylvania position instead."

Usually, added Sergeant Major George Cary Eggleston of Lampkin's Virginia Battery, the Union fought a battle, retired, obtained a new commander, then had to deal with a fresh Confederate offensive. Not so with Grant, who simply shifted position and spoiled to fight again.

By the time of Cold Harbor, "we had begun to understand what our new adversary meant…[that] the era of experimental campaigns against us was over; that Grant was not going to retreat; that he was not to be removed from command because he had failed to break Lee's resistance; and that the policy of pounding had begun, and would continue until our strength would be utterly worn away."

In short, added onlooker-participant Eggleston, "He intended to continue the plodding work till the task should be accomplished, wasting very little time or strength in efforts to make a brilliant display of generalship in a contest of strategic wits with Lee."

Eggleston had it exactly right. In what some consider the first display of modern—or total war—Grant employed overwhelming resources to wear Lee down, press home his final campaign, and, within the year, win the war for the North. Or, as Lincoln would say, for an undivided Union.

Later, though, whatever he thought of Lee as man or legend, it would largely be Grant's intervention that would derail a move to try Lee for treason.

Friendly Boost Given

FEW REPORTERS COULD EVER CLAIM SUCH A HELPFUL SOURCE, A FRIEND IN COURT, as the contact that Harry E. Wing developed inside the Lincoln administration.

Wing, a law school graduate, had served as a color corporal with the 27th Connecticut from September 1862 until the end of that year, when a wound suffered at Fredericksburg drummed him out of the Union Army. He had previously reported for the New Haven Palladium, and now, taking up residence in Washington, he began reporting on capital affairs, first for the *Norwich Bulletin* (also in Connecticut) and then for the *New York Tribune*.

He wanted action, however, and he persuaded the Tribune to assign him as a courier for the paper's reporters accompanying the Federal Army of the Potomac. That job led quickly to new status as a war correspondent, but he still was the "new boy" of the crowd at the time of the great Battle of the Wilderness in the spring of 1864. As low man on the seniority list, he carried the pooled dispatches back to the nearest telegraph station, and that journey took him through the war-torn territory of northern Virginia, which was subject to the unpredictable meanderings of John S. Mosby's guerrilla band.

Indeed, Wing was chased by Rebs of some kind, then held up by Confederate cavalrymen before finally reaching a Union camp boasting a telegraph unit. It was restricted for military use, but Wing managed to inform Secretary of War Edwin Stanton that he had the first news from the first day of battle at the Wilderness.

Stanton of course wanted to see the story, but Wing kept insisting it should go out to his newspaper as well. Never one to sit on his temper, Stanton ordered Wing arrested. It was at this stage that word of the tempest reached Abraham Lincoln in the White House.

Far more agreeable, he not only overruled Stanton, but he sent a train for reporter Wing. The two met at 2:00 a.m. in the White House, with Wing providing a full verbal report of all that he had seen and heard during the crucial day of battle. Lincoln was moved to kiss the journalist when he also conveyed a personal message from U. S. Grant (just beginning his ultimately successful "sidling" campaign of 1864 against Robert E. Lee) that there was no reason to turn back despite the heavy Union casualties.

Lincoln now told Wing to allow the Associated Press to share in the story, the only account of the battle to reach official Washington so far. Still Wing's friend in court, Abe Lincoln also furnished the reporter with an escort allowing him to retrieve a horse he had hidden in a thicket while escaping from Confederate raiders. Wing remained a war correspondent until Appomattox, then became co-publisher of the *Litchfield (Connecticut) Enquirer* and, later in life, a minister.

"Down, You Fool!"

FOR SUPREME COURT JUSTICE OLIVER WENDELL HOLMES JR., SEPTEMBER 13 WAS the day on which for many years he made an annual pilgrimage. Every year he left his workplace, the nation's highest court, to trek to Arlington National Cemetery across the Potomac. The date was a birthday, and the man he came to memorialize with flowers in hand was his divisional commander at one point during the Civil War, Major General John Sedgwick.

Appointed to his bench seat in 1902, Holmes served until retirement in 1932 and died in 1935. Holmes today is recalled as a creature of the twentieth century. We tend to forget that he was born in 1841, that he was in his twenties during the Civil War, and that he indeed did serve in the war.

Not only did he serve, but he fought at Ball's Bluff, Antietam, Fredericksburg, and Chancellorsville; he was wounded three times and at Antietam left for dead. His father, the famous New England author-poet, then published the personal story ("My Hunt After 'The Captain'") of searching out his badly wounded son after receiving word that he had been shot in the neck. Young Captain Holmes had been taken into a home in Hagerstown, Maryland, for his immediate care and treatment, and several days passed before his father, a doctor, finally tracked him down on a train bound for Philadelphia— obviously, much recovered.

Fairly famous in those days were their greetings, one to another:

"How are you, Boy?"

"How are you, Dad?"

In his article for the *Atlantic* in December 1862, the elder Holmes was moved to point out how careful people of their time and social status were to hide strong personal emotion. "Such are the proprieties of life, as they are observed among us Anglo-Saxons of the nineteenth century, decently disguising those natural impulses," wrote the Boston Brahmin.

His son, the young captain, was back in the field in short time; eventually he was promoted to lieutenant colonel. At the Battle of Chancellorsville in the spring of 1863, he was wounded one more time—a nick in his heel that kept him from remaining with his 20th Massachusetts Regiment. Still recuperating, he was assigned duty as aide to Union General Horatio Wright, who in the spring of 1864 was in command of the 6th Corps as Ulysses S. Grant moved into position to squeeze both Petersburg and nearby Richmond in an inescapable vice.

While Grant was busy in that regard, however, and while Sherman marched on Atlanta in July, Confederate Lieutenant General Jubal Early made his sudden dash with twelve thousand troops from the Shenandoah Valley into Maryland and drew up before Fort Stevens, a back door to Washington itself.

Since the nation's capital was lightly defended at best, Wright's 6th Corps hustled back from the Union lines outside Petersburg, traveling up the Potomac River by steamboat, and disembarking to a personal welcome by Abraham Lincoln himself. With Wright and his 6th Corps was the young Colonel Holmes. When Lincoln then visited Fort Stevens to see the front lines for himself, there was young Holmes again, assigned to escort the president. And when Lincoln impulsively stood up, his signatory top hat such an obvious target, shots rang out and Confederate rounds whizzed close by. The future Supreme Court justice wasted no time and minced no words as he pulled Lincoln down, while blurting, "Get down, you fool!"

In later life Holmes rarely volunteered the story of his brush with Lincoln, which may have saved the president's life but was also deeply embarrassing to the young officer. Holmes eventually did tell the story to both Supreme Court Justice Felix Frankfurter and to Professor Harold J. Laski of the London School of Economics and Political Science, if not a few others.

As events turned out, Lincoln himself had eased the colonel's possibly lasting pain—and made things all right—when upon leaving Fort Stevens, he turned and said a bit wryly, "Goodbye, Colonel Holmes, I'm glad to see you know how to talk to a civilian."

Sadly, the same General John Sedgwick whom Holmes faithfully remembered for years after the war is most famous today for a wry comment of his own. It happened at Spotsylvania, in May 1864. Warned of Confederate sharpshooters nearby, he said, "They couldn't hit an elephant at this range." The words were hardly out of his mouth when he was struck down by a sharpshooter's round.

Perhaps as a result, Holmes was more than commonly sensitive to the effectiveness of unseen snipers when he pulled Lincoln down, out of harm's way.

Brave Men Spared

THE FIERY, HOT-TEMPERED CONFEDERATE CAVALRY LEADER NATHAN BEDFORD Forrest began his unbending ways early in life—as "man of the house" while still a boy, he had to grow up in a hurry. And he did, skipping school and supporting the family as a farmhand, then as a livestock dealer, and finally as slave trader and cotton planter of moderate wealth.

An incident when he was only ten served notice of what was to come. A neighbor's bull kept breaking loose and rampaging through the Forrest family's precious stand of corn, despite repeated pleas and complaints. Finally, young Forrest told the neighbor he could expect to have his bull shot if it wandered one more time.

The neighbor let it be known that anyone shooting his bull would be shot himself.

The bull indeed broke loose one more time and again found its way into the Forrest cornfield. The lad took up his rifle and shot the beast on the spot. The neighbor then appeared with a rifle in his hand and violence in his heart. He started over the fence in between them but the ten-year-old shot again. The round whistled through the neighbor's clothing, causing him to turn and run for home.

As a full-grown man, the same Forrest was so ornery that he once threatened his own commander, General Braxton Bragg. Amazingly, with no military schooling whatsoever, he rose from enlistment as a private in the future 7th Tennessee Cavalry to general's rank, with a reputation as a genius at cavalry warfare tactics. His reputation for ferocity in battle also was great—and deservedly so. Still, one Southern woman had it slightly wrong the day he and his unit galloped through town with Union men closely pursuing. "Why don't you turn and fight, you cowardly rascal?" she shouted. "If old Forrest were here, he'd make you fight!"

This same officer may or may not have ordered the massacre of black Union troops at Fort Pillow. This controversy was never quite settled and was fueled by his apparent postwar role as a founder and possibly the first Grand Wizard of the original Ku Klux Klan.

At least once, though, Forrest showed unexpected softness of the heart. Two Union soldiers—Germans from Wisconsin—had been taken prisoner near Forrest's headquarters outside of Memphis, Tennessee. Since food rations were short and exchanges of prisoners were difficult to arrange, explained *Harper's* magazine in 1871, "orders had been issued to take no prisoners, but execute them on the spot."

The firing squad assembled, and things looked bleak for the two Union men as Forrest himself strode into sight to command the grim proceedings. Still, to the surprise of the onlookers, Forrest included, the two young Germans merely lit up their pipes and stood chit-chatting with each other, seemingly unconcerned.

Forrest barked his orders. The firing squad formed up and stood at attention. Still the two captives did not flinch or break down, but kept on smoking.

Forrest continued his drill, "Shoulder arms," he shouted. "Ready. Aim...."

The Rebels took aim, waiting for the final command to fire.

But Forrest then barked, "Ground arms" and "Right about face."

There would be no execution after all! "Git up and git!" he told the two Yankees. To his onlookers the rarely perturbed Forrest merely explained: "Brave men are too scarce to be shot down like dogs."

Christmas

What was happening during Christmas 1861, the first Christmas of the war? In Washington, the Lincolns had guests for Christmas dinner at the White House. He and his Cabinet also met at some length on this Christmas Day—in the White House, as was the custom.

In the field this first Christmas, Union and Confederate shooting—skirmish-ing, they call it—took place near Frederick, Maryland. Union ships stopped and seized a Reb blockade-runner off Cape Fear. A minor Union expedition was in motion in Missouri—no great results to report.

It was a Wednesday, and just days before there had been consternation in the Lincoln White House over Mary Todd Lincoln's spendthrift ways. She had already exceeded her congressional appropriation for interior refurbishment, and she was in tears over the embarrassing issue. Husband Abraham was upset, too, saying none too prettily, "It would stink in the nostrils of the American people" to know he approved expenses "overrunning an appropriation of $20,000 for flub dubs for this damned old house, when the soldiers cannot have blankets."

In any case, the presidential home did look much better for the holidays, and despite the tragedies of war there was momentary joy and warmth for the Lincolns in being all together one last time. Eldest son Robert was down from Harvard, and his young brothers Willie and Tad were on hand as well. Two months later, Willie, only eleven, would be dead, a victim of fever. After that shock, Mary Todd Lincoln, already subject to emotional swings, would never be the same again.

Christmas Day of 1862, the second Christmas of the war, came to a nation far more war-weary. The Lincolns marked their holiday by visiting the wounded in Washington hospitals. Fighting—no major battles, but real fighting—took place at widely scattered sites. William T. Sherman was moving down the Mississippi from Memphis to Vicksburg, and there was fighting near Brentwood and on the Edmonson Pike in Tennessee; at Ripley, Mississippi; and near Warrenton, Virginia; and at Green's Chapel and Bear Willow in Kentucky. Few could be happy with the state of the divided nation this day.

On Christmas Day of 1863, a Friday, little change in the inclinations of the belligerents would have been apparent to the unacquainted spectator looking down from on high. Except, perhaps, for more naval action. In South Carolina's Sono River, Federal gunboats dueled with Confederate shore batteries, with severe damage to the Union's *Marblehead*. A similar exchange took place between the USS *Pawnee* and shore guns at St. John's Island near Charleston. Ashore, Union troops destroyed Rebel salt works at Bear Inlet, North Carolina, and fought the Johnny Reb at Fort Brooke, Florida.

By Christmas Day of 1864, a Sunday (since 1864 was a leap year), the obvious end was now in sight—obvious except that the Union suffered ignominious defeat in its attempt to land sixty-five hundred troops, supported by nearly sixty warships, at Fort Fisher, North Carolina.

The entire assemblage had to sail back to Hampton Roads in Virginia to round after round of recriminations among the Federal commanders. The amphibious assault would be repeated three weeks later, on January 13, 1865, with far greater success.

Elsewhere on Christmas Day, John Bell Hood's shattered Army of Tennessee was hurrying as well as it could out of Tennessee, with skirmishing at Richland Creek, Anthony's Hill, and White's Station. Petersburg, Virginia, was under tight siege by the Union forces commanded by U. S. Grant. And in the western theater Sterling Price's Rebel forces were in retreat from Missouri. The Confederacy was shrinking in size and spirit day by day. What would the next Christmas Day hold for all?

By Christmas Day of 1865, a Monday, there was little joy, but the heart-rending war was over. It had been over for several months, but its stark images would linger and haunt for generations. By now the Confederacy had fallen; Jefferson Davis was a prisoner; Henry Wirz, commandant of the notorious Andersonville Confederate Prison in Georgia, had been hanged; Abraham Lincoln had been assassinated; and Tennessee-born Andrew Johnson was president. Four alleged conspirators in the Lincoln assassination, including a woman, Mary Surratt, had been hanged. And, in an interesting postscript, the Thirteenth Amendment to the U.S. Constitution—abolishing slavery—had gained final ratification, with Alabama, North Carolina, Georgia, and Oregon all voting for it since December 1.

What Does a Slave?

WHAT EXACTLY DOES A SLAVE DO? A CIVIL WAR–ERA SLAVE IN THE SOUTH, THAT IS? Far from field hand or typical household servant, but a slave nonetheless, was one Laurence, a personal valet to James Chesnut (onetime U.S. senator, briefly Confederate senator, general-rank Confederate officer, and aide to President Jefferson Davis) of Mulberry Plantation, Camden, South Carolina. Laurence and Mrs. Chesnut—the famous Civil War diarist Mary Boykin Chesnut—lived for a time right across the street in Richmond, Virginia, from Jefferson and Varina Davis.

Laurence appears often in Mary Chesnut's wartime musings. For instance, early on—during the shelling of Fort Sumter in Charleston Harbor—the cannon boomed night and day. War had come. Slavery was such a keen issue. Mary Chesnut wondered what the slaves themselves thought.

She observed no change in their manner. "Laurence sits at our door, as sleepy and as respectful and as profoundly indifferent (as all the blacks in general)." No reaction to the shelling, and as for the whites—well, "people talk before them [the slaves] as if they were chairs and tables. And they make no sign. Are they stolidly stupid or wiser than we are, silent and strong, biding their time?"

A few weeks later, Mary's husband had to pass through the newly named Confederate capital of Richmond. Here all was confusion—a crowded city, unbearable heat, overflowing hotels. The former senator had to share his hotel bed with a Confederate congressman from Louisiana, while also sharing the room with still others.

Traveling with four slaves, Chesnut had left his horse overnight in Petersburg, just below Richmond. The dependable Laurence stayed with the animal until it could be transported to Richmond the next morning. "My hands were so full with the four negroes, all green except Laurence," wrote Chesnut to his wife, "that I had no time to take a meal from the time I left Kingsville [South Carolina] until I got here."

That was in June 1861. By mid-July the two Chesnuts, husband and wife, had openly discussed the issue of Laurence's true loyalties. Laurence was in charge of his master's personal items, some of them valuable—his watch and "two or three hundred gold pieces [that] lie in the tray of his trunk." Laurence was supposed to take those things to Mary Chesnut if anything happened to her husband, then an officer in the field.

She wondered if this expectation would hold true. "Maybe he will pack off to the Yankees—and freedom—with all that."

"Fiddlesticks!" said her husband. "He is not going to leave me for anybody else. After all, what can he ever be better than he is now—a gentleman's gentleman?" To which she replied, "He is within the sound of the enemies' guns, and when he gets to the other army, he is free."

But Laurence did not run off to freedom. By August of the same year it was recorded that "[he] does all our shopping." Mrs. Chesnut was worried about the gold, however; and so she had sewn it into a money belt with her diamonds for safekeeping during an emergency.

Laurence's reaction? "Laurence wears the bronze mask." Whenever she left her trunk open, "Laurence brings me the keys and tells me, 'You oughten to do so, Miss Mary.'" And when her husband left money in his pockets, "Laurence says that's why he can't let anyone but himself brush Mars Jeems' clothes."

By October of the same year, the Chesnuts had discovered that Laurence made "an excellent tailor," and, former Alabama senator Clement Clay's wife,

Virginia, "never tired of laughing at the picture he made seated cross-legged on Mr. Chesnut's trunk darning."

Laurence did have a mind of his own, as the saying goes. Chesnut's second cousin, Mary Stevens Garnett, once said, "I thought Cousin James was the laziest man alive until I knew his man Laurence." To this, Mary Chesnut added that Laurence would "not move an inch or lift a finger for anyone but his master." One time a friend, British-born Ellen Middleton, "politely sent him on an errand—and he was very polite about it too."

Except that hours later she spied him sitting on the front yard fence. When she asked if he had gone on her errand, he replied, "No, Ma'am. I am waiting for Mars Jeems."

His master, "Mars Jeems," had taken to calling Laurence "Adolphe," after the dominating valet in *Uncle Tom's Cabin*. But Chesnut defended Laurence as "simply perfect as a servant for him." And he was indeed most dependable, as he himself would assure Mary Chesnut during the winters of 1862 and 1863. Richmond was feeling the deprivations of war, but a certain amount of entertaining was called for nonetheless. "You give me the money, I'll find everything you want," he told her. There was "no such word as 'fail' with him."

This was a time when turkeys cost $30, "but Laurence kept us plentifully supplied," she wrote.

Once, too, Mary Chesnut wanted to entertain Varina Davis and a mutual friend. Laurence had produced a basket of cherries, but wouldn't it be nice if they had some ice, too?

"Respectfully Laurence said—and also firmly, 'Give me money and you shall have ice.'"

Somehow he knew of an icehouse on the other side of town across the James River. "In a wonderfully short time we had mint juleps and cherry cobblers."

But there came a time when Laurence slipped up, with embarrassing consequences. He had gone to one of Richmond's "negro balls," as Mary Chesnut called them. He had forgotten his mandatory pass as he changed his coat for the affair. When a fight broke out at the ball, the police came. Those present were ordered to show their passes. Laurence "was taken up as having none."

A household maid and cook named Molly delighted in telling Mary Chesnut the next day why Laurence was missing. (Molly and Laurence often argued, it seems.) And so Molly appeared before their mistress in tears from laughing. "Come and look," she said. "Here is the fine gentleman, tied between two black niggers and marched off to jail."

Apparently she and Mary Chesnut were looking at Laurence from a window. "Laurence disregarded her and called to me at the top of his voice. 'Please Ma'am—ask Mars Jeems to come take me out of this. I ain't done nothing.'"

Master James did go to his rescue, a never-forgotten moment in the Chesnut household. "He was terribly chopfallen when he came home, walking behind Mr. C. He is always so respectable and well behaved and stands on his dignity."

Laurence didn't hesitate to offer his protection when the dread Yankees came close to a lightly garrisoned Richmond in 1863, but it must also be reported that on January 4, 1864, he was drunk. He and Molly "had a grand row."

In the next month, there was further mortification for Laurence. Drunk again when told to move a chair at breakfast, he lifted it high over his head and it "smashed" the chandelier above. Chesnut was so furious that he told Mary to send Laurence away, all the way back to their plantation home in South Carolina. So there he went, "gone back ignominiously," although not for long. "He will soon be back, and when he comes he will say, 'Shoo! I knew Mars Jeems could not do without me.' And indeed he cannot."

Laurence did return, but the Chesnuts had to excuse a former landlady's report that both Molly and Laurence were apt to be a bit noisy when the Chesnuts were away from home. "They went about the house, quiet as mice when we were at home," it was said. "Laurence sat at the door and sprung to his feet if we passed. When we were out they sung, laughed, shouted, danced."

Laurence nonetheless was back in the family's good graces by the time the Chesnuts entertained the Jefferson Davises at dinner in Columbia, South Carolina, in October of 1864. The Confederate dream was slipping away fast.

"Our world, the only world we cared for," wrote Mary Chesnut, was now "literally kicked to pieces." Everything would change.

She spent the last weeks of the Civil War in search of safe places to stay—out of the Yankee path. One of those unhappy stops, ironically, was at Lincolnton, North Carolina, where the unfortunate Laurence ran into an angry buzzsaw of a landlady in Mary Chesnut's entourage.

"Refugees in Lubberland," she called this section of her memoir diary, and Lincolnton's chief attraction was that it was "a thoroughly out-of-all-routes place."

Still, by Chesnut standards also it was thoroughly miserable. "Here I am brokenhearted—an exile," wrote Mary Chesnut later. "Such a place [where she had rented rooms]. For a feather bed, a pine table, and two chairs I pay 30 dollars a day. Such sheets!—but I have some of my own."

They had arrived—Mary Chesnut, a house servant named Ellen (taking Molly's place for a time), and Laurence—and "before I was well out of the hack," Laurence had encountered "the woman of the house." She attacked the startled black man. She said "she would not have him at any price." She said "his clothes were too fine for a nigger—'his airs indeed!' Poor Laurence was as humble—and silent."

He did plead, "Miss Mary, send me back to Mars Jeems." When "Miss Mary" looked for a pencil to write a note to her husband (who had remained in South Carolina with his command), it was Laurence, unfortunately, who brought forth a gold pencil case.

That set the landlady off again. "Go away," she shouted. "I wants no niggers here with pencils—and airs."

Laurence "fled before the storm"—but not before saying that "Mars Jeems" wouldn't want his wife staying there if he knew "how you was treated."

A friend and fellow refugee told Mary Chesnut not to pay attention to people like the Lincolnton landlady. "They will never comprehend the height from which we have fallen," said Susan Middleton.

Chesnut and her maidservant Ellen were more happily quartered at another rental space in Lincolnton, but it was only temporary. In the end, after the hostilities were over, the Chesnuts returned to a ruined plantation once home to a few hundred slaves and their own large family. The slaves were free now. Some left, and some stayed on. James and Mary Chesnut were left financially strapped for a while, and they never regained the great wealth they had known before the war.

Mary Chesnut's last diary reference to Laurence the slave came in a letter from James Chesnut dated March 15, 1865, still before Appomattox. James informed Mary that he was sending a Confederate officer and Laurence to Lincolnton to bring her down to Chester Court House, South Carolina, where he had found three vacant rooms with access to half a kitchen for them all. They would go home to the Mulberry family plantation outside Camden later.

There came a time, in the difficult postwar period, when the family's cash income stemmed from maid Molly's efforts at selling eggs and butter. Molly swore she would never leave her "Missis." Ellen, too, would stay. Her husband, Claiborne, one day "asked enormous wages for her," but Mary Chesnut told him, "You and your child [Ellen's, too] are living in one of our houses, free of rent. Ellen can go or stay as she pleases."

And Mary told Ellen, "I have no money, Ellen."

But Ellen said, "Claiborne is an old fool always meddling and making—I don't care for money, I gits money's worth."

More Staggering Stats

WHAT WERE THE ODDS, ANYWAY, OF BEING WOUNDED? WHAT WERE THE CHANCES of the average soldier or sailor getting by without being hurt—mortally or otherwise? After all, if 8 percent of the Union's 583 generals—sixty-five— were killed, mortally wounded, or fatally diseased, what chance stood the lower, presumably more exposed, ranks? And in the Confederacy, if 18 percent of that side's 425 general officers—ninety-two in all—succumbed to one lethal threat or another, what were the average enlisted man's odds against wounding or death?

Well, statisticians can always play games and sources can be unreliable, particularly when it comes to something as difficult to document as the American Civil War. With all the military action, the confused records, and wanton destruction everywhere, its sometimes loose organization to begin with, and all the time that has passed since then, one cannot always be sure of some of the "facts." Still, E. B. Long, who compiled the day by day *Almanac* of the Civil War, can be considered an astute student of such matters. Long said that in the Union Army chances were that one in every sixty-five men would be killed in action, that one of fifty-six would die later of wounds, and that one of every 13.5 men would die of disease. Further, an even greater one in ten would be wounded in action, while one in fifteen would be captured or cited as missing. One of every seven captured men would not survive his status as a prisoner in the hands of the Confederacy.

As Long notes, "disease in the Civil War claimed a far deadlier toll than the battlefield." The sicknesses to avoid most were those affecting the bowels; diarrhea and dysentery combined to kill at least 44,558 Union soldiers. The next leading killer was fever of various kinds under various names, not always scientifically diagnosed (or expertly treated, for that matter). Mark down 40,656 deaths to fevers, and we have more than eighty-five thousand casualties from those two areas of illness alone—far more than America lost in the twelve-year Vietnam War of the twentieth century.

Another twenty thousand or so Union deaths can be attributed to pneumonia; still others are to be blamed upon sicknesses such as smallpox, measles, and consumption (tuberculosis).

As for Confederate statistics in this area, no such records exist. But Long cites Bell Irvin Wiley's *Life of Johnny Reb* as authoritative and reliable enough in concluding that "for every soldier killed in battle or of mortal wounds, there were three deaths from disease." Once again, the bowels were the average Confederate soldier's most vulnerable area, but measles, typhoid (which was one of the Northern fevers, too), and smallpox also were prevalent killers.

When you add it all up—combat, disease, accident, what-have-you—the final Civil War casualty figures are truly staggering. In the North, total Army deaths of all causes were 360,222. Less than a third—110,100 to be exact—were caused by combat. Although the Federal Navy was active throughout the war, its records indicate that only 1,084 died in combat and another three thousand were stuck down by disease or accident.

The comparative Confederate figures are, again, not so easily or reliably obtained, but Long says, "Probably the best and most accepted estimate is 94,000 Confederates killed in battle or mortally wounded, while 164,000 died of disease. Total deaths thus came to 258,000."

Although the North won the war, it had many more dead and wounded—107,000—than the South. But then, the North entered the fray with many more men.

Often hidden in such figures are the ways that men died. Not all fell in some neat bookkeeper's row before a fusillade of bullets. No, war's actual toll—its pain and suffering—can be much more graphic. The details sting even now.

The U.S. Navy's losses, low as they were by comparison with the Army's, included 342 men scalded to death (usually when boilers on their ships were blown open) and 308 men drowned, usually when a ship broken open in combat or, otherwise damaged, spilled them into the sea or a river.

The Army's losses included executions—267 by the Union and sixty-four by the Confederates. Another 520 Federal soldiers were murdered, while nearly 5,000 were drowned, 391 took their own lives, 31,000 succumbed as prisoners of war, and 313 died of sunstroke.

How do these horrendous figures compare with those of America's other wars?

First, consider that, as Long puts it, "Total deaths in the Civil War for both sides may be placed at least at 623,026, with a minimum of 471,427 wounded, for a total casualty figure of 1,094,453."

By comparison, Americans counted 13,283 dead in the Mexican War; 2,446 in the Spanish-American War; 117,000 in World War I; 407,000 in World War II; 54,246 in Korea; and 58,000 in Vietnam. In short, more men died in the Civil War than in any other, including the more recent conflicts in Iraq and Afghanistan.

★ ENDINGS ★

Old Abe the Soldier Bird

SOMEHOW, SAYS THE LEGEND, HE ALWAYS FOUND HIS OWN ARMY—THE BLUE—AND even his own regiment, Wisconsin's 8th, when he returned from a hunting foray with a chicken, rabbit, or lamb in his clutches.

Allegedly he ranged for miles across the war-torn countryside to find his prey and was sometimes gone for as long as two or three days. When not so engaged, he would go to the nearest stream in the mornings for a splashy bath.

The reality is that he was usually kept on a sixteen-foot leash, but he sometimes broke loose. They say that from their first meeting at Madison, the state capital, he stuck by his Wisconsin regiment throughout the war, whether on the march or in the thirty-seven battles and various skirmishes they fought. He was there for the siege of Vicksburg, for the taking of Corinth, and for Sherman's march at Red River. The hotter the battle, the more likely and the more frequent his piercing scream.

Once you heard his shrill cry, you never forgot it. Hail Columbia! An apt symbol for the 8th Wisconsin—the "Eagle Regiment." "Old Abe the Soldier Bird," the bald eagle, accompanied his Wisconsin boys through their fights and marches, ignoring Rebel taunts of "Yankee Buzzard" or "Owl, Owl."

Old Abe went through St. Louis with the boys, who turned down one man's five-hundred-dollar offer for the bird and another's pledge to swap his farm for the still-young but handsome eagle. He had supped on many an unwary chicken, including the time he and his handler were invited to visit a curious farmer's barnyard and he espied a nearby fowl.

They say he not only loved his boys but their music; a favorite tune was "Yankee Doodle." He watched carefully over drill and parade, and on the march or in camp knew when to soar and when to perch. It was considered quite an honor to be a regimental eagle-bearer. He became so well known that luminaries such as Grant or Sherman routinely doffed their hat in salute when passing his mobile roost.

You could say he was also popular with the enemy, since Confederate General Sterling Price once ordered his men to capture the symbolic bird. They weren't successful; Old Abe the Soldier Bird stayed with his regiment until he returned to Wisconsin in 1864—with a somewhat cropped set of tail feathers that had been trimmed by a flying bullet.

Wisconsin was his original home. A Chippewa Indian had found him as a wee eaglet, then sold him for a bushel of corn to a white man who carried him into Eau Claire just as its men were gathering to march off to war. "An eagle!" the men shouted. "Let him enlist!"

Eau Claire's Company C then took him to Madison mounted on a perch with bunting in the colors of the Stars and Stripes. State officials gave him a new perch, and the 8th Wisconsin took him on as both a mascot and an inspiration for its name, Eagle Regiment.

Old Abe was so much a part of his soldiering outfit that he even went home on furlough—with his boys, of course. On one such visit, he took part in a fund-raising affair sponsored by the Ladies Aid Society of Chippewa Falls. That evening, Old Abe and fellow members of the regiment's Company C sat by as a minister from Eau Claire delivered a patriotic sermon.

It is also reported in the Wisconsin Historical Society's handsome book *Old Abe the War Eagle* by Richard H. Zeitlin, that, on the way back to their duty station, the eagle and his last eagle-bearer of the war period, a German immigrant named Burkhardt, encountered a train conductor who said the soldier would have to buy a ticket for the eagle "who, after all, occupied a seat." When Old Abe's bearer objected, the conductor said, "Pay for that thing or I'll put you out!" The Union soldier then stammered in his best English, adds Zeitlin, "that Old Abe was a free American eagle and, therefore, should ride for free."

Even though that didn't impress the resolute conductor, he finally backed down when Burkhardt's compatriots and other passengers in the car turned a bit stormy in his defense. Old Abe traveled for free.

About four years old by now, the bald eagle returned to duty with his head and tail feathers turned white—a mark of full and proud maturity for the species.

With the end of the war near in 1864, the question of Old Abe's peacetime future was raised. The men of his regiment debated the choices before them—send him to Washington as a gift to the Federal government, present him to the state of Wisconsin, or send him back to Eau Claire with its Company C? "The entire regiment participated in the decision-making process," reported Zeitlin, "voting unanimously to present Old Abe to the state authorities in Madison."

Thus Victor Wolf, Company C's commander, officially passed along Old Abe, who then took up residence on the grounds of the state capitol while his compatriots of the Eagle Regiment went back to war for almost another year.

Officially classified a "war relic" after the hostilities ended in 1865, Old Abe became more than a local curiosity. "As the years passed, Old Abe's fame grew," noted Zeitlin. In the meantime, he lived in a two-room "apartment" in the basement of the capitol. "He had access to a specially constructed bath tub, was fed fresh rabbits and had several sawhorses to roost upon. The 'Eagle Department' never lacked for visitors."

He escaped a couple of times, but was always recaptured. He did some traveling in the postwar years as well, appearing at various patriotic exhibitions and at the Philadelphia Centennial in 1876. Old Abe lived on until 1881, when, his lungs damaged by smoke from a fire in a nearby storeroom, he died in the arms of his last attendant.

Debate immediately arose over what should come next—a dignified burial or a trip to the taxidermist's bench. As Zeitlin said, "Taxidermy won out over burial." Although the result "did not look especially life-like," Old Abe was displayed in the capitol's Grand Old Army Memorial Hall (and was once "visited" by Teddy Roosevelt). A fire in 1904 destroyed the building, together with the eagle's remains.

Still, Old Abe did not entirely fade away. A six-foot likeness in bronze sits atop the Wisconsin memorial at the Vicksburg Wartime Military Park. Many other Old Abe likenesses appear in Wisconsin itself, and even in the Atlanta (Georgia) Cyclorama and as the logo for at least one large manufacturing company. Further, reported author Zeitlin, Old Abe's likeness is on the shoulder patch of the U.S. Army's 101st Airborne Division—"The Screaming Eagles."

Bleak Holiday

CONFEDERATE REPRESENTATIVE WARREN AKIN OF GEORGIA ARRIVED IN Richmond on November 27, 1864, to take his seat in the second session of the Second Confederate Congress. Arriving three weeks late due to the birth of a daughter at home, he entertained high hopes of returning to Georgia for Christmas.

The war wasn't going well, prices in the Confederate capital were greatly inflated, and his legislator's salary might not match his expenses, he soon noted in letters to his wife, Mary. But there was the Christmas recess to anticipate. Recently introduced Senate legislation called for adjournment on December 20, a recess that was to last until January 10. That would give Akin three weeks for the difficult journey home and the return to Richmond.

True, he also wrote on December 11, "we are getting on slowly with the business of Congress." In any case, the Georgia lawyer, farmer, and slaveholder instructed his wife that he would telegraph immediately once the Christmas recess won congressional approval. She should then send their slave Bob to meet him partway home with a wagon. "The rail roads will often fail to make connections, and I may be behind time," Akin warned. (He had ridden in a boxcar partway to Richmond the previous month.)

Three days later, on December 14, he wrote with bad news: The resolution passed by the full Senate would allow only an eight-day Christmas recess. It seemed there would not be enough time for Akin to spend any time at home.

There was one hope, however. Possibly his House chamber would amend the Senate's resolution and allow a longer Christmas break. "You know not how anxious I am to go home," this father of seven children wrote to his wife.

On December 16 Akin wrote that the House was still debating a bill to try to stabilize Confederate currency. "We are getting on very slowly." Then more bad news: "I am sorry I cant [sic] go home Christmas, but must bear it as well as I can. The Senate agreed to a recess of only eight days, and the House refused that, so the matter, I presume, is at rest."

Two days later, Akin mentioned that the food at his boarding house was fairly plain, far from hotel standards but ample. Akin and two Virginia state legislators were staying with the George Washington Gretter family, whose home at Fifth and Leigh Streets was a "pleasant walk" of about a quarter-mile to Capitol Square.

The war news was worse than ever as the last Christmas of the Civil War approached. Akin cited the recent November 30 debacle of John Bell Hood's Army of Tennessee at Franklin, with six Confederate generals among the dead. "The loss of Generals at Franklin in Hood's army was awful…and I have no doubt when we hear the truth, our loss in officers of the line and men was awful."

The disaster at Nashville, which took place about two weeks later, would be even worse—Hood's army was shattered. The battle began December 15, but in Richmond, three days later, Akin had heard only "a rumor…that Hood had another fight and has been terribly beaten."

The Georgia congressman was afraid the rumor was true, and, if so, Hood's "whole army is lost, I fear." Indeed, Hood would cross into Mississippi on Christmas Day and would soon resign his command, his army no longer an effective force.

By December 21, meanwhile, Akin again was writing home, this time with Christmas only four days away. "There will be no recess at Christmas, and I do not expect to get home until Congress adjourns, and I fear that will be March or April, and may be May."

As always seems the case, the legislative pace was slow. One important issue to the Confederacy in its final months was the proposal to open the ranks to blacks, a notion dismissed early in the war. By now, however, the South was desperate, and the prospect of additional manpower was a serious matter. The Second (and last) Congress would authorize President Jefferson Davis to ask the member states for three hundred thousand black soldiers, but not until mid-March 1865, too late to induct more than a few, much less deploy them.

Sitting at his desk in the House on December 22, Akin again wrote his wife: "O how glad I would be to eat dinner with you and my dear children Christmas." The next day he lamented the course of the war and the suffering throughout the Confederacy rather than dwelling on the yuletide, except to write at one point: "One more day and then it will be Christmas. O how glad I would be if I could go home tomorrow."

He also reported that a turkey in Richmond by now cost $125.

Finally the House decided there would be a brief Christmas recess after all, an adjournment for two business days.

It was the day after Christmas before Akin wrote his wife again. He reported that he had spent the day with "Anderson's Brigade" (probably Georgia's General George T. Anderson). "Rode out...[on horseback] and felt the effects of it last night." Akin, a good Methodist and occasional lay preacher, wrote that he preached a bit, and "I was very tired and did not get back until dark."

Akin did offer one observation of his Richmond surroundings: "The defenses are very strong, indeed, and I think the Yankees will be greatly slaughtered if they ever attack our men in their works."

He had been invited, he said, to two eggnog parties, "but have not gone to any." Instead, he tried to visit Vice President Alexander H. Stephens, also of Georgia. But, alas, Stephens was not home, and Akin returned to his lonely room and resumed writing a letter to his wife. He expressed regret that the House was not discharging its duties this day after Christmas, noting that members for some time had been determined "for going home and frolicking."

Akin remained in Richmond for the next several weeks, troubled not only by the Confederacy's declining hope of survival but also by his family's difficulties. His wife, their seven children, and six or seven slaves had been forced from their home in Bartow County, and then from a temporary abode at Oxford, southeast of Atlanta, to escape Union forces. They were now in exile at Elberton in Akin's native Elbert County.

The legislator finally rejoined his twice-displaced family on March 5 after a "long and tedious journey through the country." Congress was still in session when he left Richmond, and no reason is given for why such a dutiful member left his post after so much sacrifice earlier. It may be that his sense of duty to family finally prevailed. It may be, too, that he saw the proverbial writing on the wall—the surrender at Appomattox was barely a month away when Akin returned to Georgia.

Although his home and law office in Cassville had been burned by Union troops, Akin took his family back to Bartow County and picked up his legal practice after the war. He lived until a week before Christmas 1877. His widow lived until 1907. They were survived by two daughters and four sons.

The seventh child, another son, Elbert, had died in a pony-riding accident. Warren Akin learned that sad fact a few days later on his way home from Richmond in the bleak year of 1865.

Unlucky John Bell Hood

JOHN BELL HOOD WAS UNLUCKY IN LOVE AND WAR—INDEED, IN LIFE ITSELF. Although he built a fine combat record at a lower command level early in the war and continued in brave and dedicated service after losing a leg and suffering a crippled arm, he wound up the culprit historically (and somewhat unfairly) blamed for the loss of Atlanta to William Tecumseh Sherman.

After the war Hood found himself assailed in print again by Sherman over his mistakes and alleged shortcomings. This happened after Hood had endured the public censure of his former commander, the controversial Joseph E. Johnston, whose own dilatory deployments were a major reason the Confederacy lost Atlanta.

Hood, an 1853 graduate of West Point, started off the war well enough. Initially commander of the Texas Brigade, he fought well at Gaines' Mill outside of Richmond, at Second Bull Run, and at Antietam, all in 1862. Soon wearing two stars, he was known far and wide as a fighting general.

Unmarried and still relatively young, this Kentucky native might have been a fine "catch" for many a Confederate belle caught up in the romance of The Cause. Unfortunately, Hood chose to woo a very sophisticated young woman from South Carolina who was in Richmond with her father, the head of the Confederate conscription hierarchy. Sally Buchanan Preston (called "Buck") was known as a charming but wily "tease," and Hood was smitten by her charm and beauty until more gripping events swept him away.

He suffered in other ways, too, from the same doggedness seen in his hopeless pursuit of Sally "Buck" Preston, and unhappy personality clashes often were the result. At Antietam in September 1862 he blindly persisted in a contretemps with fellow Confederate general Nathan George Evans (like Buck Preston, from South Carolina) over a number of ambulance wagons Hood's men had captured the previous month at Second Bull Run.

Hood, it seems, had wanted his sick and wounded men to have use of the wagons, but Evans told Hood to turn them over to the South Carolina troops. "Whereas I would cheerfully have obeyed directions to deliver them to General Robert E. Lee's Quartermaster for the use of the Army," wrote Hood after the war, "I did not consider it just that I should be required to yield them to another brigade of the division, which was in no manner entitled to them."

Hood refused the order, whereupon he was "placed in arrest" and told to expect court-martial proceedings. In the meantime, Lee was moving into Maryland with the Army of Northern Virginia, with the Battle of Antietam soon to take place. At this point Hood persisted in his dispute to the point of dangerous insubordination. "I was still under arrest, with orders to move in the rear of my two brigades," recalled Hood, a popular commander in those days. At South Mountain, near Antietam Creek, shells began to burst near Hood's column. He could hear the men, as they angled up the ascent, calling out, "Give us Hood!"

At the base of the ridge, Hood came upon Lee, who told him, "General, here I am just upon the eve of entering into battle and with one of my best officers under arrest. If you will merely say that you regret this occurrence, I will release you and restore you to command of your division."

But the stubborn Hood would not back down, even before the venerated Robert E. Lee. He repeated his long-held assertion that the release of his wagons would be unjust, unless they were given up to use by Lee's entire army.

Lee repeated his request, and Hood still would not retreat from his position. An exasperated Lee finally had to concede. "Well," he said, "I will suspend your arrest till the impending battle is decided."

With that, Hood hastily remounted his horse and galloped off to lead his division. He has been credited ever since with stopping the Union attack on the Confederate left near Dunkard Church and West Woods during the Battle of Antietam Creek.

Almost a year after Antietam, Hood was badly wounded at Gettysburg, his left arm crippled. Hardly recovered from that wound, he bravely traveled to the western theater of war with his commander, James Longstreet, just in time to appear in the field at Chickamauga on September 18 through 20, 1863. There he lost his right leg to another severe wound. Hood insisted upon resuming duty, although he had to be helped in mounting his horse and needed a safety belt to keep him in the saddle. From this time on, he always traveled with an orderly in charge of the general's crutch.

After the amputation of his leg Hood was reassigned to his onetime commander (outside Richmond), General Johnston. The touchy Johnston, one of only five full generals in the Confederacy, was widely known for his dispute with President Jefferson Davis, who had ranked him fourth among those five.

Hood was reunited with Johnston in the face of Sherman's advance into Georgia, a campaign marked by successive Southern defeats and withdrawals, until finally the two were backed up close to Atlanta. At this point Davis sent the order for Hood to replace Johnston as commander of the Army of Tennessee and do what he could to stop Sherman. Although by now there was little that Hood really could do, some analysts fault the Kentuckian for his apparent confusion in some of his actions as the new head of an entire army.

Far worse would happen after Hood escaped Sherman's siege lines around Atlanta on September 1, 1864, and left the city to its fiery fate. Hood next crossed northern Alabama and struck into Tennessee, his avowed purpose to cut Sherman's supply lines from the rear.

All on his own as a full Army commander, Hood found himself approaching Franklin, Tennessee. When West Point classmate John Schofield's Federals escaped Hood's planned entrapment at nearby Spring Hill, Hood blamed his subordinate Benjamin Cheatham for failing to cut off Schofield, a feat that could easily have been accomplished by seizing the turnpike leading westward to Nashville. So enraged was Hood that he rescinded an earlier recommendation for Cheatham's promotion. When Cheatham then appeared before Hood to volunteer his error in the matter of the turnpike and to apologize, Hood rescinded again and allowed the endorsement of promotion to stand. Hood then persisted in assaulting Schofield with the most massive infantry charge of the whole war, but the Union troops held for five hours. In the end Hood was forced to retreat after losing 6,252 men, among them six generals killed outright, to the Union's 2,326 casualties.

The curtain came down for Hood at Nashville two weeks later. On December 15 his former West Point instructor, the Virginian George Thomas, dealt Hood's Army of Tennessee a final, shattering blow in two days of grim battle. On Christmas Day Hood retreated into Mississippi, where he soon relinquished command at his own request.

After the war, Hood refought many of his battles in a famous "Reply" to Joe Johnston's final depiction of Hood's failings. (The "Reply" became the centerpiece of Hood's personal memoirs.) Sherman then launched a flank attack on the ill-fated Confederate hero, listing various steps his onetime enemy Hood should have taken in response to the Union campaigns in Georgia and Tennessee.

Meanwhile, Sally "Buck" Preston had retreated from Richmond back to South Carolina before war's end. Hood apparently found marital bliss with another woman, but their marriage—and their lives—ended in New Orleans during the yellow fever epidemic of 1879. Sadly, at his death at forty-eight years of age, he and his wife were in a severe state of financial duress.

"On, Wisconsin...On!"

FEW REGIMENTS HAVE EVER HAD A HERO LIKE THE "BOY ADJUTANT" OF THE 24TH Wisconsin Volunteer Infantry, only seventeen when he and his companions marched off to war in 1862. Likewise, few heroes ever had a son as an expert—and moving—chronicler of their deeds. But this one surely did!

Three battles are the story here. At Stone's River—the first three days of 1863—his regiment lost nearly 40 percent of its men. Every mounted officer was felled, except for the youthful adjutant. The 24th Wisconsin began one day's action in a well-prepared line of rifle entrenchments, with artillery in supporting position. So fierce and swirling was the action that the Wisconsin regiment had to change frontal position fourteen times. By nightfall the regiment's men were back in their rifle pits again, but facing opposite the direction they had started out in that morning. The enemy was still in front, and the young adjutant was congratulated by Phil Sheridan, who noted: "You haven't lost a foot of ground."

The youth's finest hour was yet to come. He missed the Battle of Chickamauga due to a bout of typhoid fever, and one has to wonder if he really had his strength back by the time of Missionary Ridge on November 25, 1863. Brooding over Chattanooga, Tennessee, late that fall, the mountainlike rise presented a corrugated ground strewn with boulders, etched by gullies and ravines, and covered with difficult underbrush. From defensive lines beginning with rifle pits at the base and continuing up the steep, tough slopes to the crest, Braxton Bragg's Confederates awaited Union attack from the besieged city below.

None of it was too palatable for the Union troops under U. S. Grant's overall command and, in the case of the 24th Wisconsin, under the command of Grant's able subordinate Phil Sheridan. His troops were given the mission of taking the rifle pits at the foot of the mountain, which was done with bayonets. The rifle pits cleared, the next and far more imposing task was the steep, pitted rise itself, repeatedly swept by shot and shell. Would or could the conquerors of the rifle pits now start up the steep slope into the withering fire from the entrenched enemy?

Years later, the young Wisconsin adjutant's famous son would write his account of what happened next:

No one seems to know just what orders may have been given, but suddenly the flag of the 24th Wisconsin started forward. With it was the color sergeant, the color guard of two corporals, and the adjutant. Up they went, step by step. The enemy's fire was intense. Down went the color bearer. One of the corporals seized the color as they fell, but was bayoneted before he could move. A shell took off the head of the other corporal, but the adjutant grasped the flag and kept on. He seemed to be surrounded by nothing but gray coats. A Confederate colonel thrust viciously at his throat, but even as he lunged a bullet struck and the deflected blade just ripped a shoulder strap. There was no movement yet from the Union lines. And then, above the roar of battle, sounded the adjutant's voice: "On, Wisconsin!"

They come then—with a rush and a roar, a blue tide of courage, a whole division of them. Shouting, cursing, struggling foot by foot, heads bent as in a gale! Gasping breath from tortured lungs! Those last few feet before the log breastworks seem interminable! They falter! Officers are down! Sergeants now lead! And then, suddenly, on the crest—the flag! Once again that cry: "On, Wisconsin!" Silhouetted against the sky, the adjutant stands on the parapet waving the colors where the whole regiment can see him! Through the ragged blue line, from one end of the division to the other, comes an ugly roar, like the growl of a wounded bear! They race those last few steps, eyes blazing, lips snarling and bayonets plunging! And Missionary Ridge is won.

The adjutant then fell to the ground, "exhausted, his body retching, racked with pain." He was covered with blood and mud, "his smoke-blackened face barely recognizable, his clothes torn to tatters."

Sheridan, no novice to combat, was obviously stunned by his young officer's feat. "Sheridan, the division commander, utters not a word—he just stares at him—and then takes him in his arms. And his deep voice seems to break a little as he says: 'Take care of him. He has just won the Medal of Honor.'"

It wasn't long before the hero of Missionary Ridge distinguished himself again. At nineteen, he was a colonel, the youngest such officer in the entire Union Army. It was as one of eleven Union colonels leading eleven regiments that he took his 24th Wisconsin up the steep slopes of Kennesaw Mountain, Georgia, in 1864.

One by one, all eleven colonels went down, the youngest colonel of them all struck a crippling blow and left for dead—a shot had passed through one arm and coursed into the chest area. But there it was stopped short of mortal damage by a wadded obstruction. Halting the bullet just outside the walls of the heart was his wallet, and in it, letters from home, a Bible, and a farewell message.

The farewell message was the result of a meeting the previous night of all eleven regimental colonels. Their concerted conclusion was that their task of storming Kennesaw would be suicidal. Each then wrote a farewell message.

The former "boy adjutant" from Wisconsin, by now a full-fledged regimental commander, faced one more harsh test before the war ended for him. After recuperating from the wounds suffered at Kennesaw, he found himself at Franklin, Tennessee, a debacle for the South but a tough fight for anyone who was there. Here once again the youthful commander proved himself both hero and leader. His successor as regimental adjutant, Captain Edwin Parsons, later wrote of what happened after the Rebels suddenly struck the Federal line in front of the 24th Regiment—struck hard and fast, and indeed broke through the lines.

Not an instant could be lost. The whole army was imperilled unless the breach could be closed. I saw the Colonel swing into his saddle and heard his yell, "Up, Wisconsin!" There was no time to form lines. We just rushed pell mell to meet the enemy in a desperate hand to hand melee. I saw the Colonel sabering his way toward the leading Confederate flag. His horse was shot from under him, a bullet ripped open his right shoulder, but on foot he fought his way forward trying to bring down those Stars and Bars. A Confederate Major now had the flag and shot the Colonel through the breast. I thought he was done for but he staggered up and drove his sword through his adversary's body, but even as the Confederate fell he shot our Colonel down for good with a bullet through the knee. The other regiments of the reserve were now up and we drove the enemy back and healed the breach. When I returned to the Carter House, where they had brought the Colonel, I saw four dead Generals lying on the porch side by side.

Six generals, all Confederate, died at Franklin, Tennessee, that day, but there were more than a few Union casualties as well. What of the "boy colonel"?

Woefully stricken, he recovered and "rejoined the regiment in time to bring it home at the end of the war."

At Franklin, he had served beyond the mere call of duty. In the words of Union General David S. Stanley: "It is rare in history that one can say a certain unit saved the day. But this was the case at Franklin when the 24th Wisconsin, with no orders from higher up, by its spontaneous action, repelled the enemy and rectified our lines. In this it was bravely led by its young Colonel, Arthur MacArthur."

With the end of the war, the 24th "marched triumphantly through the streets of Milwaukee before the cheering crowds," wrote Arthur's son nearly one hundred years later. "But there was many a sob and tear in that great gathering. The regiment had lost more than two-thirds of its officers and men. They were mustered out on June 10, 1865, and Arthur MacArthur was again a civilian."

So wrote a proud son who himself was destined to be first in his class at West Point, to earn seven Silver Stars for heroism in World War I, to be awarded the Medal of Honor for his defense of the Philippines in World War II. So wrote Arthur's son, Douglas MacArthur.

Longest Siege

As THE GUNS BEGAN THEIR DEADLY DRUMBEAT, ONLY BOYS AND OLD MEN WERE on hand to fight back. In a few days, ninety thousand troops were wheeled up against the ten thousand defenders assembled here. And yet: "No lovelier day ever dawned than June 9, 1864," one of the surviving women later recalled of the first salvos.

Like all in Petersburg—even like the enemy at its gate—she was unprepared for the longest siege of any American city. For ten months they would endure shelling; blockade; economic deprivation; starvation balls; death in the trenches; lack of food; the disappearance of dogs, cats, even rats; inflated prices; daily bombardment; and death in the streets or backyards.

It lasted until April 2 or 3, 1865, just days before Appomattox. Robert E. Lee, accompanied by his horse, Traveller, was here much of the time to direct the defense of Petersburg.

The siege today is not so well known as the Battle of the Crater, the Union-triggered explosion beneath Confederate trenches just outside the city that resulted in a Union debacle.

Actor Joseph Cotten, a Petersburg native whose grandfather's farmland was a battlefield, narrated the story for a tourism film, saying: "This battle for Petersburg would be the life-and-death struggle for the entire Confederacy."

He knew so personally because, as he explained, "I was born and grew up in Petersburg, and my brother Whitford still lives here. As boys, we heard a lot of stories about life here in the siege. There are people all over town whose family histories are bound up with Petersburg's time of trial."

Cotten recited those memories in the short film, *The Echoes Still Remain*, premiered in 1978 by Petersburg's tourism experts of the twentieth century and shown at the city's Siege Museum, established in an antebellum commodities exchange and bank building.

Says Cotten in his narrative: "It would be a very personal struggle for survival as well. For now Grant's big guns began to fire directly on the city. They went on for hours that first day [June 9]—and that was only the beginning of almost daily shelling during the next 10 months. By the middle of the summer, both armies had dug in for a prolonged siege." To those trapped in Petersburg, he said, the countryside for miles around looked like "one enormous camp."

The Crater, he said, was the "most spectacular battle of the siege," but he noted also, "All the careful engineering that enabled the Union forces to tunnel under the Confederate line and blow a huge hole in it brought no advantage to either army, and both sides suffered heavy losses."

The really devastating event for Petersburg—no longer the major Southern trade and industrial center it once was—was the siege, including the daily bombardment by the Union forces outside the walls. Many have written of its effects.

"As soon as the enemy brought up their siege guns, or heavy artillery, which was only a few days after taking their positions, they opened on the city with shell without giving the slightest notice, or without giving opportunity for the removal of non-combatants, the sick, the wounded, or the women and children out of range of fire," wrote John H. Claiborne, a Confederate doctor here at the time. "To persons unfamiliar with the infernal noise made by the screaming, the ricocheting, and the bursting of the shells, it is impossible to describe the terror and the demoralization which was immediately created."

Indeed, we can wonder if any American city has ever endured as much. Besieged and starved of supplies, pounded by artillery day after day, with skirmishes and fights on every side, the Confederates were vastly outnumbered by the enemy in the not-so-distant trenches. The brave but dwindling Army, its beloved commander, the women and children—all trapped for ten months.

In recent years the city has been largely forgotten, but to U. S. Grant and Robert E. Lee it was a prize to be sought—or held—at nearly any cost, for it fed the Confederate capital of Richmond from a hub of far-flung railroad supply lines.

Grant had come at the end of his "sidling" campaign in June. Denied entry, his army encamped outside the city. By the time his siege ended, there were 125,000 Federals assembled to Lee's 57,000 or so.

The siege dictated a lifestyle for both sides. Deprivation, of course, was the order of the day for those inside the siege—that and a siege mood. Social life carried on, particularly the dances. "While we were in the trenches and matters comparatively quiet," wrote William M. Owen, a Confederate artillery officer, "we would often slip into town and get the girls together and have a dance."

If firing broke out, the tattered cavaliers "would have to scamper," but they'd be back in a hour or so to say:

"You have kept the dance for me, Miss? Only a small affair; one man killed, that's all."

"Oh, is that all!" the ladies would reply. "Come, they are forming the set."

They tell also of Confederate artillery genius Colonel E. Porter Alexander, an innovator who produced bullet-proof wooden shields for his Rebel artillerymen's guns. Wrote Owen also: "He [Alexander] introduced a system of awards for the men who could collect the largest amount of leaden bullets and fragments of shell fired by the enemy, and [he] would have the men chasing projectiles and fragments even before the former exploded."

Predictably, Alexander himself was seriously wounded one day collecting bullets in view of the enemy.

The Union side had its own frustrations. General Benjamin Butler, another innovator, seriously proposed a super fire engine that would "squirt water on earthworks and wash them all down," according to Union Colonel Theodore Lyman.

"By 1864, General Grant knew that to conquer the South he must immobilize this strategic little city," Cotten gently reminds us in his film. "The closeness of the battlefield made the siege a strangely intimate experience. Especially for the families whose men were part of the defense force. Almost daily, servants carried letters and small gifts—an apple, a bouquet of flowers—between the battlefield and the homes of the city."

The shortages extended to firewood, clothing, and shoes, but food was the worst problem as Grant's forces cut one rail line after another of the five radiating from the city.

"Many people actually starved to death during the siege," said Petersburg's director of tourism, John R. Elliott, in 1978. "The amazing thing is what Americans did to an American city."

Cotten also reported: "Eventually the pigeons disappeared from the street. Then the cats and dogs and even the rats. The suspicion grew that most of them had found their way into somebody's stew pot. It happened in the best of families."

Soon to come were "starvation" parties and dances, with hosts and guests ignoring the lack of any refreshments. Wrote Army surgeon Claiborne later on: "Ball followed ball, and the soldier met and danced with his lady love at night, and on the morrow danced the dance of death in the deadly trench."

In all, forty-two thousand Union men and twenty-eight thousand Confederates died or suffered wounds before the siege was lifted.

The end came when Grant captured three thousand Confederates and seized the last remaining rail line into Petersburg on April 1, 1865. After the Rebel lines collapsed on April 2, Lee withdrew, and on April 3 Grant and his troops entered the tired and tattered city.

"We sat all day in the front room," wrote one Southern survivor, "watching the splendidly equipped host as it marched by on its way to capture Lee. Our hearts sank within us!"

The triumphant Union forces issued a small but real newspaper on the day of their takeover: *Grant's Petersburg Progress.*

Headlines:

"Petersburg Ours!"

"We Are Here"

"Hallelujah!"

The lead paragraph in the account that followed showed that the unsigned author's sense of timing was somewhat off—

"For nearly six [sic] months the Army of the United States has kept watch and ward over the city of Petersburg. Since last June the roar of shells and the whistle of bullets have disturbed the silence of the woods in the vicinity, and today the old flag waves from the Court House. The United States armies and U. S. Grant have foreclosed and entered in possession and Petersburg is ours."

That pretty well tells it all. Richmond fell the same day as Petersburg. At Appomattox six days later, Lee's army, the heart of the Confederacy, collapsed. In those six days Abe Lincoln himself had visited Petersburg.

Petersburg's own *Daily Express* got back on its feet, and on April 13 it published this temperate advice for its readers:

"Our cause, whatever may have been the varied opinion of its justice or demerits, is now lost—hopelessly, irretrievably lost—and it is no less the part of duty than of wisdom to submit quietly and willingly to the 'powers that be,' acknowledge the supremacy of the flag that waves over us and strive, under the blessing of God, to secure all the happiness and prosperity that the symbol of the United States can confer." Fine thoughts, except that on the next day, April 14, Lincoln was assassinated, and all such fine sentiments of April 13 were suddenly and forever skewed.

Each to His Own Pathway

JAMES MCQUEEN MCINTOSH AND JOHN BAILLIE MCINTOSH WERE BROTHERS-IN-arms. James, born in Florida in 1828, graduated from West Point in 1849—at the bottom of his class. He first served with the U.S. Army's infantry, and was on frontier duty with the U.S. Cavalry when the Civil War broke out.

Brother John, born in 1829, had seen military service in the Navy during the Mexican War. He was strictly a civilian—a businessman in New Jersey—when the Civil War swept them both up.

Both brothers would reach the rank of general before the war was over.

James served in the western theater, while John, also in the cavalry branch, served in the eastern. John, in fact, collected quite a few major-battle stars. He was at Seven Days near Richmond, at South Mountain and Antietam in Maryland, at Chancellorsville in Virginia again, and at Gettysburg in Pennsylvania; then it was back to Virginia for Petersburg, Shenandoah Valley, and Third Winchester.

John did not survive the war entirely unscathed. After Gettysburg in 1863, he was injured when his horse fell, but a quiet cavalry command in the Washington defenses helped him to recuperate. At Winchester in September 1864 he lost a leg.

His brother, James, had experienced one major battle much earlier—at Pea Ridge, Arkansas, on March 7, 1862. James McIntosh, the West Pointer, fell at Pea Ridge, shot in the heart while leading the mounted troops of Ben McCulloch's Division—which had been fighting Union troops in Arkansas. James, the brother of Union general John McIntosh, had been a Confederate general.

It is said that John decided to join up on the Union side when his brother, James, joined the Confederacy. They never met in combat.

Squint to His Eye

HE WAS A JOLLY PRANKSTER, THIS HANCOCK, AND ONE COULD WONDER IF ON THIS day he had anything more than still another trick in mind. As his fellow prisoners held at Richmond knew all too well, he was likely to cut up, to mimic, to "put on" remarkable facial expressions at the slightest provocation or excuse.

He had been a Union scout under Grant, but in 1864 he was captured and accused of being a spy. As a prisoner, he had ample reason to use his diverting talents to relieve the cheerless prison life with merry song and dance. One evening, though, even as he sang for fellow prisoners, he suddenly stopped, threw up his hands, staggered, and fell like a bag of sand to the floor.

He didn't stir, and remarkably few, if any, of the onlookers thought it was a joke. The guards were solemnly told, and then the post surgeon. The man looked dead, but of course the post surgeon would make that determination

As Hancock could not have known in advance, the post surgeon was quite out of sorts, having just returned from a lengthy outing on horseback. Tired and anxious to go to his quarters for the night, he might not have looked too closely before his hasty pronouncement that Hancock was indeed dead.

In just twenty minutes, the recumbent Hancock was placed in a wagon to be sent to the hospital for preparation for burial.

The driver set off dutifully, but found upon his arrival that he was quite alone; nobody—that is to say, no body—remained in the wagon. Frantic, he retraced his path to see if the corpse had bounced out of the wagon. But…no luck there, either. He asked a few people if they had noticed a body by the roadside. Not really.

In fact, though, Hancock was entirely alive and still in Richmond. Indeed, where else could he go? If he plunged into the countryside beyond, he could run into a Rebel patrol.

Had the Union scout planned his escape? Surely not with a doctor's unexpected acquiescence. Yet he had money hidden away in his clothing, and now he simply walked through the streets of Richmond to a good hotel, checked in, and plunged into a clean bed for the night.

The next day he bought fresh clothes and wandered freely, speaking to various persons he met in his bold travels. To some he said he was in the Confederate capital as a businessman securing a government contract; to others he imparted the news that he was a Confederate secret agent.

After dinner, however, he was arrested on Richmond's Main Street. Provost troops, the equivalent of today's military police, spotted him as the man who exactly fit their fugitive's description. But he was detained for only a moment since on closer examination it appeared their prisoner was cross-eyed and his mouth pulled to one side.

With his accosters confused, Hancock then drew on the good offices of his hotel clerk. Incredibly, the clerk was passing by at the moment, and he spoke up for Hancock, who then was allowed to go free.

So far so good, but not for long. In four days, the escapee was broke. At the post office he was arrested once more, and again he resorted to his contortions. His mouth pulled, his left eye squinted, and he pretended to be deaf. He was taken in this time and returned to his former abode, once more a prisoner.

But neither the guards nor his fellow prisoners could say with any real certainty that he was the man who had escaped—that he was Hancock. They were thoroughly confused by his remarkable squint.

Every story, or course, has its end, and Hancock's was fast approaching.

"For seven long days the scout kept his mouth twisted around and his eye on the squint, and then he got tired of it and resumed his accustomed phiz," says the nineteenth-century book Stories of the Civil War, adapted by Albert F. Blaisdell. The minute he let go the squint, everyone recognized him as Hancock.

Back in custody and accused of spying, he all too soon would have been executed, as others in the same circumstance often were. It was his good fortune that Appomattox was close at hand, even though, during his moment of freedom, Richmond had not quite yet fallen. "The close of the war gave him his liberty with the rest, but 10 days longer would have seen him shot as a spy," says Blaisdell's book.

Ugly Blows Exchanged

Scuffleburg was the meeting place. Hidden away in a hollow of the Blue Ridge Mountains in Virginia, it was "a place peculiarly adapted to the meeting of partisan rangers to transact business pertaining to their system of warfare." So wrote one of Mosby's Rangers, J. Marshall Crawford.

The despised Yankees, he added, "imagined it a second Gibraltar, filled with all kinds of infernal machines and implements of warfare, and believed that none of them who got there ever returned." And so: "The foot of no Yankee soldier ever trod its magnificent thoroughfares, or reposed his wearied form under the stately oaks and chestnuts…while the mountain breeze refreshed his burning cheek with the perfume of the wild honeysuckle, and the air was musical with the songs of birds."

Whether or not a Yankee ever intruded, Scuffleburg remained a rendez-vous point typical of Mosby, the University of Virginia graduate, lawyer, and onetime cavalryman under "Jeb" Stuart who conducted harassing raids against the Union occupiers of northern Virginia. Typically, Mosby and his partisan-like troop struck, then dispersed, only to meet again by prior arrangement at hideaways like Scuffleburg.

So successful was this master of the hit-and-run attack that his hunting ground, with all its hidden lairs, became known as "Mosby's Confederacy." As the war wound down, however, it became more and more ugly for the often-romanticized Mosby and his proud rangers. Life was no lark, and the air was no longer "musical with the song of birds." Instead, in those last months, death was on the wing.

West of the Blue Ridge in the fall of 1864, Union cavalry commander Phil Sheridan was the latest target of Mosby's harassment. The "Grey Ghost's" of-ficially titled 43rd Virginia Battalion "had been having a generally bang-up time throughout October, sniping at [railroad] workers, derailing locomotives, lobbing howitzer shells into Union camps, and helping themselves to enemy paymasters' strongboxes," wrote Roy Morris Jr. in his biography, *Sheridan: The Life and Wars of Phil Sheridan.* In one such raid, they grabbed $173,000, and in another they grabbed a nice hostage, a brigadier general named Alfred Duffie.

Instead of trading purely military blows, however, the Union and Confederate antagonists often exchanged executions.

"Several members of the Fifth Michigan Cavalry, surprised that fall by Mosby's men while looting a farmhouse, were shot or hanged," writes Morris; "hams were tied to the victims' legs, along with a card promising other for-agers a similar fate." In another "hardcase" incident, a Union straggler was evidently surprised while skinning a stolen sheep. He was killed, and a hoof was jammed into his mouth. A note left with the body said: "I reckon you got enough sheep now."

This all came at a time when Sheridan was torching his way northward through the Shenandoah Valley, laying waste to fields, barns, food stores; a time for years after to be called "the Burning." Too, Ulysses S. Grant had ordered that Mosby's troopers should be treated as partisans rather than soldiers serving their cause honorably. The back-and-forth executions had been going on for weeks.

"A self perpetuating cycle of atrocities, reprisals, and counter-reprisals," Morris called it, and rightly so.

An incident in late September had inflamed feelings on both sides. When a Union lieutenant's horse bolted into a knot of Rebels, the Union man was shot and killed. His compatriots thought he was shot while trying to surrender, so they then took six newly captured rangers (one a seventeen-year-old who was not a member of Mosby's group) and executed all six in Front Royal, Virginia. Mosby "bitterly vowed retribution."

In another incident, John Meigs, son of the Federal quartermaster general, Montgomery C. Meigs, was killed in another questionable episode. Outside of Harrisonburg, Virginia, one rainy day, Lieutenant Meigs and two order-lies encountered three Rebs (all six men in ponchos covering their uniforms). Shooting broke out, and Meigs was left dead.

Told that his young officer had simply been shot down execution style, a furious Sheridan "resolved to punish the unoffending residents of Dayton, the site of the shooting, on the wrong-headed assumption that the 'murderers' lived in the area and had been visiting their homes prior to the deed." He issued orders to burn down every house within a five-mile radius. Fortunately, "cooler heads prevailed," and the order was canceled, a welcome respite for the pacifistic Mennonites who lived in the area. They had nothing to do with the three Rebs in question, all privates with Brigadier General Thomas Rosser's cavalry.

In fact, the story that emerged later was that Meigs had fired on them first, using a pistol hidden under his poncho. He had wounded one Confederate, George W. Martin. The other two, Benjamin F. Shavers and F. M. Campbell, then fired back and fatally wounded Meigs. "Ironically," added Morris, "Martin, whose own gun misfired, went into hiding for several years after the war, a one-thousand-dollar bounty having been placed on his head by Meigs's bereaved father, who mistakenly thought Martin had killed his son."

Still more ugly incidents followed the Meigs affair at Dayton, which for a time was blamed on Mosby's men. A week later a Union quartermaster officer and an army doctor were "shot dead within Union lines near Newtown," also in the Shenandoah Valley. Next, the Federals hanged a freshly captured Mosby trooper on October 13. Then, in early November Mosby acted in reprisal for the Front Royal executions of September. Erroneously blaming George Armstrong Custer for those killings, he had been collecting as his prisoners as many of Custer's men as possible. By Morris's account, he informed Robert E. Lee in late October, "It is my purpose to hang an equal number of Custer's men whenever I capture them." Lee, "without undue gentlemanly hesitation, approved the scheme."

After seven unfortunates among twenty-seven Yankee prisoners were selected by a drawing for execution, Mosby had them taken to Beemer's Woods west of Berryville, Virginia, close to Custer's camp. On the way, one Federal prisoner persuaded a fellow Mason among Mosby's men to let him go and execute another freshly captured Custer trooper instead—a switch that Mosby only learned of later and severely condemned.

In the early-morning darkness, the unlucky Union prisoners marked for execution were brought forth. Two of them escaped, but the others were executed, their bodies left with a note saying they had been killed "in retaliation for an equal number of Colonel Mosby's men hung by order of General Custer, at Front Royal. Measure for measure."

Mosby then sent Sheridan a note saying that in the future he would treat his prisoners with "the kindness due to their condition, unless some new act of barbarity shall compel me to reluctantly adopt a course of policy repulsive to humanity."

There is no historical record of Sheridan's response, noted Morris, "but the absence of any Union retaliation, then or later, strongly suggests that he took the message to heart."

In the aftermath, Sheridan did send his subordinate Wesley Merritt on a "Burning Raid" into "Mosby's Confederacy," described as that square of country "bounded on the south by the line of the Manassas Gap Railroad…on the east by the Bull Run Range, on the West by the Shenandoah River, and on the north by the Potomac." In the effort to drive off Mosby and punish the local residents who put up with his guerrilla band, Sheridan ordered Merritt to "consume and destroy all forage and subsistence, burn all barns and mills… and drive off all stock in the region." At the same time, perhaps to avoid a new round of unorthodox casualties, Sheridan also told Merritt, "no dwellings are to be burned and…no personal violence be offered to the citizens."

Merritt did his job with terrible thoroughness, burning barns and other outbuildings, purging the land of all livestock. This time it didn't matter that many locals were Quakers or Union sympathizers, noted Morris. By his account, Sheridan told one subordinate, "Should complaints come in from the citizens of Loudoun County, tell them that they have furnished too many meals to guerrillas to expect much sympathy."

While the countryside was devastated, Mosby was not yet knocked out of the contest. By the end of 1864, his 43rd Battalion had grown to eight companies. Indeed, he was still fighting as late as the day after Lee's surrender to Grant at Appomattox on April 9, 1865—a final raid conducted just prior to dispersing his troops in a review ceremony at Salem (now Marshall), Virginia. The widely hailed

Confederate hero returned to a law practice and then surprised and angered many of his fans and colleagues by turning Republican and even supporting Grant for president in 1868 and Rutherford B. Hayes, also a Union officer, in 1876. Mosby served as a U.S. consul in Hong Kong and as an assistant attorney for the Federal Justice Department. He wrote two books recalling his wartime experiences. He died in 1916 in Washington, D.C., at the age of eighty-two.

They Also Served

NOT TO BE CONFUSED WITH SECOND COUSIN THOMAS J. JACKSON, BETTER KNOWN as "Stonewall," this Jackson was also a Confederate officer. Before the war he had been a lawyer, judge, and lieutenant governor of his native Virginia. During the war, he served honorably and rose to the rank of brigadier as a cavalryman. He served as an aide on Stonewall Jackson's staff in the latter's famed Shenandoah Valley campaign and saw action in the Seven Days campaign and in the battles of Second Bull Run and Antietam. He returned to Maryland for the Jubal Early incursion, which was finally halted outside Washington. Long after cousin Stonewall's death, he returned to the valley for resumed fighting at Winchester, Fisher's Hill, and Cedar Creek.

After the war, he refused to surrender and sought refuge in Mexico for a time, then resumed the practice of law and again became a judge, this time in Kentucky. Not ever to be confused with second cousin Stonewall, this Jackson was known to his contemporaries as "Mudwall."

★★★

This son of Indiana was a Mexican War veteran, state senator, and lawyer when the Civil War broke out. Soon vaulted to the rank of brigadier and then major general, he endured what might be described as an up-and-down military career on behalf of the Union. He won accolades for routing the Rebs at Romney in today's West Virginia, and he did well as the head of a new division under U. S. Grant at Fort Donelson, but he was criticized for his slow reactions at Shiloh. Soon after, he organized a stout defense of Cincinnati. He fatally slowed raiding Confederates under Jubal Early at Monocacy, Maryland, outside Washington, late in the war. He sat on the court-martial that convicted those who participated in the Lincoln assassination and on the panel that ordered the execution of Andersonville Prison's commandant Henry Wirz. He dabbled in ventures against Mexico's Emperor Maximillian, he was governor of the New Mexico Territory, and he once served as an American diplomat in Turkey.

For none of those reasons is he best known today. Rather, the only American writer to be honored with a likeness placed in Statuary Hall in the U.S. Capitol, he was Lew Wallace, author of the phenomenally successful novel *Ben Hur: A Tale of the Christ*.

★★★

Father and son John A. and Ulric Dahlgren were an admiral and cavalry colonel, respectively, for the Union. Admiral Dahlgren was the ordnance expert whose eleven-inch Dahlgren gun was put to effective use against Charleston by the Union Navy's South Atlantic Blockading Squadron under his command. Prior to that sea-going posting, he was chief of the Navy's Bureau of Ordnance. He probably could have felt personal pride and satisfaction at war's end but for the death of his son Ulric in both heroic and controversial circumstances—and the macabre aftermath.

A lawyer as a civilian, Ulric survived several actions unscathed until wounded at Boonesboro, Maryland, right after Gettysburg. Despite his foot injury, he would not quit the battle scene until falling unconscious from loss of blood. He then lost his leg from below the knee to a surgeon's knife. He recovered to fight again, equipped with a wooden leg, this time leading a five-hundred-man detachment from Judson Kilpatrick's proposed raid on Richmond in early 1864. Equipped with a wooden leg, Dahlgren was killed March 2 in Henrico County next to the city.

The controversy arose when Confederate officials claimed that papers found on his body revealed a plan to assassinate Jefferson Davis and other highly placed members of the Confederate government. The macabre twist was that agents of Union spy Elizabeth van Lew secretly dug up the young officer's body from its battlefield burial place and spirited it to awaiting Union hands to be carried north for reburial in a family plot.

★★★

John Wise and son O. Jennings Wise were another father-and-son pair. John was a Confederate general and Jennings was a member of the Richmond Light Infantry Blues when Ambrose Burnside stormed Roanoke Island, North Carolina, in February 1862. The elder Wise had been governor of Virginia before the war, and soon after the hostilities erupted he served as commander of Wise's Legion in mountainous western Virginia. In command of the Confederacy's eastern North Carolina sector when Roanoke Island fell, he later served in the Seven Days campaign outside Richmond, fought at Drewry's Bluff, commanded Confederate elements at Petersburg, and brought his unit through the Battle of Sayler's Creek hurting but intact. Appomattox came just days later, but Wise never accepted the Union proffer of amnesty, perhaps because his son had fallen with mortal wounds at Roanoke Island.

★★★

His star did not shine very brightly during the Civil War, but before the hostilities broke out, there was no stopping the great Western adventurer, explorer, and widely ballyhooed "pathfinder" John C. Frémont. His antebellum résumé was so impressive that Abraham Lincoln gave him the Army's highest rank at war's start. Indeed, the officer from the Army's Corps of Topographical Engineers had been a real pathfinder as an explorer of the Far West. Apparently acting under secret orders from President James K. Polk, and not averse to intrigue, he had been instrumental in wresting future California from Mexico's claim. He underwent court-martial for his role in establishing the territory as an American state, but that did not stop him from amassing a fortune, serving as U.S. senator from California, or even running for president in 1856 as the new-born Republican Party's first nominee for the White House (an election won by Democrat James Buchanan).

During the Civil War, however, Frémont's star dimmed after he failed to give full support to Nathaniel Lyons at Wilson's Creek in Missouri and continued his independent ways by issuing an emancipation proclamation of his own for Missouri—months ahead of Lincoln's emancipation decree. He then eluded delivery of orders sent to relieve him of command until a disguised emissary placed the papers in his hands. Frémont was later given a chance to prove himself against Stonewall Jackson in the Shenandoah Valley, with a predictably dismal result. Assigned next to John Pope's newly formed Army of Virginia, Frémont refused to take orders from Pope and was again relieved, this time permanently.

After the war, his fortune dwindling, he served as governor of the Arizona territory for ten years. His U.S. Army retirement rank was major general, the rank that Lincoln had granted him at the start of the war.

★★★

John and Willie Pegram were sons of Virginia and brave men both. The higher ranking and older was John—West Point graduate, cavalryman, and engineer. He was a major general in the Confederate Army and served with distinction in various battles and many demanding posts in both the east and west. His wedding in Richmond in the winter weeks before Appomattox was a rare bright spot in the city's declining social life. Three weeks later, his bride, Hetty Cary, and many of the wedding guests were back in the same Richmond church for his funeral. John Pegram had been killed at a place called Hather's Run.

His brother, Willie, rose in rank from private to colonel and achieved a reputation as an artillerist with an array of impressive battle stars all his own. Just days before Appomattox and weeks after his brother's death, Willie Pegram was killed at Five Forks.

★★★

The adopted son of a ranking U.S. Navy officer, this Civil War figure went to sea as a midshipman at age nine. He briefly commanded a captured prize ship at age twelve during the War of 1812. Born James, he changed his first name to David, apparently in honor of his adoptive father, Admiral David Porter. It was as David Farragut, however, that he became a U.S. naval legend when, subduing the defenses of Mobile Bay, he uttered the famous cry (or something very close to the version known today), "Damn the torpedoes! Full speed ahead!" (He meant mines, actually.) While Farragut did subdue the bay's defending forts and drive off or defeat the defending Confederate ships by the end of August 1864, he also should be recalled as the Union's conqueror of New Orleans (April 24, 1862), vital to control of the Mississippi. He then helped blockade the lower Mississippi and the Gulf waters below and supported Grant's campaign against Vicksburg higher up on the Mississippi.

Coincidentally, as a child he had lived in New Orleans—the city he later captured for the Union.

Story with a Kick

Professor John B. Minor of the august University of Virginia was worried on March 1, 1865, as Union troops filtered into Charlottesville and the town's university precincts. He was just one member of a joint committee of university and town leaders who greeted the incoming Federal officers and asked them to prevent looting by their troops.

General George Armstrong Custer sent word by two staff officers that "no damage to the buildings would be tolerated; and that a squad would be assigned to furnish the amplest protection," wrote Professor Philip Alexander Bruce in his centennial history of the school (1819–1919).

Hardly had that assurance been conveyed than at the very edge of the university grounds Professor Minor "observed a couple of soldiers desert the main road, and turn in towards the rear of his pavilion [campus residence]."

Hurrying to his house on Thomas Jefferson's famous Lawn, Minor was relieved to find that his wife had intercepted the pair after they asked the Minor servants if any silver plate was hidden on the premises. "As soon as they were told that a guard was to be stationed on the grounds, the two men remounted their horses, and rode off."

And so, they missed the mule—Professor Minor's balky, temperamental, difficult female mule.

She might have been a bit elderly for her kind, but she was still dear to the Minor household, and no bluecoat was to grab her! "Her keeper and companion, an old servant of the house, had at the first alarm solemnly led her off to the wooded fastness of Observatory Mountain."

That sanctuary close by the university should have been safeguard enough, but it seems the stubborn mule didn't care for a stay in the rough. She let loose her strident bray and thus revealed her hiding place to one and all.

The Federal officer in charge of the campus guard—"a plain illiterate man, but courteous in his deportment and kindly disposed in spirit"—suggested it would be safer to bring her back to the campus she was so used to "as the only way to keep her out of the clutches of Federal stragglers."

Still worried, Professor Minor went the officer one better—he brought the mule back in the dark of night and without telling his Federal guardian installed the recalcitrant animal in his cellar.

She didn't care much for this arrangement either, "and soon showed a disposition to kick with great violence, and to make many strange and alarming noises at unexpected and ill-considered moments."

Still, she was in Minor's cellar, and the outside world did not hear the hullabaloo.

The next evening, the unsuspecting Federal officer (a captain from Michigan, it is believed) came to dinner at the Minors. He was seated without incident, and prevailing among all at the table was an atmosphere of "peace and serenity, in spite of the depression of the times." With the war very nearly over, it could be called a moment of reconciliation. "The captain was gracious and conciliatory, and the professor courteous and agreeable."

But the mule down below, quiet until now, was not to be ignored any longer. "In the midst of their conversation, there came suddenly the sound of some extraordinary commotion that was happening beneath the floor of the dining room."

It is not recorded whether the Federal officer actually leaped to his feet in alarm, but, "disturbed and suspicious," he did at least rise from the table. After all, "the uproar was so loud and so confused that it was impossible to distinguish its cause."

For a tense moment, the captain from Michigan "seemed to be apprehensive of a personal attack from without," but Minor, convulsed with laughter, was finally able to gasp out that it was only the old mule hidden in the cellar below. The meal was resumed, we are told, "amid hearty laughter over the one humorous episode which lit up the dark clouds that enshrouded the hour."

Two More to Mourn

FOR THE SOUTH, MAY 11, 1864, WAS ONE MORE UNFORTUNATE DAY TO MARK. Two days earlier Phil Sheridan had set out with ten thousand hard-riding Union troopers against Richmond itself, and on this day at Yellow Tavern, six miles north of the capital city, J. E. B. Stuart threw himself into the breach.

A hard-riding, legendary, ballad-singing man's man in an era of many brave heroes, Stuart had only forty-five hundred cavalrymen when he began the conflict. He then divided the forty-five hundred men, sending James Gordon after one prong of the Federal attack and taking the remainder to block the bluebellies at Yellow Tavern.

There a Union private named John Huff got off a lucky pistol shot, and Stuart was struck in the stomach while in the saddle. Reeling from the blow, he managed to turn his horse about and ride for his own lines.

Aided by his men, he was carried to Richmond, to the home on Grace Street of his brother-in-law, Charles Brewer, a doctor, it so happened. There he would linger for another day.

He was attended during his painful passage from life by several doctors and visited by fellow officers, by the Episcopal minister who would soon be burying him, and even by President Jefferson Davis, who knew him well.

Word had been sent to Stuart's wife, Flora, who was off in the country and would have some distance to travel before reaching his side. "I would like to live to see my wife," said Stuart upon being told that his wound was a mortal one. "But God's will be done."

In the meantime, Jefferson Davis spent about fifteen minutes with the Confederacy's famous cavalryman. He took Stuart's hand and gently asked, "General, how do you feel?" and Stuart answered, "Easy, but willing to die if God and my country think I have fulfilled my destiny and done my duty."

Here was an echo of another sad moment, a year and a half earlier. Stuart's five-year-old daughter had fallen ill. Busy with his war duties, he could not go to her side in Lynchburg, Virginia. "I shall have to leave my child in the hands of God," he said. "My duty requires me here." He of course wept when told little Flora had died.

Now Stuart himself was dying. As he applied ice to the wound with his own hand, he said he was resigned to his death. Close to the end, Stuart stated some last-minute bequests. He gave his horses out to his staff, stipulating that the largest horse should go to a large man among his beneficiaries. He said his sword should go to his one surviving son. For Mrs. Robert E. Lee, there were Stuart's own golden spurs, a symbol of his affection and respect for her husband, Stuart's commander.

Stuart asked the minister to lead in the singing of a hymn, with Stuart himself weakly joining in. He also took part in a prayer.

Earlier, his delirium had provoked memories of battle and command, old orders and new, imaginary ones. Now, at the end, all was so much more simple and peaceful. "I am going fast now: I am resigned," he said. "God's will be done."

His wife arrived about ninety minutes after he had passed.

In the church service that followed, fellow generals were among the pallbearers who carried his remains to the altar, while President Davis and many other luminaries of the Confederacy looked on from quiet pews. Stuart's remains then were borne to the waiting grave at Richmond's Hollywood Cemetery in a hearse decorated by black plumes and drawn by four milky-white horses.

★★★

On another unfortunate day for the South, the general's aide, Sergeant George Tucker, had to wonder why they were riding slowly, somewhat aimlessly it seemed, so close to the bluecoats who had broken through the Rebel lines at Petersburg on Sunday, April 2, 1865. A few minutes earlier, Robert

E. Lee had also wondered about the condition (mental and physical) of his devoted subordinate, Ambrose Powell Hill.

For months, A. P. Hill, the victim of venereal disease picked up in a wayward moment of his youth, had been showing the effects of the long-term illness. The West Point graduate, one of Lee's greatest lieutenants, had had to relinquish command of his army corps for a time during the great slugging matches of 1864: the Wilderness, Spotsylvania, Cold Harbor. He rode his horse in great pain and hobbled when he walked. While just about everyone in Lee's command suffered from the hardships of deprivation and fatigue, in A. P. Hill's case diseases of the prostate and the kidneys were also taking their toll.

When he painfully mounted his steed Champ that morning, wrote James I. Robertson Jr. in his biography *General A. P. Hill: The Story of a Confederate Warrior*, Lee had been "disturbed" by the "sudden and unexpected fire" he saw in Hill "after weeks of sickness." He sent an aide after Hill to tell him to be careful.

But he wasn't. When he and Sergeant Tucker a short while later saw a large cluster of men next to some huts abandoned by the Confederates defending Petersburg, Tucker asked whose men they were. "The enemy's," said Hill matter-of-factly.

He seemed in a daze, perhaps induced by uremic poisoning.

As they rode on, skirting the danger zone, the worried Tucker interrupted again. "Please excuse me, General, but where are we going?"

Hill informed him they were going to General Henry Heth's headquarters. They rode on, the countryside seemingly empty again. Hill "suddenly spoke up," adds Robertson's account. "Sergeant," he said, "should anything happen to me, you must go back to General Lee and report it."

In moments they came across more Federals and turned aside toward some screening woods, both with their revolvers in hand. In the woods, though, were a half dozen more Union soldiers. "Suddenly two of them ran behind a large tree." They aimed their muskets at Tucker and Hill. Not twenty yards lay between the two parties. Tucker called upon the two Federals to surrender. So did Hill.

Silence.

Then shots. Private Daniel Wolford of the 138th Pennsylvania missed. Corporal John W. Mauck, a carpenter in civilian life, did not. Struck in the heart, Hill "died instantly."

Tucker found Lee a short while later, astride his own horse on Cox Road, "handsomely dressed, sword buckled to his waist." As the sergeant made his sad report, Lee could not hide his sorrowful reaction. Indeed, an aide later said, "Never shall I forget the look on General Lee's face." With tears in his eyes, Lee said, "He is now at rest, and we who are left are the ones to suffer."

As Robertson also pointed out, it was only hours later that Lee's Army of Northern Virginia abandoned Petersburg and "began its death march to Appomattox."

The army left chaos in its wake. Richmond, the capital of the Confederacy, also fell that day. The city was engulfed in fire, and thousands fled the doomed city, their exodus a one-way tide across the James River bridges. Against this flow some hours after A. P. Hill's death, a ramshackle Army wagon carrying his body struggled to enter the city. "The family wish was to bury Hill in Hollywood Cemetery, the capital's 'Place of Heroes,'" wrote Robertson. But they were to be frustrated since "every road leading out of town was packed with soldiers, civilians, wagons, carriages and horses." Only the wagon carrying Hill's remains was pointed toward the city.

Family members—a pair of cousins—tried again about 1:00 a.m. on April 3. Finally succeeding in crossing the river, they found "the downtown stores were deserted and in shambles as a result of widespread looting." They needed a coffin, and after searching "from building to building," they came across "a small plain pine coffin" in a funeral home. They washed Hill's face, wrapped him in his Army coat, and placed him in the pine box. With no one available to arrange burial at Hollywood and Union troops expected to march into town at any moment, the two cousins carried their burden back to the Chesterfield County estate of A. P. Hill's uncle, Henry Hill. During an illness-imposed furlough only two weeks earlier, Hill and his wife, Dolly (the former Kitty Morgan, sister of John Hunt Morgan), had stayed there. Now this would be the slain general's burial place, at least for the time being. His body later was re-interred at Hollywood, then—and finally—beneath a monument erected in his memory in Richmond.

Prophetically, reported biographer Robertson, the forty-eight-year-old Hill had said while on a visit to Richmond with his uncle Henry in March, just the month earlier, "that he did not wish to survive the fall of Richmond." And he didn't.

Embarrassing Outing

WHEN MRS. LINCOLN WAS ON ONE OF HER JEALOUS STREAKS THERE WAS HARDLY any way to hide the embarrassing fact. On one occasion when a general's wife was given special permission by the president himself to remain at a Union encampment near Petersburg, Mrs. Lincoln was beside herself when she heard of it.

"What do you mean by that, sir?" she expostulated. "Do you mean to say that she saw the President alone? Do you know that I never allow the President to see any woman alone?"

General Adam Badeau probably didn't know. On the scene as an aide to Ulysses S. Grant and escorting officer for Mrs. Lincoln and Julia Grant as they visited the troops outside Petersburg just before the war's end, he was taken aback at the outburst, never suspecting that even worse was yet to come.

"I tried to pacify her and palliate my remark [about the special permission], but she was fairly boiling over with rage," he wrote later.

It was only with great difficulty that Julia Grant persuaded Mrs. Lincoln against stopping their carriage to go ask her husband if he had been alone with the woman in question.

The next day, the visit to the Union encampments at City Point, (Hopewell, Virginia, today), with Grant himself showing Lincoln the sights, ran aground on even more vicious shoals of jealousy. The fit began when Mrs. Lincoln, again in her carriage, saw that another general's wife, Mrs. Edward Ord, was mounted on a horse and riding next to Lincoln himself. That was only polite since she was the wife of the commander of the Army of the James—and the ambulance carrying the ladies was full in any case.

Mrs. Lincoln soon reacted. Again the raconteur is General Badeau, whose account some historians consider rather embellished.

"What does the woman [Mrs. Ord] mean," cried Mary Todd Lincoln, "by riding by the side of the President and ahead of me? Does she suppose that he wants her by the side of him?"

That was only the beginning, and this time Julia Grant was unable to pacify the president's wife, who in moments turned her wrath against even Julia herself. Badeau and another escorting officer were concerned "to see that nothing worse than words occurred." For one thing, they were afraid that Mrs. Lincoln would leap from her carriage "and shout to the cavalcade," she was so agitated.

It was at this point, apparently, that she angrily said to Julia Grant, "I suppose you think you'll get to the White House yourself, don't you?" Julia Grant maintained her calm and merely replied that she was quite satisfied with her present position; it was far greater than she had ever expected to attain.

Mrs. Lincoln wouldn't let the matter go. "Oh!" she declared. "You had better take it if you can get it. 'Tis very nice."

Four years later, Julia and Ulysses Grant indeed would occupy the White House, although one has to wonder how many people seriously thought that a likely prospect before Lincoln's death. In any case, having dispensed with Julia

Grant for the moment, Mary Todd now turned her blazing light once more on the unfortunate Mrs. Ord.

Stumbling into the fray just then was Secretary of State William Seward's young nephew, a major in the Union Army. He rode up to the ladies' ambulance-carriage to exchange pleasantries, only to say exactly the wrong thing considering the circumstances. "The President's horse is very gallant, Mrs. Lincoln," he began. "He insists on riding by the side of Mrs. Ord."

When Mrs. Lincoln reacted by crying out, "What do you mean by that, sir?" related the onlooking General Badeau later, "Seward discovered that he had made a huge mistake, and his horse at once developed a peculiarity that compelled him to ride behind, to get out of the way of the storm."

Before the day's unhappy episode was over, Mrs. Ord herself innocently approached Mrs. Lincoln's carriage. By General Badeau's account, "Mrs. Lincoln positively insulted her, called her vile names in the presence of a crowd of officers, and asked what she meant by following up the President."

The publicly branded Mrs. Ord was reduced to tears before one and all, "and everybody was shocked and horrified." Mrs. Lincoln railed on, "'til she was tired."

That evening, still unappeased, Mrs. Lincoln was hostess at a dinner for the ranking officers on hand, including the Grants, General Grant's staff, and General Ord. She took occasion at this gathering aboard the president's steamer in the James River to "berate" General Ord "and urged that he should be removed," once again creating an ugly scene. "He was unfit for his place," she said, to say nothing of his wife. General Grant sat next to and defended his officer "bravely."

Later in life, Julia Grant refuted much of Badeau's gossipy report, but she and others did leave the impression that something unpleasant took place at City Point. From all reports of this and other scenes, it seems fair to say that Mrs. Lincoln's husband had his burdens aside from the crushing weight of the Civil War itself.

Surviving to Serve Again

THE REMARKABLE THING ABOUT OHIO'S BATTLE-SCARRED COLONEL HAYES WAS not so much that one day soon he would secretly be sworn in as president while attending dinner one night at the White House of Ulysses S. Grant, but the added circumstance that on the Colonel's staff was another young officer,

William McKinley, also destined to serve one day as president. Still another future president, James A. Garfield—four Union officers in all—hailed from the state of Ohio.

The nation, unaware at the moment, came ever so close to doing without the future services of President Hayes. At South Mountain on the eve of Antietam in September 1862, he was badly wounded above the left elbow while leading a charge by elements of his 23rd Ohio. Although the injury was severe, he rose to his feet and urged his men onward until he finally became so weak and faint that he fell helplessly to the ground again. There, between the battle lines, he was trapped, possibly to be captured by the enemy or, worse, left to die of his wound.

Despite the Rebel fire, his men dashed forward and pulled him back to their own lines. Even so, it was possible that his arm would have to be amputated because of the damage from the musket ball. Fortunately, Rutherford B. Hayes was able to avoid that radical step—often fatal to the wounded of the Civil War era—and after recovering, he continued to serve.

Truly a war hero by any definition, Hayes, an attorney in civilian life, began his Civil War service as a major in the Ohio Volunteers. He ended the war as a brigadier general—and a member of Congress who had eschewed the safety of the legislative corridors to remain in uniform.

Before the shooting was over, he had survived several battles and four woundings. The first came in Virginia in a skirmish on May 10, 1862, a minor injury inflicted by an artillery shell—his right knee, he later said, was "scratched."

After escaping the surgeon's knife at South Mountain later in 1862, he was shot in the head and shoulder at Winchester, Virginia, in September 1864. He was able to rebound quickly enough to appear at nearby Cedar Creek a month later, there to have his horse shot out from under him and to suffer a wound in the ankle.

By that time Hayes had been nominated for Congress by fellow Ohio Republicans, and in the fall of 1864 he was elected to the seat. He had accepted nomination but declined to actually campaign, saying, "An officer fit for duty, who at this crisis would electioneer for a seat in Congress, ought to be scalped."

Once elected, he stuck to his brave talk and refused to serve until leaving the Army in June 1865—after the shooting had stopped—as a brigadier. His political career then led to two terms as governor of Ohio and finally to election as president in the U.S. Centennial year of 1876—not by popular vote, but only by a last-minute switch in electoral votes that gave him an edge of one electoral vote over his opponent, Democrat Samuel J. Tilden.

In the controversy that followed, the Hayes election was disputed until confirmed by an official commission just two days before he was scheduled to succeed U. S. Grant on March 4, 1877. (During the nineteenth century, March 4 was the traditional inaugural date for incoming U.S. presidents.) In this particular and touchy year, the date fell on a Sunday. With the Sabbath considered no proper day for the inauguration of a president, it was decided to wait until Monday, March 5. That would leave the nation with no president, at least technically, for a day.

The final decision was to install Hayes as president twice in two days— secretly on Sunday at a White House dinner for the incoming president and publicly the next day at the usual inaugural ceremonies.

So it was that the distinguished guests proceeding from the East Room reception area in the White House to the State Dining Room that evening momentarily "lost" the leading luminaries of their number—Grant and Hayes. Those two, it seems, had ducked into the Red Room, where Chief Justice Morrison R. Waite quietly and quickly administered the oath of office to Rutherford B. Hayes—without benefit of the customary Bible, since that item had been overlooked by all those present.

Thus, the president who sat down to a twenty-course dinner in the State Dining Room a few minutes later was not Grant, as the general public would have thought, but Hayes—who was sworn in public, with all the usual trappings, the very next day.

The new president was neither the first nor the last of the six Union officers who eventually occupied the White House in the latter half of the nineteenth century. Grant was the first. Succeeding Hayes was fellow Ohioan James A. Garfield, who had also fought well during the Civil War and had reached the rank of major general.

Garfield's best-known Civil War feat was his return to the scene of battle at Chickamauga after his superior, General William Rosecrans, retreated in disorder. Some critics said that Garfield used that occasion to undercut his commanding officer and point to his own battlefield prowess. Be that as it may, Garfield, like Hayes, had been elected to Congress during the war but chose to remain in uniform at least until after Chickamauga, which took place in September 1863.

Coming along a bit after Garfield, President Benjamin Harrison had been an officer with the 7th Indiana Volunteers. His outfit took part in Sherman's Atlanta campaign, among other activities, and Harrison left the Union Army as a brigadier general in 1865. He became a U.S. senator before reaching the presidency.

After Harrison came William McKinley in 1897, the once-young officer who had joined Hayes's staff at Antietam. Originally a private in the 23rd Ohio Volunteers, he had reached the post of commissary sergeant by the time he and his unit appeared at Antietam. He won promotion there to lieutenant and assumed command of the 23rd's Company D, serving until war's end and leaving the conflict as a major who had earned his decorations. He was only twenty-two at the time.

Finally, Chester Arthur, the vice president who succeeded popular White House occupant Garfield, held a desk job during the Civil War in the quartermaster corps of his state, New York.

Grover Cleveland was yet another Civil War–era president. Drafted for the Union Army just as he plunged into law as his lifetime vocation, he paid another man (quite legal at the time) to serve in his place.

As fate would have it, two of the men who survived combat during the Civil War and became president died in office at the wrong end of a gun. Both Garfield and McKinley were fatally wounded by gun-wielding assassins.

Hospital Town

When Union General Godfrey Weitzel's brigade entered Richmond the morning of April 3, 1865, as the vanguard of an occupying Federal Army, he rode his horse up a hill at the eastern end of the city to encounter one of the most amazing sights in the history of military medicine. There, spread out in tableau atop towering Chimborazo Hill, row upon neat row with straight streets and alleys in between, were the buildings and the tents of the largest military hospital ever known.

Five hospital divisions collected together, Chimborazo Hospital had the capacity to house eight thousand to ten thousand patients at a time. For nearly four years, the sick and the wounded from such battles as Second Bull Run, the Wilderness, or Spotsylvania had come to Chimborazo by the thousands for treatment, recovery, or death.

By the end of the Civil War, seventy-six thousand patients had been through the doors of this huge medical facility, seventeen thousand of them wounded soldiers. Of that large number, only a fraction more than 9 percent died.

As reported to the Association of Medical Officers of the Army and Navy of the Confederacy in 1904, Chimborazo had no equal in military history.

According to Dr. John R. Gildersleeve, president of the medical veterans' group, "It was the first military hospital in point of size in this country and in the world, the next largest in this country being the 'Lincoln' at Washington, D.C., which reported a total number of 46,000 patients; and the next largest in the world at large was the Scutari Hospital in the Crimea, which reported a total of 30,000 to 40,000 patients."

Amazing, too, was the fact that barely four years before General Weitzel's arrival, the hospital site had been a bare, breeze-swept hill overlooking what Dr. Gildersleeve called "the tawny James on its tortuous seaward way."

With the advent of large-scale battle early in the Civil War, however, Confederate authorities realized they would need hospitals—and more hospitals. The capital of the Confederacy soon became the chief medical center of the Confederacy. Chimborazo Hill with its fresh breezes, its view, its forty largely open acres, its water supply, and its natural drainage was an obvious and natural choice for a major medical facility. "And early in 1862, the hospital was opened, and in one week 2,000 soldiers were admitted, and in two weeks' time there were in all 4,000."

While some tents were erected for the convalescing patients, this was not a makeshift city of tents. Instead, 150 single-story buildings one hundred feet long and thirty feet wide sprang up in neat rows to create a grid of streets. With two lines of cots placed in each ward, the long, low structures held forty to sixty patients each. They were divided into five divisions, or "hospitals," of thirty wards each. In addition, there were one hundred Sibley tents for the convalescent, a guardhouse, five soup houses, five icehouses, an administration building, a cemetery, Russian bathhouses, and a bakery that turned out seven thousand to ten thousand loaves of bread a day. There also was a brewery, and a nearby farm for one hundred to two hundred dairy cows and three hundred to four hundred goats that provided nutritious "kid meat" for the patients. A canal trading boat, the Chimborazo, plied the waterways from Richmond to Lynchburg and Lexington to furnish added provisions for the hospital's clientele.

Workers in the vast complex included free blacks, whites, and black slaves. Established as a Confederate Army post, Chimborazo was supervised by Dr. James B. McCaw as Commandant Surgeon. (His doctor-son, Brigadier General Walter Drew McCaw, would later become Chief Surgeon of the American Expeditionary Forces in World War I.)

As recalled by Confederate medical veteran Gildersleeve in 1904, "The hospital presented the appearance of a large town, imposing and attractive, with its alignments of buildings kept whitened with lime, streets, and alleys clean, and with its situation on such an elevated point it commanded a grand, magnificent, and pleasing view of the surrounding country for many miles."

This, then, was the scene that greeted Union General Weitzel as Richmond fell in the last few days of the war. With him on the ride up the hill was his brigade's medical director, Dr. Alexander Mott, who spotted the Chimborazo commandant among the awaiting Southern medical officers.

"Ain't that old Jim McCaw?" Mott cried out.

"Yes," said McCaw, as recalled later by Gildersleeve. "And don't you want a drink?"

Mott's reply was yes. "The General will take one, too, if you will ask him."

Weitzel did, and in perhaps unconscious tribute to the work of the Confederate doctors, he also placed them, their hospital, and all its patients under his immediate protection.

So Very Personal

THE WAR HAD BECOME SO PERSONAL BY THE LAST DAYS BEFORE APPOMATTOX THAT as the Union soldiers began their attack on their Confederate counterparts in the Battle of Sayler's Creek on April 6, 1865, they displayed handkerchiefs as apparent invitation for their brethren in gray to surrender and dispense with any further bloodshed.

It was an eerie scene that late afternoon in the rural Virginia countryside southwest of Richmond. For their part, the Union men had marched steadily up the incline just beyond the rain-swollen creek to attack the Rebels on the heights above. The Union men were ordered to hold their fire until the last possible moment, and amazingly, they did. They "pressed forward," said a history of the 37th Massachusetts Volunteer Regiment later, "holding their fire till they were in plain sight of the enemy almost face to face."

The Southerners, for their part, contributed to the momentary silence by also holding fire until the men in blue were at one hundred yards or even less. They refused, though, to heed the imploring handkerchiefs.

Battalion commander Robert Stiles, a Confederate Army major, recollected calling out to his men, "Ready!" They then "rose, all together," he later wrote, "like a piece of mechanism, kneeling on their right knees and their faces set with an expression that meant everything."

Stiles then ordered: "Aim!" And before him, "The musket barrels fell to an almost perfect horizontal line leveled about the knees of the advancing line."

As he next barked, "Fire!" the first line of Union men went down like tenpins, and the second line visibly wavered. Another Southern volley, and the line broke, the survivors running back to the creek behind them, hotly pursued by Stiles's men, who had their bayonets fixed and poured on hot fire until meeting some of the Union soldiers at the bottom of the hill or in the creek in hand-to-hand fighting.

This was only a portion of the Federal center line, however; on both flanks the Federals were advancing. And even here at center, they reformed quickly to mount a counterattack back up the hill, despite a second charge by Stiles's battalion, which then took position once more in the main Confederate line.

Now came a second assault by the Federal line, this time in overpowering strength too great for the retreating Rebels to repel. Walter Watson, another Rebel officer on the scene that afternoon, reported that the opposing lines now "mingled in one promiscuous and prolonged melee with clubbed muskets and bayonet as if bent upon exterminating each other."

Stiles later said the fight "degenerated into a butchery…[of] brutal personal conflicts." He saw "men kill each other with bayonets and the butts of muskets, and even bite each other's throats and ears and noses, rolling on the ground like wild beasts."

In one corner of the battlefield, a Rebel officer seemed about to surrender to a Union officer but instead fired his pistol at the blue-clad officer and wounded him. They were so close that the Union man took hold of the Rebel, and they grappled in a rolling struggle that carried them down the slopes of a ravine. Shot a second time by an onlooking Rebel, the Union man was finally overpowered. His original assailant was taking aim again to deliver a final, killing shot when a Union infantryman, Private Samuel Eddy, took aim of his own and fatally shot the Southerner. As Eddy fired, still another Rebel bayoneted him in the chest so fiercely that the point emerged from Eddy's back, pinning him to the ground. His assailant now tried to wrest away Eddy's rifle. Somehow the Union private not only held on to his weapon, but also managed to place another cartridge in the chamber and fire into the chest of the Rebel, killing him. Eddy then pushed aside the Rebel's body, pulled the bayonet out of his own chest, and walked away from the scene under his own power.

The war became personal in another way, too. At one point at the conflict at Sayler's Creek (as related in *Thirty-six Hours Before Appomattox* by National

Park Service Ranger Historian Chris Calkins), a Union corporal shot and fatally wounded a Confederate officer, then hurried to his victim's side with the words, "I am sorry I had to shoot you" and "I am a Christian, and if you wish, I will pray for you; it is all I can do for you now." And so he did, with the stricken Confederate saying "Amen" before he died.

When George Armstrong Custer's cavalrymen attacked a Confederate line, a ragged Rebel volley emptied many a saddle, but the Union mounts came on anyway. As they jumped the Confederate defensive works, some of the defenders were killed not by gunfire, but by the hooves of the leaping animals.

And they weren't all horses, either. Some, seized at Amelia Courthouse a day earlier, were mules replacing lost Federal horses. One Union sergeant, Francis N. Cunningham of the 1st West Virginia Cavalry, was perfectly happy with the result. "It took my mule just about four jumps to show that he could outclass all others," Cunningham later said. "He laid back his ears and frisked over logs and flattened out like a jackrabbit."

More to the point, "He switched his tail and sailed right over the rebs, landing near a rebel color-bearer of the 12th Virginia Infantry." What happened next was certainly an oddity of war: The color-bearer was big and brawny, but to Cunningham's hot-headed mule, no matter. The Reb "put up a game fight, but that mule had some new side and posterior uppercuts that put the reb out of the game."

George Custer's brother, Tom, a young second lieutenant, did his best to seize a Confederate set of colors. He didn't find it very easy, being shot in the face and neck by the color-bearer and left with a cheek spotted by burned powder. Nonetheless, Tom Custer grabbed and held on to the colors while fatally shooting his adversary, then took fourteen prisoners. Both Lieutenant Custer and Private Eddy, in fact, were awarded the Medal of Honor for their efforts in the Battle of Sayler's Creek, in which the retreating Robert E. Lee lost seven thousand men, including six generals taken prisoner, to the relatively low Union casualty count of 1,180 men captured, killed, or wounded. (For Tom Custer, incidentally, it would be his second Medal of Honor earned in the Civil War. Like his brother, George Armstrong Custer, he was destined to be killed by the Sioux at the Little Big Horn.)

So very personal was Sayler's Creek, just days before Lee's surrender at Appomattox down the road, that George Custer shared his blanket with newly captured Confederate General Brevard Kershaw that night. Likewise, Union General Phil Sheridan shared his bivouac supper with his Confederate captives.

Lee, on seeing some of his men streaming to his own headquarters after the battle of Sayler's Creek, said: "My God! Has the Army dissolved?"

Back at City Point outside Richmond and Lee's recently vacated bastion of Petersburg, a visiting Abraham Lincoln was told of a messate from Sheridan to overall Union Commander Ulysses S. Grant that said, "If the thing is pressed, I think that Lee will surrender." Lincoln replied in that personal way all his own: "Let the thing be pressed." It was, and three days later, Lee surrendered at Appomattox.

No Opportunity for Surrender

HE SAID IT THREE TIMES TOWARD THE END, AND IT WAS TRUE. "THEY'LL NEVER take me alive, they've sworn to kill me if they capture me again."

After an initial burst of excitement and downright adulation for John Hunt Morgan following his remarkable escape from the Ohio State Penitentiary in late 1863, nothing had gone right for the Confederacy's famed raider. After months of confinement, he returned to a South clearly running out of steam. Political enemies such as Braxton Bragg had Jefferson Davis's ear in Richmond, and there were questions as to why Morgan had disobeyed orders and crossed the Ohio River into the state of Ohio, no matter how spectacular or effective the raid that ensued.

He was now based in southwest Virginia's rugged and poor mountain country with ill-suited troops and stronger, better-equipped and better-manned Federal forces edging his way. His beloved Mattie awaited his occasional visits—and his many letters—in lovely Abingdon, Virginia.

In the last year of the Civil War, unfit men often had taken the place of those killed or disabled in the many previous battles. Desperate recruiting measures had dragged in the misfits, and Morgan had to use the personnel assigned to him, even though he could have filled his ranks with many others. Richmond denied Morgan better-suited, eager volunteers who wanted to transfer into his command from their own units.

Ragged as they were, he and his men mounted an expedition into eastern Kentucky by way of a difficult mountain trek. But this final raid by John Hunt Morgan was marred by the thievery and outright robberies associated with it.

It is almost certain that when Morgan marched through Mount Sterling, Kentucky, it was his own brigade's surgeon who robbed the local bank of $72,000 and disappeared, last suspected of fleeing for his native Germany. Then, too, wrote Morgan biographer Cecil Holland, "At least a half-dozen

Mount Sterling stores were forcibly entered, and goods valued at several thousands of dollars—goods privately owned and in private hands—were hauled away."

Even private homes were stripped of valuables, noted Holland. "The riffraff and the criminals out of the backwash of the South who had found their way into Confederate uniforms were showing their stripe." Some soldiers reportedly took jewelry from local women at gunpoint. "A Mrs. Hamilton, riding into Mount Sterling with delicacies for the wounded, was robbed of her money and horse." Then, too, at nearby Lexington, another bank lost $10,000, more stores were broken into, and more individuals were robbed.

Morgan was outraged by such behavior, but, intent on confronting nearby Federal forces, unwisely put off his own investigation and discipline measures until later. This mistake gave his enemies in Richmond and in the North fresh ammunition to undermine his reputation.

At the same time, Morgan did not really concentrate on the military situations ahead of him. Failing to fully assess his enemy's capabilities, he was taken by surprise near Cynthiana and, due to poor tactical planning, was badly defeated. Morgan and his men then limped back to their base in Virginia.

The summer of 1864 came and went, with the Confederacy as a whole limping visibly by now. For Morgan, the clouds left by his last raid would not blow away. Subordinate officers of his command were demanding investigation by higher authority, and once again—as in the case of his Ohio raid in 1863—a burning issue was Morgan's authority for setting out on the ill-fated Kentucky raid to begin with. Morgan promised to cooperate after his Richmond superiors decided to look into the excesses attributed to the foray. There is strong evidence that at the outset of the raid he "had issued strict orders...against depredations and had made his subordinate officers responsible for the good conduct of his men," wrote Holland.

Before an investigation could get under way, however, Morgan moved south from Abingdon to counter a Union move northward from Knoxville, Tennessee. Taking a train to Jonesboro, where the rail line stopped, Morgan led his sixteen hundred cavalry troopers into Greeneville, Tennessee, home before the war of Abe Lincoln's vice president, Andrew Johnson. Greeneville, and indeed, much of eastern Tennessee, was pro-Union territory.

Morgan's plan was to stay at the spacious residence of Mrs. Catherine Williams, whom he knew to be pro-Southern herself, even though she had a son serving in both of the opposing armies and the wife of her "Union son" was living with her. Morgan should have used better judgment. On a previous visit, he had had a run-in with Mrs. Joseph Williams, the daughter-in-law whose husband was a Union soldier. At the time, a wounded Yankee had been staying at the Williamses' home, and despite being on parole, he'd tried to send information on Morgan's force to the Federals at Knoxville via a letter in a prayer book carried by the younger Mrs. Williams. Morgan had revoked the man's parole and sent him to Abingdon under guard. The younger Mrs. Williams had been furious.

The old episode did not stop Morgan from now choosing the same overnight abode. He sent a subordinate ahead to clear the way with the elder Mrs. Williams while he sat astride his horse on a road leading into town, his men filing by on their own mounts. "Much of the glory and prestige of Morgan's old command was gone," wrote biographer Holland, "but Morgan's presence was still inspiring. Cheer after cheer rang out as the wearied troops marched by; unknown to them they were taking farewell of their beloved commander."

To the north in Abingdon, Mattie awaited her husband's return from yet another combat. She carried his child in her womb.

That night rain fell in torrents on Greeneville and on the outposts Morgan had established all around the town. With the younger Mrs. Williams absent, ostensibly visiting a family farm not far away, Morgan and members of his staff slept comfortably in the big brick house on Main Street (Andrew Johnson's homestead is also located on Main Street).

Earlier in the day Morgan had told his staff officer Major A. C. Withers that he didn't expect to be taken alive by the Federals again. That evening, while his compatriots talked or sang songs in the Williamses' parlor to pass the time, Morgan was not himself. He was moody and again remarked, "Do you know that they have sworn never to take me prisoner again?"

It was early the next morning, right after daybreak, that the Union troopers struck; slipping into town under cover of the rain and darkness, they had surrounded the Williamses' house. When rifle fire was heard nearby, Mrs. Williams alerted Morgan, who pulled on a few clothes and hastily retreated to the garden with another staff officer.

Trying to slip unseen to the nearby stables where their horses were quartered, they found Union soldiers blocking the way. They retreated to a space beneath a small adjoining church, but the rifle fire was by now heavy, ripping through the air all around. Major Withers joined Morgan and the other staff officer after "creeping through the shrubbery." Withers then momentarily returned to the nearby house and found, by looking through the windows, that the streets all around were infested with Union troopers. No avenue of escape presented itself.

He returned to the hideyhole beneath the church and told Morgan he ought to surrender. "As he spoke there was a sudden clatter above them as the Federals smashed in the door of the church," wrote biographer Holland.

Morgan said surrender was out of the question. Once more, for a third time in the past twenty-four hours, he said, "It is useless. They have sworn never to take me prisoner."

He was not far wrong. Seconds later, the three officers crept out of their hiding place and started for the house—Morgan thought they might barricade themselves in it and hold out until his troops deployed around the town could come to the rescue. He and his two officers separated for the short passage.

Then a woman's voice rang out from across Main Street. "That's him—that's Morgan, over there among the grape vines."

By the account Withers later provided, Morgan then shouted, "Don't shoot. I surrender."

A Union soldier was sitting astride a horse outside the yard fence, just twenty feet away. His was the third voice. "Surrender and be God damned. I know you."

He fired his rifle. Morgan gave a stifled "Oh God!" as he fell forward, fatally wounded.

The exultant trooper yelled, "I've killed the damned horse thief!"

In seconds, a crowd of Union soldiers rushed to the spot, pressed right through the fence, and draped Morgan's body on the back of a horse to be paraded through the town. Withers was shocked a while later, after himself being taken prisoner, to have the Yankees show him his chief's body tumbled into a roadside ditch, nude except for underdrawers and besmirched with mud and blood.

After Withers protested to a pair of Union commanders, Morgan's body was finally carried to the Williamses' home, "where Withers and Captain James Rogers of Morgan's staff were permitted to wash and dress it."

It was a humiliating and unworthy end for one of the Confederacy's greatest heroes, even if he had fallen a step or two from grace by his own ill-considered decisions. In the inevitable postmortems, it was fairly well established that the younger Mrs. Williams, obviously suspect as an informer, really had been out of town and returned late the next morning unaware that Morgan had been in her mother-in-law's home once again.

In the North, the newspapers were predictably exultant, the Chicago Tribune saying, for instance, that the Rebel raider "has suddenly passed unto death, much to the regret of associate horse thieves and peace sneaks." Predictably, too, but a bit too late, the Southern press mourned the passing of a great hero: "One of the noblest Southern soldiers and gentlemen," proclaimed the *Richmond Examiner.*

A week after funeral services in Abingdon, Mattie attending, Morgan's body arrived in Richmond encased in a pine box covered with a Confederate flag. Escorted to the State Capitol (also the Confederate Capitol) it was viewed by thousands shuffling past in an attitude of sorrow and respect. Neither Jefferson Davis nor Morgan's old commander Braxton Bragg was among those who attended the last rites before the box was placed in a vault to await reburial in Morgan's hometown of Lexington, Kentucky, after the war.

*Note: Historian James A. Ramage's 1986 book *Rebel Raider* offers additional detail on Morgan's death at Greenville that sometimes conflicts with Cecil Holland's 1943 biography cited here.

Parallel Spies

THE SOUTH MAY HAVE HAD ITS ALLURING FEMALE SPY BELLE BOYD, BUT THE NORTH had a bold beauty of its own whose life story largely paralleled that of Belle Boyd. Both were captured and quite correctly accused of their activities. Of the two, though, the Union's Pauline Cushman came closer to the hangman's noose.

In reality "Pauline" was Harriet Wood, native of New Orleans. Raised in Michigan and a Union loyalist through and through, she began her espionage career as a Union agent nosing about St. Louis, Missouri, for Confederate spies. "She did this with aplomb," wrote Donald E. Markle in his book *Spies & Spymasters of the Civil War.*

She accomplished her missions early in the war in secret, without fanfare. Assigned next to Nashville, again to pinpoint Rebel spies in the Union-held town, she resorted to a safe form of fanfare—as an actress she could appear on stage without creating suspicion. She was always careful to maintain her actress "cover."

In the East, Belle Boyd was just the opposite. Arrested several times during the war as a spy for the Confederacy, she was bold and brassy about her activities. She loved the notoriety and left no doubt as to her affiliations. Sent to

Baltimore from Virginia after one arrest, she proudly displayed the Confederate flag from her railroad car's window. In Baltimore, she so dazzled the warden that he set her loose.

That was her way. Known for her activities, she somehow still got her man among Union soldiers—and his information—time and time again. Arrested another time, she sang "Dixie" from her jail cell at the top of her lungs.

In the war's western theater, a much more subtle Pauline Cushman and her spymasters arranged to have her offer a toast to Jefferson Davis on her stage in Nashville (some accounts say Louisville, Kentucky). As a result, she was "thrown out of town"—exactly the cover she sought. Her spying behind Confederate lines followed; she produced much more vital intelligence than Belle Boyd ever did, said Markle.

In 1863, however, while seeking information on Braxton Bragg's Army of Tennessee, she was captured. Documents on her person proved her true role to the satisfaction of Bragg, who ordered her hanged forthwith. If the sentence had been carried out, noted Markle, "Miss Cushman would have become the only female spy hanged by either side during the entire Civil War."

As events turned out, a Union raiding party descended on the area—Shelbyville, Tennessee, and environs. They were just in time to scatter the Rebels holding the brave actress-spy, and she was released.

Her cover was "blown," but a grateful Union Army—some of its officers, anyway—gave her the honorary title of "Major." As "Major Cushman" she continued with her stage career during the last years of the war and afterward.

Belle Boyd, who had even married and conscripted a Union officer during the war, also pursued a postwar stage career. Both women were able to boast of their wartime spying activities as a drawing card for their audiences, but Pauline's fortunes gradually declined, and she died in San Francisco—some say a suicide—after stints as a dressmaker's assistant and charwoman. Her gravestone, supplied by the Union veterans of the Grand Army of the Republic, gives a simple but appreciative epitaph: "Pauline Cushman," it says. "Federal Spy and Scout of the Cumberland."

Belle Boyd lived until 1900, six years beyond her Union rival. She died on a visit to Kilborn, Wisconsin, for a stage appearance. By then she had written a book on her wartime exploits and married twice more. Her burial in Wisconsin, wrote Markle, "was funded by the women's auxiliary of the Grand Army of the Confederacy."

Acquiring a New Name

FREEDOM, SURPRISINGLY, WAS NOT ALL JOY FOR THE SOUTHERN BLACKS WHO HAD been slaves. They were used to being slaves, according to a black man raised on a Virginia plantation and called "Booker" in slavery days.

One of the first things many newly freed blacks wanted to do, quickly, was to take on a new name—any name other than the master's. "In some way," wrote Booker later, "a feeling got among the coloured people that it was far from proper for them to bear the surname of their former owners, and a great many of them took other surnames."

Only a boy at the time, Booker recalled the very moment that freedom was announced to the slaves at his plantation in Franklin County, Virginia, where his mother was the cook and where their cabin (he slept there on rags on the floor) was the plantation kitchen. His father was unknown but was thought to be a white man from another farm-plantation nearby, and his stepfather was a slave from a neighboring plantation who came visiting once in a while. His stepfather, in fact, hadn't been seen for a while, because he had run away and found sanctuary in West Virginia, where he had a job in the salt mines outside Charleston.

The morning that young Booker and his fellow slaves heard about their freedom, they were told to gather at the "big house."

"All of our master's family were either standing or seated on the veranda of the house, where they could see what was to take place and hear what was said. There was a feeling of deep interest, or perhaps sadness, on their faces, but not bitterness."

A stranger, probably a Union officer, "made a little speech and then read a rather long paper—the Emancipation Proclamation, I think." Next, "we were told that we were all free, and could go when and where we pleased."

The reaction among the former slaves at first was excitement, joy, and more, which was to be expected. Young Booker's mother leaned down and kissed her children "while tears of joy ran down her cheeks." Among the other newly freed slaves, "for some minutes there was great rejoicing and thanksgiving, and wild scenes of ecstasy." In this case there was "no bitterness," and in fact "there was pity among the slaves for their former owners."

Booker noted that the "wild rejoicing on the part of the emancipated coloured people lasted but for a brief period, for I noticed that by the time they returned to their cabins there was a change in their feelings."

What had happened? "The great responsibility of being free, of having charge of themselves, of having to think and plan for themselves and their children, seemed to take possession of them....In a few hours the great questions with which the Anglo-Saxon race had been grappling for centuries had been thrown upon these people to be solved. These were the questions of a home, a living, the rearing of children, education, citizenship, and the establishment and support of churches." Remarkably, in just a few hours "the wild rejoicing ceased," replaced in the slave quarters by "a feeling of deep gloom."

Many of them realized that being free was a serious thing. The older people, in particular, found it frightening. After all, "their best days were gone." They had spent their lifetime as slaves. Where would they go? What would they do?

"Besides, deep down in their hearts there was a strange and peculiar attachment to 'Old Marster' and 'Old Missus,' and to their children, which they found it hard to think of breaking off." Was it any wonder then, that "gradually, one by one, stealthily at first, the older slaves began to wander from the slave quarters back to the 'big house' to have a whispered conversation with their former owners as to the future?"

Young Booker and his family did not stay around very long. And he would soon take steps to remedy the fact he had only one name to his name.

First, though, his mother and her children had to journey to West Virginia to join Booker's stepfather. They left their Virginia home and crossed over mountains, streams, and valleys on foot; the trip took several weeks. One day in the future Booker would reverse the trek—five hundred miles on foot—to attend school and work as a janitor at Virginia's Hampton Institute. Then, after other important stops on the way, he would go on to operate Tuskegee Institute in Alabama as its widely esteemed president and become a towering leader among American blacks.

First, though, before any of these things could come to pass, he had to attend elementary school classes in West Virginia, then settle the issue of his name. At school, "I noticed that all of the children had at least two names and some of them indulged in what seemed to me the extravagance of having three."

The youngster from Virginia was ready the first time the schoolmaster called the roll and asked for his full name. "I calmly told him 'Booker Washington' as if I had been called by that name all my life; and by that name I have since been known."

Well, not quite—for later in life the black educator found out his mother had actually given him another name soon after he was born in 1858 or 1859: Taliaferro. And so, as he recounted in his autobiography, he became Booker T. Washington finally and forever more.

Close Connections

RELATIVES AND RELATIONSHIPS (PLUS A WEE BIT OF NEPOTISM) AMONG THE CIVIL War's principal figures crop up so frequently you would think we were a tiny European principality going through an internal shakeup of the royal court rather than a bloody division that split an entire continent.

So it was that briefly visiting in the "King's Palace" in the national capital—the Lincoln White House, that is—was the grieving widow of a recently killed Rebel general. Twice, that is.

Among the generals still living, a leading "Royalist" commander, George McClellan, was married to the former love of a leading Rebel officer, Ambrose Powell ("A. P.") Hill. Thomas J. ("Stonewall") Jackson was married to Daniel Harvey ("D. H.") Hill's sister. Both men were generals, but at least they fought together, as fellow Confederates.

For that matter, the South's great and reliable General A. P. Hill was married to the Southern cavalry raider John Hunt Morgan's sister Kitty, more fondly known (to Hill, at any rate) as Dolly.

National division was seen in the familial connections of "Jeb" Stuart, who died at the home of his brother-in-law Charles Brewer, future surgeon general of the Confederacy. Stuart's wife, the former Flora Cooke, counted a brother as a brigadier in the Confederate Army and a brother-in-law (married to her sister Julia) as a general in the Union Army. For that matter her own father, Phillip St. George Cook, was a Union general.

On the opposite side, Robert E. Lee was the son of the Revolutionary War hero Henry "Lighthorse Harry" Lee. Robert E. Lee's wife, Mary Custis Lee, was the daughter of George Washington Parke Custis, adopted son of George Washington—grandson, actually, of Washington's wife, the Widow Martha Custis.

Ulysses S. Grant, commander of the Union armies late in the war, enjoyed the services of his brother-in-law (and West Point roommate) Frederick T. Dent on his staff. Indeed, Officer Dent later served President Grant in the White House as Grant's military secretary. Grant's father-in-law, former Mississippi slaveowner Frederick Dent and father to Julia Grant and her brother, young Fred, was a White House occupant until his death.

On the south side of the Potomac—in Richmond—not only did Robert E. Lee's eldest son Custis serve as an aide to Confederate President Jefferson

Davis, but so did the president's nephew Joseph Robert Davis, like Custis also a Confederate brigader.

The son of a former U.S. president fought on the Rebel side: Louisiana's Dick Taylor, son of the late Zachary Taylor (once father-in-law to Jefferson Davis during Davis's first marriage to Taylor's daughter Knox, who died of a fever shortly after their wedding).

Robert E. and George Washington Custis Lee, father and son, were not the only members of the Lee family to take part in the Civil War. Robert E. Lee's other son in Confederate service was cavalry officer William Henry Fitzhugh "Rooney" Lee, while General Fitzhugh Lee was a nephew of Robert. Confederate General Stephen Dill Lee was not a relative, but the Confederacy's Admiral Sydney Smith Lee was Robert's brother. Still another distant relative was Samuel Phillips Lee—a Union naval officer.

Among the "lesser nobility" of the war, many brothers took part on opposite sides—witness Kentucky's two army generals named Crittenden, Thomas and George, one Union and one Confederate.

Friends also split along similar lines, especially among the many West Point graduates who served on both sides of the battlefield. Confederate General James Longstreet, for instance, had attended future Union General Grant's wedding to Julia in 1848. The Jefferson Davises, for that matter, had kept lingering Northern friendships from their antebellum days in Washington and other ties. Mrs. Davis, Varina Howell by birth, was the grandchild of a New Jersey governor.

It was the Lincolns, though—Mary Todd Lincoln especially—who may have endured the most painful and complex genealogy chart of any principal player in the Civil War. With both Lincolns born in Kentucky, itself a state of competing loyalties, it was inescapable that relatives would land on opposite sides of the conflict. Consider the complications implicit in the number of Mary Todd Lincoln's Southern-leaning siblings. Born of Robert Smith Todd's first wife, Eliza, she counted five siblings from that marriage, while another eight siblings (half brothers and sisters) were the result of her widowed father's second marriage, to Elizabeth Humphreys.

Not only did Mary Todd, as first lady of the land, have a half sister, Elodie, living in Selma, Alabama, and married to a Confederate officer during the war, but her half sister Emilie was married to a Rebel brigadier general, Benjamin Helm, whom Lincoln had appointed as a paymaster in the Union Army shortly after Fort Sumter. Helm turned down the proffered commission, however, and joined the Confederate Army. A graduate of West Point himself, he advanced to the rank of brigadier general and was killed in the Battle of Chickamauga in September of 1863. At the time Emilie was living in Selma also.

Not only did the White House mourn the likable Helm, but President Lincoln was left in a delicate spot. Just as George McClellan had once allowed Robert E. Lee's wife safe passage through Union lines, now Lincoln was asked to allow Confederate General Helm's widow to pass through Federal-held territory after attending her husband's funeral in Atlanta. She wished to go home with her children to her mother in Lexington, Kentucky.

Even more sensitive for Lincoln, she was apparently halted by Federal officers who wanted her to take the Union oath of allegiance. Lincoln had to intervene and order her forwarded to Washington. In Washington the Rebel widow, together with daughter Katherine, stayed for a period of time in the White House with the Lincolns.

Emilie also wanted the president's help in safeguarding her investment in supplies of cotton stranded down South. Lincoln, no doubt with misgivings, wrote a note giving her amnesty (based on her taking the oath) and said, "Mrs. Helm claims to own some cotton at Jackson, Mississippi, and also some in Georgia; and I shall be glad upon either place being brought within our lines, for her to be afforded the proper facilities to show her ownership, and take her property."

Safely home, Emilie kept asking for favors. Now she wanted to provide clothing for Rebels held prisoner at Camp Douglas. She returned to the White House for another visit in the fall of 1864, still desirous of protecting her cotton. Shortly after that visit, upon learning of the death of her half brother Levi, she turned on Lincoln, calling Levi "another sad victim to the powers of more favored relations." She also charged in a letter to Lincoln, "Your minnie [sic] bullets have made us what we are." She said that fact gave her "additional claim" in seeking Lincoln's favors and called herself "a woman almost crazy with misfortune."

Lincoln tried to help her with the cotton, but was frustrated when it accidentally burned up. After the Civil War and the assassination of her in-law in the White House, Emilie Todd Helm had to eke out a living as a musician until another Lincoln, Abraham's oldest son, Robert, came to the rescue. He used his influence to obtain her an appointment as postmistress in Elizabethtown, Kentucky.

Meanwhile, Mary Todd Lincoln's half brothers David, Alexander, and Sam and her brother George all served in the Southern armies. Still another half sister, Martha, allegedly took advantage of a Lincoln pass to smuggle medicines to her favorite side in the war—the Confederacy.

Lee's Final Order

General Order #9
Hd Quarters
Army of Nor. Va.
10 April 1865
After four years of arduous service marked by unsurpassed courage and fortitude, the Army of Northern Virginia has been compelled to yield to overwhelming numbers and resources.

I need not tell the brave survivors of so many hard fought battles, who have remained steadfast to the last, that I have consented to this result from no distrust of them.

But feeling that valor and devotion could accomplish nothing that could compensate for the loss that would have attended the continuance of the contest, I determined to avoid the useless sacrifice of those whose past services have endeared them to their countrymen.

By the terms of the agreement, officers and men can return to their homes and remain until exchanged. You will take with you the satisfaction that proceeds from the consciousness of duty faithfully performed, and I earnestly pray that a Merciful God will extend to you His blessing and protection.

With an unceasing admiration of your constancy and devotion to your country, and a grateful remembrance of your kind and generous consideration for myself, I bid you an affectionate farewell.

R. E. Lee
Gen'l

Julia Reads a Note

IT WAS JUST A FEW DAYS AFTER THE SURRENDER AT APPOMATTOX, AND JULIA DENT Grant thought it all so very odd. First was the man who came to her hotel room with a message from Mrs. Lincoln. Then there were the four "peculiar" men sitting together at lunch. Finally, there was the angry-looking man, "dark, pale," who galloped past the Grant couple's carriage late that day and "glared in a most disagreeable manner." And last, there was the mysterious letter.

It was Good Friday, April 14. The Grants—still buoyed by the excitement of great events—had begun their day in a room at Willard's Hotel (today's Willard International Hotel) after returning the day before from City Point on the James River opposite Richmond. Julia Grant was anxious to return to their cottage in Burlington, New Jersey, outside Philadelphia, for a few days of quiet and rest—in short, for resumption of a normal life.

Her husband (she called him "Ulys") wasn't sure he could wind up his affairs in Washington quite in time. "I wish I could," he told her, "but I have promised Mr. Lincoln to go up this morning and with him to see what can be done in reference to the reduction of the army."

That appointment was scheduled for nine o'clock in the morning, but before the Union's victorious general could leave his hotel quarters there came a tap at the door. It was a message from Abraham Lincoln—one of his last ever. It said to please come at eleven o'clock instead of the earlier hour because his son Robert had just returned from his own army duty, "and I want to see something of him before I go to work."

Although this would make it even more difficult for the Grants to get away in time for the train trip to New Jersey, the general still promised his wife to do whatever was possible about leaving that day.

After he left their room another rap came at the hotel door. When Julia Grant innocently said, "Come in," there appeared "a man dressed in light-colored corduroy coat and trousers and with a rather shabby hat of the same color."

When she told the stranger she had expected a bellboy bringing cards, he "reddened," bowed to her, and asked if she indeed were Mrs. Grant.

Assured that she was, the man said he had been sent by Mrs. Lincoln, "to say she will call for you at exactly eight o'clock to go to the theater."

Perhaps this odd messenger didn't know it, but Julia Grant was not all that enamored of Mary Todd Lincoln's ways. They had had a couple of run-ins, you might say, while the Lincolns visited the Grant headquarters at the Richmond-Petersburg apex just days earlier.

Julia Grant related her own reaction: "To this I replied with some feeling (not liking either the looks of the messenger or the message, thinking the former savored of discourtesy and the latter seemed like a command), 'You may return with my compliments to Mrs. Lincoln and say I regret that as General Grant and I intend leaving the city this afternoon, we will not, therefore, be here to accompany the President and Mrs. Lincoln to the theater.'"

You would think that a White House messenger at that point would bow out of the room and hurry on back with the reply. After all, why should he care who went to Ford's Theatre with the Lincolns? But there was no bowing for this messenger.

By Julia Grant's own account (*The Personal Memoirs of Julia Dent Grant*, first published in 1975), he hesitated, then was bold enough to say: "Madam, the papers announce that General Grant will be with the President tonight at the theater."

Julia Grant wasn't going to debate with the man. She simply told him to deliver her reply as given and dismissed him. Oddly, he smiled as he left. Oddly, too, it was only a short time before she would see the same strange messenger again—as she had lunch that day with General John A. Rawlins's wife and two of their respective children.

Four men came into the dining room together. "I thought I recognized in one of them the messenger of the morning, and one, a dark, pale man, played with his soup spoon, sometimes filling it and holding it half-lifted to his mouth, but never tasting it."

The same slow-eater "seemed very intent on what we and the children were saying." He was so disconcerting that Julia Grant thought he was "crazy." When Julia asked Mrs. Rawlins to take a furtive look at the four men, she agreed that there was "something peculiar about them." Julia then suggested they might be Southern partisans, "a part of Mosby's guerrillas." She told her friend the suspect men "have been listening to every word we have said."

The incident only added to Julia Grant's unease on this fateful day. In the morning, after dismissing the "messenger" from Mrs. Lincoln, Julia had sent word to her husband "entreating him" to take her home to New Jersey that evening and stressing that she did not wish to go to the theater. "I do not know what possessed me to take such a freak," she wrote later, "but go home I felt I must." And again at lunch, Julia Grant blurted out to her friend Mrs. Rawlins, "I believe there will be an outbreak tonight or soon [of guerrilla or partisan activity, apparently]. I just feel it, and I am glad that I am going away tonight."

By the time of her late lunch, Julia Grant had heard back from her husband. He had been attending a Cabinet meeting, but his message was: Pack the trunks. They indeed would take the late afternoon train for Philadelphia.

So it was that in the late afternoon they were leaving Willard's in a carriage bound for the railroad depot. Just then, "this same dark, pale man rode past us at a sweeping gallop on a dark horse—black, I think." The "same" dark pale man as at lunch.

The mysterious rider forged twenty yards ahead, turned, and swept back, "and as he passed us both going and returning, he thrust his face quite near the General's and glared in a disagreeable manner."

Grant was startled enough to "draw back" as the stranger made his return circuit. In reply to a pleasantry offered by their companion in the carriage, General Daniel Rucker's wife, Grant said, "I do not care for such glances."

Neither of the Grants knew it then, but they had just brushed up against John Wilkes Booth. As Julia Grant said in her memoirs, she was "perfectly sure" her mysterious, corduroy-clad "messenger" was one of the four men at lunch, as was Booth, the very same man who had ridden past the Grants' carriage with such glaring countenance.

That night Booth shot Lincoln at Ford's Theatre, as is well known. But what had the assassin been doing all day? That morning Booth's crisscrossing travels around the Federal capital included a stop to visit fellow conspirator Lewis Paine, who later said his assignment from Booth was to assassinate Ulysses S. Grant.

Booth encountered theater owner James Ford, who excitedly told the actor that a large crowd was expected at the theater that night—to see Grant.

Booth made other stops and conducted other errands, but he also dropped out of the sight of latter-day historians for an hour or two. Could it have been for a late luncheon with three coconspirators in view of Julia Grant's nearby table?

Publicly in view again late in the afternoon, Booth hired a lively horse from Pumphrey's Livery Stable at the Mall and then was seen riding the mare, sometimes at a canter, on nearby streets. He allowed her to race a few blocks up Pennsylvania Avenue.

He made a stop at the theater, spoke to property man James Maddox, then raced off again.

He was soon at the corner of 14th Street and Pennsylvania, location of the Willard's hostelry. He encountered a fellow actor, one John Matthews, and asked him to deliver a letter to the editor of the *National Intelligencer*.

While they were talking, they saw across the street a company of Union soldiers marching along as escort for a column of prisoners. "My Great God, Matthews! I have no longer a country!" Booth exclaimed.

Just then, wrote Theodore Roscoe in his book *Web of Conspiracy*, Grant's carriage, with a small cavalry escort, was leaving Willard's for the rail depot. "Booth angled the nimble mare over for a closer look at the General." Then, as the carriage continued on its way, he rode back to the Willard—quite likely passing the carriage coming and going, as Julia Grant later wrote.

Booth found out from the "curbstone loungers" that the Grants were off to the Philadelphia train and New Jersey. That meant one less target would be available at the theater that night—but also fewer escorting soldiers and officers to get in the way.

The Grants, safe on their train, had not quite reached their destination of Burlington that night when they heard of the horrifying events at Ford's Theatre. They had passed through Philadelphia and were waiting for the ferry to take them across the Delaware River to their next train in New Jersey. As they ate dinner in a restaurant near the ferry landing, Grant was handed three telegrams, one after the other. "The General looked very pale."

When Julia asked what had happened, Ulysses told her Lincoln had been assassinated (although he actually didn't die until the next morning). Grant then accompanied his wife and their daughter Jesse to the cottage at Burlington and returned during the night to Washington by special train.

The very next morning, a still-stunned Julia Grant found a chilling letter in the flood of telegrams and mail that reached the Grants in the immediate aftermath of the assassination. "General Grant, thank God, as I do," it said, "that you still live. It was your life that fell to my lot, and I followed you on the [railroad] cars. Your car door was locked, and thus you escaped me, thank God!"

Could the letter have been from Lewis Paine, whose real name was Lewis Thornton Powell? It is unlikely, since it was without a doubt Paine-Powell who brutally attacked and almost killed Secretary of State William Seward and his son Frederick at their Washington home the night of the Lincoln assassination.

Paine-Powell, along with four others who took part in the Lincoln plot, was hanged for his own bloody deed, and Booth died in a fire marking the end of his escape attempt. But no one knows who the writer of the mysterious letter to General Grant was, even today.

Freedom Still Denied

FREEDOM WAS AT HAND, WITHIN HER GRASP, BUT SLAVE CHILD ARMACI ADAMS didn't know it. Richmond had long since fallen; the slaves were free; and Lincoln was dead. Still, on a lone farm in Tidewater, Virginia, the young black girl slaved on. No one had told her.

Dey never give me my age. White folks kept hit an' never give it ter me.

She might have been five years old when Richmond fell in 1865. Then again, she might have been about fifteen.

Before Emancipation, life as a slave to Isaac Hunter and his "Missus" was sheer hell. You could call both of them "hell cats." The old Marse was a preacher, but he was wicked. *Las' time I seed 'im he was comin' f'om a revival drunk.* Mean and wicked.

That time, before Emancipation, when poor Uncle Toney ran away and was caught, *Ole man Hunter an' hi son beat 'im all de morning. Dey took turns. After a while dey got tired an' went in ter dinner and lef him hanging 'dere. He was tied up in de air wid his han's crossed an' his toes jes touchin' de groun'.*

The father and son went back to beating Uncle Toney again—until the middle of the afternoon. They then "pickled" him, soaking him with salted water, and let him down. He "mos' nigh" died, but he did live, only to be sold down South upon his recovery.

Meanwhile, most of the Hunter slaves were being sold off. Armaci probably would have been, too, but for an accident. As she told it many years later, the Hunters never provided enough to eat, and she used to sit by the side of a fireplace poaching corn. One day her dress caught fire and she was badly burned on the neck and legs before a passerby saw her running with her dress blazing, threw his coat around her, and smothered the fire. She was on crutches "fur a lon' time."

One day the slave cook, Aunt Rose, was looking at young Armaci and crying. And she said, "Honey, I don' never 'spect ter see you anymo.'" Armaci was too young to understand at first.

The next day, the Marsa took her and a team of pretty claybank ponies to Norfolk—to sell both Armaci and the animals. As they proceeded down Main Street, the girl saw a man up on a block and people "jes a-hollerin' 'roun' him"—bidding. The next thing she knew, her "ole man" took her into the back of a vacant store and took off her clothes. Then he and another man looked her over—"examined me." But the prospective buyer balked *'cause he 'fraid I won' be no good on account o' de burn scars.*

Armaci went back to Huntersville and never was sold. Soon only two men were left to work the farm, while the young, unsalable girl, not yet into her teenage years, was left to do all the housework.

In time another of her jobs was minding the turkeys, a thankless task because "dey runs eve'y which-a-way." One day after Richmond had fallen to the Union armies, there were some Union soldiers across a creek at some fairgrounds. She noticed one of the soldiers "patrolin' by" with his rifle on his shoulder, and soon she heard a loud bang. Seconds later, the soldier came into view again, with a turkey slung across his shoulder.

One o' dem turkeys done got 'cross de creek an' dat sojer done shot 'im.

Here was trouble, real trouble, for the slave girl. She was "scared weak" when she realized it. She herded the rest of the turkeys together and hustled them back to the farm, but she was too late. The Missus was standing outside and counting the big birds. All at once she yelled, "Isaac! One o' dem yaller turkeys is gone!"

Dat man grabbed me an' strip me naked—after freedm min' you—an' whupped me wid a bull whup ontill I fainted. Atter dat I don' know how long he beat me. When I come 'roun dey were washin' me down in pickle.

At the time of that incident, Armaci was "free" in theory. All slaves were free in theory by the end of the Civil War in April 1865, if not earlier by Lincoln's Emancipation Proclamation. All but a handful, that is, who didn't know and weren't told—like Armaci. In a 1930s interview transcript subsequently published in *Weevils in the Wheat: Interviews with Virginia Ex-Slaves*, edited by Charles L. Perdue Jr., Thomas E. Barden, and Robert K. Phillips, she calculated she was about thirteen before she escaped the Hunter farm in Huntersville.

"How long I been free, I don' know," she said so many years later. "I wondered why eve'body done gone, but dey kept me so close in de house I couldn' fin' out." By their former slave girl's account, the Hunters clearly did their best to keep her from learning she could walk away free at any time. She finally did find out and ran away.

She found refuge with a black family named Foreman at nearby Norfolk Mission College, found work, and never went back to the Hunter place.

Surprisingly Kind Fate

When, at the tender age of sixteen or seventeen, Dorence Atwater went off to the American Civil War with the 1st Connecticut Cavalry Squadron in August of 1861, he surely had no idea that he was destined to become a prisoner, at one time or another, of both warring governments. Sometime later he became a good friend and literary model for Robert Louis Stevenson in the South Sea Islands.

Such destiny was not yet clear even after his unit was taken over by the 2nd New York Cavalry, nor yet when young Dorence managed to survive the fiercely fought battles of Second Bull Run, Cedar Mountain, Fredericksburg, Chancellorsville, Brandy Station, Chantilly, and even Gettysburg.

Right after Gettysburg, though, he was captured while on courier duty. He spent eight slow months as a prisoner in Richmond, then was sent to the Confederacy's notorious Andersonville Prison, where Zurich-born Commandant Henry Wirz, a doctor, allowed Union prisoners to die of neglect and/or starvation. After two months in the stockade at Andersonville, the Connecticut youth became ill and was transferred to the prison hospital. Upon his recovery, he became clerk to the hospital surgeon.

Dorence now sat at a desk beside Wirz himself. His clerical job was to post the paperwork on the deaths of his fellow prisoners.

Unknown to Wirz and his cohorts, Dorence Atwater maintained a duplicate list that he took with him when he was paroled in March of 1865, less than a month before the Civil War ended. That list eventually allowed the Federal government to identify and mark thousands of Union graves in what is now known as Andersonville National Cemetery. However, the same Federal government in 1865 fought young Dorence Atwater's attempts to publish his list for the sake of the POW families. Court-martialed and dishonorably discharged, he was briefly sentenced to hard labor in prison for his efforts.

In the meantime, Clara Barton, future founder of the American Red Cross, took up the fight and the graves were marked after all. Journalist Horace Greeley of the *New York Tribune* published the list in 1866; as happy end to the story, young Atwater was vindicated in his efforts.

Well, not quite. His story does not end there. He managed, for instance, to win appointment in 1871 as U.S. consul in Tahiti. There he became a friend of Robert Louis Stevenson; he even appears in the Scots-born author's *Ebb Tide*. They were partners in a small steamship business, but Atwater also compiled a personal fortune in pearls and gold. He married into South Seas royalty as well.

It wasn't until 1898, however, that the Federal government finally relented and gave him an honorable discharge from military service. A few years later his hometown of Terryville, Connecticut, dedicated a memorial to its native son. He traveled back to New England from his South Sea island to visit the memorial in 1908 and was on his way back to Tahiti when, stricken ill, he suddenly died in California.

Burial was in the islands, where another memorial—a monument—was erected in further tribute to Dorence Atwater, the lad from Connecticut. While he was at Andersonville in those difficult years of the war, who would ever have guessed how his life story would wind up?

Always a Clear Course

IN THE VIEW OF THE UNION GENERAL WHO PROSECUTED THE CIVIL WAR MORE successfully than anybody else, there was one reason for the Civil War and one reason only. "The cause of the great War of the Rebellion against the United States," wrote this ex-general, ex-Union commander, and ex-president many years later, "will have to be attributed to slavery."

Ulysses S. Grant, on his deathbed (from throat cancer) as he completed his memoirs, minced no words and held back no feelings. "There were two political parties, it is true, in all the states," he said, but in the South "the slaveowners, even as a minority, governed both parties."

Not only that, wrote Grant: "The fact is, the Southern slave owners believed that in some way, the ownership of slaves conferred a sort of patent of nobility—a right to govern independent of the interest or the wishes of those who did not hold such property." Further, "They convinced themselves, first, of the divine origin of the institution and, next, that that particular institution was not safe in the hands of any body of legislators but themselves."

Grant found it most illogical that supposed states' righters would insist upon reluctant states joining the Confederacy. In some of the states following South Carolina's secession course, wrote Grant, "the Union sentiment was so strong that it had to be suppressed by force." In this vein, Grant listed Maryland, Delaware, Kentucky, and Missouri, "all slave states…[that] failed to pass ordinances of secession…[and yet] they were all represented in the so-called congress of the so-called Confederate States."

In short, Grant summed up, "the South claimed the sovereignty of States, but [also] claimed the right to coerce into their confederation such States as they wanted, that is, all the States where slavery existed."

Grant was afraid of civil war as early as 1856, when the presidential election of that year gave him his first opportunity to vote even though he was already in his thirties. He voted for a Democrat, despite the Republican Party's reputation as the party of abolition. Throughout the country, he later wrote, "Treason to the Government, was openly advocated and was not rebuked." He feared the election of a Republican as president would mean "the secession of all the Slave States, and rebellion."

Reluctantly, Grant cast his ballot for James Buchanan. "Under these circumstances [the probable secession of Southern states] I preferred the success of a candidate whose election would prevent or postpone secession, to seeing the country plunged into a war the end of which no man could foretell. With a Democrat elected by the unanimous vote of the Slave States, there could be no pretext for secession for four years." Over that period, Grant hoped, "the passions of the people would subside."

But they didn't, and in 1860 the Republican Abraham Lincoln was voted into office. This time Grant couldn't vote (and would have voted for Lincoln's opponent, Stephen Douglas) because he had also recently moved to Galena, Illinois, to help operate his father's leather-goods store there. Grant's hope for declining passions regarding slavery were unrequited.

Even so, Grant felt that most people expected the more extreme Southern states to pass "ordinances" of secession but stop there. "The common impression was that this step was so plainly suicidal for the South, that the movement would not spread over much of the territory and would not last long," he said.

Even in the South itself, he was convinced many years later, "the prevailing sentiment" was against actual secession. But the slave-owners and demagogues held sway, and unnecessary tragedy was the result, he clearly felt.

Grant did not directly criticize Buchanan for any of his actions—or inactions—in the last months of his presidency. He merely said that the Buchanan administration "looked helplessly on and proclaimed that the general government had no power to interfere [with secession]; that the Nation had no power to save its own life."

Grant saved his heat especially for a key Cabinet member under Buchanan—his Secretary of War, a "secessionist" who, in Grant's view, acted treasonably.

War Secretary John B. Floyd (former governor of Virginia and later a Confederate general), Grant said, "scattered the army so that much of it could be captured when hostilities should commence." He shifted cannon and small arms from Northern arsenals to supply centers in the South "so as to be on hand when treason wanted them." The Navy "was scattered in like manner," and Buchanan did nothing to stop his Cabinet from "preparing for war upon their government, either by destroying its resources or storing them in the South until a *de facto* government was established with Jefferson Davis as its President and Montgomery, Alabama, as the Capital."

By that time, the two Southern sympathizers had left the Cabinet—"Loyal men were put in their place. Treason in the executive branch of the government was estopped."

But "the stable door was locked after the horse had been stolen."

Grant didn't mention that Floyd was found innocent by a congressional committee on the charge that he dispersed arms to the South in anticipation of the coming hostilities. The Virginian (his middle name Buchanan) later met Grant himself in battle at Fort Donelson, Tennessee, a famous Grant victory over the Rebels. But Floyd escaped capture at Fort Donelson (as did Confederate Generals Nathan Bedford Forrest and Gideon Pillow). A good thing, too, in Grant's strongly held view. "Well may he have been afraid to fall into the hands of National troops," Grant wrote. "He would no doubt have been tried for misappropriating public property; if not for treason, had he been captured."

As events unwound, Floyd died of natural causes in August 1863 before the charge could be put to the test and before the war itself was over.

In the meantime, Grant's victory at Fort Donelson was a major battlefield success for the Union. He had yet to weather the public clamor over casualties incurred at Shiloh (Never mind, said Lincoln afterward. "He fights."), but his reputation grew with his victories at Vicksburg and Chattanooga, and during his relentless, casualty-strewn campaign, from spring 1864 to the surrender at Appomattox in April 1865, to wear down Robert E. Lee's Army of Northern Virginia.

Whatever personal resources he drew upon to withstand the truly staggering losses in men that were the price of his victory, Grant's memoirs leave no doubt as to his motivation: The South had rebelled, and its rebellion was treason so far as he was concerned. The Civil War had been "a fearful lesson," he wrote at the end of his memoirs and close to the end of his life, but still, "It is probably well that we had the war when we did."

Just a week after finishing his work, he was dead, succumbing finally to cancer of the throat. He had fought off death to finish his memoirs, which raised $450,000, money badly needed by his estate to pay off his debts and provide for his surviving family.

War's Sting Delayed

The Civil War spared Danville, Virginia, any real grief until the very end—past the end, if you count Appomattox as the penultimate moment of all.

To be sure, the war took the lives of some Danville boys. But the community was spared, for there was little fighting here on the Dan River at the borderline of Virginia and North Carolina. Danville was a part of the overall picture; in the Confederate government's last days, it stopped here in its flight from Richmond and made a third capital out of Danville—but only for a week. Richmond fell on April 3, 1865, and Lee surrendered at Appomattox, not seventy miles from Danville, on April 9. On April 10 Jefferson Davis and his government, what was left of it, took to the rail lines again and headed farther south and into history (after one more stop at decidedly unwelcoming Greensboro, North Carolina).

All of this left Danville alone again, shaken and still agog at what had passed so suddenly. The small city had no idea, no inkling, that the wartime tragedies scarring so many communities over the past four years, especially in the South, were about to leave scars on Danville as well.

It may have been children, small boys at play.

The arsenal was located at the low end of Craighead Street, against the river and below the Richmond and Danville railroad station. Here, carefully stored away and usually well guarded, were gunpowder, cartridges, and various other munitions and explosives. Not the sort of thing, normally, to concern two local women who left home that morning fully expecting to return later to hearth and family.

"No one knows how the powder was ignited," said L. Beatrice W. Hairston in her 1955 book, *A Brief History of Danville, Virginia: 1728–1954*, "but suddenly a tongue of flame gushed up and a tremendous explosion shook the town. Crash followed crash as one after another the explosives went off, and the building itself leaped into the air, to fall in pieces."

The shame was that at least fourteen persons were killed, including the two local women—"drowned when they flung themselves into the river to extinguish the flames in their clothing." Fourteen bodies, "terribly mangled," were recovered on the site and nearby, and still others injured in the explosion died later.

Just one day earlier Danville had heard of the war's probable end with Lee's surrender to Grant on April 9—and now this!

Few outside of Danville heard or spoke of the city's terrible loss, so intent was the nation on the larger events that were quickly unfolding. In Mobile, Confederates were leaving their fortresses. In North Carolina, Sherman was still advancing northward, but he and Confederate General Joseph Johnston soon would come to terms. In Washington, Abraham Lincoln made a speech at a White House window stressing reconciliation—his last public speech, it so happens.

There were many in Danville, Virginia, the night of April 11 who didn't care for a moment what was going on elsewhere. While it seemed that everywhere else the war was ending or had ended, in Danville, Virginia, its sting had just been felt.

Pair for Two

A FEW MORE STATS ILLUSTRATE THE EXTENT OF VIRGINIA'S ROLE IN THE CIVIL WAR before all the shooting ended. As reported by editor Kenneth H. Phillips in the magazine *Great Battles*, Virginia furnished the site of the first real (albeit small) battle of the war—at Phillipi, on June 3, 1861. The Old Dominion was the location for the war's first major land battle, First Bull Run. It was the scene of the world's first engagement between ironclads at Hampton Roads. And while Petersburg may have been under siege longer than any other American city in history, is there any place other than Winchester, Virginia, that changed hands more than seventy-two times?

As Phillips noted, Virginia led the way in several other wartime departments as well. "Thirty-eight percent of all battalion-size units of the Southern army hailed from Virginia," he wrote. "More men, Northerners and Southerners alike, spilled their blood on Virginia's terra firma than in any other state involved. Of all the railroad lines in the South—a major mode for moving men and supplies—Virginia dominated, with 1,771 miles of track, 20 percent of the total in the Confederacy. Virginia also led the way in producing war products, with a resounding 32 percent of all manufactured goods used to support the war effort."

Finally, Virginians still boast that their seventy-nine generals outnumbered—almost two to one—the number of generals from any other Southern state.

Himself Virginia-born and -raised, Phillips had another sort of stat to report—more a tale than a stark fact, but true nonetheless.

Two Virginians served in Stonewall Jackson's fabled "Stonewall Brigade." In time each was wounded in the leg, and each then lost his injured leg.

They went home, and by the turn of the century, "having become related by marriage," they were living in the same Nelson County home. For one, it was his father's home. For the other it was his father-in-law's home.

"Once a year they traveled by train to Lynchburg to buy supplies they were unable to raise on the farm. The two Rebel veterans would buy one pair of shoes—one man wore the left and the other wore the right."

How would Ken Phillips know such an intimate detail? "They were my great-grandfathers."

Final Glimpses

OVER THE "SMOKE-BLACKENED" STREETS OF RICHMOND, WROTE "MRS. GENERAL Pickett" in *Lippincott's* magazine of May 1906, right up to the front door of "the old Pickett house" in that dramatic April 1865, came a surprising figure— Abraham Lincoln. He was looking for Confederate General George Pickett's uncle, an old friend and law associate. On the same visit to the freshly defeated city, Lincoln had passed through the White House of the Confederacy and walked the downtown streets with crowds of cheering blacks around him and his soldier escort.

To be sure, "Mrs. General Pickett" was surprised to see the Union president at her doorstep. He asked for her husband, famous for Pickett's Charge at Gettysburg, "perhaps wishing," she wrote forty years later, "in his generous heart to offer the comfort of a cordial handshake to the soldier he had once known in his ambitious youth, whose hopes had gone down with the pride and glory of Richmond."

When Lincoln was told neither gentleman was in, he asked for Mrs. Pickett. "The inquiry was answered by a lady who came forward with a baby in her arms and saw at the door a tall, strong-visaged stranger, with earnest, careworn features and a kindly look in his tender, melancholy eyes."

She spoke. "I am George Pickett's wife, sir."

He spoke. "And I am Abraham Lincoln."

"The President?"

"No; Abraham Lincoln. George's old friend."

They chatted, and before Lincoln turned to go he held the baby, "Little George" by name, and submitted to "a dewy baby kiss."

Handing the child back, Lincoln spoke again "in that deep and sympathetic voice which was one of his greatest powers over the hearts of men." Pretending to address "Little George," he said, "Tell your father, the rascal, that I forgive him for the sake of your mother's sweet smile and your bright eyes." And then he was gone.

★★★

A little-known hero of the Lincoln assassination on April 14, 1865, was Lincoln's guest in the presidential box at Ford's Theatre, Major Henry Riggs

Rathbone. He and stepsister Clara Harris, daughter of U.S. Senator Ira Harris of New York, had agreed to join the Lincolns after General and Mrs. Ulysses S. Grant and others declined the presidential invitations.

When John Wilkes Booth entered the Lincolns' booth and shot the president, Rathbone jumped to his feet, trying to stop him. He was stabbed in the arm for his efforts but struggled with Booth anyway—and may have been responsible for Booth losing his balance in the leap to the stage that broke the assassin's leg. In any case, the combat veteran of Antietam and Fredericksburg is credited as the man who shouted, "Stop that man!" and thus gave the alarm at Ford's that night.

Rathbone then helped the nearly prostrate Mary Todd Lincoln to the Peterson House across the street, where the dying Lincoln had been taken. Rathbone had lost so much blood by now that he fainted.

Two years later, Rathbone and his step-sister married. Unfortunately, the story doesn't end there. After moving to Germany as a U.S. consul in 1894, a now-insane Rathbone, said to be jealous of their children, murdered his wife, Clara. He was convicted and committed to an asylum for the rest of his life.

His son Henry, a congressman from Illinois, later authored the bill that authorized the Federal government's fifty-thousand-dollar purchase of the Osborn Hamilton Ingham Oldroyd collection of Lincolnia destined to become the nucleus of the Lincoln museum at the restored Ford's Theatre in Washington.

Incidentally, Oldroyd was such a dedicated collector of Lincoln memorabilia that he once rented Lincoln's home in Springfield, Illinois, for ten years, married a woman from Springfield, became custodian of the same home when it was acquired as a historical site by the state of Illinois, and then somehow arranged to move his collection—and himself—into the Peterson House in Washington where Lincoln died and Rathbone fainted from loss of blood.

★★★

After slowly riding his horse, Traveller, home to Richmond and to the house on Franklin Street where Mary Custis Lee awaited him, Robert E. Lee had a few days to think. He then wrote to a friend, "I am looking for some little, quiet home in the woods, where I can procure shelter and my daily bread....I wish to get Mrs. Lee out of the city as soon as practicable."

The city was ruined and occupied by Federal troops. Mrs. Lee herself had made note that it was a dreary place. "Gen'l Lee," she wrote to cousin Mary Meade on April 23, "is very busy settling up his army matters & then we shall all probably go to some of those empty places in the vicinity of the White House [their son "Rooney's" plantation on the Pamunkey River, which had been turned into a Union supply depot early in the war]."

Richmond, she said, "is an utter scene of desolation."

There had been excitement when Lee first appeared, approaching the city on his horse with an escort of five companions a few days after the surrender at Appomattox. He had hoped to slip into town without fanfare, but people spotted the familiar figure, and news of his return flew ahead of the slow-moving party. By the time he reached the borrowed house on Franklin Street, a crowd had gathered. People cheered and waved handkerchiefs, pushing forward in hopes of shaking the great man's hand.

He mounted the front steps of the row house, turned to salute his well-wishers with a tip of the hat, then went inside to greet his invalid wife and other family members.

The Robert E. Lee who came home to his wife that April day was the same highly principled man she had known before, always calm and supportive, but quieter than ever. And he was worn, both emotionally and physically. Neither one's health was what it once was. She was now an invalid confined to a chair; he had heart problems dating back at least to the weeks before Gettysburg. Then he had been fifty-six; now he was only fifty-eight.

They couldn't go home to their Arlington House, which had been seized by the government and turned into a cemetery by then. They didn't want to stay in Richmond, and Lee thought he should set an example for his compatriots in defeat by finding work and beginning a new life.

A savior now stepped forward. Mrs. Elizabeth Randolph Cocke offered refuge in a small cottage on her Derwent estate in Powhatan County, a short drive today from Richmond. The Lees were glad to accept and escape the torn capital city. They traveled together by slow canal boat in early June. Their packet left one evening and arrived at dawn the next day, putting in at Pemberton Landing on the James River canal system above Richmond.

Their eldest son, Custis, had ridden the faithful Traveller out from the city. He and the son of their patron, Captain Randolph Cocke, were waiting to greet the Lees as they arrived—just in time for breakfast at Mrs. Cocke's nearby home of Oakland. They stayed there a full week, then moved into the four-room cottage, accompanied by daughters Agnes and Mildred.

In the wake of her final weeks in war-battered Richmond, Mrs. Lee wrote that she and her family now encountered "a quiet so profound that I could even number the acorns falling from the splendid oaks that overshadowed the cottage."

As Lee rebuilt his strength at Derwent, all kinds of offers came to him. He was less a defeated general than the general of a defeated South. Said one daughter: "They are offering my Father everything but the thing he will accept; a place to earn honest bread while engaged in some useful work."

One useful work that Lee heartily endorsed was education, and it was at Derwent that he received the offer to come to Lexington, Virginia, as president of Washington College, for an annual salary of fifteen hundred dollars and housing in the President's House—on the campus of today's Washington and Lee University. Lee accepted, arriving to take his place as head of the small school on the afternoon of September 18.

Wrote a student: "I went to the window and saw riding by on his old war-horse Traveller the great soldier. Slowly he passed, raising his brown slouch hat to those on the pavement who recognized him, and not appearing conscious that he more than anybody else was the center of attention."

Not only that, he wore a military coat, but with all signs of rank, even the military buttons, removed. "He doubtless would have laid it aside altogether, but it was the only one he had, and he was too poor to buy another."

Mrs. Lee waited until the campus residence was ready later that fall, then made the journey to Lexington by canal boat again, a trip that took several days. Lee greeted her while seated on Traveller, and at her new home their youngest son, Robert, carried the invalid Mary Custis Lee up the stairs to her room—the only room in the house completely furnished. The furniture had been made by a one-armed Confederate veteran of the Civil War.

★★★

Both Robert E. Lee and "Stonewall" Jackson called upon another legendary Confederate general on their respective deathbeds. That man was A. P. Hill. Not only did Jackson call for Hill as he died in 1863, so did Lee years later—in 1870—in his home on the campus of Washington College. Fading now, Lee said: "Tell Hill he must come up." And then those famous, final words that Lee uttered as, like so many others before him, he passed: "Strike the tent."

An Arlington Postmortem

Final Visit to the Old Homestead

STOOPED AND GNARLED BY ARTHRITIS, THE AGING WOMAN STOPPING BY THE OLD estate could see it never would be the same again. They could restore shrubs, trees, lawns and drives all they wanted, but it still could never be the home she and the "Gen'l" once had known so well.

"It was so changed," she later wrote, "it seemed but as a dream of the past—I could not have realized that it was Arlington but for the few old oaks they had spared and the trees planted on the lawn by the Gen'l and myself which are raising their tall branches to the Heaven which seems to smile on the desecration around them."

It was June of 1873, the only time Mary Custis Lee, Robert E.'s widow, ever saw their beloved Arlington estate after the Civil War had driven her from it. And "they" of course was the Federal government that had taken possession and turned it into a gigantic cemetery.

And so, she left, and with her an old order was gone, never to return.

But there were others left at Arlington from the old days—former slaves, among them "Uncle Jim" James Parks, a former slave not only born and raised at Arlington but also destined to live out his whole life there, even to die and to be buried there.

In the 1830s, Parks was born a slave to the Arlington mansion's first owner, George Washington Parke Custis, adopted grandson of George Washington— and Mrs. Robert E. Lee's father. Choosing the now-familiar bluff across the Potomac River from Washington, D.C., Custis built Arlington House in 1802 as a living memorial to the first president. Custis, in fact, once planned to name the imposing, eight-columned structure "Mount Washington," but instead settled on Arlington, from a Custis ancestral home on the Eastern Shore of Virginia.

Born just a few years after Mary Anna Randolph Custis's marriage in 1831 to Robert E. Lee, the young slave Jim Parks in effect grew up on the Arlington estate with the Lee children—three sons and four girls.

In later life, he often recalled the pre–Civil War days of the 1840s and '50s. "We used to go to Washington 'cross the long bridge, or we'd dress up and row across," he liked to relate. "People would look at us and say: 'Who's them fine folks?' Then some'd say: 'They's the Custis coloreds. They have their own horses an' cows, an raise their own stuff.' Some [of the Custis 'coloreds'] owned houses in Washington when they were slaves."

The plan back in those pre-war days apparently was for Parks and his fellow slaves to expect their freedom just ahead. "Maj. Custis left his will in 1857," Parks also recalled, "saying we was to be free in five years—everyone, from the cradle up, was to be given $50 and be free. Col. Lee [Robert E. himself] was to administer the estate, but when the five years were up, they [Union troops] were here, and there weren't no estate; but Col. Lee give us our freedom."

What happened, of course, was the intrusion of the Civil War. Lee left, first to command Virginia's military forces, then to take over his vaunted Army of Northern Virginia on behalf of the Confederacy. His wife Mary left her beloved ancestral home soon after, and the Union troops moved in. They erected military installation at various points around the 1,100-acre plantation, among them Fort Whipple, nowadays known as Fort Myer.

Going beyond mere military occupation, the Federal government soon confiscated the Custis-Lee estate when Mrs. Lee couldn't cross the lines and pay her property taxes in person, as required by law. A tax commissioner seized the property in early 1864 for "government use," and later that very year, Union Brig. Gen. Montgomery Meigs, commander of the garrison at Arlington House, appropriated its grounds for use as a military cemetery. His goal, no secret about it, was to make the onetime Custis-Lee home uninhabitable, in case the Lee couple ever hoped to return.

The first burial—in May 1864—was that of Private William Henry Christman of the 17th Pennsylvania Infantry, but the first battlefield casualty buried there was Private William Blatt of the 49th Pennsylvania Infantry, interred the day after Christman. Since the very first graves at today's Arlington National Cemetery were reportedly dug by former slave James Parks, it's likely that he dug both of their graves.

By now in his thirties, he had chosen to stay on at Arlington even after he was given his freedom. Not only did he dig graves and do other odd jobs for the Army, he helped to build Fort Whipple.

Park is also associated historically with another little known facet of today's Arlington National Cemetery: its Civil War–era Freedman's Village, home to an estimated 1,500 to 3,000 former slaves and other blacks, some of them runaway slaves, others former slaves freed as a result of Union incursions in the South. No longer visible, it was located in the southeast section of the cemetery, according to the Arlington National Cemetery website.

Meanwhile, the fate of the Lee couple's onetime home had been sealed by the construction of a stone and masonry burial vault in their rose garden. The vault became final destination for the remains of 1,800 men as just "one of the first monuments to Union dead erected under Meigs's orders," says the same website. Meigs, himself would later be buried "within 100 yards of Arlington House with his wife, father and son."

The property, by now irreparably become a vast cemetery, did briefly return to Lee family ownership in 1882, thanks to a U.S. Supreme Court ruling on a claim by General Lee's son Custis that the property had been illegally confiscated. Indeed, the court said, it had been seized without due process. Custis then quickly sold the property back to the U.S. Government for $150,000.

"Uncle Jim" Parks, however, would be staying on…and on. During his ninety-three years at Arlington, he would outlive slavery, the Civil War, the Spanish-American War, and World War I. In the meantime, too, he outlived two wives while fathering twenty-two children—with five of his sons serving in World War I.

It was not until 1929 that he would finally pass from the scene…but not entirely from Arlington. While it's rare for a civilian with no military or governmental background to earn the right to burial at Arlington, "Uncle Jim" Parks was granted that exception by the secretary of war. And there he lies, still at Arlington: Grave Number 2 in Section 15.

★★★

Additional note: In more recent years, of course, Arlington National Cemetery has become known as a hallowed burial ground for America's greatest heroes, both political and military—a reputation only enhanced with the interment of Senator Edward M. ("Ted") Kennedy (D-Mass.) in August 2009 close to the final resting places of his two assassinated brothers, President John F. Kennedy and Senator Robert F. Kennedy (D-N.Y.). Possibly surprising to some, however, only one other president is buried there, William Howard Taft, who also served as chief justice of the U. S. Supreme Court.

Until the burial in 1963 of the slain John F. Kennedy on the hillside just below the old Custis-Lee mansion, across the Potomac from the Lincoln Memorial, the best known memorial at Arlington was its Tomb of the Unknowns, final resting place of unidentified American war casualties. In all, the cemetery in recent times held the remains of more than 300,000 persons, among them nearly 3,800 former slaves like "Uncle Jim" Parks.

The Lincoln Memorial:
A Postscript

By now, he has been there so long, we tend to think he's been an essential piece of Washington, D. C. forever. And indeed, there he sits, day after day, at one end of the national mall stretching from the banks of the Potomac to the great, domed Capitol. There he has been, there will be, belonging to the ages, inseparable from the Federal city and capital overall.

Simply, stolidly there...immutable, eternally wise, strong, and yet so kindly looking. Obviously too, a man who had suffered.

At nineteen feet high, Lincoln in his Memorial.

What contrast with a day only a few generations ago, when the newly seated, real-life Abraham Lincoln presided in the same Federal City...but then, in 1861, a city and capital isolated, cut off from the Union he extolled so mightily.

Can we today recall mid-April of 1861, just days after Fort Sumter in that watershed year that began the Civil War?

To the south, just across the Potomac River, Virginia had voted to join the secession states in leaving the Union. Loyal son Robert E. Lee, offered command of the Union armies, would go with Virginia instead, loyal to his state rather than to Lincoln's ideal of Union above all. But seemingly more of a threat to Washington at the moment was Maryland, immediately to the north of the city. For here was another slave state rife with Southern sympathizers; here, too, was the pathway for Northern armies coming to the defense of Washington by rail.

"Ringed by rebellion," was how Margaret Leech so aptly described the Federal city's plight in her book *Reveille in Washington, 1860–1865.*

Imagine the fear and consternation that April 19 as the Massachusetts 6th Infantry Regiment's anxiously awaited troop train pulled into town, only to discharge four dead and thirty-one wounded, many carried off on stretchers. What had happened? Needing to go from one rail station to another, they had marched through the streets of Baltimore. A mob hurling stones, even firing guns, had greeted them.

Still, it shouldn't have been a total surprise. The night before, but far less famously, a Pennsylvania volunteer contingent and a company of Union regulars from Minnesota also had been assaulted by the Baltimore hooligans.

No lives were lost in their case, and they joined the local District of Columbia militiamen bedded down in the Capitol itself for the night, while over at the White House, the newly ensconced Lincolns slept on the second floor with citizen volunteers camping out in the East Room one floor below.

Nothing was certain. Not with the Federal city itself teeming with Southern sympathizers. By contrast, Southern-born Regular Army and Navy officers were leaving in droves, headed back to their home states. One such officer was the quartermaster of the entire U.S. Army, General Joe Johnston. He would turn up later, fighting for the Confederacy but wounded outside Richmond, to be replaced and then eclipsed in fame by Robert E. Lee. Months later, even after Lee's surrender at Appomattox, Joe Johnston would command in the last major battle of the Civil War, against one William Tecumseh Sherman. Still later, supposedly while attending Sherman's funeral, the same Joe Johnston would catch cold—fatally.

Even with the men of the Sixth Massachusetts now sleeping in the Senate chamber of the Capitol, the city was wide open to attack that Friday night, April 19, 1861.

No more troops appeared Saturday the 20th. No trains from the North, either. No mails or newspapers from above Maryland. Only a Baltimore delegation pleading against any further troop deployments passing through their aroused city. By Sunday night, even the telegraph link through Baltimore would fail.

On Monday the 22nd, Lincoln exploded in anger when presented a fresh request to have any further troops bypass Maryland altogether. "You would have me break my oath and surrender the Government without a blow," he protested. 'There is no [George] Washington in that—no [Andrew] Jackson in that—no manhood nor honor in that."

In case anyone hadn't noticed, "Our men are not moles and can't dig under the earth; they are not birds, and can't fly through the air."

Go home, he told his Maryland visitors. "Go home and tell your people that if they will not attack us, we will not attack them; but if they do attack us, we will return it, and that severely."

Empty words? *Return an attack severely.* Really?

In Maryland, the rail bridges from the North were destroyed, telegraph lines were cut as well.

In Washington, Lincoln anxiously paced the White House, biographer David Herbert Donald noted in his *Lincoln.* "A Confederate assault from Virginia was expected daily. And everyone predicted that it would be aided by the thousands of secessionist sympathizers in the city." Peering down the Potomac, hoping to see ships carrying troops, Lincoln repeated, "Why don't they come, why don't they come?"

On Wednesday the 24th, he visited the Sixth Massachusetts' wounded and said—only half-jokingly, one supposes—"I don't believe there is any North. The Seventh Regiment is a myth…You are our only Northern realities." He was talking about the Seventh New York, supposedly on its way to Washington also.

Incredibly enough, Northern troops, plenty of them, the Seventh New York included, had been standing by, not fifty miles away, since midnight the previous Saturday.

In this case, Lincoln's missing reinforcements had traversed the Chesapeake Bay by ship, bypassing troublesome Baltimore, had reached Annapolis, but then had been unable to ride the short rail line into Washington, due to torn-up tracks. With the tracks restored, the missing New Yorkers and others finally arrived in the Federal capital on Thursday, April 25.

After Washington's six days—nearly a full week—of dangerous isolation, noted Leech in her *Reveille* book, "Crowds came running, and housetops, windows and balconies swarmed with people."

The war, just started with the Confederate bombardment of Fort Sumter in Charleston Harbor, now would go on…and on, interminably for its participants. In April of 1861, no one yet had witnessed, nor even imagined, bloody Bull Run (First Manassas) just outside of Washington itself, with the Federal capital again weakly exposed to possible assault. And so much more pain to follow. Four long years of brother against American brother; of more than 600,000 left dead; of men, women, even children, on both sides so sorely tried. And, at the end, Lincoln would be assassinated, his rival president, Jefferson Davis, would be briefly imprisoned. Both would be hated in many quarters. Many a soul forever would be embittered.

Still, at fearful price, slavery in this country would be brought to a stop and the Union preserved.

Today, it is a benign Lincoln who sits in his temple-like Memorial, modeled upon the Greek Parthenon as a bow to the birthplace of democracy in ancient Greece. The 36 exterior columns symbolize the 36 states of the freshly reunited nation at the time of his death. Their names appear on the frieze above the columns.

Inside architect Henry Bacon's Lincoln "temple" are three chambers. Two flank the main chamber, which is dominated by the oversized statue of Lincoln. The two smaller chambers display key words from two of Lincoln's most memorable speeches: the Gettysburg Address of November 19, 1863, and his second inaugural address of March 4, 1865.

Inside those two chambers also, canvas murals by Jules Guerin, each sixty feet long and twelve feet high, show an "Angel of Truth" above both the Gettysburg address selection and Lincoln's inaugural statement calling for "malice toward none, charity for all." In the latter case, the "Angel of Truth" joins hands with two figures representing North and South. Since the first "Angel of Truth," seen above the Gettysburg quotation, is depicted releasing slaves from their shackles, the two themes here are Emancipation and Unity, each certainly a hallmark of Lincoln's sorely tried presidency.

As for the statue itself—majesty in marble, we might call it—the credit goes to American sculptor Daniel Chester French, who spent years studying the Lincoln story in preparation for the solemn task ahead. The result, in the words of the care-taking National Park Service, is a Lincoln depicted "as a worn but strong individual who had endured many hardships."

And look at his hands. One is clenched, "representing his strength and determination to see the war through to a successful conclusion." The other is "a more open, slightly relaxed hand representing his compassionate, warm nature."

To achieve his masterpiece in marble, sculptor French "viewed photographs, read eyewitness descriptions, and studied Leonard Volk's 1860 castings of Lincoln's hands, then sculpted several models until he [French] rendered a perfected final product." Ecumenically enough, the giant figure we see today is sculpted from marble quarried in the South...in Georgia.

Not that the Massachusetts-born French did it all, either...for such a vast undertaking he needed the help of the Piccirilli marble-cutting workshop of New York, where the six Piccirilli brothers of the firm their father founded "transformed twenty-eight blocks of white Georgia marble into intricately carved pieces that French himself perfected." Thanks to their "collective efforts," close examination will show that "the pieces fit together with nearly invisible seams."

As for authorship of the short inscription to be found right above the timeless marble Lincoln—"In this temple, as in the hearts of the people for whom he saved the Union, the memory of Abraham Lincoln is enshrined forever"—try *New York Herald Tribune* art critic, columnist and lecturer Royal Cortissoz. They say that out of the thousands upon thousands of words he wrote in his lifetime, these few were his proudest accomplishment.

So, there you have it, the Lincoln Memorial, under construction—under creation, really—from 1914 to its completion and dedication in 1922, just one of the many, many stories emanating from the Civil War a century and a half ago.

THE CIVIL WAR'S
TWO FIRST LADIES

by Ingrid Smyer

Varina:
Forgotten First Lady

EVERYONE KNEW HER—THIS FEISTY, ELEGANT, AND, AS SOME DESCRIBED HER, often regal First Lady of the Confederate States of America. But not everyone loved her.

A true Southern belle and so much more, Varina Howell Davis, wife of Confederate President Jefferson Davis, was a devoted wife, a conscientious mother, an astute manager of plantation affairs, and a keen student of current events. In time this survivor of severely difficult years matured to become the writer of a comprehensive biography of Jefferson Davis.

Her dark beauty and vivacious personality could have propelled her straight from the pages of a romance novel. She was a captivating, fictionlike heroine always committed totally for or against a person or idea. This trait, coupled with her dynamic abilities in so many areas, may explain the devotion she stirred among so many of her contemporaries and the vehement hatred seen in so many others.

A mere girl when she met the distinguished but older Davis (she was seventeen and he was thirty-six), she came away with a rather mixed first impression. "I do not know whether this Mr. Jefferson Davis is young or old," she wrote her mother. "He looks both at times." Varina decided, to her dismay, that he must be old since he was only two years younger than her own mother.

Years later, while writing her memoirs, she remembered the first time she and Jefferson went riding together. It was during a Christmas holiday when she was a guest at "The Hurricane," the plantation that belonged to Joseph Davis, the elder brother who filled the role of father for the younger Jefferson. "He rode with more grace than any man I have ever seen and gave one the impression of being incapable either of being unseated or fatigued," wrote Varina.

What she didn't mention was that she, too, was a polished rider who kept up with the best. That particular day she made a fetching picture in her bonnie-blue riding costume with plumed hat.

Born into a prominent family of Natchez, Varina was accustomed to the good things of life. Raised at "The Briers" on the outskirts of town, she led a sheltered life typical of a plantation girl of her day, but she longed for wider horizons. She once wishfully described the extent of her travels as *autour de ma chambre.*"

Then, in 1843, came the invitation from close family friend Joseph Davis for Varina to spend the Christmas holidays with his family at The Hurricane, thirty miles below Vicksburg. Perhaps the elder Davis hoped that this vibrant young lady would shake his widower brother from his long grief over the death of Sarah Knox Taylor (daughter of future President Zachary Taylor) just months after their marriage. In the eight years since then, he had shown no interest in remarriage. With his best years slipping away, he remained in isolation on a Mississippi plantation, and his recent interest in the male-dominated politics of the day was not likely to find him a new wife.

Enter Varina Howell, tall, attractive, full of energy and grace. She had just changed her little-girl curls for a more sophisticated, smooth hairdo, with her long tresses parted in the middle and swept up on either side. Her thick, dark hair crowned an oval face with soft features and dark eyes. Those eyes—a dominant feature—often danced with fire; at other times they were soft and friendly.

This striking young lady was also highly intelligent—although she had attended a female seminary in Philadelphia for two terms, she later in life gave full credit to her home-bound tutor of twelve years' standing, Judge George Winchester, for "the little learning I have acquired," and for his "pure, high standard of right." Thanks to the good judge, she excelled in Latin and the English classics. Always well informed, she read the *National Intelligencer* regularly and rarely was loathe to express her thoughts on the issues of the day. A Whig and Episcopalian, as were most of her social set, she held strong opinions. Thus her observation to her mother about the younger Davis at their first meeting: "Would you believe it, he is refined and cultivated, and yet he is a Democrat!"

Politics aside, theirs was an immediate attraction, followed by a whirlwind romance. Varina fell in love with the stately, serious-minded soldier-turned-planter; he in turn was entranced by her stimulating conversation, her quick wit, and her good looks.

In those few weeks at his brother's plantation they spent many happy hours together. He also took her to "Brierfield," his land adjacent to the vast Hurricane holdings, to show her the fields he had turned into a plantation of his own. Before she returned to Natchez in January, they became engaged. Thus began a lifelong devotion that took them through good times and bad.

Although Varina's new love came from a moneyed family, Varina could boast an impressive pedigree all her own. Grandfather Richard Howell served with distinction under General Washington as both soldier and secret agent. He subsequently became governor of New Jersey. His third son, Varina's father, William Burr Howell, left home at an early age to seek his fortune, served in the Navy during the War of 1812, and eventually settled high on a bluff of the Mississippi River at Natchez. Here he was befriended by Joseph Davis, who later served as groomsman at his wedding to one of the belles of Natchez, Margaret Louisa Kempe. She was the daughter of Colonel James Kempe from Dublin, Ireland, who fought alongside Andrew Jackson in Alabama and New Orleans, then settled in Mississippi, amassed a fortune, and married a Virginia girl, Margaret Graham. Grandmother Kempe was to be a role model for young Varina—both had fiery tempers matched with worldly charm and strong convictions.

Jefferson and Varina were married in a simple ceremony at her home, with little time spent on formal arrangements. The wedding had been put on hold for many months due to a lingering fever that weakened the bride-to-be. Still recovering, she was determined that they should wed at once. For the wedding on February 26, 1845, she wore a white embroidered Indian muslin trimmed in lace and set off by a pink rose from the garden in her hair. A breakfast followed in a drawing room filled with white hyacinth.

Then came a wedding trip by river boat to visit his sister's house in Louisiana, the very place Sarah Knox Taylor had died. The sojourn also included a stop at that unfortunate woman's grave. (This may have been done at Varina's suggestion, since throughout her life she always honored the memory of her husband's first love.) After a visit to husband Jefferson's mother at the family home in Woodville, it was on to New Orleans before settling into life on the plantation. Here, at her husband's Brierfield, Varina made a gracious transition from teenager to capable wife.

But politics had entered their peaceful picture. Davis, who had taken part in a political meeting for the first time in his life the same week that he and Varina met, soon acquired a seat in Congress. Next, war intervened, too—the West Point graduate marched off to the Mexican War, where he would earn a hero's spurs and reunite with his former father-in-law, General Zachary Taylor.

With Mexico soon defeated, it wasn't long before Taylor rode his own military coattails straight into the White House. Joining the Taylors in Washington just as quickly were Senator and Mrs. Jefferson Davis of Mississippi—first appointed to the Senate to complete a deceased member's unexpired term, Davis won the same seat in his own right in the election of 1848, coincident with Taylor's election.

The move to Washington was to tap Varina's social skills as never before, but she was not intimidated in the least by capital society. She soon was a familiar figure in the most prestigious salons of Washington. Her political astuteness won her many friends—and some obviously jealous enemies. Her powers of observation would serve her well as she made mental notes of the famous and not-so-famous, passing along her insights to her idealistic husband, still a neophyte in the political game and somewhat unbending in manner. Her vivacious personality made up for his native aloofness, and it certainly did not hurt their social standing to be embraced as intimates of the first family in the White House. In fact, Senator Davis and his wife would be with the family as the president lay dying from a stomach ailment in July 1850.

It wasn't long before the Mississippi couple would be seen as close friends of still another White House occupant—Franklin Pierce, a bona fide Yankee by virtue of his New England background and a sharp contrast to the late President Taylor's Virginia heritage. Davis would serve in Pierce's Cabinet as Secretary of War from 1853 to 1857.

Returning to their Mississippi plantation whenever possible, Varina and Jefferson tended to their flower gardens and improved their land. They took daily rides on fast racing horses and "enjoyed the exercise exceedingly," she wrote. "Nothing could be more pleasant than the dense shade through which we could ride for miles in air redolent of the perfume of the moss, flowers, wild crabapple and plum blossoms." As the specter of politics continually intruded, she "began to know the bitterness of being a politicians's wife," she wrote many years later. Her situation "meant long absences, pecuniary depletion from ruinous absenteeism, illness from exposure, misconceptions, defamation of character; everything which darkens the sunlight and contracts the happy sphere of home."

Even so, Varina blossomed in motherhood with the birth in 1852 of a son named Samuel. She still missed her husband, who was off campaigning for his "Yankee" friend Franklin Pierce, and in a very human, surprisingly candid, letter for her day, she wrote him that "your wife's courage is giving out about your staying away for such a time. I feel the want of you every hour, though I try not to be so selfish."

With the elections of 1852 past, the Davises returned to the nation's capital as Jefferson joined Pierce's Cabinet. These days in Washington were happy ones for the Mississippi couple, he enjoying his work in the War Department and she participating in social and political affairs even while developing a satisfying role as serious helpmate to her husband.

Varina would often wait up for Jefferson. Then they would burn the midnight oil working on a project together, she doing double duty as researcher and secretary. It was during this time of working alongside her husband that

Varina came to idealize him—perhaps too much. At least one historian, Clifford Dowdey, has written that she was helpmate in the true sense of the word, but where she "failed him" was in "never turning her analytical gaze on the man she regarded as perfect, virtually godlike."

Mr. Dowdey's words were true. Varina's historic 1890 memoir of their days together glorified her husband and offered justification for all he had accomplished…or tried. Her *Jefferson Davis: A Memoir by His Wife* also was her repudiation of detractors from both North and South. And if her writing is often valued for the sketches peppered throughout of the leading figures of her times, it provides insights, some unintended, into Varina's own makeup.

Her husband lost his Cabinet post with the arrival of the James Buchanan administration in 1857, but no great matter—Jefferson Davis was back again as a senator from Mississippi. And Varina, for her part, had already become one of the newly installed president's favorite Washington ladies. For her the social swim merely continued, except that too soon the inevitable was upon them all.

The long debate was over. It was now a *fait accompli*. South Carolina, soon followed by five more Southern states, Mississippi among them, seceded from the Union.

The Southern legislators would of course be taking their leave very shortly. Like his fellow solons, Jefferson Davis delivered a final speech in the Senate of the United States, his address stressing a plea for peace. "There was scarcely a dry eye in the multitude as he took his seat," noted Varina.

These were dramatic times, and nowhere was it more obvious in the next few days than in Washington, where the streets were crowded with teary-eyed friends bidding good-byes. "As the planters' coaches went rumbling off to the South, laden with the fine trappings of their luxurious existence," wrote Varina biographer Ishbel Ross in her book *First Lady of the South*, "the Davises made a quiet and unostentatious departure but were greeted at many stops as they traveled South." They were returning to their beloved land to prepare for what he predicted would be "a long and severe struggle."

That was in January 1861. In February Varina and Jefferson, at home once again, were tending their roses at Brierfield when they received the historic message that was to change their lives forever. Indeed, the rocky road ahead would never lead them back to their cherished rose garden as they knew it at that moment.

As Jefferson Davis read the message saying that he had been selected for the presidency of the newly formed Confederate States of America, "he looked so grieved," said Varina, "that I feared some evil had befallen our family." He left the next day for Montgomery, Alabama. Varina was to follow later with the children—Margaret, six (oldest child Samuel had died in 1854); little Jeff, four; and Joseph, two; plus Varina's sister Maggie, now a permanent member of the family. Varina put her house in order and left by riverboat to join her husband in the capital of the new Confederacy.

A seven-gun salute announced Varina's arrival as she sailed up the Alabama River on the *King*. While she was warmly greeted by old friends from Washington days, the general public now showed a great deal of curiosity about this stately woman of thirty-five, elegantly dressed and coiffured, her dark hair in Grecian braids.

These were heady days. Her husband and his associates were inventing a new nation. Varina, with much expected of her on the social scene, set a pace that quickly established the same tradition of hospitality she had enjoyed in the national capital. She entertained in a formal and sophisticated way, her receptions and dinners impressing the Confederates who crowded into Montgomery. But there would be critics to decry her fancy soirees and eventually to dub her "Queen Varina."

For all her own new responsibilities, she was more sensitive than ever to the towering problems her husband had been called to shoulder. Diarist Mary Chesnut, a good friend throughout the war and after, made an entry in her journal about this time that is revealing: "Mrs. Davis does not like her husband being made President." Apparently Varina also told Mary Chesnut, "General of the Armies would have suited his temperament better." For one thing, Varina was afraid her husband was not yet adept in the art of politics.

Varina, herself by now quite polished in the political realm, won the respect of the men who surrounded the president, especially Confederate Cabinet member Judah Benjamin, with whom she developed a lasting friendship. As Varina became known for her sparkling wit and quick mind, critics of her president-husband suggested he leaned too much on his wife in matters of state. But she, better than anyone, understood the need to smooth the way for her Jefferson, who still struck some associates as inordinately stiff, even cold.

The move from Montgomery to Richmond, new capital of the Confederacy, presented a hurdle of a different kind for Varina. Accustomed to the warm, open manners of the deep South, she found a sometimes chilly reception from the established social leaders of the very traditional Richmond. However, her natural resilience still stood her in good stead as, despite the grim backdrop of a horrifying war, she pursued a social agenda in support of Jefferson Davis.

Indeed, a darkness descended upon Varina's beloved South. Forts Henry and

Donelson fell. Then came the disaster at Shiloh. New Bern, North Carolina, and New Orleans were soon in the hands of the Union. The naval yards of Virginia were lost. Gettysburg and Vicksburg became twin benchmarks in the sad litany for the struggling nation.

Personal tragedy struck, too. In April of 1864, five-year-old Joe Davis, playing on an open porch at the White House of the Confederacy in Richmond, climbed a railing and fell to his death on the brick walk below. Varina wandered around in a daze while Jefferson Davis, besieged by the South's troubles on every front, had no time for personal grief—except for the pain in his heart.

The loss seemed to soften the antagonism some still held for Varina. "People do not snub me any longer," she wrote to Mary Chesnut, "for it was only while the lion was dying that he was kicked; dead, he was beneath contempt." And an afterthought: "Not to say I am worthy to be called a lion, nor are the people here asses."

Varina was underestimating herself, for if not a lion, she had the heart and courage of one. She continued to give her strong shoulder to Jefferson as disaster begat disaster on the war front—the siege of Petersburg, the fall of Atlanta, Sherman's march to the sea.

One ray of sunshine did lighten the grim days—a baby girl was born to Varina on June 27, 1864. Named Varina Anne, she was called "Winnie" (a pet name Jefferson had used for his wife) and would soon be known as the "Daughter of the Confederacy."

"She looks like a little rosebud," wrote the proud mother.

After the fall of Atlanta, the president went to visit his troops and make speeches around the South to shore up confidence. Along the way he stopped off in Columbia, South Carolina, to visit the Chesnuts, who were renting a small cottage there. Mary Chesnut had to scrimp and save to put together a decent repast in the face of ever-worsening shortages and her family's reduced financial fortunes. As she did her best to provide fitting hospitality, she told the visiting Jefferson Davis, "It is the wind-up, the Cassandra in me says: and the old life means to die royally."

In Richmond, Varina, too, was trying to make ends meet, no longer able to indulge in her sometimes regal ways. As she sold off some of her elegant cloth-ing, she gave up the most colorful dresses. Especially painful to part with was a favorite green silk, but she did not expect to wear it again anytime soon since she was always in mourning. Indeed, for the rest of her life Varina was rarely seen in any color but black.

In those final days in Richmond, Varina coped as best she could with her limited largess and the mounting pressures created by the South's looming defeat. She won over many more of her critics, while strengthening the respect that others already accorded her. Robert E. Lee, for instance, remained loyal to both Davises until the very end; he always treated Varina with unusual respect, even admiration. He quite obviously understood the burdens she carried along with the "menfolk"; he saw the constant attention she gave her husband, along with her readiness to help her friends. She often caught Lee's ear with some special plea on behalf of friends concerned for a son, brother, or husband. Lee was aware, too, that Varina sometimes sat in on meetings her husband held with various delegations come to discuss serious matters such as the exchange of prisoners.

As calamity followed calamity, the very heart of the South bled. "Darkness seemed now to close swiftly over the Confederacy, and about a week before the evacuation of Richmond," Varina wrote later, "Mr. Davis came to me and announced the necessity for our departure." She begged to stay and be near him, but he was adamant that she must seek safety, saying, "I have confidence in your capacity to take care of our babies." In the end, Varina packed away a few things, while many of their household goods (which Davis called "trumpery") were sold to a dealer who wrote a large draft on a Richmond bank for the items. Never cashed, the check remained among Varina's personal effects after her death.

The first lady of the Confederacy now gathered her teenage sister and the four Davis children—Margaret, age nine; Little Jeff, age eight; Little Billie, age three; and Winnie, still an infant—"to go forth into the unknown."

The huddled, despairing group of Davises and three daughters of close friends, escorted by presidential secretary Burton Harrison, left Richmond on a train pulled by a "worn-out engine." Twelve hours later—with no arrangements for sleeping quarters—they reached Danville, Virginia. Then it was on to Charlotte, North Carolina. After a brief reprieve in a rented house that had been arranged for in advance, their flight continued across South Carolina at Chester and Abbeville to another Abbeville via tiny Washington, Georgia. They at last arrived in Irwinville in south Georgia. The trip was hectic and harried, uncomfortable and uncertain, but throughout their separate flights— Jefferson Davis was now on the run also—the two fugitives kept in touch by courier, their letters stating and restating their abiding love for one another.

Jefferson Davis had just missed his wife when he arrived in Charlotte with his Cabinet. At the "dreadful" news of Lee's surrender on April 9, Varina had continued on her southward journey. After a harrowing train ride as far as Chester and a five-mile walk in the darkness through mud while carrying a "cheerful little baby in my arms," Varina and her entourage had arrived in Abbeville, South Carolina. Here, her gloom was momentarily dispelled when a courier delivered a long letter from her husband dated April 23. "Dear Wife," it began, "this is not the fate to which I invited [you] when the future was rose colored to us both; but I know you will bear it even better than myself and that of us two I alone will ever look back reproachfully on my past career.... Farewell, my dear, there may be better things in store for us than are now in view, but my love is all I have to offer and that has the value of a thing long possessed and sure not to be lost."

Varina at once responded: "It is surely not the fate to which you invited me in brighter days, but you must remember that you did not invite me to a great Hero's home, but to that of a plain farmer. I have shared all your triumphs, been the only beneficiary of them, now I am but claiming the privilege for the first time of being all to you now these pleasures have past [sic] for me."

Before they would meet again, Varina heard about the Lincoln assassination, news that came like a thunderclap just days after Lee's surrender at Appomattox. Her response had been immediate: "I burst into tears," she later wrote, "tears which flowed from the mingling of sorrow for the family of Mr. Lincoln and a thorough realization of the inevitable results to the Confederates, now that they were at the mercy of the Federals."

This prediction was to prove true over and over again for Varina and her beloved South. But for now the dark clouds over the separately fleeing Davises lifted ever so slightly—suddenly they were reunited. In the vicinity of Milledgeville, Georgia, Varina's party had paused and was under guard because of the constant danger of marauders when up rode her worn but still stately horseman. Jefferson and Varina were together again.

But not for long. Exhausted, the two had little time to talk. While the children danced around in joy, husband and wife—historic figures now—made plans for her to escape to Nassau and to join him wherever and whenever possible. But Davis had to leave her briefly. And after his return one night, encamped by a stream, Jefferson and Varina were awakened next morning by the sound of horses' hoofs—Union cavalrymen—then gunfire. By mistake they were firing at each other, and two troopers were killed. Jefferson stepped out of the tent, hesitated a moment, then, disguised by a shawl Varina threw over him, attempted to walk quietly away. But he had no such good fortune—he was seized and captured. Thus, on May 10, 1865, began the long, dreadful months of imprisonment for the president and Varina's long struggle to free him.

Transported over rutted roads in broken-down carriages and then by train to Macon, Georgia, next hustled onto a rusted river tug, and finally placed aboard the ocean steamer *William P. Clyde* at Savannah, the weary and bedraggled captives arrived in a few days at Hampton Roads, Virginia. Here, without so much as a moment's warning, Jefferson Davis was removed from his loving wife. Varina wrote that he had only time to approach her and say, "It is true, I must go at once." But he was also able to whisper quickly, "Try not to weep, they will gloat over your grief." His body trembled as he embraced her—then he was gone, to be incarcerated at Fortress (Fort) Monroe on May 22, 1865.

Jefferson Davis was treated harshly. He was placed in a cold, damp cell and for a few days was held in leg irons. Not even Varina's words can quite convey the deprivation and humiliation he suffered: "Worn down by privation, over-exertion, and exposure, my husband was in no condition, when thrown into prison, to resist exciting causes of disease." Said she also: "The damp walls, the food too coarse and bad to be eaten, the deprivation of sleep caused by the tramping of sentinels around the iron cot, the light of the lamp which shone full upon it, the loud calling of the roll when another relief was turned out, the noise of unlocking the doors…[all] produced fever, and rapidly wasted his strength." Davis was refused his mail—even a trunk containing a change of clothes.

Varina and the children were taken back to Savannah, where she had no family connections or friends. Here, without funds, she momentarily was held under house arrest at the Hotel Pulaski. Many citizens of the grand old Georgia city welcomed her, but any attempt to help her husband fell on deaf ears. For months, the only news she received of him came from newspapers. As Mrs. Robert E. Lee wrote to a friend, "She [Varina] writes very sadly, as well she may, for I know of no one so to be pitied."

Finally, with no really meaningful response to the pleas she directed in letters to government officials of all kinds, friends or even remote acquaintances in Washington and elsewhere, she contacted Horace Greeley, famous as a New York newspaper editor—and also known to champion lost causes. Even though he had reviled Jefferson Davis in his newspaper, he also had called for the due process of law in dealing with the Southern leader, whose very life hung in the balance in the hysteria still lingering from the Lincoln assassination. Varina now hoped that a public outcry over her husband's treatment would prompt even greater support from Greeley. She wrote to him: "How can the honest men and gentlemen of your country stand idly by to see a gentleman maligned, insulted, tortured and denied the right of trial by the usual forms of law?" Greeley did take up the cause to the extent that he engaged legal counsel on behalf of the imprisoned Jefferson Davis. And in time the Federal government's prosecutors found no evidence of complicity in the Lincoln plot and even backed off the charges of treason based on secession. Still, Jefferson was kept confined.

Varina would stop at nothing to win her husband's freedom. Now she went to the top. She wrote President Andrew Johnson, who himself faced legal problems in the form of impeachment proceedings.

Her efforts having positive effect at last, she soon was on her way to Washington. It was in late May 1866 that Varina returned to the capital where once she had been sought after and admired as the wife of the young senator from Mississippi. This time appearing as the wife of the world's most famous prisoner, she created a sensation. Her friends of old were quick to notice the changes wrought by the years of suffering. Her eyes, once so sparkling, were now deep set and sad. Yet those who studied her could sense a new dimension about Varina, a depth that seemed to sustain her in all her anguish.

The president received her cordially—she even felt sorry for such a political innocent now being demeaned by his own party. She was gratified that the immediate result of the meeting was that Davis was allowed more freedom within his prison walls. Soon Varina was even allowed to move in with him.

Many months would pass, however, before Jefferson Davis was granted his freedom. After the better part of two years, he was finally released on bail in Richmond. "Strangely enough," wrote Hugh MacCulloch in his book *Men and Measures of Half a Century*, "Horace Greeley and Gerrit Smith, the distinguished abolitionists, were among the signers of his bond."

All of Richmond took to the streets to greet the reunited couple the day of his bond hearing in the city that had played such an important role in their lives. They were given the very same suite at the Spotswood Hotel that they had shared in happier (if uncertain) days here so long ago. And after the bond hearing—free at last!

More tests lay ahead as Varina set out to find a place in the sun—both figuratively and literally—for herself and her weary, wounded husband, now a man without a country. As pleased as the Davises were, Richmond was a city of painful memories, and they were anxious to rejoin their children in Lennoxville, Canada.

After a stopover in New York, the Davis couple at last had a joyful family reunion in Canada. Staying to enjoy the company of family, friends, and a few Southern compatriots, Varina and Jefferson found solace in the simple pleasures. For Varina, soothing her husband's proud soul was demanding. The long, cold Canadian winter of 1867 left her restless; she was not content to sit out the rest of their lives on the sidelines, and she persuaded her husband to join her in a search for new horizons. The "king and queen in exile" would move on.

First it was to Cuba for a brief sojourn, then to New Orleans, with a rousing welcome there from old friends and Confederate diehards. Finally came the heartbreaking return to Brierfield—the buildings burned, the fields overgrown, the roses covered in bramble. Since it could no longer be home to them, they returned to Lennoxville, where they had established residence in a pension. The next summer, at Varina's urging, they sailed for England.

Here the old conviviality and flair of her earlier days had to be held in abeyance, since Varina found it hard to accept invitations from wealthy lords and ladies while she could not reciprocate in expensive Victorian style. Traveling on the Continent, Varina and Jefferson soon found their financial resources low, and he reluctantly accepted a position as president of an insurance company in Memphis.

And so this Southern city on the Mississippi River became home for a while. Varina again made many new friends, but much of the stimulating social scene, once so much a part of her life, eluded her there. Things did not go so well for Jefferson, either. Deciding there was no future for him in the business world, he once again took his wife off to England.

As fate would have it, a wealthy plantation owner whose husband had recently died was traveling in England. Sarah Dorsey, another vivacious, ambitious woman and an old Mississippi acquaintance, heard about Jefferson's wish to write his own memoir. She had recently bought Beauvoir, a beautiful estate on the Mississippi coast, and she offered the wandering former president of the Confederacy a place to come home to.

Bidding Varina good-bye—a chronic heart condition, more and more troublesome these days, apparently prevented her from attempting the ocean voyage at this time—Jefferson returned alone to his native Mississippi. There, in the fresh air and ocean breezes of an idyllic setting, he began to unwind. A pavilion set off from the main house became his haven, and the story he had already lived began to unfold on paper. Thus began his two-volume tome, *The Rise and Fall of the Confederate Government*.

Many months would pass before Varina was strong enough to leave England. When she did return to America, for once she did not rush into the arms of her husband. She went to Memphis to be with her daughter Margaret, who had lost her first baby.

But more than concern for her daughter kept her away from Jefferson.

Sarah Dorsey, whom Varina had known when they were both young girls in Natchez, now posed an intrusive threat. By midsummer, Varina, hoping to squelch gossip about her husband and Mrs. Dorsey, moved to Beauvoir and achieved a truce with Sarah. Never doubting the unabiding love of her husband nor her enduring devotion for him, Varina made her peace with Jefferson, too. But she would carry her resentment toward Sarah to the grave.

Jefferson, who had been none too happy over their separation, needed her now more than ever. She stepped naturally into the role she had filled so often as his assistant and collaborator.

Most of the Confederate government papers had been lost or destroyed, making it difficult to set forth the history of the fallen nation. For three long years they interviewed principal players, taxed their own memories, and worked side by side. Finally, the book was finished. It was four o'clock in the morning, and Varina had been taking dictation since eight in the evening.

Though never a financial success, the memoir accomplished the end for which they so long had labored: "setting the righteous motives of the South before the world," Varina wrote later.

During these years Mrs. Dorsey had died in New Orleans, where she had moved to receive medical attention. Before she left, she sold Beauvoir to Jefferson and made him the executor of her estate.

Beauvoir proved to be the haven the Davises needed in their golden years. Son Jefferson had died and daughter Winnie, also settled at Beauvoir, was a constant companion to her father. Jefferson Davis never took his Federal oath of allegiance and never attempted to have his American citizenship restored (although during Jimmy Carter's presidency he was at last restored as a citizen of the United States of America).

After Jefferson died in 1889, Varina lived on into the twentieth century. She wrote her own two-volume memoir, which was widely acclaimed. Ironically, she moved to New York, where she—predictably—soon became a grande dame in the social, cultural, and literary world. On October 16, 1906, she died there, far from the river country of Mississippi where she and a handsome, graceful rider twice her age had met so many years before—to begin a life together more dramatic than any fiction.

Mary Todd Lincoln: Troubled First Lady

BY THE TIME SHE WAS FIVE, SHE HAD LOST HER LILTING DOUBLE NAME TO A newborn sister, Ann. From now on, "Mary Ann" would simply be Mary… Mary Todd.

So began a lifetime of losses for perhaps the most troubled and certainly one of the most maligned first ladies ever to step across the White House threshold. Even as first lady, she would encounter truly crushing losses… along with bizarre reminders of the childhood difficulties that began with the loss of her name to a sibling. Unbelievably, in the midst of the Civil War, married to the president of the United States, commander in chief of the Union armies, she would find herself playing hostess—in the White House—to a much younger half sister who was the widow of a recently killed Confederate general!

Not only "politically incorrect," the weeks-long visit of Emilie Todd Helm to the Lincoln White House, coming after her pleas for safe passage through Union lines, was a sharp reminder for Mary Todd Lincoln of her days as a little girl in the Todd home in Lexington, Kentucky—as a child who hardly had time to enjoy being the baby of the family. Baby brother Levi arrived barely a year after Mary. Then, a year after Levi, came Robert Parker Todd, but in fourteen months he died of natural causes. His death from a common childhood illness left "Mary Ann" with a deep sense of loss, aggravated only a short time later by the bestowal of half her name to a newborn sister.

Years later Mary, in her unforgiving way, described this unfavorite sister (named for a childless and favorite aunt) as "poor unfortunate Ann, inasmuch as she possesses such a miserable disposition and so false a tongue."

Ironically, Mary herself would be the one to go down in the history books as having a sharp and even shrewish tongue, not always a fair judgment.

Meanwhile, after losing a baby brother at the tender age of four, and shorn of half her name at the age of five, Mary at age six encountered the worst loss yet—her mother died from childbirth complications after delivering another son, who was named George Rogers Clark Todd.

Compounding this loss, Mary was only seven when a stranger would claim the affections of her father—young Mary had to endure yet another upheaval as her father brought a new wife into the Todd family.

Like the wicked stepmother of fairy tales, Betsey Humphreys Todd was de-
tested by all six of Mr. Todd's children, but in age and temperament, Mary apparently was the most vulnerable to the effects of all this family trauma. Mary's
two older sisters, Elizabeth and Frances, had long ago bonded and would remain
close friends throughout their lives, while Ann, the youngest sister, would be
a favorite of Aunt Ann, who came to run the household for a while before
Mary's father, Robert Smith Todd, remarried. Mary's two brothers, in an age
that tended to honor boys more than girls, could expect to be treated as the
future standard-bearers of the proud and prominent Todd name.

Betsey Humphreys came from the wealthy and prominent Humphreys family
of Frankford, Kentucky. Her mother, Mary Brown Humphreys, absolutely
ruled Frankford society. But Betsey, at age twenty-five, was well on her way to
spinsterhood until she met the widower Robert Todd in 1826. Since she could
be adept at hiding her age, some say she may have been as old as twenty-eight!
Years later her five daughters would omit her birthdate from both her obituary
and her tombstone.

Whatever her true age, Mr. Todd's new wife demanded her own standards
of order and elegance in the Todd home and would not be daunted by a
household full of stepchildren. Though she would never endear herself to
the first Todd children, it was not totally her fault. The children's formidable
grandmother, who lived in the big house on the hill above the Todd house, had
prepared her grandchildren to reject any substitute for her daughter and their
mother, Eliza Parker Todd, who was connected to the Todd clan not only by
marriage but also through their other grandmother…who herself was a cousin
of the Todds.

The Widow Parker, as the maternal grandmother was known, to distinguish her from the many Parker relatives of Lexington, often reminded her
grandchildren of the patriotic exploits of their ancestors on both sides of the
family. At the time of the Revolution, Robert Parker and Levi Todd, along
with brothers Robert and John Todd, had come to the Kentucky wilderness
and established the beginnings of a town that was little more than a fortification
against the Indians. The year was 1775, and they named their newborn village
after a distant battle just past in Massachusetts, the double battle of Concord
and Lexington. As family legend would have it, these men served with valor
in the Revolutionary War that followed. John in particular was a hero at the
battle of Blue Licks, Kentucky, in 1782 as he joined Daniel Boone and fellow
frontiersmen in a desperate fight against a marauding force of British soldiers
and Chickasaw and Miami Indians. Riding on a white horse—family stories

were always a bit bigger than life—he paid the ultimate price by laying down his life for country, for family, and for fellow Kentucky settlers.

After serving in the Revolution, Robert Parker and Levi Todd proceeded to promote their town with glorious and exaggerated accounts of the prospects in their frontierland. Both men accumulated vast land estates spread over three counties of Kentucky, but unlike the plantation owners of the Deep South, they did not create their wealth and prominence by planting crops and managing farms. Todd once emphasized his bent for other enterprises in a letter to a friend: "I believe you have as little taste for farming as myself."

Much of Levi Todd's wealth came about after Kentucky's first governor, Isaac Shelby, appointed the younger brother of the hero of the battle of Blue Licks to the important position of clerk of the Fayette County Court. In this position from 1780 until his death in 1807, Levi Todd was keeper of all important records, from road surveys to deed registrations—in essence, he was a one-man government.

Robert Parker, meanwhile, was busy making his own mark as surveyor, miller, merchant, and clerk of the city's governing body. According to Jean H. Baker's biography *Mary Todd Lincoln*, in this capacity Robert Parker "collected four shillings every time a property exchanged hands in Lexington, just as Levi, in a similar annuity, collected a fee on all legal documents processed in Fayette County."

Then, too, if ambition and hard work rewarded these two pioneers, so did their extensive family connections—Sisters marrying into prominent families, sons, brothers, and nephews also finding their way into important positions—all made the saying "first families" a truism. Thus, young Mary Todd's grandfathers and grandmothers represented two thriving branches of a leading Kentucky family.

In keeping with the family's storied success, Robert Parker built the first brick house in Lexington, and Levi Todd built the first one in Fayette County. According to family legend also, Levi named his estate Ellerlie for the Scottish village of his sixteenth-century Todd ancestors.

Into this promising and secure world Robert and Elizabeth Parker's daughter Eliza—later to become Mary's mother—was born in 1794. When she was only six years old, her father died and her mother built a large two-story house near the center of town. Here, from the second-floor window, most of Lexington could be seen, wrote biographer Baker, adding that the view included "the expectant eighty-foot-wide Main Street, the brick-pillared courthouse, and Cheapside Market." Even Lexington's slave markets could be seen and heard from this vantage point. Here too, in this prominent house, the formidable Widow Parker would spend the rest of her long life.

Life was circumscribed for "little misses" in this town of Southern graciousness. Young girls had only one vehicle to success and that was to marry well. Known as a "rising beauty," Eliza attended tea parties, cotillions, theater, and the inevitable round of gossip sessions with her girlfriends. Schooling for girls was not stressed even though the family had endowed the local university for men, Transylvania.

In the meantime Robert Smith Todd, the third of Levi's six sons, lost his mother but soon acquired a young stepmother. He graduated from Transylvania and went on to study law under the famed jurist George Bibb. Then, with his law studies under his belt, he was ready to start out—some say "like a house afire"—to capture the lovely "Liza" Parker. But as new winds of war stirred the men of this frontier state to action against the British and their ally, the Indian chief Tecumseh, even before the official opening of the War of 1812, Robert was ready to serve. In the tradition of oft-told stories of father Levi's role in the same fight at Blue Licks that cost the life of Uncle John Todd, young Robert now asked one of the Parkers to recommend him to U.S. Senator Henry Clay for a commission.

Many frontier families boasted oral histories that endowed each generation with a need to further serve the cause of patriotic glory. But the Todds and Parkers raised such historical imperative to rare heights. Even the women had their family stories of bravery in wartime roles. Eliza Parker's own grandmother had brought food and clothing to her husband, Capt. Andrew Porter, during the terrible winter that George Washington and his men spent at Valley Forge, Pennsylvania. She often rode out with provisions to the log-hut encampment, "where one day she met an unfamiliar officer who led her to her husband, complimenting her, as they rode through the snow on a bitter cold day, on her devotion to her husband and, through him, the Republican cause." The officer was none other than George Washington.

Meanwhile, Eliza Parker accepted her cousin Robert Todd's proposal, and they were married in 1812. Despite the latest war and the fact that he would be away with Kentucky's volunteer forces part of the time, they went to live with the Widow Parker, who gave them the lower half of her lot. There, in 1814, the newlyweds established their own home in the family compound.

Into their world a third daughter was born in 1818—Eliza and Robert named her Mary Ann, but she soon would be just Mary...Mary Todd.

With babies arriving every two to three years, Eliza often needed help running her household, and the Widow Parker sent her slaves down the hill to assist with the chores. One such slave, the house servant called Mammy Sally, became a parent-like presence for the little third daughter, a role that was even more pronounced after the death of Mary's mother a few years later.

Mammy Sally was the archetypal Southern mammy whose terrifying stories of ghosts, spirits, devils, and phantoms, often invoked while also calling upon the good name of the Christian God, were certain to keep her wards on their good behavior. One of Mammy Sally's especially terrifying stories was the West African myth about the jaybird who kept records of all the bad children and reported to the devil every night. For a sensitive and impressionable child like Mary, these stories loomed as entirely true. Mammy's mix of Christian theology and transplanted African tales reinforced her little ward's cherished hope that the dead, perhaps even her mother who had abandoned her, would return in spirit.

But it was to the affairs of the world, specifically political affairs, that Mistress Mary turned her thoughts as time passed. And here she hoped to gain her busy father's ear. At the tender age of nine she joined his political party and as a Whig refused to attend a public rally in Lexington for the visiting Democrat Andrew Jackson on the eve of his election in 1828.

For this young miss to follow a political bent was most unusual. Proper ladies of her generation and her social standing, young or old, were expected to remain in the domestic sphere, and Mary, constantly surrounded by sisters, half sisters, stepmother, mammy, and other female servants, was expected to prepare herself accordingly. The women of Lexington, it should also be noted, were known for their high fashion. As the wife of the president of Transylvania, Mary Holley, a proper New Englander, once noted, after the ladies of town had paid their obligatory morning social calls, "I was astonished to see callers arrive in satin and silk as if they were going to an evening function." Drawing a fetching word-picture of the same visiting ladies, she added that they would "adjust their flounces, scarcely touching their backs to the parlor chair lest they form a wrinkle or disturb a hair."

The small demands on women, especially unmarried ones in Mary's society, left plenty of time on their hands to indulge in idle gossip, parties, and pretty dresses, until such time as a husband would rescue them from the dread of spinsterhood. Politics and education were of the man's realm.

For all of Mary's own desire to fill her wardrobe with pretty clothes, she was also eager to fill her head with more than idle gossip. Fortunately, her father was of like mind that women should not be boring. Robert Todd, who probably had been exposed to many books in his father's library, was aware of early feminist Mary Wollstonecraft's revolutionary ideas that education was a natural right for girls. He saw to it that his daughters as well as his sons had a formal education. Accordingly, Mary at age nine entered Shelby Female Academy, or Ward's' as it came to be called after the Reverend Ward and his wife. Here, and later at Madame Mentelle's boarding school, Mary excelled. While most of her contemporaries finished their schooling at about age fourteen, Mary stayed in school.

The eccentric Madame Mentelle and her husband had escaped with their heads from the excesses of the French Revolution and made their way to Lexington, where Madame opened her "select family school." In this environment Madame made a lasting impression on her pupils. In addition to introducing Mary to a lifetime fluency in French, plus a love of reading and writing, Madame opened young Mary's eyes to theater. Here, in school plays, Mary Todd became a "star actress," as one cousin put it, and began to develop an uncanny ability later used to mimic friends and, most hilariously, her hated enemies. It was also Madame Mentelle, according to biographer Baker, who left Mary with "an unshakable fascination with royalty, indelible images of female independence, aristocratic snobbishness, and individual eccentricity."

The year 1832, meanwhile, had brought about three major changes in Mary's life. She entered Madame Mentelle's boarding school, which was good. Soon afterward, her father, stepmother, and entourage moved to a new house in Lexington. This was painful for Mary, since she was losing the home that held memories of her earliest childhood, the very place where she had lived with her mother. And the third upheaval was the marriage of her favorite sister, Elizabeth, to the young lawyer Ninian Wirt Edwards, son of an Illinois governor. As a result, Elizabeth would be moving away, to his home in Illinois.

In the fall of 1839, seven years later, Mary herself left Lexington and moved to Springfield, the new capital of Illinois, to live with Elizabeth and her husband Ninian—a sensible arrangement if only because it meant escape from a home presided over by the stepmother Mary had not yet learned to like. Further, Mary's sister Frances in an earlier visit with Elizabeth had had the good fortune to meet her own future husband, local physician and druggist William S. Wallace. As described in Ruth Painter Randall's book *Mary Lincoln*, the convivial Edwards home was the "center of the aristocratic 'Edwards clique.'" All the most distinguished visitors in town, "especially when the legislature was in session, found their way up the gentle slope to the house on the hill where hospitality was on a lavish, old-fashioned scale."

Just in case Mary expected to match the matrimonial experience of sister Frances, the Edwards mansion was the right and proper place to be.

Mary quickly made friends with another visitor to this bustling capital city, Mercy Levering of Baltimore, also destined to be swept up in the "lively coterie," as the younger set called themselves. Soon after Mercy's arrival at a brother's local home, she was being courted by a young lawyer, James Conkling, an arrangement that then blossomed into an engagement. "Dear Merce," as Mary called her, had to return home temporarily in the spring of 1840, but the young women kept in touch by mail, with Mary filling in Mercy on the latest gossip and changes taking place since her departure.

Revealing a serious side, Mary responded to one of her friend's letters by saying, "Would it were in my power to follow your kind advice, my ever dear Merce, and turn my thought from earthly vanities, to one higher than us all."

Apparently feeling a bit guilty over the frivolity of the coterie, Mary continued, "Every day proves the fallacy of our enjoyments & that we are living for pleasures that do not recompense us for the pursuit."

All well and good, but the fact was that Springfield, a little town so young, so vigorous, so fast growing as a new state capital, could itself at times ring with the sounds of excitement and frivolity. As historian Randall wrote, it was a burgeoning community "full of young people and their enthusiasms and love affairs."

Into this town in 1837 a young lawyer not much given to frivolity had ridden with all his worldly possessions packed in two saddlebags.

It was not long before the unlikely Abraham Lincoln, tall, thin, awkward, uncouth and even ugly, was included in the smart set around town. Seemingly a contradiction in terms, yes, but then, as noted by one observer who had heard him in the legislature, this Lincoln "spoke with such force and vigor that he held the attention of all." More important, he was well known as the man most responsible for the removal of the state capital from Vandalia to Springfield.

The day of course came when Mary Todd, one of the belles squired about town by several eligible bachelors, first saw the up-and-coming legislator across a dance floor. It was not love at first sight, but, wrote Ishbel Ross in her book *The President's Wife*, "by some magic a fire was lit [that day in 1839] that burned through a quarter of a century of love and sorrow."

And here was another seeming contradiction—that popular Mary Todd, described by sister Elizabeth as having "clear blue eyes, long lashes, light brown hair with a glint of bronze, and a lovely complexion," should be smitten by the poor country lawyer with few of Mary's own social graces. And it certainly did make for an odd match—the tall, gawky Lincoln alongside such a sophisticated young lady associated with the "lively coterie."

That Lincoln should find Mary alluring was far less a surprise. Consider the fetching picture that Mary made that year, as somewhat lavishly described by an obviously loving niece: "Mary, although not strictly beautiful, was more than pretty. She had a broad white forehead, eyebrows sharply but delicately marked, a straight nose, short upper lip and expressive mouth curling into an adorable slow-coming smile that brought dimples to her cheeks and glinted in her long-lashed blue eyes."

The same niece went on to say: "Those eyes, shaded by their long silky fringe, gave an impression of dewy violet shyness contradicted fascinatingly by the spirited carriage of her head."

As Lincoln soon would discover, there was an intellectual side to this beguiling young woman, who had been better educated than most of her distaff contemporaries, was well read, and was even given to a real understanding of politics. In a letter to Mercy in late 1840, for instance, Mary confessed to her strong interest in the recent election of William Henry Harrison as president: "This fall I became quite a politician, rather an unladylike profession, yet at such a crisis, whose heart could remain untouched while the energies of all were called in question?"

Sometimes what is not written tells more than the actual script, for Mary did not mention that her heart by then belonged to Lincoln. She said only that they had reached an "understanding." And, in her chatty way, that his "lincoln green" suit had gone to dust, apparently a reference to an unbecoming suit the two women had laughed over in the past.

But then, just as the unlikely lovers were making marriage plans, the informal engagement was off! And to this day no one really knows why. Most probably the socially attuned Edwards couple did not consider the raw Lincoln a suitable husband for their Mary. Then, too, Lincoln himself felt he was a dreary prospect as a future husband.

While Mary Todd held her head high during the eighteen months the star-crossed lovers were apart, Lincoln became depressed, even physically ill. In a letter to his law partner at the time, Congressman John Todd Stuart, Lincoln lamented: "I am now the most miserable man living. If what I feel were equally distributed to the whole human family, there would not be one cheerful face on the earth." And worse: "Whether I shall ever be better or not I can not tell; I awfully forbode I shall not. To remain as I am is impossible, I must die or be better, it appears to me."

If Mary were able to put up a brave face during their schism, in her heart of hearts she, too, felt the sting of their separation, as confided by letter to "Dear Merce" in mid-1841. "Summer in all its beauty has come again," she wrote, while departing winter had left her with "some lingering regrets over the past, which time alone can overshadow with its healing balm."

The Edwardses aside, there were some in Springfield who were determined to bring Mary and Abraham together again. According to Justin G. Turner and Linda Levitt Turner in their book *Mary Todd Lincoln*, such a person was their mutual friend Simeon Francis, editor of Springfield's Whig newspaper, the *Sangamo Journal*. During the summer of 1842, Francis and his wife would be the healing balm that Mary had invoked. They invited the two unhappy people to their home, unbeknownst to either one, with the result that the onetime lovers "were shyly delighted when Mrs. Francis urged, 'Be friends.'"

After two years of romantic ups and downs, love and breakup, family pressures and political interventions, Mary Todd and Abraham finally made a whirlwind decision to wed. Delighted to flout tradition and do without a big, "showy" wedding, Mary at first thought to be married at an Episcopal rectory—destined later to become the couple's first real home—but then accepted sister Elizabeth's insistent offer to hold the wedding at the Edwards home instead.

If the newly married Mary Todd Lincoln was seeking glamour, a continuation of parties and pretty clothes, a showy home and life of ease, well, she had chosen the wrong man.

There would be no elegant trips to Saint Louis and down the Mississippi River to New Orleans—the preferred vacation mode of her Kentucky kinfolk—no travels abroad for these newlyweds. A drive across town to a boarding house called the Globe Tavern would be their wedding trip. Here they would live until the birth of their first child in August 1843, just three days short of nine months from the night they had wed.

It was assumed that Mary would seek the comforts of her sister Elizabeth's ample home for the birthing, but no, Mary's long-smoldering streak of independence, so much a part of her nature and only further nurtured at the knee of Madame Mentelle, caused Mary to manage on her own, without Big Sister. No harm was done, as Mary produced a fine, strong, and healthy baby boy. They named him Robert Todd Lincoln after her father.

Now, of course, with the responsibility of a newborn on her hands, loving as Mary might be, surely she realized the contrast with her happy-go-lucky days as a member in good standing of "the coterie." Rather than the gay parties she helped to organize at her very social sister's home, Mary and Abraham now enjoyed all the amenities of a frugal boarding-house existence, for which they paid $4 a week.

★★★

There is no doubt that Mary married for love, yet with her intuitive powers she saw in her man, already standing tall in local politics, a potential for achievement, even the hope of greatness. Her competitive spirit found the political arena exciting—an arena where she, along with husband Abraham, could fill a heretofore somewhat empty life of frivolity and satisfy that nebulous but utterly human longing "to be somebody."

Lincoln, too, was ambitious, if in a quieter way. "Nearly always between these two there was a moving undertow of their mutual ambitions," wrote Carl Sandburg in his sentimental biography, *Mary Lincoln*. Their temperaments were startlingly different, but both had a burning desire to achieve. "And between these mutual ambitions of theirs might be the difference that while he cared much for what History would say of him, her anxiety was occupied with what Society, the approved social leaders of the upper classes, would let her have."

Imagine her thrill as she saw predictions come true when, in 1846, Lincoln was elected to Congress! Her husband was going places and she with him. Unlike other congressmen of that day, Lincoln was taking his family—now two sons, the younger one named for a friend and fellow politician, Edward Dickinson Baker—with him to Washington. Not so incidentally either, Mary decided it at last was time to take her husband to meet her family and friends in Lexington. For one thing, stepmother Betsey Todd had never met the rising young politician who was her stepson-in-law.

So it was that before they set out on the long journey to Washington, the Lincolns first went to Mary's hometown, where they spent three weeks. Here Lincoln experienced southern hospitality, and here he saw with glaring clarity slavery at its worst and at its best.

From the porch of the Widow Parker's down past sweeping lawns, he viewed the peaceful scene of the town, but not too far away, beyond a spiked fence, he could hear the moans and groans of runaway slaves housed in a grim-looking structure run by William Pullum, Lexington's leading slave dealer. Here, in vermin-infested slave pens, poor black souls strained to see out from the high-barred windows. Slave trading went on almost every day, but on Saturdays and court days special auctions were held. Here half-naked men, women, and children were on view and bids were made for human flesh and blood.

And yet at the Todd home, Lincoln could almost believe the stories of contented slaves as he watched the house servants—mostly female—go about their capable management of the household and their gentle handling of children.

The first visit to the state where he was born was an eye-opener for the soon-to-be congressman. But Lincoln enjoyed being with his wife's family—he and his father-in-law were on friendly terms, and he was pleased to see that even his wife and her stepmother seemed cordial to one another. Relatives and friends rallied to the visitors. They were graciously entertained—after all, Mary was a Todd, and that carried weight in Lexington.

Robert Todd saw that Lincoln met important people, one of them Mary's hero of her youth, Henry Clay, then mourning the death of his son in the Mexican War. The war was doubly painful for the elder statesman, for he felt that the war was an action of "unnecessary and offensive aggression." Lincoln heard a speech made by Clay claiming also that to take over Mexico would open new territory to slavery. Lincoln could see why the venerable Clay had been such an influence on his wife, even inspiring much of her early interest in politics.

While Lincoln was taking in the lavish estates and grand lifestyle of Mary's family, he must have felt that had she not married him, she would surely be living in luxury such as this, in a style he could never even aspire to match. Mary delighted in the parties and seeing old friends, while also enjoying unaccustomed leisure afforded when old Mammy Sally took charge of the two Lincoln boys. But Mary also was anxious to leave for Washington.

Mr. and Mrs. Lincoln and their two sons arrived in Washington on December 2, 1847, a great day in Mary's eyes. If Mary had visions of grandeur, however, they were quickly thwarted—not only because Lincoln housed his family at Mrs. Ann G. Sprigg's simple boarding house, but because Mary would hardly have time to find her way around before her congressman-husband would send her back to Lexington.

As far as Lincoln himself was concerned, Mrs. Sprigg's was the place to be. It was ideal if one were in a hurry to get to the Capitol building. The lodging place was strategically situated where the Library of Congress now stands, so close to the Capitol that another congressman-boarder once explained, "The iron railing around the Capitol comes to within fifty feet of our door." In those days, most congressmen boarded with fellow delegates from their state, but Lincoln originally choose Mrs. Sprigg's on the recommendation of Mary's cousin and former House member John Todd Stuart because it was a Whig stronghold, and he was the lone Whig sent to Congress from Illinois. (But he was only one of the four Lincolns crowded into a single room!)

Hardly a metropolis, Washington in 1847, with a population of thirty-eight thousand, nonetheless was the biggest city Mary—or her husband, for that matter—had ever seen. Newly built on swampland on the banks of the Potomac between Maryland and Virginia, the capital at the center of the old thirteen colonies was hardly on a par with Paris or London, but it was the seat of government, and for Mary that meant an exciting, stimulating center of power.

The weather on the flats of the Potomac was muggy, rainy, or generally uncomfortable, hardly the place for a young wife with two youngsters. Sharing one room with two boisterous boys in tow was no easy feat for the new congressman—or for his wife. Particularly with these two boys, onlookers commented on the undisciplined behavior of the Lincoln boys often.

Mary both helped and hindered her congressman in their crowded quarters at Mrs. Sprigg's. She demanded his help with the children and yet was able to help him as she read over the legislative reports and gave him her quick analysis. Still he sent his brood back to Mary's family in Kentucky in the early spring.

If he felt that his family interfered with his work when they were with him, without them he was lonely for them. His letters to her were filled with longing, and Mary's expressed equal pining for him. "How much I wish, instead of writing, we were together this evening," she wrote one May evening, and she assured him that his "codgers," as he teasingly referred to their boys, had not forgotten him. "I feel very sad away from you," she wrote.

Thus, on June 12, Lincoln wrote that he would welcome her on one condition: "Will you be a good girl in all things, if I consent?" A rather demeaning way to put it, but he had often referred to Mary as his child-wife. The letter continued, "Then come along, and that as soon as possible. Having got the idea in my head I shall be impatient till I see you."

Joyfully packing her beautiful new dresses, she (and the boys, too) later joined Lincoln on the campaign trail of 1848 for Zachary Taylor, who subsequently won the presidency while Lincoln's own state went for Taylor's opponent, Lewis Cass. This was a real disappointment for the hopeful Lincoln, who would receive little recognition for the part he had played in Taylor's successful run for the presidency.

Mary had not rejoined him in the capital, and when the Thirtieth Congress adjourned in March 1849, he returned to Springfield. These were dark days for the Lincolns. Feeling that his political career was over, he sank into deep depression. Mary suffered from recurring headaches but refused to give up her dreams of someday returning to Washington. According to legend at least,

Mary even then declared she would not have married Mr. Lincoln had she not believed he was destined to be president.

During these seemingly hopeless times for Lincoln came an offer for the governorship of Oregon. If Lincoln thought seriously about this opportunity, Mary said no. She held to her belief that her husband was destined for greatness; Oregon would be a political dead end.

Lincoln continued his law practice, traveled the Eighth Circuit, and kept in touch with the people. Mary, meanwhile, kept up with local politics.

But sad events enshrouded the Lincolns during this time. On July 16, 1849, Mary's father, Robert Todd, died of cholera, and soon after Christmas, in January 1850, Mary's grandmother, the Widow Parker, who had outlived her husband by half a century, also died. It was especially hard for Mary to lose two members of her family in a span of six months—the very two who probably had exercised the most influence on her early life. But still worse was to come—less than a month later, her own son, little Eddie, her pride and joy, died of diphtheria.

Mary mourned her little one with an outpouring of grief that was an ominous prelude to the uncontrollable emotions she would display years later upon another young son's death, this time in the White House. Lincoln, for his part, mourned little Eddie inwardly, as evidenced by his deep gloom.

Over the next few years, meanwhile, there were few developments in Lincoln's life and activities to encourage the deep conviction that Mary still harbored of a great destiny awaiting him…and her.

One bright spot in this otherwise uneventful period was a visit in 1854 of Emilie Todd, now a lovely young lady of eighteen. Four married Todd sisters who now lived in Springfield began a gay round of parties, which of course delighted Mary. "Little Sister" Emilie, as Lincoln liked to call Mary's favorite half sister, was a keen observer of people and events who years later would write one of the best accounts of the home life of the Lincolns. According to historian Randall, Little Sister not only spent a good deal of time with the Lincolns but kept a diary noting no unhappiness between them. Emilie went so far as to record the pride she saw in Lincoln's eyes as they rested on his comely little wife, and the pains that same little wife took to dress prettily, the effort she made to sparkle and bring that look to her husband's eyes.

But this observer was also aware that sister Mary was nervous and often let her Todd temper run uncontrolled. "Her little temper was soon over," Emilie once wrote, "and her husband loved her nonetheless, perhaps all the more, for this human frailty which needed his love and patience to pet and coach the sunny smile to replace the sarcasm and tears—and, oh, how she did love this man!"

Emilie married Ben Hardin Helm, a popular choice with both Mary and her husband, especially when they discovered his mutual interest in politics, albeit not always of their persuasion. Some of the correspondence between Emilie and Mary over the years fortunately survived the calamitous events of the 1860s to offer a glimpse into the political talk of their day. In November 1856, for instance, Mary wrote to her sister that Lincoln absolutely was not an abolitionist. "All he desires is that slavery not be extended, let it remain where it is," Mary explained. Both she and Lincoln believed in gradual emancipation, she added, with compensation to slaveholders.

But now, suddenly, came a major change in the lives of the Lincolns. The year 1858 would give the busy wife, mother, and letter-writer much to celebrate and to write about. At the Republican state convention on June 16, Lincoln was selected to be his party's candidate for the U.S. Senate! He made an acceptance speech that same evening that included the now-famous line, "A house divided against itself cannot stand."

His Democratic opponent was none other than Mary's own onetime beau, Stephen A. Douglas. Mary of course was proud and excited when her candidate challenged her old suitor to a series of debates. Now, at last, Mary's confidence in her man was dramatically reinforced...and she was ready to realize her dream.

The debates gained Lincoln national recognition and followers, but now would come Mary's own turn in the limelight. On the day of the last debate Lincoln's wife would make a grand appearance. It was agreed that the charming Mrs. Douglas, who had been traveling with her husband, needed the competition of a pretty, beautifully dressed, intelligent, and refined lady on the Republican side. Mary's excitement that day was reflected in her comment while watching the two debaters on the platform: "Mr. Douglas is a very little, little giant by the side of my tall Kentuckian, and intellectually my husband towers above Douglas just as he does physically."

At this final debate, too, she heard Abraham repeat his warning that "a house divided against itself cannot stand," uttered with the amendment, "I believe this Government cannot endure permanently, half Slave half free."

Despite all the hurrahs, though, Lincoln was defeated in his bid for the Senate. Of course Lincoln was disheartened, to say the least, but what of his wife who had held such confidence in their political destiny? They had fought long and hard, and yet she was not totally disheartened. Writing to Emilie, she said, "One feels better even after losing, if one has had a brave, whole-hearted fight."

Then, too, "fizzle-gigs and fire-works" was the surprising, almost cheery phrase Lincoln used to describe the campaign to a friend. But his disappointment was obvious in a letter to another friend. "I now sink out of view, and shall be forgotten," he wrote, but more prophetically he continued, "I believe I have made some marks which will tell for the cause of civil liberty long after I'm gone."

Like Mary, in fact, he was not yet ready to give up the quest for the political grail. Lincoln also told a downhearted follower: "Quit that. You will soon feel better. Another 'blow-up' is coming; and we shall have fun again."

Blowup, yes; fun, no—not in the true sense of the word. Excitement aplenty, yes! In May 1860, at the national Republican convention held in nearby Chicago, Abraham Lincoln was nominated to be the Republican candidate for president. Suddenly—was it really possible?—the impossible dream could be, might be, realized!

The firing of a hundred guns in Springfield that November election night indeed did proclaim Lincoln's victory, and as he turned to leave the State House he remarked, "There's a little woman down at our house [who] would like to hear this. I'll go down and tell her."

That night, the Lincoln home became the center of attention for all Springfield—it seemed the whole town had arrived on the doorstep.

Fireworks and rockets, bands blared their music in the street, and, as one observer said, "even the Democrats, who all liked Lincoln personally, joined in the jubilee." What a night it was for Springfield, adopted home for both Lincolns!

Now the "little woman" who had not so patiently awaited her turn to continue the Todd-Parker saga of legendary feats of patriotism and bravery was ready to march on to her own glory, along with her own triumphant man.

Somehow, though, it wasn't destined to work out quite that way.

The two-story house at Eighth and Jackson Streets that had been their home for fifteen years was rented out; furniture was stored. If there were pangs of nostalgia, Mary brushed them aside as she made ready for a new life of bigger and better things. But already her elation was clouded by ugly threats directed at her husband and by the ominous rumbles of approaching war. Danger would now be a constant companion, making their leave-taking for Washington less than joyful for all in the family. Mary, if she were present at the rail depot that morning of February 11, 1861, must have felt a chill as she listened to her husband say his farewell to Springfield—"I now leave, not knowing when, or whether ever I may return, with a task before me greater than that which rested upon Washington."

Lincoln's special Great Western railroad train then rolled out of town, leaving Mary and the younger boys—Willie and Tad—to catch up with him and Robert the next day in Indianapolis. That day, February 12, after all, was his birthday, his fifty-second.

The journey east was to be a campaign-like tour taking days and passing through small-town and big-city America alike. The *New York Herald* noted that men carrying American flags were stationed along the tracks at half-mile intervals. "Every town and village passed was decorated." Thousands awaited a glimpse of the gangling giant—their president-elect. Mary, for her part, happily, even dreamily, wandered about the special train, chatting with one and all. As one onlooker said, "She was tickled to death with all she had seen since leaving home." No doubt, too, all talk of dangers aside, she was thrilled to be going back to Washington once again, this time at the side of the most important man in the country.

Always longing to travel and see other places, other people, Mary now had the opportunity—she thoroughly enjoyed the ride through the countryside. Many of her women relatives were in the Lincoln entourage, but it had been a sore subject that few of her Todd relatives had supported her husband in his quest for the presidency. In all of Lexington only two votes were cast for Lincoln. On the other hand, her sister Elizabeth, who once opposed Mary's marriage to Lincoln, was now very much present to share in Mary's triumph, as were Elizabeth's two daughters and a niece, Elizabeth Todd Grimsley—who later wrote an informative account of her time with the Lincolns in the White House.

Along the whistle-stop tour Lincoln would step out on the back platform and greet the well-wishers. Sometimes, heeding cries from the crowd to see Mrs. Lincoln, Mary made her appearance as well. As she stood by his side at one such stop, the president-elect tenderly held her hand as he quipped to the onlookers, "Now you see before you the long and short of the Presidency." Mary Lincoln of course was only five feet, three inches, not unduly petite, but next to her giant of a man she did appear very short. In fact, she would never allow a photograph made of the two of them together, since she was aware of the absurd contrast they made.

The train rolled merrily on, but trouble lay ahead. Fortunately, Lincoln's advisers had engaged the services of Allan Pinkerton, a former Scottish barrel maker who had founded one of the first private detective agencies in America. He had placed spies along the train route, and he was informed of a plot to sabotage the railroad somewhere near Baltimore, "a hotbed of secessionist agitation and notorious for lawless gangs," as Dawn Langley Simmons described the Maryland city in her biography *A Rose for Mrs. Lincoln.* It was decided that the president-elect would secretly switch trains and arrive in Washington ahead of schedule. Mary and the children would follow on without Lincoln.

★★★

Mrs. Abraham Lincoln, soon to be the first lady of the land, thus arrived in Washington rather unceremoniously and not on the arm of her husband, the president-elect. Once again, any dramatic dreams of glory she may have held were thwarted. Arriving in the nation's capital with no fanfare, she was quietly escorted to the hotel where they were to stay until the inauguration, although she at least was greeted in person by the Willard brothers, owners of the hotel that is still a Washington landmark today as the Willard Inter-Continental. Reunited with her husband, she found him "sprawled out in an armchair in their suite upstairs." In seconds, the children had left her side for their father's lap, ready for a good round of play.

The family's split arrival, and the ugly threats imposing these unusual arrangements, were an unpleasant harbinger of the ill feelings that the Lincolns would encounter in Washington's Southern-dominated society. Feelings of resentment ran high as Southerners took their leave, as these new Republicans came in, and as Washington took on the appearance of an armed camp. "The 'aristocrats' who remained looked upon their Southern-born First Lady as a traitor for being married to the champion of anti-slavery, and the leader of a new social revolution," wrote Simmons.

Unfortunately for Mary, and Mary alone, the town's Yankee residents were just as vicious and vitriolic in their conviction that a Southern spy was taking up residence in the White House.

Despite all the unpleasantness, Mary was excited to be in Washington with her now-famous husband and their three sons. Robert, by this time a student at Harvard, was on hand for the family gathering. He was often the life of the party and was playful with his friends. Two chums from school had met him in Indianapolis to bid him farewell on his journey to Washington. They had both hugged him and playfully suggested that he be a good boy in Washington, and then, before Robert knew what they were doing, they triumphantly left with a lock of his hair. Now old enough to join the men in the smoking room downstairs at the Willard, he was known to smoke a cigar or two. He also enjoyed listening to the music in the hotel, but he complained when some anti-

Unionists persuaded the band to strike up "Dixie," even then the well-known air associated with newly formed Confederacy. The music-makers diplomatically followed up with "Hail Columbia," noted Simmons.

In preparation for becoming the president's lady, Mary had gone to New York on a shopping spree the month before leaving for Washington. And quite a spree it was! While a Springfield housewife she had been frugal, some say even parsimonious, but in her new role she insisted on the very best no matter the cost. She was especially fond of fancy hats and had found a milliner in New York who could create headpieces that suited her. For the first time in her life she did not have to pay on the spot, since credit was gladly extended to the now-prominent Mrs. Lincoln.

Ready to claim her place in Washington, she was anxious to demonstrate that she was no backwoods matron from Illinois. She in fact had already received approving notices calling her the fashionable Mrs. Lincoln—the *Home Journal* was calling her the "Illinois Queen."

Safe and secure in one of her prettiest new hoop-skirted dresses, the newly arrived Mrs. Lincoln received guests in the parlor of their hotel suite. Here she held court not only as a fashionable lady but as one knowledgeable about politics, which she could and did discuss candidly and intelligently. An admiring Lincoln at one such reception commented to a guest, "My wife is as handsome as when she was a girl, and I a poor nobody then, fell in love with her, and what is more, I have never fallen out."

Inauguration Day arrived. Mary and her sons took their seats on the special platform built out from the Capitol's east portico. At any moment her husband would officially become the sixteenth president of the United States. Chief Justice Roger Taney, for the seventh time in his long career, would do the swearing-in. Could anyone have foreseen the extreme irony in the fact that Taney's Dred Scott decision basically declared that slaves were nonpersons with no rights, and here he was, swearing in the very man destined to become known as the Great Emancipator of slaves in America?

Irony or no, Taney would be the one to hold the red velvet–covered Bible for this unpopular Republican come to place his hand upon the Good Book and take the oath of office.

Anyone looking on could not help but feel the air of sadness that permeated the city. This new adventure in government was taking place in a capital that was barely sixty years old and raw as a construction site. The soldiers lining the streets were there more in their capacity as guards than as celebrating marchers. The Capitol was topped with scaffolding awaiting its cast-iron dome and the bronze figure of Liberty. Closer to the White House, the great obelisk designed to become the foremost monument honoring the father of his country was a mere one-third finished, with high grass obscuring unplaced stonework all around the foot of the future Washington Monument.

Despite all this, Mary surely felt a surge of pride as she watched the new president, her Abraham, begin his inaugural address: "In your hands, my dissatisfied fellow countrymen, and not in mine, is the momentous issue of civil war."

"Mary was still half in a dream, carried away by her husband's words, when she realized that he was kissing her," according to biographer Simmons's vision of the moment— "the most solemn kiss of their entire years together." And before Mary knew it they were on their way to the White House while the cannon were booming.

For her first inaugural ball the president's wife wore a watered blue silk gown and trimmed her throat with her ever-present pearls. During the grand promenade, incidentally, she would not be on the arm of her husband, since protocol dictated that she have another partner. Stepping forward to do the honors was none other than her husband's famous debating rival of old—and her early beau— Sen. Stephen A. Douglas. A scene out of an epic movie could not be more perfect than the real-life sight of the first lady accepting the offered arm of her former suitor and gliding across the floor with him. All who knew must have wondered if she wasn't congratulating herself on having chosen the right suitor so long ago.

Settling into the White House after the big day, the new mistress quickly saw that her new home was—to put it bluntly—shabby. With her usual energetic approach she wasted no time. Not only would she dress herself in elegant silks and lace and ribbons, but she determined to refurbish the White House in like style. She was aware that Abigail Fillmore, shy as she was, had unabashedly asked Congress for appropriations for the start of a library and even had spent funds to install a coal cookstove in the kitchen. And during the administration just departed, President James Buchanan had installed a conservatory!

Thus it was, despite the soon-erupting war, that Congress appropriated $20,000 to refurbish the Executive Mansion. What a delight for this first lady, who in all her life had never had so much money to spend as she pleased! This precipitated, even necessitated, a trip to New York to order the various fabrics, furniture, rugs, dishes, and other accouterments. Elizabeth Grimsley, Mary's niece, who was on a prolonged visit to the first family, also went on this shopping excursion. Yet it was her aunt, naturally, who made the major decisions to dress the nation's mansion in finery. Not only did Mary enjoy shopping for her new abode, but it couldn't hurt her standing with the social critics who, she had already discovered, were always watching. Naively, she felt compelled to prove that "westerners" like Lincoln and herself were not uninformed country bumpkins. Nor even boors.

For all her best efforts at providing the White House new elegance, however, Mary was horrified at the eruption of newspaper accounts criticizing her extravagance, with her newly chosen china a special target. That elegant dinnerware of solferino and gold with an eagle featured in the center and rimmed in purple was such a favorite of the first lady that she ordered a set for herself with her initials emblazoned on it. According to Elizabeth, this personal set was not on the official bill, although various critics said that it was.

Throughout her four years in Washington, Mary Lincoln lived in two worlds not always of her own choosing. She had married a man in whom she saw great career potential, by modern terminology, yet a man she loved. And through her marriage she was catapulted into the limelight to her unfettered delight. Yet, for all her own drive and intelligence, she was very much a part of the female sphere, too, having been surrounded by sisters, half sisters, nieces, and women friends all her life. As biographer Jean H. Baker pointed out, Mary once thanked *New York Herald* editor James Gordon Bennett for a complimentary reference to her "female amiability and reticence" by telling him, "My character is wholly domestic."

At the same time an article in the *New York Times* commented, "Mrs. Lincoln is making and unmaking the political fortunes of men and is similar to Queen Elizabeth in her statesmanlike tastes." This irritated her.

Irritated or not, the truth of the matter is that Mary Lincoln had always been drawn to the stimulating conversations of men—her interest in politics and willingness to express her opinions set her apart from most of her female contemporaries. She once admitted that most women's talk bored her.

Still, she had always relied upon the women among family and long-time friends as a support system, but now she found that women, especially, were in the enemy camp, socially speaking. Now, Washington's social leaders ridiculed her every attempt at hospitality. And there was also the jealousy invariably directed at the wife of just about every president. Among others sharpening their knives, the beautiful and ambitious Kate Chase, daughter of Treasury Secretary Salmon Chase, himself a would-be candidate for president, was adamant in her dislike...and perhaps more than a bit envious as well?

Mary was jealous of other women who flocked around the president. To her dismay, she found that her rough-hewn Springfield man, always popular with the menfolk, now was surrounded by sophisticated and flattering Washington ladies who delighted in access to such an important figure. Perhaps a bit of flirting went on, and though Mary herself was good at coquetry, it must have been unbearable for her to see these women fawning over her husband. "Her intense love was possessive," historian Ruth Painter Randall wrote. And indeed quite smothering on occasion, too.

After a time in Washington, Lincoln came to rely less and less upon his wife's astute political insights. Perhaps losing the ear of her president, plus her jealousy over the attention he received from flattering females, plus all the criticism aimed her way, publicly and privately, simply combined to fuel new self-doubts in Mary. She suffered chronic, debilitating headaches more and more frequently. Often, too, she lost control and impulsively said things she later regretted, apologizing with real remorse.

"In the bitter politics of wartime, there was a deliberate launching of a whispering campaign against Mrs. Lincoln as a way of injuring her husband," was Randall's explanation for a good bit of the hostile publicity the first lady faced. William Stoddard, one of the young presidential secretaries living in the White House, befriended the well-meaning Mary and later pointed out she was constantly surrounded by "a jury empaneled to convict on every count of every indictment which any slanderous tongue may bring against her."

But Mary Lincoln had brought a lot of emotional baggage to Washington with her, much of it bound to stir wagging tongues in the restless capital. That she was impulsive, impudent, and emotionally immature there is hardly any doubt. In the words of her friend Stoddard, "Her personal antipathies are quick and strong, and at times they find hasty and resentful forms of expression." But then, hear also the words of a distaff journalist who wrote under the pen name Howard Glyndon, who was sent to Washington as correspondent for the *St. Louis Republican*, and who, after attending a reception in the Blue Room, recorded keen observations of Mrs. Lincoln's dress and very white complexion. Said this writer: "At all events, the charm of her [Mary's] face was not owing to cosmetics. It was a chubby, good-natured face. It was the face of a woman who enjoyed life, a good joke, good eating, fine clothes, and fine horses and carriages, and luxurious surroundings; but it was also the face of a woman whose affectionate nature was predominant."

For all the good and bad said and written about this first lady, she herself did provide grist for the gossip mill. Under the guise of helping her husband, she took an active hand in political affairs. Having spent years advising him in his clothes, social etiquette, and even urging the reluctant eater to finish his vegetables, she felt equally qualified to advise him in such things as Cabinet appointments. The president having encouraged her participation in certain areas, she was quick to take an active role. Quite often she wore her official prestige like a uniform, for all to see, even representing her husband in reviewing troops and inspecting ships!

Mary felt so strongly about their Republican cause that she wrote letters to editor Bennett of the *New York Herald*, himself not always to be counted in their corner. On one occasion she was brazen enough to write him concerning Cabinet posts.

Fully convinced of the importance of her womanly suggestions, Mary ever so sweetly said, "I have a great terror of strong minded Ladies, yet if a word fitly spoken and in due season, can be urged, in a time, like this, we should not withhold it." The president, though, once told her, "If I listened to you, I should soon be without a Cabinet."

From her schoolgirl days, Mary of course had been intrigued by royalty and the grandeur in which they lived. And now, she was the grand lady living in the Republic's grand Executive Mansion…and she would make sure it was turned into an appropriate setting for the leader of a great nation—and, of course, for his wife as well. Approaching the challenge with characteristic energy, she found an ally in the form of William S. Wood, a man of less than impeccable reputation whom she insisted upon having named a commissioner of public buildings. That done, off they went to New York to invade the city's finest shops.

Quite naturally, reporters followed Mary wherever she went, and even though her niece Lizzie Todd Grimsley went with them, tongues now wagged furiously back in Washington. Soon, the president received an anonymous note warning him of the "scandal of your wife and Wood" and asserting, "If he continues as commissioner, he will stab you in your most vital part."

Even though Lincoln reportedly had words with his wife over Wood, she and the commissioner soon had overspent the entire $20,000 allowance Congress had given her for the White House refurbishments. In all, Mary made eleven trips to New York, but Wood eventually became too controversial to remain a companion.

In any case, despite wartime shortages and delays, the White House interiors did sparkle with a new look as Mary held court. She organized various White House receptions and attended them even when miserable with headaches. Enjoying the spotlight that entertaining gave her, she impressed the diplomats with her bright and knowledgeable conversation. The ambassador from Chile and his wife were most grateful to the first lady when she conversed with them in French because they spoke no English. Then, too, a contemporary historian came away from one evening soiree so impressed that he wrote: "She told what orders she had given for renewing the White House and her elegant fitting up of Mr. Lincoln's room, her conservatory and love of flowers . . . and ended with giving me a gracious invitation to repeat my visit and saying she would send me a bouquet. I came home entranced."

But Mary's importance to Lincoln as a political counsel or really did diminish—quite understandably, his preoccupation with the war tended to pull him away from their congenial companionship of old.

Seeking ways to compensate, Mary not only staged formal state dinners and receptions, but she also held her own private salons, attended by stimulating patrons, mostly men. To be sure, a few brilliant women were included in these affairs . . . but only if they could hold their own in the political conversation sure to take place. Though Mary was knowledgeable on women's concerns, she turned a cold shoulder to the idea of women's suffrage—she never lent her name to the feminist causes of the fair sex.

Still, she joined an association to boycott international goods, which put a damper on the elegant and expensive fabrics used in ladies' dresses. Even without European materials, however, the first lady would not be daunted in her quest to be the best-dressed lady in Washington. Her old fascination with royalty, stemming from her school days under Madame Mentelle's tutelage, drew Mary to the fashions favored by the beautiful redheaded Empress Eugénie of France, who had married Napoleon III in 1853. War or not, the American press itself was fascinated with the two "fashion queens."

One member of her salon, Nathaniel Willis, columnist for *Home Journal*, wrote of Mary Lincoln as the "Republican Queen in her White Palace." What he didn't say was that she was an insecure and lonely queen in need of constant companionship. And soon this role was filled by a former slave, a mulatto seamstress who became the first lady's confidante and closest friend.

In fact, on Mary's second day in the historic "White Palace," her first visitor was the same Elizabeth Keckley, one of Washington's most treasured dressmakers. She came recommended by several well-known customers, and ironically she had made gowns for the first lady of the Confederate States of America, Varina Davis, wife of the former senator from Mississippi who now was president of the Confederacy, Jefferson Davis.

The fact is, the Union's first lady had been raised in the presence of family slaves, had once looked upon her Mammy Sally as a surrogate mother helping to fill the void in her little-girl life after her mother's death. Thus, it was only natural that Mary welcomed Keckley with open arms. In response, the newcomer draped her patron in beautiful clothes and soothed her worried brow through many of the troubles and sadnesses of the first family. And Mary in turn lent a helping hand in 1863 to her trusted seamstress in the latter's campaign to help the "contrabands," newly freed blacks pouring into the city from Union-liberated areas down south.

Keckley convinced Mrs. Lincoln of the desperate situation of these former slaves, many of them dying of want. The president's wife responded so positively, she set herself apart from many other Union women of goodwill, recalled biographer Baker, not for "her attention to good causes but rather her commitment to an unpopular one."

As if such an unpopular cause were not trouble enough for an already much-maligned first lady, she added more fuel to the critical fires by soliciting help from her male friends, most of them counted among what she called "my beau monde friends of the Blue Room." She meant the steady attendees of what is thought to be the first salon in America. Notoriously to some onlookers, she had included interesting men, not all of them boasting an impeccable past. They ranged, wrote biographer Baker, from those who could discuss love, law, literature, and war, to those able to talk of philosophers and kings of the past, of the great writers, of commerce, the church, even of the boudoir.

If Mary stubbornly sought to have her way—and Abraham, too, on a larger, national scale—they could not always shake the always-pursuing shadow of tragedy in their lives. As first lady, Mary was determined to show the political and social forces of Washington that she could bring gracious galas to the White House, grand events reminiscent of Dolley Madison's hospitality. To this end in 1862 she planned with great care her first large party since moving into the White House. Five hundred invitations went out—to a "dancing party," a decided break with tradition. Although the guests arrived in their best ballroom attire, they learned the dancing itself had been canceled.

Despite the ban on dancing, a bow to those critics who viewed such activity in the White House as inappropriate in time of war, the attempt at gaiety, the music, and the serving of fabulous food all went forward as planned. Upstairs earlier that evening the president had come into his wife's dressing room as Keckley was helping her into her new gown. "Whew!" was his reaction to Mary's bold finery. "Our cat has a long tail tonight. Mother, it is my opinion if some of that tail was nearer the head, it would be in better style."

But Mary was determined that her best features—her white shoulders and arms—should be shown, and Keckley agreed. Minutes later, Mr. and Mrs. President walked down the stairs to greet their guests, then together began the traditional promenade around the East Room. Mary of course made a fetching picture in her low-cut gown of white satin. A train of black chantilly lace trimmed in crepe myrtle flowed behind her, while a matching wreath of crepe myrtle crowned her dark hair. Her jewelry—as always—was pearls. But for the war, it should have been a happy occasion for Mary, the hostess, especially. All around her, ladies in jewel-bedecked gowns, hoops, and crinolines swished as they moved about the floor…without dancing.

This was to be Mary's triumph, a platform to display her knowledge of fashion and grace. But upstairs in this perfect White Palace a dark cloud hovered ever lower and lower.

In the private family quarters little Willie lay ill, very ill with a fever. The Lincolns had considered calling off the party, but the doctor had assured them that their young son was better. Throughout the evening both parents slipped away to check on their child, who was later diagnosed as suffering from typhoid. Along the hall and stairwells flower-scented air wafted up to the sick room, and music could be dimly heard…as Mary came again and again to see her Willie. Keckley, who was at the bedside, reported that his fever had dropped.

But it wouldn't be for long. Both Keckley and Willie's faithful playmate Bud Taft kept the hard vigil in the days ahead with Mary. The end came on February 20. The president, in and out of his son's room for days, said, "It is hard, hard to have him die!" and buried his face in his hands.

"Mrs. Lincoln alternated between bouts of convulsive weeping and total prostration," reported historian Ishbel Ross. Mary couldn't face the funeral that followed, nor would she ever again enter the guest room where her Willie had died.

Mary in fact displayed such paroxysms of grief that her despairing husband finally sent for Mary's sister Elizabeth because she usually had "such a power & control, such an influence over Mary." He knew Elizabeth would have little patience with such incessant grief, especially with the nation at war, its casualty lists growing day by day.

Now emulating Queen Victoria, who had recently lost her dear Prince Albert, Mary draped herself in black taffeta. More than a year later, a visiting Emilie Helm, herself just left a widow by Confederate Gen. Ben Helm's death in battle, was startled by Mary's hallucinations and seemingly serious talk of trying to communicate with Emilie's dead husband. Mary also claimed to have nightly visitations with her departed sons, Willie and Eddie. Emilie felt obliged to discuss Mary's condition with the president, who had already warned her that Mary was highly nervous.

As if the Lincolns didn't have enough to worry about, oldest son Robert's relations with his family were strained. He was anxious to join the ranks with his friends and do his duty for the Union. But his mother was putting every obstacle in the way of his joining the army. She continued to use Willie's death as an excuse, saying, "We have lost one son, and his loss is as much as I can bear, without being called upon to make another sacrifice."

The split nation, North and South, saw the death tolls mounting day by day. Mary herself could count a brother, three half brothers, and three brothers-in-law as casualties, and all on the side of the Confederacy—Rebels in her eyes whom she refused to mourn. She did feel her sister Emilie's loss of her husband, even if he had been a Rebel general. And Mary told Emilie that in his "visitations," Willie had let her know that he was in touch with their brother Alexander, also recently killed in battle.

While Lincoln's religious faith deepened over the profound experience of Willie's death, Mary's nighttime visitations with her dead sons convinced her that a medium could put her in touch with her lost loved ones. It is easy to understand that she would fall into the hands of a charlatan who went by the alias of Colchester. After several séances, the so-called medium was exposed as a fraud, an episode that only added to Mary's many humiliations.

Lincoln desperately needed help in caring for his sick wife and his youngest son Tad, also ill with raging fever. Tad was not only sick, he was prostrate with spasms of crying over his lost brother and playmate. Fortunately, he recovered, but Lincoln in the meantime found a well-recommended nurse, Mrs. Rebecca R. Pomroy, who had lost loved ones of her own…and had found consolation in her religious faith. She appeared to be just what the doctor ordered, and a relieved Lincoln greeted her with the words, "I am heartily glad to see you, and feel you can comfort us and the poor sick boy." And indeed she did win over the hearts of everyone in the household.

Mary Lincoln, of course, was more sick at heart…an emotional or mental illness, rather than a physical malady. In modern times she or her family would surely have sought help from mental health specialists, but in her day women especially were expected to carry the burden of tragedy stoically. That attitude clearly comes through in letters written by stern older sister Elizabeth, who had hurried to Mary's side right after Willie's death then stayed on in an effort to ease Mary's obvious pain. "Your aunt Mary's manner is very distressed and subdued," Elizabeth wrote to her daughter. "It is a serious crush to her unex-ampled frivolity, such language sounds harsh, but the excessive indulgence, [it] has been revealed to me, fully justifies it."

Mary might have felt not only the censure of family members, but outside the family circle, the ever-ready hostile tongues also were finding fault with everything she did. As Randall so aptly put it, "Newspapers on all sides were denouncing the invalid who wept in the White House." Mary herself forever felt remorse over the ball that went on despite little Willie's illness. She had wanted to cancel the invitations, she lamented. "I have had evil counselors," she shrieked in front of a friend.

Adding one more cruel blow, Eleanor G. Donelly wrote a widely read poem called "The Lady-President's Ball." The poem was supposedly written by a poor dying soldier who through glazed eyes could see the bright lights of the White House. A typical stanza of it went like this:

What matter that I, poor private,
Lie here on my narrow bed,
With fever gripping my vitals,
And dazing my hapless head!
What matter that nurses are callous,
And rations meagre and small,
So long as the beau monde revel
At the Lady-President's ball!

These heartless verses were printed in a newspaper four days before Willie's death. Mary Lincoln had rallied from her little Eddie's death, "with the help of youth," Randall noted. "But now youth was behind her, health was impaired, and she was in the midst of war, suspicion, criticism, slander and hate. The future was dark and uncertain. She would never recover from this blow."

★★★

It wasn't until ten long months later that Mary would finally emerge from this dark period and stand by her husband's side at their New Year's Day reception of 1863. As the guests passed through the reception line, they no doubt studied with added interest this woman who had been so removed from the public eye, yet not the public's curiosity. Fashionably attired for the occasion but clad in her ever-present mourning clothes, her black hair coiffed in a severe style, Mary was the very picture of a somber Victorian mourner. No lively coterie now, no wonderful White House entertainments in view…she had visibly changed.

Perhaps there was a moment's cheer for Mary not long after, when who should come avisiting at the White House but "Gen. Tom Thumb" (real name, Charles Sherwood Stratton), whose recent marriage to the equally petite Miss

Lavinia Warren had momentarily pushed the war news aside (with a little help from that early public relations genius P. T. Barnum of circus fame). Tom Thumb, one of the shortest adult visitors ever to walk into the presidential abode, stood all of three feet, four inches tall. He and his tiny bride had been married in New York's Grace Episcopal Church on February 10, 1863.

But this was also the year of Gettysburg, Vicksburg, and so many other confrontations, with unthinkable slaughter taking place even in the Union victories such as those two benchmark battles. Gen. Ulysses S. Grant was emerging as the man of the hour. War-fattened nouveau riche were flocking into the capital, helping to swell the population from 60,000 to 200,000. Hotels were crowded, gambling flourished, restaurants did a booming business, and the money flowed accordingly. The theater flourished also—Ford's and Grover's were sold out at every performance.

At the very moment that the battle was raging in Gettysburg, Mary Lincoln was out for a ride in her carriage. Suddenly the coachman fell from his seat. The first lady was thrown to the ground and hit her head on a rock. It was later discovered that the seat had been deliberately tampered with. Regardless of the cause, however, the mishap was still another setback for the anguished mourner. Her son Robert believed that his mother never recovered from the accident.

Mary did emerge again to perform her hostess duties and care for Tad, long since recovered from his bout with fever. Now, too, her concern was for her husband's health, since the pressures of the presidency and the war were taking an obvious toll. Even the press began to notice the tired, strained face of the president. So it was a welcome turn of events in 1865 when General Grant invited the Lincolns to view the front at Petersburg and Richmond, where the war was grinding down to its inevitable end. They embarked on the *River Queen* for City Point, Virginia, with a large official party on board, plus the ever-present Keckley. It was an especially happy time for the dressmaker because she would be visiting newly emancipated friends in her birthplace of Petersburg.

While at City Point the Lincolns took a carriage ride by the side of the James River and came upon an old tree-studded graveyard. According to Simmons, the couple walked hand in hand among the peaceful graves. "Suddenly the President, overcome with emotion, said, 'Mary, you are younger than I. You will survive me.'" The next few words he uttered were startlingly prophetic: "When I am gone, lay my remains in some quiet place like this."

The Lincolns' visit to City Point (today's Hopewell, Virginia) unfortunately was marred by embarrassing emotional outbursts on the part of the overly possessive first lady. Mary had always been jealous of the attention showered on the president by other ladies. When she learned that the wife of a young officer had been granted permission to remain at the front, she could not restrain herself. She flew into a rage…but that was just her first display of uncontrolled jealousy.

Due to review the troops with the commander in chief and arriving in a carriage with Julia Dent Grant, she was shocked and dismayed to find post commander Edward Ord's beautiful wife riding a handsome mount beside the president. The first lady screamed at Mrs. Grant, "What does this woman mean by riding by the side of the President? Does she suppose that he wants her by the side of him?"

According to biographer Simmons, Mrs. Grant tried to quiet the outraged Mrs. Lincoln, but Mary only retorted to the general's kind wife, "I suppose you think you'll get to the White House yourself, don't you?" Mrs. Grant (a slave owner's daughter who later did get to the White House as a first lady herself) was stunned and said nothing.

As if the altercation were not yet enough of a scene, Mary Lincoln then dressed down the patient president in front of his officers and men. He tried to calm her by gently calling her by the pet name he often used, "Mother." The next day the president made excuses for his wife, saying she was not well.

The Lincolns returned to Washington on April 9, the very day that Gen. Robert E. Lee surrendered the Army of Northern Virginia to Grant at Appomattox. On Tuesday evening all government buildings in the Federal capital were ablaze with lights to mark the beginning of peace. From a window of the White House the exultant president addressed a jubilant crowd and magnanimously ordered the musicians to play "Dixie."

Just ahead, obviously, would be heady days for the first family. The war was just about over, the family was safe, and Robert had just arrived from Virginia in his Union army uniform. One night that week, however, Lincoln, awoke from a terrible dream. In it, he had wandered into the East Room and saw a coffin with a corpse inside. "Who is dead in the White House?" he asked the soldier in attendance, and the chilling answer was: "the president."

Perhaps it was to shirk the gloomy remembrance of the dream (if he told her about it), that the first lady on Friday evening—Good Friday, it was—planned an outing for her tired husband. Knowing how much he enjoyed the theater, she decided on a party at Ford's Theatre, where the renowned Laura Keene was appearing in *Our American Cousin*. Mary invited the Grants to join them, but Julia Grant, still smarting from the recent outburst at City Point, sent her regrets. Maj. Henry Rathbone and his fiancée, Clara Harris, accepted Mary's last-minute invitation.

Earlier that day the president and his lady took their usual afternoon drive in their carriage, just the two of them. "I have never seen you so happy since before Willie's death," she said.

His answer: "Mary, we have had a hard time of it since we came to Washington, but the war is over, and with God's blessing we may hope for four years of peace and happiness, then we will go back to Illinois and pass the rest of our lives in quiet."

It was not to be.

The lights were already dimmed when the Lincolns arrived at the theater. He seated himself in the red upholstered rocking chair that Harry Ford had placed in the presidential box and had once used in his own bedroom. A guard, John F. Parker, was assigned to protect the president. The Lincolns should be snug and secure in their box. Between acts the president and his wife chatted.

In these last few happy moments together, Mary drew closer to her beloved Abraham and took his hand in hers. "What will Miss Harris think of my hanging on to you so?" she whispered.

"She won't think anything about it," her husband the president answered.

His last words.

The assassin's bullet entered the back of Lincoln's head. He would never regain consciousness.

Mary Lincoln began screaming. "Why didn't he kill me? Why wasn't I the one?"

And so it all ended. Many of Mary's hopes and ambitions had been granted and many taken away. As she herself described her plight to a friend after the assassination, "My own life has been so chequered; naturally so gay and hopeful—my prominent desires, all granted to me—my noble husband, who was my 'light and my life,' and my highest ambition gratified—and that was, the great weakness of my life. My husband—became distinguished above all. And yet owing to that fact, I firmly believe he lost his life and I am bowed to the earth with Sorrow."

She indeed became the epitome of mourning. She lived many lonely years and suffered more losses and abandonments. She buried her son Tad in 1871 and felt betrayed by her remaining son Robert when he had her committed for a short time to a mental institution. She exiled herself to Europe, then returned to her America. And in the end she returned to Springfield.

Mary Todd Lincoln died on July 16, 1882, in the home of her sister Elizabeth Edwards. Forty years before, a gay young woman and her tall gangly husband had left this very house to begin their chequered life together.

The Civil War—A Short Chronology

★ 1861 ★

First year: Confederate States of America formed, February. Inauguration of Lincoln, March 4. Firing on Fort Sumter, April 12. Philippi, in western Virginia, first real battle, June 3. Rich Mountain, also in western Virginia, July 11. First Battle of Bull Run (First Manassas), July 21. Confederates enter Kentucky, September 3–4. Battle of Ball's Bluff, Virginia, October 21. Provisional Confederate President Jefferson Davis elected president for a six-year term November 6.

★ 1862 ★

Second year: Fort Donelson falls to U. S. Grant, February 16. Battle of Valverde, future New Mexico, February 21. Jefferson Davis inaugurated in Richmond, no longer "Provisional President," February 22. Ironclads *Monitor vs. Virginia* battle in Virginia's Hampton Roads, March 9. Shiloh, April 6–7. Virginia's Peninsular campaign, April–July. Stonewall Jackson's Shenandoah Valley campaign, April–June. Second Bull Run, August 28–30. South Mountain and Antietam, Maryland, September 14–17. Lincoln issues his Emancipation Proclamation, September 22 (to be effective January 1, 1863). Fredericksburg, December 13. Battle of Murfreesboro, Tennessee, begins December 31.

★ 1863 ★

Third year: Chancellorsville, May 1–4, Stonewall Jackson mortally wounded by his own men. Vicksburg campaign under way. Cavalry battle of Brandy Station, Virginia, June 9. Gettysburg, July 1–3. Vicksburg falls to U. S. Grant, July 4. Draft riots in New York City, July 13–15. John Hunt Morgan captured in Ohio, July 26. Chickamauga, September 19–20. Chattanooga, November 23–25.

★ 1864 ★

Fourth year: The Wilderness, May 5–6, begins U. S. Grant's sledgehammer campaign to wear down Robert E. Lee's Army of Northern Virginia. Spotsylvania, May 8–21. Jeb Stuart mortally wounded at Yellow Tavern, Virginia, May 11. Battle of New Market (with VMI Cadets), May 15. Cold Harbor, June 1, as Grant approaches Richmond. Petersburg battle and siege begin, June 9. Battle of Atlanta opens, July 22. Petersburg's crater explosion, July 30. Battle of Mobile Bay, August 5. Winchester and Cedar Creek mark continuing struggle in Virginia's Shenandoah Valley, September and October. Lincoln reelected, November 8. Sherman's March to the Sea, November 16–December 21. Battle of Franklin, Tennessee, November 30. Battle of Nashville, December 15–16.

★ 1865 ★

Fifth and last year: Second Union amphibious assault takes Fort Fisher, North Carolina, January 13–15. Lincoln reinaugurated, March 4. Siege of Mobile, March 25–April 12. Lee abandons Petersburg, Richmond falls, Lee surrenders to Grant at Appomattox, Virginia, April 3–9. Lincoln assassinated, April 14. Confederates under Joseph Johnston surrender to William Tecumseh Sherman in North Carolina, April 26. More surrenders, May 4–26. Jefferson Davis captured, May 10. The Civil War is over.

ACKNOWLEDGMENTS

THE AUTHORS WISH TO ACKNOWLEDGE THE CONTRIBUTION TO THIS VOLUME OF several invaluable advisers, fact-checkers, and other helpers without whom we never would have been able to bring forth the foregoing. Thus, our thanks to Ron Pitkin and staff at Cumberland House Publishing, to Sara Kase, an editor at Sourcebooks, and to Shirley Burke Cunningham, our original production manager par excellence and editor (and husband, Jack, not only for enduring many interruptions to a once-tranquil home life, but also as our "Murfreesboro Connection"); to our original production assistant, Ruth Estep for faithful, often "hurry-up" service; and as fact-checkers, proofers, design-and-production mentors, etc., to the late Champ Clark and the Cowles History gang (Jon Guttman, Ken Phillips, Greg Lalire, Gregg Oehler, Lori Flemming).

Equally important, but in most cases a faceless crowd not known to us except through their works, are all those whose careful, painstaking efforts before ours have produced the great body of literature available on the American Civil War. We thank and acknowledge them with due humility. Since we make no claim to present brand-new material unearthed from previously unknown primary sources, but instead rely upon the narrative nuggets to be mined from previously published material, we hasten to commend to our readers all those who have gone before us as authors in this field, whether as historians, participants who told their stories in print, or historical journalists like ourselves.

—C. Brian Kelly
Ingrid Smyer-Kelly

SELECT BIBLIOGRAPHY

Albert, Don E., ed. *Rebels on the Rio Grande, The Civil War Journal of A.B. Peticolas.* Albuquerque, New Mexico: University of New Mexico Press, 1984.

Alexander, E. Porter. *Military Memoirs of a Confederate: A Critical Narrative,* with introduction by Gary Gallagher. New York: Da Capo Press, 1993.

Baker, Jean H. *Mary Todd Lincoln: A Biography.* New York: Norton, 1987.

Ballard, Michael B. *A Long Shadow: Jefferson Davis and the Final Days of the Confederacy.* Jackson, Mississippi: University Press of Mississippi, 1986.

Bergeron, Arthur W. *Confederate Mobile.* Jackson, Mississippi: University Press of Mississippi, 1991.

Blaisdell, Albert F. (adapted). *Stories of the Civil War.* Boston: Lothrop, Lee & Shepard Co., 1890.

Boykin, Edward, ed. *The Wit and Wisdom of Congress.* New York: Funk & Wagnall's Company, 1961.

Browning, Robert M. Jr. *From Cape Charles to Cape Fear: The North Atlantic Blockading Squadron during the Civil War.* Tuscaloosa, Alabama: University of Alabama Press, 1993.

Bruce, Philip Alexander. *History of the University of Virginia, 1819–1919,* Centennial Edition, Vol. III. New York: Macmillan Company, 1921.

Butters, Pat. "From the Fields of Battle to the Oval Office," *Washington Times,* 19 February, 1994.

Catton, Bruce. The *Coming Fury; Terrible Swift Sword; Never Call Retreat,* The Centennial History of the Civil War, Vols. I–III. Garden City, New York: Doubleday & Company, 1961.

Clark, Champ and the Editors of Time-Life Books. *Decoying the Yanks: Jackson's Valley Campaign.* Alexandria, Virginia: Time-Life Books, 1984.

Coco, Gregory A. *War Stories: A Collection of 150 Little Known Human Interest Accounts of the Campaign and Battle of Gettysburg.* Gettysburg, Pennsylvania: Thomas Publications, 1992.

Connell, Evan S. *Son of the Morning Star: Custer and the Little Big Horn.* San Francisco: North Point Press, 1984.

Coulling, Mary P. *The Lee Girls*. Winston-Salem, North Carolina: John F. Blair, 1987.

Dabney, Virginius. *Virginia: The New Dominion*. Charlottesville, Virginia: University Press of Virginia, 1971.

Davis, Varina. Jefferson Davis, *Ex-president of the Confederate States of America: A Memoir by His Wife*, 2 vols., reprint, with introduction by Craig L. Symonds. Baltimore: Nautical & Aviation Publishing, 1990.

Davis, William C. *The Orphan Brigade: The Kentucky Confederates Who Couldn't Go Home*. Mechanicsburg, Pennsylvania: Stackpole Books, 1980.

Dedmondt, Glenn. *Southern Bronze*. Columbia, South Carolina: Palmetto Bookworks, 1993.

Donald, David Herbert. *Lincoln*. New York: Simon and Schuster, 1995.

Douglass, Frederick. *Narrative of the Life of Frederick Douglass, An American Slave, Written by Himself*. New York: New American Library, Inc., 1968.

Dowdey, Clifford. *Lee Takes Command*. New York: Barnes & Noble, 1993.

Dufour, Charles L. *Nine Men in Grey, with introduction by Gary W. Gallagher*. Lincoln, Nebraska: University of Nebraska Press, 1993.

Duke, Duer. *Alabama Tales*. Northport, Alabama: Vision Press, 1994.

Eisenschiml, Otto and Ralph Newman. *The Civil War, The American Iliad as Told by Those Who Lived It*, with introduction by Bruce Catton. New York: Grosset & Dunlap, 1956.

Freeman, Douglas Southall. *Lee*. Abridgement by Richard Harwell of *R. E. Lee*. New York: Scribner's, 1961.

Fretwell, Jacqueline K., ed. *Civil War Times in St. Augustine*. St. Augustine, Florida: St. Augustine Historical Society, 1986.

Gallagher, Gary, ed. *Two Witnesses at Gettysburg*. St. James, New York: Brandywine Press, 1994.

Grant, Julia Dent. *The Personal Memoirs of Julia Dent Grant*. New York: Putnam, 1975.

Grant, Ulysses S. *Personal Memoirs of U. S. Grant*, with introduction by William S. McFeely. New York: Da Capo Press, 1962.

Grimm, Herbert L., Paul L. Roy, and George Rose. *Human Interest Stories of the Three Days Battle of Gettysburg*. Gettysburg, Pennsylvania: Gem Inc., 1983.

Hay, Peter. *All the Presidents' Ladies: Anecdotes of the Women Behind the Men in the White House*. New York: Viking, 1988.

Hendrick, Burton J. *Statesmen of the Lost Cause: Jefferson Davis and His Cabinet*. Boston: Little, Brown and Company, 1939.

Hennessey, Joseph, ed. *The Portable Woolcott*. New York: Viking, 1946.

Holland, Cecil Fletcher. *Morgan and His Raiders*. New York: Macmillan, 1943.

Hood, John Bell. *Advance and Retreat*, with introduction by Richard M. McMurray. New York: Da Capo Press, 1993.

Johnson, Robert Underwood and Buel, Clarence Clough, eds. *Battles and Leaders of the Civil War*, Vols I–IV. New York: The Century Co., 1884–1888.

Jones, Katharine M., ed. *Heroines of Dixie: Spring of High Hopes; and Heroines of Dixie: The Winter of Our Discontent*. New York: Ballantine Books, 1974.

Kelly, C. Brian. "Warren Akin's Christmas in Richmond." *Washington Times*, 25 December, 1993.

———— and Ingrid Smyer. *Best Little Stories from the White House*. Charlottesville, Virginia: Montpelier Publishing, 1992.

————, et al. *Military History* magazine. Leesburg, Virginia: Cowles History Group, 1984–1994.

Lawliss, Chuck. *The Civil War Sourcebook, A Traveler's Guide*. New York: Harmony Books, 1991.

Lewis, Lloyd. *Sherman: Fighting Prophet*. New York: Harcourt Brace, 1932.

Long, E.B. and Barbara Long. *The Civil War Day by Day: An Almanac 1861–1865*. Garden City, New York: Doubleday, 1971.

Luvaas, Jay and J. P. Cullen (photos by W. A. Bake). *Appomattox Court House*. Washington, D.C.: National Park Service, 1980.

MacArthur, Douglas. *Reminiscences*. New York: McGraw-Hill, 1964.

MacDonald, Rose Ellzey. *Mrs. Robert E. Lee*. Reprint of 1939 edition by Ginn & Co, Boston. Pikesville, Maryland: Robert B. Poisel, 1973.

Mallinson, David. "Drummer Boys," *America's Civil War* magazine. Leesburg, Virginia: Cowles History Group, November 1992.

Manarin, Louis H. and Clifford Dowdey. *The History of Henrico County*. Charlottesville, Virginia: University Press of Virginia, 1985.

Markle, Donald E. *Spies & Spymasters of the Civil War*. New York: Hippocrene Books, 1994.

McHenry, Robert, ed. *Webster's American Military Biographies*. New York: Dover Publications, 1984.

Mitchell, Patricia B. *Cooking for the Cause*. Chatham, Virginia: Sims-Mitchell House Bed & Breakfast, 242 Whittle Street, SW, 24531, 1988.

Mobley, Joe A. *James City: A Black Community in North Carolina, 1863–1900*. Raleigh, North Carolina: North Carolina Division of Archives and History, 1981.

Morris, Roy, Jr. *Sheridan: The Life and Wars of General Phil Sheridan*. New York: Crown Publishers, 1992.

Neely, Mark E. Jr. *The Abraham Lincoln Encyclopedia*. New York: Da Capo Press, Inc., 1984.

Perdue, Charles L., Thomas E. Barden, and Robert K. Philips, eds. *Weevils in the Wheat, Interviews with Virginia Ex-slaves*. Charlottesville, Virginia: University Press of Virginia, 1976.

Phillips, Kenneth. *Great Battles* magazine. Leesburg, Virginia: Cowles History Group.

Ramage, James A. *Rebel Raider: The Life of General John Hunt Morgan*. Lexington, Kentucky: University Press of Kentucky, 1986.

Randall, Ruth Painter. *Mary Lincoln, Biography of a Marriage*. Boston: Little, Brown and Company, 1953.

Riddle, Albert G. *Recollection of War Times*. New York: G. P. Putnam's Sons, 1895.

Roberts, Nancy. *Civil War Ghost Stories and Legends*. Columbia, South Carolina: University of South Carolina Press, 1992.

Robertson, James I. Jr. *The Stonewall Brigade*. Baton Rouge, Louisiana: Louisiana State University Press, 1963.

———. *General A.P. Hill: The Story of a Confederate Warrior*. New York: Random House, 1987.

Roscoe, Theodore. *The Web of Conspiracy*. Englewood Cliffs, New Jersey: Prentice Hall, 1959.

Ross, Ishbel. *First Lady of the South: The Life of Mrs. Jefferson Davis*. New York: Harper & Brothers, 1958.

———. *The President's Wife: Mary Todd Lincoln—A Biography*. New York: Putnam, 1973.

Ryan, D. David. *Four Days in 1865: The Fall of Richmond*. Richmond, Virginia: Cadmis Marketing, 1993.

Sandberg, Carl. *Mary Lincoln, Wife and Widow*. New York: Harcourt, Brace, and Co, 1932.

Sifakis, Stewart. *Who Was Who in the Civil War*. New York: Facts on File, 1988.

Simmons, Dawn Langley. *A Rose for Mrs. Lincoln: A Biography of Mary Todd Lincoln*. Boston: Beacon Press, 1970.

Simon, John Y., ed. *The Personal Memoirs of Julia Dent Grant* (introduction by Bruce Catton), including *First Lady as an Author*, by Ralph Newman. Carbondale, Illinois: Southern Illinois Press, Carbondale, 1975.

Snyder, Louis L. and Richard B. Morris, eds. *A Treasury of Great Reporting*. New York: Simon & Schuster, 1962.

Sterkx, H.E. *Partners in Rebellion, Alabama Women in the Civil War*. Rutherford, New Jersey: Fairleigh Dickinson University Press, 1970.

Taylor, L. B. Jr. *The Ghosts of Fredericksburg…and Nearby Environs*. Copyright 1991 by L. B. Taylor, Jr.

———. *The Ghosts of Charlottesville and Lynchburg…and Nearby Environs*. Copyright 1992 by L. B. Taylor, Jr.

Taylor, Richard. *Destruction and Reconstruction*, with introduction by Edwin C. Bearss. New York: Bantam Books, 1992.

Turner, Justin G. and Linda Levitt Turner. *Mary Todd Lincoln: Her Life and Letters*. New York: Knopf, 1972.

Vaughan, Mary C. and L. P. Brocker. *Women at War: Civil War Heroines*. Reprint of 1867 edition by Longmeadow Press, Stamford, Connecticut. Woodbury, New York: Platinum Press, 1993.

Wamsley, James S., with Anne M. Cooper. *Idols, Victims, Pioneers: Virginia's Women from 1607*. Richmond, Virginia: Virginia State Chamber of Commerce, 1976.

Washington, Booker T. *Up from Slavery: An Autobiography*. New York: Doubleday, 1901.

Waugh, John C. *The Class of 1846: From West Point to Appomattox: Stonewall, McClellan and Their Brothers*, with foreword by James M. McPherson. New York: Warner Books, 1994.

Wert, Jeffrey. *General James Longstreet, The Confederacy's Most Controversial General*. New York: Simon & Schuster, 1994.

Wheeler, Richard. *Lee's Terrible Swift Sword*. New York: HarperCollins, 1952.

Wiley, Bell Irvin, ed. *Letters of Warren Akin, Confederate Congressman*. Athens, Georgia: University of Georgia, 1959.

Williams, Frederick D., ed. *The Wild Life of the Army: Civil War Letters of James A. Garfield*. East Lansing, Michigan: Michigan State University Press, 1964.

Wills, Brian Steel. *A Battle from the Start: The Life of Nathan Bedford Forest*. New York: HarperCollins, 1992.

Woodward, C. Vann, ed. *Mary Chesnut's Civil War*. New Haven, Connecticut: Yale University Press, 1981.

Zeitlin, Richard. *Old Abe the War Eagle*. Madison, Wisconsin: State Historical Society of Wisconsin, 1986.

INDEX

ABOUT THE AUTHORS

T. *Michael Knasel*

C. BRIAN KELLY, A PRIZE-WINNING JOURNALIST, is first, the editor and longtime columnist for *Military History* magazine. He is also a lecturer in newswriting at the University of Virginia. As a reporter for *The Washington Star*, he was named 1976 Conservation Communicator of the Year by the National Wildlife Federation; he was also cited for his political reporting by the American Political Science Association and for local reporting by the Washington-Baltimore Newspaper Guild.

Ingrid Smyer has been a freelance writer and editor, ballet teacher, and civic and political activist. She is a member of the Charlottesville (Va.) Historical Resources Committee and former member of the board for the Lewis and Clark Exploratory Center of Virginia in Charlottesville, Virginia.